D1074264

Chang Chih-tung and Educational Reform in China

Harvard East Asian Series 54

The East Asian Research Center at Harvard University administers research projects designed to further scholarly understanding of China, Japan, Korea, Vietnam, and adjacent areas.

Chang Chih-tung and Educational Reform in China

William Ayers

Harvard University Press

Cambridge, Massachusetts

1971

Distributed in Great Britain by Oxford University Press, London
Preparation of this volume has been aided by a grant from the Ford Foundation.
Library of Congress Catalog Card Number 71–129121
SBN 674–10762–4

Printed in the United States of America

To My Parents

Contents

Preface

To the historian there is a familiar ring to some of the dramatic events that have affected Chinese education since 1966. In the summer of that year, as Mao Tse-tung's "great proletarian cultural revolution" gathered momentum, the nation's educational system came under heavy political attack—in a manner reminiscent of an onslaught mounted nearly three-quarters of a century before. On June 13, 1966, the Central Committee of the Chinese Communist Party and Peking's State Council decreed that all university enrollment should be suspended until the entrance standards, curriculum, and teaching methods of higher education could be thoroughly reformed. Middle schools followed the colleges in temporarily closing their doors. University presidents and professors were pilloried for opposing the thought of Chairman Mao. Students, soon to emerge as militant Red Guards, published officially inspired protests against the "vicious" and "criminal" nature of their education. Pedantry was honored in the schools and politics ignored, they charged. Practical work was despised. Courses were too long. Examinations "put school marks in command," gave preference to children of the exploiting classes, promoted individualism, hindered moral culture, prejudiced intellectual development, and affected physical health.

Underlying these protests was a dilemma that had plagued the Chinese Communist government since its establishment in 1949. Should priority be given to "redness" or to "expertness" in China's advance toward modernization and socialism? Should the demands of ideology or technology take precedence? At stake were problems of perpetuating the power of the Communist regime as well as increasing the strength of the nation. Several times before, the pendulum had swung between "redness" and "expertness." Events in the summer of 1966 signified a renewed determination to place Maoist "proletarian politics" in full command, ensure ideological conformity through "class struggle," eliminate "antiparty" and "bourgeois" tendencies from the schools, and destroy the vestiges of educational autonomy—even at risk of lowering academic standards and, in the short run at least, slowing the pace of modernization. The outcome remains in doubt.

In imperial China of the late nineteenth and early twentieth centuries, the dispute raged over "Confucianism" versus "Western arts," over the substance (t'i) versus utility (yung)—the "redness" and "expertness" of those years. The basic concern of Chinese officials, then as now, was how education might best help prolong the life of the constituted state and contribute to its power. The in-group of imperial leaders, like the contemporary supporters of Mao Tse-tung, was reluctant to criticize the state philosophy on which their institutions were grounded or to question fundamental ideological premises. But many were fully prepared to heap abuse on the "deviationists" and "revisionists" of their era, those who were remiss in expounding the philosophy or who would supplant it with foreign creeds.

In the field of education the controversy centered on the thousand-year-old civil service examination system, which provided the chief motivation for schooling. Reformers regretted that the system had lost contact with reality, becoming instead an empty literary exercise, inadequate as a basis for recruiting officials capable of meeting China's urgent needs. "Solid learning" (*shih-hsüeh*), equated with practical studies, had disappeared from the land, they complained. Corruption was rife in the administration of the system. They clamored for new learning, new methods, new institutions, and even for a new blend of the Chinese *t'i* with the Western *yung*. The protesting students included the 1,200 second-degree graduates (*chü-jen*) who in 1895 presented a 10,000-word memorial to the throne setting forth their reform demands.

Ten years later, in 1905, China's hard-pressed court opted for "expertness," abolished the ancient examination system, and replaced the traditional Confucian academies (*shu-yüan*) with a network of schools patterned after Western models—though not in time for education to make the contribution to political stability desired by the debilitated Ch'ing dynasty (1644–1911). Under the Chinese Republic that followed, schools were restructured, and the concept of multidisciplinary, public education began to spread. In the universities, the principle of academic independence gained support. Another major reorganization of education succeeded the establishment of the present Communist government. As shown by events since 1966, however, the void left by the overthrow of the old examination system still has not been filled to the satisfaction of Chinese leaders, who persist in viewing education primarily as training for direct and immediate service to the state.

The following study is concerned with the breakdown of the old system and the beginnings of the new. Through the career of one man, I have attempted to identify and describe major issues and developments in Chinese education at the end of the Ch'ing dynasty. Chang Chih-tung figured as both a mirror and a maker of history, a worthy product of the old system and a prime mover in fashioning its replacement. Probably no other official of his time exerted so strong an influence on the processes of educational change. Through an examination of Chang's personal struggles with the civil service examinations, the workings of the system itself become apparent. Through an analysis of his thought, insights are gained into the main intellectual currents of his age. And through an account of his activities, a picture is formed of the pressures and problems faced by Chinese statesmen striving to prevent, through educational reform, the collapse of an empire. If I have wandered afield from education as an institutional study, it is in an effort to relate the topic and the life of a prominent educator to broader social and political movements of the period.

The Ch'ing system of education that Chang Chih-tung was destined to alter was based chiefly on the Confucian classics. Theoretically, it was believed, knowledge of the classics would help build personal virtue, foster morality, and produce a contagious goodness in the scholar that would infect others and ultimately create a harmonious world. Along with classical learning went an eclectic study of Chinese history designed to show the advantages of adhering to, and the dangers of diverging from, Confucian principles in the exercise of statecraft. "The classics and the histories" were the marrow of the Chinese educational system. They embraced the disciplines of literature and philosophy, government and economics. They affected the approach to science and technology, commerce and finance, war and diplomacy, and the creative arts. Although some specialists or nonconformists sought knowledge from unhallowed texts, even from foreign sources, and "heterodox" schools of thought could always claim adherents, the majority of Chinese students was limited to the Confucian interpretation, the Confucian-oriented historical precedent, and the Chinese experience, developed in majestic intellectual isolation during the centuries of China's undisputed cultural superiority over all known neighbors.

Students in China were limited partly by the force of habit, the sheer strength of traditions which, once established, were hard to change. But they were limited also by expectations of the state and by personal or familial preference. The state encouraged study of the Confucian canons, which provided sanction for the imperial form of rule, stressed loyalty and obedience, and fostered acceptance of other values conducive to social order. The state also based the selection of its officials on the classics and the histories. The civil service examinations, requiring knowledge of the Confucian texts, dominated the educational system of the Ch'ing dynasty. These examinations dictated the specific goals and molded the methods of China's schools. Private tutors, public teachers, and state educational officials bent their efforts toward training men to pass the tests and fill the requirements of the bureaucracy.

Most Chinese students willingly accepted guidance toward this end, and their families were equally anxious that they pass the state examinations. The students were less concerned with social order and universal harmony than might be suggested by their occupation with the classics, for they were also concerned with success in life, in a down-to-earth sense. The classics, the schools, and the state were among the influences that over the centuries had helped to create and perpetuate a stratified Chinese society and definite social ideals. The top place in the social hierarchy was popularly accorded to the scholar-official. The ambitious youth, or one pushed on by his family, strove to become a scholar as the means to becoming an official and sharing in the preference, prestige, or actual power of the bureaucracy. Even if he passed only one of the three major civil service examinations, he could become a member of the gentry, set apart from the ordinary masses and permitted to enjoy certain legal privileges denied to commoners. Except for the few whose families engaged in professions defined as dishonorable, all men in China could theoretically aspire to this success. In reality, the requirements of leisure and money for study tended to restrict education and the examinations to sons of men who were already members of the gentry and the bureaucracy. But as there was no hereditary privilege, some commoners did rise, and under the system the sons of gentry and educated commoners alike were required to meet identical standards.

The principle of merit on which the system was founded was an estimable one, and the operation of the system was often admirable. When it worked well, there was little demand for change. In general, it functioned most smoothly when its administrators were honest or liberal and when alien ideas and methods were too weak seriously to threaten its Confucian bases. By the nineteenth century, however, the system was suffering badly from internal paralysis and decay. At the same time, formidable external challenges appeared from the West to suggest further that the system was failing to fulfill the expectations of the state.

The evidence of internal decay included an increase in illegal practices by examination candidates and probably an increase in the bribery of examining officials. The sale of civil service degrees and the allotment of degree quotas to districts in exchange for contributions to the state also tended to debase the system. However, these and other phenomena were manifestations of a deeper affliction—the rigidity that had overtaken the examination system. The Han dynasty had contributed the classics to the system; the T'ang and Sung added poetry of five words to a line (*shih*) and prose-poetry (*fu*). The Ming then contributed the eight-legged essay (*pa-ku wen*), a name derived from the eight parts into which the artificial exercise was divided. The Ch'ing faithfully preserved these principal literary ingredients.

Prior to the nineteenth century, complaints were made that the solid learning originally represented in the system was gradually being eroded, leaving the examinations mere literary exercises, with little or no bearing on the essential teachings of the sages or on the practical ability to conduct affairs of state. Protest was revived in the nineteenth century, with the addition of a new factor. China was experiencing ever more painful contact with the West—in diplomacy, trade, and war. The West was conquering China, apparently because of its material strength in contrast to China's weakness. Although foreigners did not appreciate the teachings of Confucius, they clearly excelled in knowledge of practical arts and practical affairs. Somehow, to combat the influence of the West, Chinese education must be restored to the path of solid learning.

During the latter half of the nineteenth century there were numerous attempts to meet the Western challenge and overcome the enervation of the Chinese educational and examination systems. Efforts to effect reform went through three general stages. First, there was an attempt to purify and improve the administration of the examination system through traditional means of reform, without basically altering its structure. Second, there was an effort to build new schools, specializing in foreign-type studies, planned in conjunction with the old schools and the old examination system, and intended to supplement rather than displace the old. Finally, there was a sweeping change that resulted in the abolition of the examination system and the transformation of the old schools.

In exploring these various phases through the career of Chang Chih-tung, I have received help and encouragement from many quarters. Portions of the research and writing were made possible by fellowships or grants from the Ford Foundation, the American Council of Learned Societies, and the East Asian Research Center of Harvard University. Among the individuals who have given assistance, I am most deeply indebted to John K. Fairbank of Harvard. His knowledgeable guidance has been surpassed only by his infinite patience since this project was first begun as a doctoral dissertation in the 1950's.

W.A.

Washington, D.C.
March 1970

Abbreviations

CC: Chang Chih-tung, *Chang Wen-hsiang-kung ch'üan-chi*
CSL: *Ta-Ch'ing li-ch'ao shih-lu*
CSL:KH: *Ta-Ch'ing Te-tsung Ching-huang-ti shih-lu*
HNP: Hsü T'ung-hsin, *Chang Wen-hsiang-kung nien-p'u*
JWCK: T'ang Chih-chün, *Wu-hsü pien-fa jen-wu-chuan kao*
PG: *Translation of the Peking Gazette,* reprinted from the *North China Herald*
WCSL: *Ch'ing-chi wai-chiao shih-liao*

1 The Man and the System

Chang Chih-tung (1837–1909) was one of the great viceroys of imperial China during the late Ch'ing dynasty. History has ranked him on a level with other famous governors general of the nineteenth century, leaders such as Tseng Kuo-fan, Tso Tsung-t'ang, Li Hung-chang, and Liu K'un-i. A man of diverse interests and abilities, he was an admired "generalist" of the Chinese bureaucracy: an astute official keenly attuned to the throne; a scholar renowned for his literary skill; an untiring administrative reformer, military organizer, industrial promoter, and educational innovator.

At the height of his influence, he involved himself deeply in the controversy boiling over the question: "Whither China? To the West or to the past?" Conservatives debated with more daring or flexible men about the sources that China should tap to regain her lost national strength and international prestige. Chang's place in the controversy was prominent but puzzling. One of his earliest biographers, writing in 1909, began his book with a question. Alas, he asked, how could he describe this recently deceased official who for more than a decade had been regarded as an ally by both the advocates of the new and the guardians of the old? Chang had at times been praised and at other times cursed by two opposing political camps. It was impossible to say that the part-new, part-old Chang Chih-tung did not represent the aspirations of the Chinese people. This paradox arose, the biographer continued, because obviously neither side had perceived the true image of Chang Chih-tung, who appeared in contrasting guises because he was actually a man in the middle.[1]

Chang's stance, while median, was also militant. Immured in traditional thought during his early career, subsequently aroused to the challenge of "Westernization," he moved into his final intermediate position as a result of experience, evolving convictions, and even, some said, political expediency. Having taken that position, however, he defended it with vehemence.

Chang arrived at his views during a momentous but painful period of Chinese history, when China was being brought into intimate contact with aggressive Western nations and Japan. His life spanned almost all of the bitter era extending from the Opium War of 1840 to the Revolution of

---

1. See opening lines of T'ing-yü-lou chu-jen, *Hsin-ch'u Chang Wen-hsiang-kung shih-lüeh*, ed. T'ao Tso-t'ing (Shanghai, 1909).

1911.[2] During those seven decades, the Middle Kingdom suffered one humiliation after another. Repeatedly, the Chinese were defeated in battle and outwitted in diplomacy. They were forced to open their doors to traders, missionaries, and other "barbarians." They witnessed the invasion of their tributary states and endured losses of territory within their own borders. During the same period, rebels arose to threaten the state—the Taipings, the Nien, the Miao and Moslem tribesmen, and finally the crusaders for a constitutional monarchy or a republican government. Remedies for the Ch'ing dynasty were prescribed by the thousands, in private writings and in memorials to the throne. When armed resistance failed, internal reforms were tried, in quantitative progression but with limited success.

Chang Chih-tung took part in the wars and in the series of political movements that were aimed fundamentally at halting the foreign inroads and the internal decay that abetted intrusion. He participated in military campaigns against the British, French, and Japanese. He identified himself with the T'ung-chih Restoration, embraced the Self-Strengthening Movement, helped touch off the Reform Movement of 1898, and was a leader in the subsequent Manchu Reform Movement.

Chang came to concur in an assessment of his times that was not uncommon among scholars and officials of the empire. According to this view, the West was conquering China because the West was materially strong, whereas China had lost its compensating spiritual vigor. Foreigners excelled in the "practical arts," even though they failed to respect the fine philosophical and governmental principles of Confucianism. The means to stop the West, some scholars and officials believed, was a revival of Chinese learning, a rededication to Chinese principles of government, and a purification of the Chinese regime. Basically, they argued, nothing was wrong with traditional ideas and methods. If only the application could be corrected, China would regain its vigor and the West would be overawed and repelled. Other observers, however, proposed mastering the scientific and mechanical secrets that enabled the West to create superior weapons of war, build better means of communication, and manufacture more desirable goods for trade. They favored imitating Western political and economic institutions that seemed to be working well and abandoning Chinese ideas and methods that seemed to have lost their vitality or pertinence.

2. For brief English biographies of Chang Chih-tung, see Meribeth E. Cameron, "The Public Career of Chang Chih-tung, 1837–1909," *Pacific Historical Review*, 7.3 (September 1938), 187–210; and her sketch in *Eminent Chinese of the Ch'ing Period*, ed. Arthur W. Hummel (Washington, 1943), I, 27–31.

Chang Chih-tung eventually placed himself between these two groups, becoming a vociferous proponent of the mean. He emerged as a studied compromiser or self-appointed umpire, now seeking to push the reluctant toward reform, now restraining the radical from the excesses of what he believed to be a "wild freedom." His hope, as he explained it during the later years of his life, was to protect the Chinese state from foreign threats without demolishing the Confucian bases of the state. He urged that Western practical knowledge and Western tools be adopted to build China's military and economic strength, which in turn would be employed to defend the Chinese heritage, representing a cultural and political strength.

Chang reduced his thought to a series of dualisms, the best known of which has been called the *t'i-yung* dichotomy. He maintained that Chinese learning should be preserved as the *t'i*, the foundation or substance, while Western learning should be selected for its relation to *yung*, utility or function. For his *t'i-yung* terminology, Chang Chih-tung was indebted to philosophers before his time, especially to the Buddhists of the T'ang dynasty and the Neo-Confucianists of the Sung.[3] In Chang's political usage of the terms, however, he diverged from his predecessors, whose emphasis was metaphysical. To the philosophers of Buddhism and Neo-Confucianism, *t'i* and *yung* were inherent in a single being or object. In man *t'i* was his hidden nature or the essence of his mind, and *yung* was the manifestation of *t'i* in action. The *t'i* and *yung* of Chang Chih-tung were external to man and separate in objective embodiment. Man could draw his *t'i* from one source (Chinese) and his *yung* from another source (Western). In a discussion of the concept, Joseph R. Levenson points out that "Chang's sum of a *t'i* from here and a *yung* from there never added up to be Chu Hsi's indivisible entity."[4]

Although Chang Chih-tung departed from the metaphysical thinkers in his adaptation of *t'i* and *yung*, he nevertheless kept within the mainstream of Chinese philosophical tradition. As Derk Bodde has observed, the desire to merge seemingly conflicting elements into a unified harmony is "basic among Chinese thought patterns." Chinese philosophy is filled with dualisms in which the two component elements are regarded as complementary and mutually necessary, rather than as hostile and incompatible. A common feature of such dualisms, furthermore, is that one of their two elements is held in higher regard than the other. Chang Chih-

3. See Hellmut Wilhelm, "The Problem of Within and Without: A Confucian Attempt in Syncretism," *Journal of the History of Ideas*, 12.1 (January 1951), 48–60.

4. Joseph R. Levenson, *Confucian China and Its Modern Fate* (Berkeley and Los Angeles, 1966), I, 68–69.

tung's *t'i* and *yung* fit this fundamental pattern. Chang assigned a higher position to the Chinese *t'i* than to the Western *yung*, but he insisted that both were necessary and sought to harmonize the two. His dualism, in fact, was similar to one of the most ancient of Chinese dualisms, the *yin* and *yang*, described by Bodde as follows: "Inferiority of the *yin* to the *yang* is accepted—explicitly or implicitly—by all thinkers who adopt the *yin-yang* ideology. Never, however, is the suggestion made by them that the one can or should wholly displace the other. Hence there is no real analogy with the dualisms based on conflict (light vs. darkness, etc.) so familiar to us in the West. On the contrary, the *yin* and *yang* form a cosmic hierarchy of balanced inequality in which, however, each complements the other and has its own necessary function."[5] In presenting his ideas on the interaction of *t'i* and *yung*, Chang Chih-tung, too, stressed the factor of proper balance or "balanced inequality." He did not advocate complete coalescence of the two elements. Rather, the Chinese was assigned one course and the Western an adjacent course, and the two were to doubletrack indefinitely through the ages.

Did Chang really believe that his proposal would work? Could Western *yung* be introduced in separation from Western *t'i* without robbing a *yung*-less Chinese *t'i* of relevance? Would the classics speak to a Western-trained Chinese engineer as they had to his scholar-official father? Would not Western science, commerce, and industry, in time, automatically alter the Chinese social structure and leave Confucian social values suspended in an anachronistic void? Was Chang actually aware of the fallacies of the *t'i-yung* concept and merely using the concept to cloak the introduction of Western methods in a garb that would be acceptable to the traditionalists? Several of Chang's contemporary critics asked such questions, and later scholars have repeated them.[6]

Chang surely acted as if he believed in the feasibility of a *t'i-yung* balance. The weight of Chinese philosophy was a significant factor in his makeup. *T'i* and *yung* did not spring suddenly from the pages of his *Ch'üan-hsüeh p'ien* (Exhortation to learning) in 1898 but were evident from his earliest public expressions. His preoccupation with getting things into immediate balance took precedence over hard forethought on a possible imbalance in the distant future. For the short run, he fully recognized the danger that one of the *t'i-yung* elements could exclude or ab-

5. Derk Bodde, "Harmony and Conflict in Chinese Philosophy," in *Studies in Chinese Thought*, ed Arthur F. Wright (Chicago, 1953), pp. 54, 61.
6. For example, see criticism by Yen Fu cited in Jerome Chen, *Yüan shih-k'ai (1859–1916)* (Stanford, Calif., 1961), p. 246; also Levenson, *Confucian China*, I, 64.

sorb the other, even before a balance had been achieved. From his viewpoint, this outcome would be disastrous. It was necessary to assure that neither element be allowed to displace the other.

Chang often painted optimistic and Utopian pictures of intended results. Initially, he appeared confident that *t'i* and *yung* could be harmonized through official manipulation and state control of men, ideas, and institutions. His method required pressure against both the Westernizers and the traditionalists; thus it was not merely a palliative offered to the traditionalists by a crafty advocate of Westernization. Before his death, however, he was dismayed to discover that the state's ability to maintain an equilibrium was dwindling, with the *yung* apparently gaining dominance over the *t'i*, which was supposed to have been master in the balanced inequality.

Chang Chih-tung's *t'i-yung* formula, although professedly designed to uphold Confucianism, did in one respect reflect a lack of confidence in a fundamental Confucian tenet. He betrayed distrust in the efficacy of righteousness (*i*), by endeavoring to support righteousness with wealth and strength—factories and railroads, ships and guns—the materials of profit (*li*) demeaned by Confucian orthodoxy. Among Chang's own subordinates were men who complained that he misconstrued the correct object of education, which was "to attain a true standard of right conduct without seeking for any material benefit." According to one of his secretaries, when Chang was confronted with the charge that he placed *li* above *i*, he stoutly argued for a distinction between public and private interests. "Individual and selfish interests should not be regarded," he maintained, "but public interests must be considered." This led Chang's secretary to comment tartly: "After much hesitation and consideration he finally hit upon the following compromise: for the good of the State, might was to be maintained and right tabooed; in the life of the individual, right was to prevail and might to be tabooed."[7]

Individual and selfish interests apparently motivated Chang Chih-tung to the extent that he was concerned with maintaining his position as a political leader in a highly competitive bureaucracy. Selfish interests, however, did not lead him to acquire personal wealth. Even his critics paid Chang the compliment, all too unusual for his age, of being a scrupulously

---

7. Ardsheal, tr., "Reminiscences of a Chinese Viceroy's Secretary," *Journal of the North China Branch of the Royal Asiatic Society*, 45 (1914), 108. See also pp. 104–105. Although this translation is stated to be from the *Chang Wen-hsiang-kung fu chi-wen*, published in 1910, it appears to be from Ku Hung-ming's *Chang Wen-hsiang-kung mu-fu chi-wen* (1910).

honest official. He died a poor man, leaving no inheritance for his large family.[8]

Public interests dominated Chang's life to the extent that he was fervidly and persistently concerned with preserving and improving the Chinese state under the leadership of the ruling Manchu dynasty. Chang's critics accused him of opportunism and disloyalty, for going too far or not far enough in reforms, and for sometimes placing considerations of his own political survival above principles. There is little doubt that Chang temporized during his career, and ambition to acquire and retain political influence was probably a factor in the process. Ultimately Chang devised the master temporization, his *t'i-yung* formula, embracing two main currents of thought in a single doctrine of the mean, and thereafter his actions were remarkably consistent with his stated beliefs. Those who then accused him of opportunism were most often partisans who desired that he be more than a middleman. If Chang was not with them, he was against them; they held no brief for conciliatory attitudes.

As a minister serving his sovereign, Chang was guilty not of disloyalty but of misplaced loyalty. To Chang, the sovereign was the de facto ruler of China and not the titular chief of state. Chang was intensely and consistently loyal to the Empress Dowager Tz'u-hsi but not to the Kuang-hsü emperor, the Son of Heaven over whom she domineered. This personal loyalty was both a weakness and a strength for Chang within the bureaucracy. He could not always successfully guide the obstinate Tz'u-hsi along the paths of gradual progress that he himself wished to follow. But had he broken with the empress dowager, he probably could not have accomplished what he did, short of leading a revolution, which was too abhorrent an idea for him even to consider.

As a governor general, in which capacity he served for more than twenty years, Chang displayed great energy and imagination. In periods of stress, his imagination sometimes soared too high, on preposterous flights of fancy, his urgent desire to act leading him to mix frenzied and utterly impractical suggestions with sounder proposals. He consistently maintained a grandiose vision of his desired ends, or at least expressed such a vision as part of the salesmanship practiced by Chinese officials to gain imperial support. However, Chang's planning to achieve his ends was usually erratic and sometimes nearly nonexistent. He was continually launching reform projects, altering their aims, reorganizing them, merging them, or dropping one altogether to concentrate on another.

8. Ardsheal, p. 107; Chang's biography from the *Ch'ing-shih kao,* comp. Chao Erh-hsün (Peiping, 1927–1928), in *CC, chüan-shou shang,* p. 28.

As a budgetary juggler, Chang showed considerable skill in the face of financial hardship. He possessed an uncanny ability to ferret out knowledge of surplus sums of money in distant places and request grants-in-aid for his own use. Within his own domains, he was continually soliciting contributions from the merchants and the gentry, inventing new sources of revenue, negotiating loans, and transferring funds from one office to pay the bills of another.

Chang's many economic schemes led J. O. P. Bland to characterize the viceroy as a " 'scholarly bungler,' the stupid, honest visionary and patient pursuer of industrial wild geese." Alexander Michie was somewhat kinder but still concluded that Chang's many schemes "would in any Western country have relegated their author to the custody of the Commissioner for Lunacy."[9] Neither commentator gave Chang credit for what he frankly admitted were experiments, and neither fully considered the obstacles in his path. In his experimentation, Chang differed from those whom the Westerners contemptuously called the lethargic, run-of-the-mill Chinese officials. Chang failed in some of his specific projects, as well as in his over-all plan of developing an invincible strength to preserve the Chinese empire. The partial successes, however, that he achieved in the modernization of China's armed forces, railroad building, the establishment of industry, and the founding of schools were impressive.

As a man, Chang was "grandly proper" in manners and deportment.[10] He was small in stature and in his old age wore a long white beard. He was fond of receiving guests, kept irregular work hours, and preferred to write at night.[11] As a memorialist, he was long-winded but convincing, and the style of his essays was widely admired. An index to his productivity is provided by the four-foot shelf of his collected works, the *Chang Wen-hsiang-kung ch'üan-chi*, containing 229 chüan of memorials, official correspondence, telegrams, essays, poems, and personal letters.[12]

Chang was paternalistic and generally benevolent, although he was capable of quick flashes of anger. He attracted to his staff many "men of

9. J. O. P. Bland, *Li Hung-chang* (New York, 1917), p. 327; Alexander Michie, *The Englishman in China* (Edinburgh, 1900), II, 381.

10. Chang's biography in *CC, chüan-shou shang*, p. 28.

11. Ardsheal, "Reminiscences of a Chinese Viceroy's Secretary," *Journal of the North China Branch of the Royal Asiatic Society*, 46 (1915), 61–62; entry for 1845 in *HNP*.

12. The *CC*, ed. Wang Shu-t'ung, was published in 1928 in Peiping, in 20 han, 120 ts'e. and 229 chüan. It comprises introductory material, 2 chüan; memorials, 72 chüan; telegraphic memorials, 13 chüan; official correspondence, 36 chüan; telegraphic correspondence, 80 chüan; the *Ch'üan-hsüeh p'ien*, 2 chüan; the *Yu-hsüan yü*, 2 chüan; the *Shu-mu ta-wen*, 4 chüan; the *Tu-ching cha-chi*, 1 chüan; *ku-wen* prose, 1 chüan; letters, 8 chüan; parallel prose, 2 chüan; collected poetry, 4 chüan; the *Pao-ping-t'ang ti-tzu chi*, 1 chüan; and family letters, 1 chüan.

talent" (*jen-ts'ai*), both Chinese and foreign, whose special knowledge and skills he made use of up to a point—beyond which point he dictated. In fact, he was a regional autocrat, personally shouldering many responsibilities of his own provincial administrations. For instance, he located his iron and steel works at Hanyang, where he could see the smokestacks from his yamen window in Wuchang. The location, he explained to the throne, would make the governor general's inspection very easy.[13] "Ease of control by officials" was a yardstick applied by Chang to many of his projects.

Chang's career itself fell roughly into periods of *t'i* and *yung*, with more attention accorded to Chinese learning during the early part of his life, and more attention paid to Western learning during the later part. Between 1837 and 1867, Chang acquired a classical education and advanced through the examination system. As a provincial director of education from 1867 to 1877, he attempted to reform the examination system by traditional means. Assigned to the Hanlin Academy during 1877–1882, he reached his peak as a traditionalist, encountered defeats in foreign affairs, and thereupon reversed his course. From 1882 to his death in 1909, Chang served as governor of Shansi, as governor general of Liangkwang (Kwangtung and Kwangsi) and then Hukwang (Hupeh and Hunan), twice as acting governor-general of Liangkiang (Kiangsu, Kiangsi, and Anhwei), and as a senior adviser to the throne in Peking. During these years, he gave precedence to innovations and reforms based on Western models, although after the Reform Movement of 1898 he became particularly insistent that the Chinese substance be preserved.

Traditional Education and the Examination Structure

Of all the reforms that Chang Chih-tung advocated or undertook, he regarded those in the field of education as most basic. Without an effective educational system, the "men of talent" so desperately needed in government could not be produced. Nor could the secrets of Western strength be fathomed and applied self-reliantly in China's own interests. In Chang's projections of the future of China, a learned man was always shown standing in the background behind each Chinese gunner, steel smelter, or scientific farmer. Yet in seeking to introduce new content and form into education, Chang confronted a formidable and ancient established system. Its schools and examinations existed for the primary purpose of training and selecting officials for the state. And by the late nineteenth century it had developed a structure of infinite complexity.

13. *CC*, 29:23–24.

The examination system as a means of recruiting public officials prevailed from the T'ang dynasty (618–906 A.D.) almost to the end of the Ch'ing dynasty (1644–1911). Seeds of the system, however, were planted as early as the Han dynasty (221 B.C.–220 A.D.), when recommendation was the principal method of recruitment. Emperors of the Han dynasty on at least fifty-six occasions ordered their subordinates to recommend for employment men reputed to be "capable, good, square, and upright" (*hsien-liang fang-cheng*), "filial and incorrupt" (*hsiao-lien*), possessed of other admirable moral qualities, or imbued with special knowledge of the Confucian classics, literature, statecraft, law, or military affairs. Officials of the Han dynasty also made recommendations on their own initiative.[14]

In 165 B.C the practice of the emperor giving written examinations was begun, as a means of determining the worthiness of candidates recommended for appointment. Initially examinations were required only for men seeking to qualify on the basis of special knowledge, but by an edict of 132 A.D. examinations also were extended to cover those recommended for outstanding virtues. At first the Han examinations tested practical knowledge of running the government, but as time passed, more attention was accorded to mastery of the Confucian classics, with their political philosophy that good government in the final analysis depends upon the good character of those governing. In 85 A.D. each prefecture and kingdom of the empire was ordered to recommend three to five men "understanding the classics" (*ming-ching*).[15]

Although only a few men were recruited by these methods during the Han dynasty, a relationship between bureaucratic appointment, examinations, and the Confucian classics became established. Also forged in the Han dynasty was a link between civil service examinations and Confucian-oriented state educational institutions. In 124 B.C. fifty students were selected to study under "doctors of the Five Classics" (*Wu-ching po-shih*) in an institute called the Supreme School (T'ai-hsüeh). After completing a course of study, disciples of the *po-shih* were examined before being admitted to the bureaucracy. Before the end of the Sui dynasty (581–618), the Supreme School had evolved into the Imperial College (Kuo-tzu-chien), an institution that lasted until the final years of the Ch'ing dynasty, although by then it had lost most of its original teaching functions.[16]

14. Teng Ssu-yü, *Chung-kuo k'ao-shih-chih-tu shih* (Nanking, 1936), pp. 1, 31–34. See also Franklin H. Houn, "The Civil Service Recruitment System of the Han Dynasty," *Ch'ing-hua hsüeh-pao*, n.s., 1.1 (June 1956), 138–164.

15. Teng, pp. 33, 407; Houn, pp. 142, 144, 149.

16. Houn, pp. 151, 163; Chang Yü-ch'uan, "The Kuo Tzu Chien," *Chinese Social and Political Science Review*, 24.1 (April–June 1940), 69–106.

Laxity developed in the administration of the incipient examination system during the later Han dynasty, and political influence tended to become more important than honest evaluation of a candidate's reputation and ability. In the period of disunion (220–589 A.D.) following the Han dynasty, further decline occurred. Rulers of the Wei, Chin, and other states of the period occasionally issued edicts calling for the recommendation of "filial and incorrupt" men or "accomplished talent" (*hsiu-ts'ai*). Other edicts stressed knowledge of the Confucian classics as a criterion for recommendation, and within this period some examinations were given. However, powerful aristocratic families dominated the political life of the times, and hereditary right or connection with those families were more important than examinations for gaining entry to the bureaucracy.[17]

The Sui dynasty, which reunified the empire, attempted to revive the Han systems of recommendation and examination. Schools of Confucian studies were founded, and in 587 A.D. it was decreed that each province should send three scholars a year to the capital to be tested for official appointment. In 606 A.D. the Sui originated an examination for "presented scholars" (*chin-shih*), or scholars to be presented to the throne.[18]

The greatest development occurred in the T'ang dynasty, when a number of different examination categories (*k'o*) were established. Tests were offered in law, calligraphy, mathematics, history, and for a short time in Taoism. Most important, however, were examinations on understanding of the classics (*ming-ching*) and examinations in the *hsiu-ts'ai* and *chin-shih* categories. The requirements of these three examinations varied, but together they included transcribing classical passages from memory (*t'ieh-ching*), a practice begun in 680 A.D.; preparing essays (*wen-chang*) on the classics, or dissertations (*ts'e*) and discussions (*lun*) on history and government; and writing poetry of the *shih* and *fu* varieties, a practice begun in 754 A.D. Examinations were generally held in the capital once a year, and candidates were selected from schools of the empire or put forward by departmental and district officials after undergoing preliminary local examinations. Beginning in 736 A.D., the metropolitan examinations were administered by the Board of Rites. Candidates who passed were sent to the Board of Civil Appointments for additional judgment before being awarded employment.[19]

17. Houn, p. 156; Teng, pp. 21–23, 51–73; Wolfgang Franke, *The Reform and Abolition of the Traditional Chinese Examination System* (Cambridge, Mass., 1960), p. 3.
18. Arthur F. Wright, "The Formation of Sui Ideology, 581–604," in *Chinese Thought and Institutions*, ed. John K. Fairbank (Chicago, 1957), p. 91; Teng, p. 409.
19. Teng, pp. 76–78, 83–84, 86, 89–90. For the T'ang system, see also Robert des Rotours, *Le traité des examens, traduit de la nouvelle histoire des T'ang* (Paris, 1932).

During the Sung dynasty (960–1279) successful candidates passed directly from the Board of Rites examination into the bureaucracy. Tests at the local level were institutionalized after the pattern of examinations held in the capital. Examinations in a number of the T'ang categories were offered during the early years of the Sung dynasty, but they gradually diminished in importance or were abolished, leaving the *chin-shih* examination as the only category of significance. In 1066 it was decreed that examinations would be held every three years. Methods of administering examinations became more highly refined during the Sung. Reexaminations (*fu-shih*) were instituted as a double-check on candidates chosen. These included a test called the palace examination (*tien-shih*), given by the emperor himself. In order to ensure impartiality, the names of candidates were concealed (*mi-feng*) on their essay papers, and essays were recopied (*t'eng-lu*) by scribes to prevent the graders from recognizing the handwriting of candidates.[20]

The examination system declined during the Mongol Yüan dynasty (1260–1368), when most important offices were filled by non-Chinese, but it was revived during the Ming dynasty (1368–1644), when the eight-legged essay became entrenched as the form for examinations on classical interpretation (*ching-i*).[21] Forms assumed by the examination system in the Ming were carried over to the Ch'ing dynasty.

Under the Manchu state, examinations consisted of writing eight-legged essays on the Four Books and Five Classics, composing *shih* and *fu* poetry, and preparing dissertations in answer to a series of questions on government.[22] The dissertation, although usually confined to standard Confucian themes, was a freer style than the eight-legged essay. In grading papers, however, examining officers assigned less weight to the dissertation than to the eight-legged essay on the Four Books. Since the Four Books had been used in examinations for hundreds of years, the possibilities of devising new questions and original elucidations was

---

20. Teng, pp. 77, 145–146. For a special study of this period, see E. A. Kracke, Jr., *Civil Service in Early Sung China* (Cambridge, Mass., 1932). For a study of another period, see K. A. Wittfogel, "Public Office in the Liao Dynasty and the Chinese Examination System," *Harvard Journal of Asiatic Studies*, 10.1 (1947), 13–40.

21. On the structure of the eight-legged essay, see Chang Chung-ju, *Ch'ing-tai k'ao-shih chih-tu* (Shanghai, 1932), chüan 2, pp. 1–3. Actual documentary examples of essays on the Four Books and Five Classics, *shih* and *fu* poetry, and other examination forms may be found in chüan 2 of that work, pp. 9–42. All page numbers given hereafter from Chang's work refer to chüan 1, the descriptive analysis of the Ch'ing system, distinct from the documentary supplement, chüan 2.

22. The Four Books were the *Analects of Confucius (Lun-yü)*, *Great Learning (Ta-hsüeh)*, *Doctrine of the Mean (Chung-yung)*, and *Mencius (Meng-tzu)*. The Five Classics were the *Classic of Poetry (Shih-ching)*, *Classic of History (Shu-ching)*, *Classic of Changes (I-ching)*, *Book of Rites (Li-chi)*, and the *Spring and Autumn Annals (Ch'un-ch'iu)* with the *Commentary of Tso (Tso-chuan)*.

practically exhausted by the nineteenth century. Examiners resorted to bizarre devices in assigning topics, and students writing essays were inclined to accept ready-made patterns, plagiarizing those who had gone before them. Detailed rules defined acceptable methods of writing poetry and essays, the latter not being allowed to exceed seven hundred characters in the provincial and metropolitan examinations. In the highest examinations, skill in the writing of small characters was a criterion in judging success or failure. In general, examination candidates were judged just as rigorously upon compliance with stylistic formulas as upon the content of their writings.[23]

By the nineteenth century, examinations were offered at the district, prefectural, provincial, and national administrative levels of government.[24] At the lower levels, a series of "youth examinations" (t'ung-shih) was held first. Candidates were tested initially by the magistrate of their native district, then by the chief of the prefecture to which the district was subordinate, and finally by the provincial director of education visiting the prefectural town.[25] In the main session of the examination before the director of education, the candidates were required to write two essays explaining passages from the Four Books and one poem (shih). The best candidates were selected according to a fixed quota governing the number of students admissible to the government schools of the locality.[26] Those chosen became "government students" (sheng-yüan), or first-degree graduates popularly called hsiu-ts'ai. They were entitled to enroll in government schools, were exempted from labor service and corporal punishment, and enjoyed other privileges that accrued to members of the lower gentry.

Next came the "annual examination" (sui-k'ao), actually a triennial test, given to sheng-yüan every three years by the provincial director of education. Through this examination, the sheng-yüan were ranked in three classes and became either "supplementary students" (fu-sheng), "extra students" (tseng-sheng), or "salaried students" (lin-sheng).

23. Chang Chung-ju, p. 19, presents a list of forty-one stylistic defects looked for in grading examination essays.

24. The following English equivalents for common Chinese administrative terms are used throughout: province (sheng), circuit (tao), prefecture (fu), subprefecture (t'ing), department (chou), and district (hsien).

25. For more complete descriptions of this and other Ch'ing state examinations, see Chang Chung-ju, pp. 3–41; Etienne Zi, Pratique des examens litteraires en Chine, in Variétés sinologiques no. 5 (Chang-hai, 1894), pp. 3–208; Shang Yen-liu, Ch'ing-tai k'o-chü k'ao-shih shu-lu (Peking, 1958); Ho Ping-ti, The Ladder of Success in Imperial China: Aspects of Social Mobility, 1368–1911 (New York and London, 1962).

26. Chang Chung-li, The Chinese Gentry: Studies on Their Role in Nineteenth Century Chinese Society (Seattle, 1955), p. 77.

Highest were the salaried students, who received a monetary allowance from the government. The *sui-k'ao* consisted of writing two essays, one on the Four Books and the other on the Five Classics, and composing one poem. Men who wished to retain their *sheng-yüan* status without obtaining a higher degree were never released from the obligation to take this test. One who neglected three times to appear for the test would be disenrolled as a *sheng-yüan*.

Another test before the provincial director of education was the "category examination" (*k'o-kao*), a preparatory trial also held triennially. Its purpose was to qualify *sheng-yüan* for the higher provincial examination (*hsiang-shih*). In content, it differed from the *sui-k'ao* mainly in requiring the writing of a dissertation on questions related to government instead of an essay on the Five Classics.

The provincial examination was held in a provincial capital once every three years during the eighth lunar month. It was presided over by a chief examiner and assistant examiner sent from Peking. The examination was given in three sessions over a one-week period. During the later Ch'ing dynasty, candidates in the first session wrote a poem as well as essays on topics from the *Analects of Confucius*, the *Doctrine of the Mean*, and *Mencius*. In the second session, essays on themes from each of the Five Classics were required. The third session consisted of writing answers to five questions on government. Successful candidates were divided into two groups. Those in the first group became "elevated men" (*chü-jen*), the second-degree graduates under the examination system. They were awarded degrees according to a quota system that allowed about forty to fifty *chü-jen* for the small provinces, seventy to eighty for the middle-sized provinces, and one hundred or more for the large provinces. Men receiving the *chü-jen* degree were entitled to participate in the metropolitan examination (*hui-shih*) or might be assigned to the less important positions in the bureaucracy. Candidates on the secondary list became "supplementary tribute students" (*fu-kung-sheng*). Their names were removed from the school rolls of *sheng-yüan*, they were released from the obligation of the *sui-k'ao*, and they could sit for the next provincial examination without taking the *k'o-k'ao*.

The metropolitan examination was held triennially in Peking during the third month of the year following the provincial examinations. Presided over by specially appointed high officials, it was preceded by a reexamination of the assembled *chü-jen*. The metropolitan examination proper was divided into three sessions with requirements similar to those of the provincial examinations. Successful candidates were selected according to a quota set for each province, with the total number varying from examination to examination. As few as 96 men and as many as 406 were chosen in the early Ch'ing period, but the figure was in the neighborhood of 300 during the latter part of the nineteenth century. Men who passed the metropolitan examination were designated "tribute scholars" (*kung-shih*). They then sat for a reexamination. Those who passed proceeded to the palace examination.

The palace examination was held in the month following the metropolitan examination and was presided over by the emperor. It consisted of writing a dissertation, averaging about a thousand words in length, on four questions concerned with history or government. Men who passed the palace examination received the highest degree of "presented scholar" (*chin-shih*). On the basis of their dissertations, they were divided into three groups, the first group being composed of the three men accorded the highest honors. The new *chin-shih* then took the court examination (*ch'ao-k'ao*).

The court examination helped to determine the position a *chin-shih* would receive in the bureaucracy. This test consisted of writing a discussion, a memorial (*shu*), and a poem, or sometimes a discussion and a dissertation. Successful candidates were divided into three classes and then appointed to office. The top man in the palace examination was assured of an appointment as a first-class compiler (*hsiu-chuan*) of the Hanlin Academy, while the two men ranking just below him became second-class Hanlin compilers (*pien-hsiu*). Other *chin-shih* were assigned according to a final score based on their standings in the metropolitan reexamination, the palace examination, and the court examination. Thus, if a man had been placed in the first class in the reexamination, in the second class in the palace examination, and in the first class in the court examination, his total score would be four, and he would be assigned as a student or bachelor (*shu-chi-shih*) of the Hanlin Academy. Those with a score of five (or sometimes higher) could also entertain hope of assignment as Hanlin bachelors. Others would be awarded jobs, in declining order of importance, as secretaries of the Six Boards, secretaries of the Grand Secretariat, or district magistrates.

In addition to the main *sheng-yüan*, *chü-jen*, and *chin-shih* classifications of the examination system, there was a variety of "tribute student" categories. The *fu-kung-sheng* have been mentioned. Every twelve years a difficult examination was held by provincial directors of education to choose "tribute students by virtue of special selection" (*pa-kung-sheng*) from among the ranks of the *sheng-yüan*. Every three years "tribute students by virtue of special merit" (*yu-kung-sheng*) were chosen in another hard test. The *pa-kung-sheng* and *yu-kung-sheng* could proceed directly to court examinations to qualify for lower level official positions. A few men were examined irregularly for the degree of "tribute student by virtue of seniority" (*sui-kung-sheng*), and upon joyous occasions a few might be promoted to become "tribute students by virtue of imperial grace" (*en-kung-sheng*).[27] "Students of the Kuo-tzu-chien" (*chien-sheng*) held a degree that could be purchased and were nominal enrollees of the Imperial College.

Since the T'ang dynasty a military examination system had developed parallel to the civil service examination system. Under it candidates could become military *sheng-yüan, chü-jen,* and *chin-shih* by passing tests at the prefectural, provincial, and metropolitan levels. At the prefectural level, for example, this examination began with an exercise in mounted archery. From horseback, candidates were required to hit a target with three arrows. Those who succeeded were then tested in dismounted archery, again being required to hit a target two or three times. Next came a test in drawing heavy bows, weighing from 80 to 120 catties. Those who could pull the 100-catty bow to its full stretch passed on to tests in brandishing heavy swords and lifting stones weighing from 200 to 300 catties. Finally, the candidates were required to write from memory a hundred words or more from a military classic. The provincial and metropolitan examinations had more difficult standards but followed the same basic pattern.[28] Shot through with corruption and outmoded by the age of firearms, the military examination system came under severe fire from critics and reformers earlier in the Ch'ing dynasty than did the civil service examination system.

Candidates for the Ch'ing examination system were prepared by the schools of China. While special schools were maintained for sons of the Manchu nobility, Chinese elementary education was entirely a matter of private initiative. Boys who had not yet obtained the status of *sheng-yüan* were trained either by private tutors or in clan schools, village schools, and charitable schools (*i-hsüeh*) supported by the local gentry. Government schools, usually sharing quarters with local Confucian temples, were maintained at the district, departmental, and prefectural levels of administration. In these schools the *sheng-yüan* were registered

27. Chang Chung-li, pp. 27–28.
28. Chang Chung-ju, pp. 12–13, 25–27, 31. The military system is described more fully in Etienne Zi, *Pratique des examens militaires en Chine,* in *Variétés sinologiques* no. 9 (Chang-hai, 1896).

and were required to take periodic examinations. But the institutions were loosely administered, with no regular attendance required, and aside from occasional lectures by staff members or visiting scholar-officials, there was no definite curriculum.[29]

Provincial governments patronized semiofficial academies (shu-yüan) and encouraged private ones. The semiofficial academy, which originated as a private institution in the Sung dynasty, had by the Ch'ing become "an integral if more or less informal, part of the government education system focused on the civil service examination."[30] Each province had at least one academy where practice tests were given under government auspices to help prepare sheng-yüan for higher examinations. Such academies were subsidized by the government, their students received a stipend from the government, and their presidents were "invited" to serve by the governor general or the governor. Officials recruited the students from the subdivisions of the province.[31] Like the district and prefectural schools, provincial academies were loosely organized, as the following description makes clear:

> A Shu-yüan consisted usually of an endowment of land, a library, a well-known scholar as director, and a number of students, who were given a small allowance to cover at least part of their expenses. The expenses of the academy were defrayed from the proceeds of the land endowment and, in some cases, a subsidy was granted by the local authorities. No lectures were given [regularly] in the academy: the function of the professor was only to advise the students as to their reading and criticize the results of their researches. Occasionally the professor or an outside scholar would lecture on some selected topic, but, on the whole, the Shu-yüan was a place of self-study, and a center of research under expert guidance.[32]

In outline, these were the examination and education systems with which Chang Chih-tung coped throughout his lifetime. He was first a student under the systems, then helped administer them, and was finally instrumental in radically altering the school system and abolishing the examinations. How the systems affected the Chinese student is exemplified in the story of Chang's own youth.

29. Chang Chung-li, pp. 186, 201–202; Theodore E. Hsiao, *The History of Modern Education in China* (Shanghai, 1935), pp. 16–17; Franke, p. 14; Ho Ping-ti, p. 171.
30. David S. Nivison, "Protest against Conventions and Conventions of Protest" (mimeo., 1957). See also Sheng Lang-hsi, *Chung-kuo shu-yüan chih-tu* (Shanghai, 1934).
31. The academies having semiofficial status in each province are listed by name in Chang Chung-ju, pp. 57–58.
32. T'ang Leang-li, *China in Revolt* (London, 1927), p. 33.

2 The Examination Candidate
(1837–1867)

Chang Chih-tung was born on September 2, 1837, during the seventeenth year of the Tao-kuang reign of the Ch'ing dynasty.[1] At the time of his birth, the Chinese government was engaged in an antiopium movement designed to stop drug imports that were said to be draining the country of silver. Crises involving foreign traders were mounting in Canton. The dispute over opium and more fundamental problems of Sino-Western intercourse led to war with Great Britain in 1840. Other conflicts followed closely within the Chinese empire—the Taiping Rebellion (1850–1864), the Nien Rebellion (1853–1868), revolts by the Miao tribes and the Moslems of the Southwest (1854–1873), and revolts by the Moslems of the Northwest (1862–1873).[2] Between 1856 and 1860, Great Britain, joined by France, waged another war with China for additional trade and treaty privileges. Chang Chih-tung spent all of his youth amid battles and uprisings as both Western invaders and Chinese insurgents challenged the declining Ch'ing dynasty.

Members of Chang's family participated in the defense of the dynasty, and for a short time, Chang himself led a militia group. His entry into the bureaucracy was delayed because of the warfare. Nevertheless, the main accounts of his youth reveal little intellectual response by Chang to the turmoil that raged around him during the first thirty years of his life. This is partly the fault of the materials available. Two *nien-p'u* or chronological biographies are the principal sources of information on Chang from 1837 to 1867. They present a procession of biographical facts and anecdotes, without explicit interpretation and with sketchy historical background.[3]

1. Courtesy names (*tzu*) for Chang Chih-tung were Hsiao-ta, Hsiang-t'ao, and Hsiang-yen. His literary names (*hao*) included Hu-kung, Pao-ping, and Wu-ching chü-shih. After Chang left Wuchang in 1907, his subordinates erected a hall called the Pao-ping t'ang, so in his last days Chang used the literary name Pao-ping lao-jen. Hummel, I, 37. The literary name Wu-ching chü-shih, roughly meaning "Nonquarreling retired scholar," alludes to a T'ang poem by Chang Chiu-ling. An explanation appears in T'ing-yü-lo chu-jen, p. 2. Chang was canonized as Wen-hsiang after his death on October 4, 1909.

2. Dating follows Mary C. Wright, *The Last Stand of Chinese Conservatism* (Stanford, Calif., 1957), pp. 98–118.

3. *HNP*; Hu Chün, *Chang Wen-hsiang-kung nien-p'u* (Peiping, 1939), 2 ts'e. Although published earlier and containing a few additions, Hu's work was based mainly on a manuscript by Hsü completed before 1921. Hsü had once been an associate of Chang Chih-tung and served as an editor of his complete works (*CC*). He spent fifteen years compiling the *nien-p'u*, receiving editorial assistance from Ch'en Pao-ch'en. Hummel, I, x, points out: "Though the *nien-p'u* is a biography, it is hardly so in the Western sense, for in it the facts are brought together in a strict chronological order under each year of the person's career—with no embellishment and without emotive suggestions."

If the *nien-p'u* are deficient in these respects, however, they do succeed in depicting a young mind being shaped in the traditional cast of
Chinese classical studies and adjusting to the behavioral routines expected of a son of the Chinese gentry. For the *nien-p'u* facts, though set
forth with a seemingly objective aridity, fit rather neatly into a time-
honored pattern of Chinese biographical writing, one that reflects a high
evaluation of scholarly achievement and bureaucratic success.[4]

By a simple substitution of names in the *nien-p'u,* Chang Chih-tung
could quite easily be made to appear as a genteel youth of the T'ang,
Sung, or Ming dynasties. Like many other well-known men of Chinese
history, he had a self-sacrificing parent, ambitious that his son become
famous as a scholar and official. As a boy, Chang himself was assiduous
in studying the classics and the ways of the ancient sages. A great future
was predicted for him. He began working his way up the ladder of the
civil service examination system, and between examinations he studied,
wrote poetry, and traveled extensively. Finally he achieved governmental position.

The particular emphasis of the *nien-p'u* is on Chang's diligence and
precociousness, applied within the context of the examination system.
This stress cannot be considered completely misplaced, for, after all,
Chang Chih-tung became a *sheng-yüan* at the age of thirteen and won
first place in a provincial examination when he was only fifteen years
old.[5] In the final analysis, he successfully met other challenges of the
difficult system that dominated his youth before entering the bureaucracy
at the age of thirty.

Boyhood Studies

Chang Chih-tung began his education in Kweichow province, where he
was born at the official residence of the Hsing-i prefecture, headed by
his father. Despite his place of birth, he was considered to be a native of

4. Scholarly achievement and bureaucratic success were considered the qualities of a
sage. Historically the tendency in Chinese biographical writing has been to present a
subject as "either demagogue or infallible sage," a practice dating back to Ssu-ma Ch'ien of
the Han dynasty, who treated individuals as "mere illustrations of the greater events and
ideals of the times." See Shih-hsiang Chen, "An Innovation in Chinese Biographical Writing," *The Far Eastern Quarterly,* 13.1 (November 1953), 49–62; "The Biographical Approach to Chinese History: A Symposium," with contributions by Howard L. Boorman,
David S. Nivison, Richard C. Howard, William Ayers, and John A. Garraty, *Journal of
Asian Studies,* 21.4 (August 1962), 453–489.

5. Chang was 14 *sui* and 16 *sui* at the time of these events. Whenever possible, *sui* are
hereafter converted to the Western method of reckoning age. On the average, examination
candidates obtained the title of *sheng-yüan* at about 24 years of age, the *chü-jen* degree at
about 30, and the *chin-shih* degree at about 35. Chang Chung-li, pp. 94–95, 121–122,
125–126.

Nan-p'i, a district town near Peking in eastern Chihli province.[6] His first ancestor to live in Chihli had migrated there over four hundred years before. The move occurred early in the fifteenth century when the Yunglo emperor transferred the Ming capital from Nanking to Peking and ordered a shift of population from Shansi province in order to "solidify the imperial domain." Succeeding heads of the Chang family included minor officials who departed from Chihli for service elsewhere in the empire, in accordance with the bureaucratic regulation that a man could not hold office in his native province.[7]

Chang Ying, the father of Chang Chih-tung, was born in 1793. Possessed of "a powerful physique, a loud voice, a broad forehead, and a bold countenance," he earned a reputation for stern probity.[8] Chang Ying had been left fatherless at an early age, and the *nien-p'u* state that "although poor, he studied hard; although he suffered, he excelled." Nevertheless he did not distinguish himself in the civil service examinations. After becoming a *chü-jen* in 1813, he never was able to pass the metropolitan examination. He was finally admitted to the bureaucracy through a special procedure known as the "great selection" (*ta-t'iao*). By this method, imperial dispensation was occasionally granted to choose officials from among candidates who had failed the metropolitan examinations at least three times.[9] Rewarded at last for his long struggle with

6. Unless otherwise specified, facts and quotations in the remainder of this chapter are drawn from the first chüan of *HNP*, pp. 1–11. This *nien-p'u* incorporates stories of Chang's youth appearing in the *Pao-ping-t'ang ti-tzu chi*, published in *CC*, ch. 228. It also duplicates information on Chang's youth appearing in five historical and biographical collections: the *Ch'ing-shih kao*, 443:3; *Ta-ch'ing chi-fu hsien-che chuan*, comp. Hsü Shih-ch'ang and others (Tientsin, 1917), 7:1; *Ch'ing-shih lieh-chuan*, comp. Chung-hua Book Co. (Shanghai, 1928), 64:3b; *Pei-chuan chi pu*, comp. Min Erh-ch'ang (Peiping, 1932), 2:8b; *Kuo-ch'ao shu-hua-chia pi-lu*, ed. Tou Chen (Soochow, 1911), 4:32a. Biographies of Chang Chih-tung from the first two collections listed above are reprinted in *CC, chüan-shou shang*, pp. 24–28; *chüan-shou hsia*, pp. 1–48. In the *Ch'ing-shih*, comp. Chang Ch'i-yün et al., (Taipei, 1960), the biography of Chang Chih-tung appears in vol. 6, pp. 4905–4907. A listing of other *Ch'ing-shih* references to Chang appears in vol. 8, pp. 192–193.

7. The Chang line has been traced back to an ancestor identified as Chang Pen, who migrated from Hung-tung in Shansi province to K'uo-hsien in Chihli. His grandson, Chang Tuan, a subdistrict deputy magistrate (*hsün-chien*), moved the family from K'uo-hsien to Nan-p'i. Chang Tuan's son, Chang Huai, became a *chin-shih* in 1508 and later served as a provincial judge (*an-ch'a shih*) in Honan. Chang Chih-tung's great-grandfather I-hsiung was a district magistrate at Shan-yin, Chekiang. His grandfather T'ing-chen became a *kung-sheng* during the Ch'ien-lung period (1736–1796) and served in Peking as a copyist of the Imperial Library (Ssu-k'u-ch'üan-shu kuan), before transferring to Fukien province as a salt official and subsequently a district magistrate. In addition to information in the *nien-p'u*, data on the Chang family may be found in two gazetteers of the same title, the *Nan-p'i-hsien chih*, comp. Wang Pao-shu (1888) and Liu Shu-hsin (1932). See also the epitaph by Ch'en Pao-ch'en in *CC, chüan-shou shang*, pp. 22–22b.

8. From a memorial biography (*hsing-chuang*) of Chang Ying by Chang Chih-ch'ing, an elder brother of Chang Chih-tung. It appears in Hu Chün, 1:5, but not in *HNP*.

9. Chang Chung-ju, pp. 50–51; Chang Chung-li, p. 25; Shang Yen-liu, *Ch'ing-tai k'o-chü k'ao-shih shu-lu* (Peking, 1958), pp. 94–96.

the examination system, Chang Ying was ordered to Kweichow to become the district magistrate of An-hua. He filled several other positions in the province before being assigned as the prefect of Hsing-i.

Chang Ying married three times and had fourteen children. Chang Chih-tung was the fourth of six brothers.[10] His mother, the third wife of Chang Ying, was the daughter of Chu Shao-en, a native of Kiangsi and a *chin-shih* of 1814, who served as a department magistrate in Szechwan. Chang's mother died in 1840, and the boy was placed under the care of a concubine named Wei, a native of Kweichow. Chang became fond of his stepmother and remained loyal to her until she died at Nan-p'i in 1887.

At the age of four Chang Chih-tung entered a Hsing-i school under a teacher named Ho Yang-yüan. From the beginning, Chang studied words closely until he had fully grasped their meanings. Between the ages of eight and ten he finished reading the Thirteen Classics and began to study poetry and essay writing. During these years, Chang meditated over problems until they became clear in his mind. If he grew weary by midnight, he would bow over his table and doze, then wake up and think some more—until at last he obtained the answers to his questions. His persistence was marked, though not quite so extreme as that of a Han dynasty student, Sun Ching, who tied his head to a beam to keep from falling asleep at his studies.[11]

Determined that his sons should succeed where he had failed, Chang Ying closely supervised their education. He impressed upon them the poor standing of the Chang family and instructed the boys that they should study hard so as eventually to raise the family's status. He taught them to adopt frugality (*chien-yüeh*) and knowledge of propriety (*chih-li*) as guides. Because Kweichow was a rustic province and had poor educational facilities.[12] Chang Ying stretched his salary to buy books for his sons—historical works, the writings of Chu Hsi, and commentaries on the classics. Chang Ying insisted that his sons read these works even though they could not understand them. He believed that if one absorbed much when young, understanding would come naturally with adulthood.

On one occasion, when Chang Chih-tung was ten years old, his budding literary talent caused his father particular delight. The Hsing-i director

10. The sons of Chang Ying were Chih-wu, Chih-ch'ing, Chih-yüan, Chih-tung, Chih-ch'eng, and Chih-yung. Four daughters married, three died before marriage, and one remained single after the death of her fiancé. For further details on the family, see Hu Chün, 1:5; *HNP*, pp. 4–5.

11. H. A. Giles, *A Chinese Biographical Dictionary* (Shanghai, 1898), p. 688.

12. The *sheng-yüan* quota for Kweichow before 1850 was only 753. All other provinces had quotas exceeding 1,000. The highest quota of 2,845 was allotted to Chihli. Chang Chung-li, pp. 79, 142.

of schools (*chiao-shou*) had composed a poem in the ancient style, and Chang Ying ordered his son to match it. The boy took up his brush and did so at once. The pleased father poured wine to drink and rewarded Chang Chih-tung with an antique ink-slab.

In 1848 at the age of eleven (twelve *sui*), Chang Chih-tung compiled his first book. As he was fond of studying in the Pavilion of Heavenly Fragrance that his father had built on the grounds of the Hsing-i prefectural office, he entitled this collection of poems and essays the *T'ien-hsiang-ko shih-erh-ling ts'ao* (Pavilion of Heavenly Fragrance jottings of a twelve-year-old). The volume was shown to an uncle, who wryly advised the boy that such talent should be stored and not exposed. Later Chang Chih-tung burned all of his childhood writings, but for the rest of his life he could recite them.

The First Examinations

When he was twelve years old, Chang Chih-tung began intensive preparation for his first civil service examinations. In 1849 he and three of his brothers were tutored by Han Ch'ao, an official awaiting appointment in Kweichow, who later became governor of the province.[13] Chang received training in history and government from Han Ch'ao and training in the classics, classical commentaries, and ancient prose (*ku-wen*) from other teachers.[14] Han Ch'ao soon took up service under Hu Lin-i, an official who was to win prominence as a general operating against the Taiping rebels. Hu was then a prefect at Li-p'ing in Kweichow, and Chang Chih-tung reportedly sought his advice on writing. A brilliant student who had done well in the civil service examinations, Hu Lin-i was well-qualified to offer assistance.[15]

13. Han Ch'ao was a native of Chihli and became a *fu-kung-sheng* in 1834. Following service as a district judge in Chihli, he was transferred to Kweichow, where Chang Ying employed him as a tutor. For a biography, see *Ch'ing-shih kao*, 426:1; *Ch'ing-shih*, 6:4808–4809.

14. *Pao-ping-t'ang ti-tzu chi, CC*, 228:27. This source also states that Chang studied the classics under Lü Hsien-chi, commentaries under Liu Shu-nien, and ancient prose under Chu Ch'i. Lü, a native of Anhwei and a senior vice president of the Board of Works, was an examiner when Chang Chih-tung took his provincial examination in 1852. In the following year Lü was killed in action while serving as a militia leader against the Taipings. Hummel, II, 949; *Ch'ing-shih kao*, 405:19; *Ch'ing shih lieh-chuan*, 54:1; *Ch'ing-shih*, 7:5535. Liu, a native of Chihli, was an intendant and the father-in-law of Chang Chih-tung's eldest sister. In 1861 Chang served as a tutor to Liu's second son. For a biography, see *Ch'ing-shih*, 6:4590–4591. Chu, a *chin-shih* of 1835, served as a censor in the capital but established his reputation later as a defense force leader in Kwangsi.

15. For information on Hu Lin-i, see Hummel, I, 333–335; Mary C. Wright, p. 118. *HNP*, p. 3, lists twelve other men under whom Chang studied, of whom Chang once said that the most capable was Ting Chia-mou, a *chin-shih* of 1838 and a reader of the Hanlin Academy. See also Hu Chün, 1:2b–3.

Government regulations stipulated that all "men of promise" (*chün-hsiu*) or candidates for the first examinations (*t'ung-shih*) had to register in their native districts.[16] They were required to verify that they came from "pure" families who had resided in the locality for at least three generations.[17] Each candidate was also required to enlist locally five fellow-candidates and a student on government stipend (*lin-sheng*) to serve as guarantors.[18] These regulations demanded that Chang Chih-tung sit for his first examinations in the Nan-p'i district, his ancestral home in Chihli province. Chang left Kweichow for Chihli in 1849. Traveling by wheelbarrow, he was accompanied by three of his brothers. After Chang reached Chihli, he earned the approbation of the provincial director of education (*hsüeh-cheng*), Ch'eng T'ing-kuei, and in 1850 was enrolled by the Nan-p'i district school. Additional information is lacking on Chang's experience with the local tests, but entering a government school was the mark of success in the series of examinations and reexaminations before the district magistrate, prefect, and director of education.[19] Thus, in 1850 Chang Chih-tung became a *sheng-yüan,* and a member of the gentry in his own right.

By 1852, the second year of the Hsien-feng reign, Chang Chih-tung was ready to enter competition for the *chü-jen* degree. In Chihli the examination for this degree was not solely for Chinese *sheng-yüan* from the various prefectures of the province. Held in Peking and known as the Shun-t'ien *hsiang-shih* (after the metropolitan prefecture Shun-t'ien *fu*), the examination was also open to Manchu and Mongol bannermen; *chien-sheng* (students of the Imperial College or those who had purchased the *chien-sheng* degree); *kung-sheng* who chose to take this test rather than one in their native provinces; candidates from Ch'eng-te prefecture in Jehol and Hsüan-hua prefecture in Chihli where the Manchus maintained alternate courts; and *sheng-yüan* of Fengtien province in Manchuria. The examination courtyard in Peking contained 13,000 to 14,000 cells to accommodate these various students writing their essays during

16. Chang Chung-ju, p. 3.
17. Among the "mean people" excluded from examinations were the sons and grandsons of actors, prostitutes, and servants. For a listing of others legally or practically excluded, see Chang Chung-ju, p. 3; Chang Chung-li, pp. 10, 12; Hsieh Pao-chao, *The Government of China (1644–1911)* (Baltimore, 1925), pp. 143–145.
18. Chang Chung-ju, p. 3. For a detailed discussion of the procedures of registration and guarantee, see Etienne Zi, *Pratique des examens litteraires,* pp. 19–31.
19. Until 1850 quotas for 122 district schools of Chihli province permitted the enrollment of 2,110 *sheng-yüan.* The highest number for a single school was 26, and the lowest was 10. Chang Chung-li, Table 15, p. 142.

the three sessions of the Shun-t'ien examination. Yet quota provisions permitted the award of fewer than 300 *chü-jen* degrees, of which about 100 were reserved for Chihli provincial candidates.[20]

Chang Chih-tung took the Shun-t'ien test under three chief examiners: the Manchu president of the Board of Works, Lin-k'uei, and two Chinese officials, Chu Feng-piao and Lü Hsien-chi. These examiners judged Chang's paper to be the best submitted and placed his name first on the list of new *chü-jen*. By this success, Chang Chih-tung, at age fifteen, gained the honorary title of *chieh-yüan*, awarded to the candidate winning top honors in a provincial examination.[21] A report of his success was quickly transmitted to Kweichow, and Hu Lin-i wrote to Chang Ying: "When we received news of your son's winning first honors, Nan Ch'i (Han Ch'ao) and I were joyful for many days." It was an unusual distinction for so young a scholar.

An Interlude of Rebellion and War

Ten years were to pass before Chang Chih-tung took the metropolitan examination for the *chin-shih* degree. National events began to impinge on his life and were partly responsible for delaying his advance through the examination system. The Taiping Rebellion had begun in Kwangsi in 1850, the year that Chang became a *sheng-yüan*. When Chang took the Shun-t'ien examination in 1852, the rebels were advancing toward the Yangtze Valley. Following the examination, Chang spent a year with relatives in Peking. In the summer of 1853, five months after the Taiping capture of Nanking, he began a journey to Kweichow to visit his father. There he found Chang Ying busy with problems of defense against the rebels.

20. Zi, *Pratique des examens litteraires*, pp. 105, 115–117; Shang Yen-liu, p. 50; translation from the *K'o-ch'ang t'iao-li* (Examination regulations) in Robert Morrison, *A Dictionary of the Chinese Language* (Macao, 1815–1823), p. 763; Chang Chung-li, pp. 22, 124–125, 167–170. According to Zi, the original Shun-tien quota (*yüan-o*) of 270 degrees was increased by 10 in 1853 when the Hsien-feng emperor augmented the quotas of all provinces in consideration of donations to the state during the opening years of the Taiping rebellion. Chang Chung-li reports the quota was 229 in 1881, and he does not include Chihli among provinces that had won a permanent increase of 10 degrees by 1874.

21. Literally, *chieh-yüan* means "first to be sent forward." In the T'ang dynasty scholars to be presented to the court were "sent forward" from the various localities. Later the provincial examinations were called the *chieh-shih*, "examinations of those to be sent forward." *Tz'u-hai* dictionary; Zi, *Pratique des examens litteraires*, p. 156. For biographies of Lin-k'uei and Chu Feng-piao, see *Ch'ing-shih*, 6:4640–4641, 4645–4646.

In 1850 Chang Ying had recommended that higher authorities adopt a plan of attack once used against other rebels in Southwest China by a Ming general, Li Hua-lung (1554–1611). While a decision was pending, Chang Ying was permitted to begin raising volunteer forces to guard the Kwangsi-Kweichow border near Hsing-i. His men experienced their first action when routing a group of Taiping rebels who had tried to cross the river forming the boundary between the two provinces. About the time that Chang Chih-tung reached Kweichow in 1853, his father submitted a lengthy plan for a militia to the Yünnan-Kweichow governor general, Wu Wen-jung. The governor general was impressed and placed Chang Ying in temporary charge of the Western Kweichow Circuit as a military administrative intendant (*ping-pei tao-t'ai*). Chang Ying's jurisdiction bordered an area of Yünnan province harboring Moslem groups who had also begun to rise against the government. Chang Ying raised funds privately, mustered troops, and made a foray across the border into Yünnan to pacify the town of Tung-ch'uan.

In 1854, when a rebel named Yang Feng attacked Hsing-i, Chang Chih-tung and other relatives mounted the parapet to help in the defense. The rebels took Hsing-i, but the Chang family escaped before its fall. Chang Ying then formed an encampment about ten miles beyond Hsing-i and appealed to the people for more recruits. He offered tax exemptions and rewards as inducements to enlist. In a short time he had raised a large force and reoccupied Hsing-i. He defeated the rebels and executed some of their commanders. Later he pursued Yang Feng to a river northeast of Hsing-i and destroyed his forces there.

Chang Chih-tung served alongside his father during part of 1855. However, when Chang Ying began to campaign against the dissident Miao tribes of Kweichow, he sent his eighteen-year-old son back to North China. Chang was accompanied on this trip by his first wife, whom he had married in 1854. A daughter of Shih Hsü, the prefect of Tu-yün, Kweichow, she died in 1865. In 1870 Chang married a daughter of T'ang Shu-i, a Hupeh provincial official who was a native of Tsun-i, Kweichow. Chang's second wife died in 1872, and in 1876 he married a younger sister of Wang I-jung, the noted scholar who committed suicide during the Boxer Uprising. Chang's third wife died in 1879, the same year that her father, Wang Tsu-yüan, became governor of Szechwan. Before 1885 Chang took a concubine named Li, and in 1891 he took another concubine, named Ch'in. He had six sons and four daughters. The daughters were T'an (b.1855), Jen-chun (b.1877), Jen-hui (b.1888), and Jen-chi (b. 1890). The sons were Ch'üan, originally named Jen-ch'üan

(1860–1930), Jen-t'ing (1871–1895), Jen-k'an (1885–1945), Jen-shih (1892–1930), Jen-yüeh (1898–), and Jen-li (1900–1949?).[22]

Soon after Chang Chih-tung returned to Chihli in 1856, he took a Board of Rites examination to qualify as an instructor for the Gioro Official Schools (Chüeh-lo kuan-hsüeh). These schools were established for sons of the Aisin Gioro clan, to which the ruling Manchu family belonged. One school was maintained for each of the Eight Banners, and with a single exception, each school had two Manchu and two Chinese instructors. Chinese *chü-jen* or *chin-shih* could qualify as instructors by taking an examination that consisted of writing an essay on the Four Books and composing a poem of five-word lines.[23] As a reexamination, the candidates were required to write portions of their earlier essay and poem from memory. Men passing the examination were eligible to fill vacancies occurring on the faculties of the Gioro schools. Chang succeeded in the examination but was not appointed to a teaching job.

Several months after this test, Chang learned of the death of his father. Chang Ying had been placed in charge of the Eastern Kweichow Circuit to fight against the Miao tribesmen. His initial support from higher provincial authorities was poor, and he reportedly pawned his own clothing and other effects to help provide for the militia. When adequate official funds were finally forthcoming, he led several attacks against the Miao. But fighting during rainy weather in a season of high humidity

22. Chang T'an died in 1868, but the younger daughters grew to adulthood and married. For a biography of the eldest son, Chang Ch'üan, a *chin-shih* of 1898 who served as a secretary at the Chinese Legation in Washington, 1904–1906, see *Nan-p'i-hsien chih*, 8:62b. Chang Jen-t'ing was given in adoption to relatives, had difficulties with his father and aunt, and committed suicide at an early age by jumping into a pond (according to Chang Jen-yüeh, interviewed in Tokyo in 1967). For a biography of Chang Jen-k'an, who held positions in the Ministry of Communications and other government offices in the early Republic, see Yang Chia-lo, *Min-kuo ming-jen t'u-chien* (Nanking, 1937), I, 5:45. Chang Jen-shih (also known as Jen-sou) served as a tax department official in Fengtien; he died following an operation for appendicitis. Chang Jen-yüeh, better known by his literary name of Jen-ch'ing, served as Minister of Industry and Minister of Foreign Affairs of Manchukuo in 1932–1937 and as chairman of the People's Reform Society (Hsin-min hui) in Peking during the Japanese occupation. He was briefly imprisoned as a collaborator after World War II, as reported in the Tientsin *Ta-kung pao*, September 19, 1946. He escaped from China in 1951 and now lives in Japan. For a biography, see *Who's Who in Japan, with Manchukuo and China, 1941–1942*, ed. Tsunesaburo Kameska (Tokyo, 1941). For a sketch of Chang Jen-li, under the name of Chang Jen-yüan, see the same source. He served as mayor of Hankow and chairman of the Wuhan Sino-Japanese Cultural Association under the puppet regime in World War II, was later imprisoned for life, and was reportedly executed by the Chinese Communists in 1949 or 1950. On Chang's family, see also *CC, chüan-shou shang*, pp. 22–22b; *HNP*, pp. 5, 6, 11, 13, 14, 15, 19, 20, 21, 49, 61, 73, 77, 96, 113, 140.

23. Manchus took a test in translating from the Manchu language to the Chinese. For the Gioro and other schools maintained for the imperial family and the Eight Banners, see Chang Chung-ju, pp. 51–53; Shang Yen-liu, pp. 215–216.

caused the recurrence of a former illness. He was released from active duty and died shortly thereafter, on August 24, 1856. His body was escorted back to Chihli for burial in a temple grove at Nan-p'i, and Chang Chih-tung began a period of mourning for his father.[24]

After Chang emerged from mourning in 1858, he spent another four years marking time until he could take an examination for the *chin-shih* degree. Early in 1859 he prepared for the regular triennial metropolitan examination (*hui-shih*), and in 1860 he went to Peking planning to take an extraordinary metropolitan examination offered by the emperor's grace (*en-k'o hui-shih*). But each time he made application for the test, he discovered that one of the examiners appointed by the throne was a relative, Chang Chih-wan.[25] According to regulations, Chang Chih-tung could not sit for the examination for fear of favoritism.[26]

While awaiting another opportunity to take the metropolitan examination, Chang had a second experience in military affairs. Returning to Nan-p'i in 1859 after his unsuccessful attempt to enter that year's test, he took charge of a militia force, the Ch'ing Pacification Corps (Ch'ing-p'ing t'uan-lien), which guarded more than twenty villages in his native district.[27] This occurred after the British and French had brought the war to Chihli in 1858 and had forced acceptance of the Tientsin treaties. Their insistence that ratifications of the treaties be exchanged at Peking had led to a renewal of hostilities in 1859. In 1860, following Chang's return to the capital, the foreign allies stormed the Taku forts and pushed on to Peking. The Hsien-feng emperor fled to Jehol with his court, and Lord Elgin burned the Summer Palace. At this time Chang Chih-tung

24. For several years after Chang Ying's death, Chang Chih-tung nourished a feeling that his father had not been sufficiently recognized. In 1862 he petitioned his old tutor Han Ch'ao, by then governor of Kweichow, to memorialize for posthumous honors for Chang Ying. He eloquently outlined his father's contributions toward rebel suppression and his sufferings on behalf of the dynasty, while defending him against criticisms by the Yünnan-Kweichow governor general. As a result of Han Ch'ao's intercession, the throne conferred upon Chang Ying the posthumous title of Director of the Court of the Imperial Stud (T'ai-pu ssu ch'ing). Chang Ying's main scholarly accomplishment was a compilation of the *Hsing-i-fu chih* (Gazetteer of Hsing-i prefecture).

25. In Western writings Chang Chih-wan has sometimes been identified erroneously as an elder brother of Chang Chih-tung. Actually they were distant relatives, both being descended from Chang Huai, who lived in the sixteenth century. *HNP*, p. 6. Chang Chih-wan (1811–1897) received highest honors in the *chin-shih* examination of 1847. After filling a number of provincial posts, he became a member of the Grand Council and Grand Secretariat and was one of the most prominent officials in Peking from 1882 until 1894. Hummel, I, 32.

26. If an examiner had relatives among the candidates, he was required to post a notice on the outer wall of the examination court and order the relatives to withdraw. For the degrees of relationship affected by this ruling, see Chang Chung-ju, p. 30.

27. Similar instances of gentry members organizing militia corps are cited by Chang Chung-li, pp. 66–68.

wrote a dirge in which he lamented the recent course of events. In his collected works this poem represents Chang's earliest comment on foreign affairs.[28]

The Final Examinations

Later in 1860 Chang Chih-tung went to Tsinan to serve as a secretary on the staff of Wen-yü, the Shantung governor.[29] But an illness the following year caused him to return to Chihli. There he took a position as tutor to the younger son of an official named Liu Shu-nien, the father-in-law of Chang's eldest sister. As this job allowed Chang time for reading, he declined a friend's offer to recommend him for employment by the Manchu general Sheng-pao. Chang wrote that he was occupied with the study of "important points concerning the successes and failures of ancient and modern kings and nobles" and that his mind was in a rather peaceful state.

His tranquillity was soon shattered. In 1862, the first year of the T'ung-chih reign, he finally sat for the metropolitan examination—and failed. Metropolitan examinations, at which about eight thousand candidates presented themselves, were presided over by four chief examiners (*tsung-ts'ai*) and eighteen assistant examiners (*t'ung k'ao-kuan*), in addition to a host of lesser functionaries.[30] It was customary for the examiners to inscribe judgments on the essay papers under their scrutiny, whether the papers were finally chosen or not.[31] An assistant examiner named Fan Ming-ho was extremely enthusiastic about Chang Chih-tung's effort. Weng T'ung-ho, whose important diary covered forty-six years of late Ch'ing history, recorded that he saw Fan's judgment on the paper. Chang's essay on a theme from the Four Books was described as "deeply profound and decidedly beautiful." The essay on a theme from the Five Classics was "fully substantiated and amply supported by quotations." The general style was considered worthy of Ssu-ma Ch'ien's *Shih-chi* (Records of History) or the *Han-shu* (History of the Han Dynasty). Despite Fan Ming-ho's opinion, however, one of the chief examiners, Cheng Tun-chin, did not consider the effort highly meritorious, and the paper was finally eliminated. According to Weng T'ung-ho, its rejection "caused men to grasp their wrists (in great regret)."[32]

28. *CC*, 224:14–14b.
29. For a biography of Wen-yü, see *Ch'ing-shih*, 6:4639.
30. Chang Chung-ju, pp. 28–29; Chang Chung-li, p. 126.
31. Zi, *Pratique des examens litteraires*, pp. 68–69, 152–153.
32. *Weng Wen-kung kung jih-chi* (The diary of Weng Wen-kung kung), quoted in *HNP*, p. 7.

Following this failure, Chang Chih-tung traveled to Honan, where he became a private secretary to Mao Ch'ang-hsi, a former Peking official who was then directing the provincial militia forces.[33] At the end of 1862 Chang's relative Chang Chih-wan was appointed governor of Honan. Chang Chih-tung joined the governor's staff to help draft memorials. The documents submitted thereafter to the throne were said to have caused the regent empresses, Tz'u-hsi and Tz'u-an, "to change countenance and sigh in admiration."

By the spring of 1863, Chang was back in the capital to sit for another metropolitan examination offered by imperial grace.[34] This time he suc-ceeded and thereupon became a *kung-shih* or "tribute scholar." But he did not repeat the superior performance of his provincial examination. When the passing candidates were announced on May 26, 1863, Chang's name was 141st on the list of 198 successful candidates.[35] Chang was nevertheless grateful, and in thanking those who had helped him, he visited Fan Ming-ho, the examiner who had supported his cause a year earlier. The two men exchanged poems in celebration of the occasion.[36]

A series of more advanced and specialized examinations now awaited Chang Chih-tung before he could receive his first appointment to office. On May 31, 1863, he sat for a repetition (*fu-shih*) of the metropolitan examination. This usually consisted of writing a poem and an essay on a topic from the Four Books. Successful candidates on this test were graded according to three classes.[37] Having rallied his wits for the *fu-shih*, Chang Chih-tung was ranked first in the first class when the results were announced.

On June 6, 1863, Chang took the palace examination (*tien-shih*), writ-ing a 2,000-word dissertation in reply to four questions on government. In theory, the emperor chose questions for the palace examination, pre-sided over the test, reviewed the papers, and determined the final ranking of candidates after receiving recommendations from the several essay examiners (*yüeh-chüan ta-ch'en*), whom he had appointed earlier by special decree. However, when Chang Chih-tung took the palace exam-

33. For a biography of Mao Ch'ang-hsi, see *Ch'ing-shih,* 6:4799–4801.
34. The chief examiners on this occasion were Li T'ang-chieh, Shan Mao-ch'ien, Shen Kuei-fen, and the Manchu official Tsai-ling. For a biography of Li, see Hummel, I, 485–486. For Shan, Shen, and Tsai-ling, see *Ch'ing-shih,* 6:4646, 4899, and 4918.
35. The total number of *kung-shih* chosen in 1863 is taken from Chang Chung-li, Table 27, pp. 157–159.
36. *CC,* 224:19b–21.
37. This *fu-shih* originated in 1712. Shang Yen-liu, p. 107. See also Chang Chung-ju, p. 32.

ination, the T'ung-chih emperor was still a minor, and decisions on his behalf were being made by the Empress Dowager Tz'u-hsi.

Chang's palace examination essay created a small controversy. By comparison with prevailing standards, it was a presumptuous and forthright critique of current policies and in part a bold attack on the very examination system whose pinnacle Chang was then approaching. Some of the imperial essay examiners were displeased, finding Chang's paper "contrary to tradition and out of harmony with precedents." *Kung-shih* who passed the palace examination were grouped in three classes, the first class being composed of only three men, who won the honorary titles of *chuang-yüan, pang-yen,* and *t'an-hua*.[38] The essay examiners originally planned to place Chang last in the third class of graduates. However, a Manchu examiner, Pao-yün, appreciated Chang's dissertation. Upon Pao-yün's recommendation, Chang was moved up to first place in the second class. The essays of the various candidates were then submitted to the throne for approval. Tz'u-hsi was instrumental in raising Chang another notch. He finally placed third in the first class and was awarded the honorary title of *t'an-hua*.[39] The incident is noteworthy, for it was possibly the origin of that strong personal loyalty which Chang later demonstrated toward the empress dowager.

On June 10, 1863, Chang Chih-tung was confirmed as a *chin-shih*.[40] Four days later he finished second in the first class of graduates who took the court examination (*ch'ao-k'ao*), a contest for admission to the

38. The term *chuang-yüan,* loosely meaning "first in exposition," originated in the T'ang dynasty to describe the top man in the palace examination. It was applied to the three highest-ranking candidates during the Sung dynasty, but later again referred only to the highest man. *Pang-yen,* "the eye of the examination list," originated in the Northern Sung period. At first it was applied to the second and third ranking men—the two eyes of the list. But by the end of the Southern Sung period, the third man was being called *t'an-hua* or "searcher for flowers," which evolved from a practice at the "Ch'ü River feast," given for successful *chin-shih* at Ch'ang-an during the T'ang dynasty. Dotted along the river were pavilions, temples, parks, and pleasure gardens frequented by residents of the capital. The two or three youngest *chin-shih* present at the feast were designated *t'an-hua shih* or "commissioners to search for flowers." They accompanied the rest of the *chin-shih* on a tour of the famous parks, and if the others plucked flowers first, the "commissioners" were "punished." *Tz'u-yüan* and *Tz'u-hai* dictionaries; Shang Yen-liu, p. 118.

39. *Pao-ping-t'ang ti-tzu chi, CC,* 228:1. The *chuang-yüan* of 1863 was Weng Tsengyüan, a son of Weng T'ung-shu and a nephew of Weng T'ung-ho. The *pang-yen* was Kung Ch'eng-chün, who later became a censor. Fang Chao-ying and Tu Lien-che, *Tseng-chiao Ch'ing-ch'ao chin-shih t'i-ming pei-lu* (Peiping, 1941), p. 193; Hummel, II, 858–859; Zi, *Pratique des examens litteraires,* p. 236. For biography of Pao-yün, see *Ch'ing-shih,* 6:4630–4631.

40. Two hundred men became *chin-shih* in 1863. Fang Chao-ying and Tu Lien-che, p. 159; Chang Chung-li, Table 27, p. 159.

Hanlin Academy and for initial rank in the bureaucracy. Chang was presented at court on June 23 and was appointed a second-class Hanlin compiler (*pien-hsiu*), a seventh-rank post in the system of nine official grades.[41] Chang received an automatic promotion a year later when by imperial decree all officials were raised one grade to celebrate the recapture of Nanking from the Taiping rebels, a victory marking the practical end of the fourteen-year-revolt.

Three additional examinations awaited Chang Chih-tung before receiving his first provincial assignment. New Hanlin scholars entered the academy's Department of Study (Shu-ch'ang kuan) for periods of research and reading. At the end of the term they were given an "examination for release from the department" (*san-kuan k'ao-shih*). Those who were successful were retained at the academy and those who failed were released to fill positions as secretaries in various Peking boards or as district magistrates elsewhere.[42] When Chang Chih-tung took this examination in 1865, he placed first in the first class.

In 1866 Chang took the *Han-Chan ta-k'ao* or "great examination for the Hanlin Academy and the Supervisorate of Imperial Instruction (Chan-shih-fu)." This examination originated early in the Ch'ing dynasty to check up on the competence of capital officials concerned with documentary and literary matters. Successful candidates achieving the first and second classes were promoted, recommended to fill vacancies, or awarded with gifts of satin. Those in the third and fourth classes were demoted, fined a part of their salary for one or two years, or degraded and transferred. Unsuccessful candidates were cashiered.[43] Because he omitted one character from his essay, Chang Chih-tung fell to thirty-second place in the second class when he took the test. It was his first error of this kind. Attesting to Chang's ability as a writer is the fact that, from the local examinations through the court examination, he used no scratch paper, and later his essays were printed without the revision of a single character.[44]

41. H. S. Brunnert and V. V. Hagelstrom, *Present Day Political Organization of China* (Shanghai, 1912), p. 73.

42. Chang Chung-ju, p. 42; Brunnert and Hagelstrom, p. 73; Shang Yen-liu, pp. 130–131. Requirements for this examination varied before the first year of the Ch'ien-lung reign. From 1736 to 1865, according to Shang, p. 130, the test consisted of *shih* and *fu* poetry writing. In 1865 the requirement was changed to *ts'e* and *lun*, but the *shih* and *fu* were restored in 1868.

43. Shang Yen-liu, pp. 134–135; Chang Chung-ju, p. 46.

44. *CC*, 228:1 The best papers of various examinations were sent to the Board of Rites for final review and revision. Selected essays from the provincial, metropolitan, and palace examinations were published in collections such as the *Hsiang-shih lu*, the *Hui-shih lu*, and the *Teng-k'o lu*.

The final examination taken by Chang before leaving Peking was the "test for commission" (*k'ao-ch'ai*), given to form a register of men qualified for commissions as chief and assistant officers to conduct provincial examinations.[45] Chang passed this test and on August 19, 1867, was appointed assistant examiner for a forthcoming provincial examination in Chekiang. Thus, at the age of thirty, Chang had successfully completed his passage through the examination system. For six of the next eight years he was to help administer the system, as a provincial examiner in Chekiang and Hupeh and as a provincial director of education (*hsüeh-cheng*) in Hupeh and Szechwan.

Early Views on Reform

Although this account of Chang Chih-tung's youth provides little insight into his personality, it shows the complexity of civil service recruitment in the late Ch'ing dynasty. The honors achieved by Chang in several of the tests were extraordinary, and he entered the bureaucracy at an earlier age than average. But his subjects of study, the sequence of examinations, and the delays he endured were typical of the experiences of many young men of his day.

The vital statistics of Chang's youth make it clear that learning acquired from Chinese literature and applied in the civil service examinations was a main ingredient in his intellectual development between 1837 and 1867. The spectacle of Chinese governmental weakness and decline, made patent by war and rebellion, may be assumed to have been another outstanding influence. Applying the sanctions of Confucian philosophy and the traditions of Chinese statecraft, Chang gradually came to realize that the empire was imperiled, and this condition indicated to him a need for reform.

Chang at first thought that adequate prescriptions for reform could be found in the Confucian classics and the standard histories. Good government depended chiefly upon the character of the rulers and officials, as the classics made clear in propounding the power of moral example. Yet Chang felt that the examination system alone was inadequate as a means of obtaining men of high moral quality and "solid learning." Modification of the system was therefore one of the reforms to which the emperor should give priority. Chang Chih-tung presented these views in his palace

45. On the *k'ao-ch'ai*, see Shang Yen-liu, pp. 133–134; Chang Chung-ju, pp. 43–45. The examination was held in the Pao-ho Palace and usually consisted of *fu* and *shih* poetry writing. Candidates were not ranked in classes, but the names of those who passed were recorded.

examination essay of 1863. Among the documents preserved in his complete works, this essay gives the best glimpse into Chang's political thought at the outset of his official career.[46]

Since the late eighteenth century, examination candidates had been encouraged to dwell upon philological issues in their discussion essays and to avoid analysis of current affairs.[47] When Chang Chih-tung received questions on current affairs in his palace examination, however, he failed to give his answers the proper philological twist that would have pleased some of his examiners. Although Chang remained within the extreme bounds of Chinese tradition, his ideas nevertheless seemed bold. He began his essay with a dramatic flourish, stating that he would discuss contemporary affairs frankly and risk the executioner's axe in behalf of one honest word for the emperor.[48]

Chang's palace examination consisted of four questions, each expected to lead toward textual exegesis. First, Chang was asked to present quotations from the classics and commentaries to support the statement that the Two Sovereigns (Yao and Shun) and the Three Kings (Yü, T'ang, and Wu, founders of the Hsia, Shang, and Chou dynasties) strictly adhered to the mean in their important policies. The second question called for suggestions on the examination system and bureaucratic recruitment, in view of the statement that order would prevail throughout the empire if worthy talent were obtained. In the third and fourth questions, Chang was asked to suggest how extravagance could be controlled and how oppression of the people by rapacious minor officials could be checked.

In answering the last two questions, Chang Chih-tung drew a bleak picture of the empire. He diagnosed China's problems bluntly, even if too simply: "Today the greatest evil in the empire is poverty. The officials are poor and therefore corrupt. The people are poor and therefore become bandits. The army is poor and therefore unable to fight." Conspicuous consumption was rampant among the populace and bureaucracy. Among the people there was wasteful expenditure for personal adornment, and proper status differentiations were overlooked in favor of lavish ostentation in the ceremonies of capping (for initiating boys to

46. For text of the palace examination essay, see *CC*, 212:1–5b.
47. Chang Chung-li, p. 176.
48. Chang was speaking figuratively, for criticism of high officials and official policies was permitted during examinations. Regulations forbade students to criticize on other occasions, offenders being subject to execution, confiscation of property, and enslavement of their families. Chang Chung-li, p. 176 *n*.51.

adulthood), marriage, mourning, and sacrifice.[49] Demands of the luxury-loving high officials for food, household equipment, carriages, and servants were ultimately paid for by the people.[50] Taxes were too heavy, and prefects and intendants extorting illegal fees from department and district magistrates left the latter gasping for breath.

Although Chang proclaimed that the Chinese government was functioning badly, he was unwilling to admit that the Confucian philosophy upon which the government rested was inherently at fault. Practitioners of Confucianism (*ju-shu*) were shooting wide of the mark, he charged, but the philosophy itself was not to blame. Confucianism would work if its adherents respected the law, revered the sages, and thoroughly understood the past and present. Within the Confucian framework, it was only necessary to "nourish the roots and improve customs" (*p'ei pen-ken hou feng-su*).

In answering the last two questions of his palace examination, Chang Chih-tung proposed two specific improvements. First, he suggested that the throne take the lead in an austerity campaign.[51] The emperor should revive ancient prohibitions against waste, remind the imperial kindred to adhere to their ranks in performing ceremonies, and reduce levies of silk to provide relief for the farmers of China. Second, Chang suggested that a new source of wealth be developed. He proposed the establishment of military-agricultural colonies similar to those sponsored occasionally by past dynasties since the Han period.[52] Wastelands, forests, grasslands, and dried-up river beds should be reclaimed by farmer-soldiers. Military-agricultural colonies could help supply food for other

49. Chang's terminology suggested classical injunctions on status and rites, quoted hereafter from James Legge, *The Four Books.* For example, *Lun-yü*, bk. III, 4:3: "In festive ceremonies, it is better to be sparing than extravagant. In ceremonies of mourning, it is better that there be deep sorrow than a minute attention to observances." Or *Chung-yung*, ch. 14: "The superior man does what is proper to the station in which he is; he does not desire to go beyond this. In a position of wealth and honor, he does what is proper to a position of wealth and honor. In a poor and low position, he does what is proper to a poor and low position."

50. Cf. *Meng-tzu*, bk. I, 4:4: "In your kitchen there is fat meat; in your stables there are fat horses. But your people have the look of hunger, and on the wilds there are those who have died of famine. This is leading on beasts to devour men."

51. Cf. *Lun-yü*, bk. VII, ch. 35: "Extravagance leads to insubordination, and parsimony to meanness. It is better to be mean than to be insubordinate."

52. Military-agricultural colonies were referred to as early as the *Han-shu*: "At the time (111 B.C.) when the provinces of Chang-yeh and Tun-huang were first established, *k'ai-t'ien-kuan* (officers in charge of cultivating land) and [conscripted] soldiers (*tsu*) numbering six hundred thousand men . . . were [stationed] there to expand frontier walls and watch towers, and to garrison and cultivate the land." Nancy Lee Swann, *Food and Money in Ancient China* (Princeton, N.J., 1950), p. 307.

areas; likin and duties could be levied on their produce; and a number of China's worthless troops could be given productive employment.

While advocating these particular economic reforms, Chang Chih-tung indicated elsewhere in the palace examination essay that the fundamental question facing the empire was how to improve the caliber of its officials.[53] In attempting to draw a moral for his own day from the example of the Two Sovereigns and Three Kings, Chang stressed the need for the minor T'ung-chih emperor to "nourish virtue" (*yü-te*).[54] In the process of "nourishing virtue," the emperor should learn the difference between good and evil, reverence and unscrupulousness, reason and desire, so that he could distinguish between "superior men" and "mean men." He should cultivate objectivity, allowing neither his own pleasure nor anger to dictate the acceptance or disregard of suggestions made by his worthy advisers.[55] Chang called upon the emperor to pay special attention to a saying of the Sung philosopher Ch'eng I: "Increase affection for men of virtue and worthy officials." Reiterating a tenet of orthodox Confucian political theory, Chang wrote, "Relying upon men creates order; relying upon law creates disorder" (*jen-jen che chih, jen-fa che luan*).[56]

Unfortunately, according to Chang, too many unworthy officials were creeping into the bureaucracy, while too many talented recluses remained hidden away in the mountains and forests. The existence of talent in the empire could not be doubted; the problems were how to attract it to the bureaucracy and how to bar admission of the untalented. The problems had arisen, Chang argued, because the original purpose of the examination system was being overlooked and the methods of the ex-

53. Cf. *Chung-yung*, 20:2–4: "Let there be the men and the government will flourish; but without the men, their government decays and ceases. With the right men the growth of government is rapid, just as vegetation is rapid in the earth; and moreover, their government might be called an easily-growing rush. Therefore the administration of government lies in getting proper men. Such men are to be got by means of the ruler's own character. That character is to be cultivated by his treading in the ways of duty. And the treading of those ways of duty is to be cultivated by the cherishing of benevolence."

54. Cf. *Ta-hsüeh*, 10:6–7: "The ruler will first take pains about his own virtue. Possessing virtue will give him the people. Possessing the people will give him the territory. Possessing the territory will give him its wealth. Possessing the wealth, he will have resources for expenditure."

55. Cf. *Chung-yung*, 20:13: "By the ruler's cultivation of his own character, the duties of universal obligation are set forth. By honoring men of virtue and talents, he is preserved from errors of judgment. By showing affection to his relatives, there is no grumbling nor resentment among his uncles and brethren. By respecting the great ministers, he is kept from errors in the practice of government. By kind and considerate treatment of the whole body of officers, they are led to make the most grateful return for his courtesies."

56. Cf. *Lun-yü*, bk. II, 3:1–2: "If the people be led by laws, and uniformity sought to be given them by punishments, they will try to avoid the punishment, but have no sense of shame. If they be led by virtue, and uniformity sought to be given them by the rules of propriety, they will have the sense of shame, and moreover will become good."

amination system were being perverted. It was important that men of true learning be introduced into the government. An example of true learning was provided by the Two Sovereigns and Three Kings, who "understood the substance and comprehended the function" (*ming-t'i erh ta-yung*) and knew how to "influence the people and perfect customs" (*hua-min erh ch'eng-su*).[57] These rulers had differed radically from petty scholars who could only write essays harking back to the past. "Speaking in abstractions and neglecting realities most definitely was not the way of the sages," Chang declared.

When the examination system originated in the Han dynasty, Chang continued, its purpose was to seek out learned men who were capable of "straightforward speech and unflinching remonstrance" (*chih-yen chi-chien*). In the interests of good government, the classics came into use as a means of uncovering virtue and exalting frugality. But formerly when the emperor went to the pavilion to ask questions, the scholars could answer fully and freely. Men such as Tung Chung-shu of the Han, Liu Fen of the T'ang, Wang P'u of the later Chou, and Su Shih and Ch'en Liang of the Sung dynasty were able to expound upon the ills of their ages fearlessly and honestly. In the early dynasties, Chang Chih-tung stated, examinations "were not for the purpose of comparing the polished essays of many scholars but for learning of the court's deficiencies." The lack of talent in the nineteenth century government reflected the fact that standards for entering the bureaucracy had become too rigid and topics of the examinations had become too narrow. Chang asserted, "Attainment in composition is insufficient (as a basis) for obtaining extraordinary scholars." The exclusively literary criterion resulted in the rejection of ardently devoted men and the selection of hypocrites. The introduction of hypocrites into the bureaucracy accounted for weak and fearful officials. Even scholars who railed against the eight-legged essay tended to become silent the moment they donned official robes.

To remedy this situation, Chang did not go so far as to suggest a thoroughgoing reform of the examination system. Rather, he suggested that the Han system of recommendation be revived and practiced concurrently with the examination system, as formerly proposed by Su Ch'e of the Sung dynasty.[58] Chang maintained that recommendations had

57. This is the earliest instance of the *t'i-yung* dichotomy in Chang's complete works. See *CC*, 212:1b.

58. Recommendation had never died out completely as an avenue to public office. However, it was infrequently used in the Ch'ing dynasty, and those recommended were often already *sheng-yüan*, classically educated members of the lower gentry. Chang Chung-li, pp. 30–31.

characterized an era when the phrase "judging ability and conferring office" (*liang-neng shou-chih*) still had real meaning. In former times, hiding worthiness was a disgrace, and failing to recommend filial and incorrupt men was a crime. Even during the Ch'ing dynasty there were noted precedents for recommendation, which had not resulted in admitting "coarse illiterates" into the bureaucracy. Chang pointed to the two special examinations known as the *po-hsüeh hung-tz'u k'o*, one given in 1679 during the K'ang-hsi reign, and the other in 1736 during the first year of the Ch'ien-lung reign.[59] Candidates for those examinations had been recommended directly to the throne by high officials, who made their selection from men reputed to be superior in learning and conduct as well as in literary skill. Chang also pointed to the examples of T'ien Wen-ching and Li Wei, two famous officials of the Yung-cheng reign.[60] Neither had been a product of the examination system, yet each had established his merit. If recommendations were practiced widely again and punishments for nonrecommendation were revived, hidden military genius would be revealed and scholarly recluses would be brought out of retreat. In time there would be a stampede of talent to the capital.

The emperor need not worry about dissemblers appearing among the men recommended, Chang added, for if recommendations were made openly, fear of public opinion would serve as a check upon sponsoring officials. Moreover, if the throne wished to judge the conformance of report and reality, it could test the persons recommended, as in 1679 and 1736, and thereby ascertain whether they were capable of living up to their reputations for competence or virtue.

Chang Chih-tung summarized his arguments in the palace examination essay as follows:

> Today if we wish to punish greed and nourish goodness, we must have responsible high officials. If the high officials know the great principles of propriety and righteousness, they will surely look askance at book examinations as the only criterion of talent. If the high officials restrain cruel customs, then strong and daring exactors will have to flee into exile and cannot endure. However, if we wish to stop their greed and do not first adopt means of nourishing their incorruptibility, I fear the outcome will be like trying to reduce the heat by fanning boiling water! Killing one bandit

59. For these examinations, see Chang Chung-ju, pp. 47–50; Hellmut Wilhelm, "The *Po-hsüeh Hung-ju* Examination of 1679," *Journal of the American Oriental Society* (January–March 1951), pp. 60–66.
60. For these officials, see Hummel, II, 719–721.

is not as effective as causing the people to reduce the number of bandits by one. It is better to pick a good civil official than to find a good general.[61]

Chang's palace examination essay was a vigorous protest against the examination system, official extravagance and corruption, and the economic hardships suffered by the people. The paper may be considered as the opening blow in Chang's long struggle against those problems of domestic administration. Nevertheless, there was little originality in the essay. The main proposals, imbedded in a mélange of allusive clichés, repeated standard principles of Confucian political theory and envisaged the re-creation of practices at least as old as the Han dynasty. Chang showed concern for the moral character of the emperor and officials within a government that demeaned legalism as an ideal. He was preoccupied with questions of imperial benevolence, individual frugality, and the observance of rites in accordance with status gradations, as conducive to economic and social order. His ideas on state revenue did not extend beyond the most widely recognized concept of agriculture as the foundation of the state fiscal structure. His ideas on the examination system revealed as little novelty. Indeed, Chang Chih-tung protested against convention with conventional protests. As early as the T'ang dynasty critics of the examination system had stressed the point that there was something comparatively empty and frivolous about mere literary accomplishment, and that examinations which placed value on such talent would fail to bring into the government just those persons who had the kind of knowledge and skill of greatest use to the state. Proposals that the Han system of recommendation be resuscitated had also been offered from the T'ang through the early Ch'ing periods.[62]

On the eve of entering the bureaucracy, Chang Chih-tung thus displayed the zeal of a young reformer who remained strictly within the Chinese tradition. His early dissatisfaction with the examination system was to fester and grow, however, and eventually bring forth more radical suggestions for reform than the Han method of recommendation. Furthermore, when Chang eventually turned to the West for ideas on reform, it was significant that he himself was a man of great literary skill and classical learning, as well as an outstanding product of the examination system.

61. *CC*, 212:5–5b.
62. David S. Nivison, "Protest Against Conventions and Conventions of Protest," in *The Confucian Persuasion* (Stanford, Calif., 1960), pp. 186–187.

In speaking of the system and Chinese education, he stood on sure ground and could ably draw from the classics and histories in an effort to justify change and convince others. As a Hanlin scholar, a well-known member of the gentry, and a high official advocating reforms based on foreign models, Chang could command greater respect and influence than many men with broader or more precise technical knowledge of the West, but subject to criticism for their inadequate commitment to Chinese values— men such as the linguists and translators, the missionary converts, the compradors, or the students returning from the West. Nearly twenty years would pass, however, from the time Chang became a *chin-shih* until he evinced a serious interest in borrowing from the West, and in the meantime he served two tours of duty as a provincial director of education.

3 The Provincial Director of Education (1867–1877)

In his palace examination essay of 1863 Chang Chih-tung had emphasized the need for discovering "men of talent" for government service. Although he was then concerned with recruitment by means external to the examination system, his first official assignments required that he seek able men within the framework of the system. As a provincial director of education for six years, he held the government job most directly involved in perpetuating Chinese culture as revealed through Chinese literature, and most intimately related to preserving the cohesiveness of Confucian ideals through maintenance of local schools and administration of civil service tests. He was in a uniquely responsible position to foster Confucian scholarship and shape the attitudes of future officials. By controlling lower level examinations, he held the power of excluding candidates from gentry rank and government service if they failed to meet established standards or engaged in irregular practices.

In carrying out his duties as a provincial director of education, Chang Chih-tung attempted to improve the administration of the examination system about which he had complained in his essay. His earlier reform proposals had been traditional ones, and the remedies he tried as a provincial director of education were also time-honored tactics. Chang's efforts were essentially a part of the T'ung-chih Restoration (1862–1874), that conservative reform movement which sought to revive the glory of the Ch'ing dynasty. In her study of the T'ung-chih Restoration, Mary C. Wright has written: "In the Confucian view the prime essentials of stable government were the ability and integrity of officials, and this view was reflected in proverbs and common sayings as well as in formal writing. To get men of the highest native ability, train their minds and mold their characters, appoint them to office on the basis of merit, and reward or punish them effectively—this was the Restoration's primary task."[1] The task was pursued in hopes that the old order could be improved, not that a new order would be established. The changes sought involved methods and not goals. The stress was upon change *within* Chinese society, the principal aim of the T'ung-chih Restoration being "the revival of Confucian values and institutions, but so *modified* that they might endure."[2]

1. Mary C. Wright, p. 69.
2. See Mary C. Wright, pp. 60–65.

Chang Chih-tung began contributing to the T'ung-chih Restoration soon after he was appointed an assistant officer to help administer a provincial examination in Chekiang.[3] In the fall of 1867 he and the chief examiner, Chang Yün-ch'ing, traveled to Hangchow and presided over a test for more than ten thousand candidates.[4] The small percentage of candidates awarded *chü-jen* degrees after the three-day competition included about fifty students who later distinguished themselves in letters or public affairs.[5] Following the examination, Chang Chih-tung devoted himself to recreation in this popular resort city. He described his unofficial activities in Hangchow as the enjoyment of "good company, rare books, and fine scenery."[6] Chang's virtual vacation was soon cut short by an imperial decree appointing him the Hupeh director of education.[7] He left Hangchow for his new post in Wuchang, where he served from December 8, 1867, until the expiration of the usual three-year term of office in the fall of 1870. Chang then returned to Peking to resume work at the Hanlin Academy.

In the capital Chang served for about two and one-half years as a professor (*chiao-hsi*) assigned to the Hanlin Academy's Department of Study.[8] In 1871, on behalf of a commission headed by Prince Kung, Chang wrote descriptive summaries of the Taiping and Nien rebellions, to be presented to the throne along with two large historical collections on those uprisings.[9] He helped select the music for the wedding of the T'ung-chih emperor on October 16, 1872.[10] His official duties were not heavy, however, leaving him time for other activities. He wrote poetry,

3. *HNP*, p. 11.

4. According to Wang Hsien-ch'ien, who served as chief examiner in Chekiang upon another occasion, there were more than 10,000 candidates in each of the six provincial examinations held there between 1865 and 1876. Wang Hsien-ch'ien, *Hsü-shou-t'ang wen-chi* (The Hsü-shou-t'ang literary collection; 1900), 2:8, quoted in Chang Chung-li, p. 170.

5. *Pao-ping-t'ang ti-tzu chi,* in *CC,* 228:2b; *HNP,* p. 12. The men included Yüan Ch'ang, who later served in the Tsungli Yamen for eleven years, effected noteworthy financial reforms in other positions, and was executed in 1900 for opposing the Boxer movement; Hsü Ching-ch'eng, who served as Chinese minister to all leading European capitals 1884–1898 and was executed with Yüan in 1900; and Sun I-jang, a prominent scholar who did important work on Mo-ti and was one of the first students of the Yin oracle bones. See biographies in Hummel, I, 312–313; II, 667–679, 945–948.

6. *HNP*, p. 12.

7. *CC*, 71:1–1b.

8. This period in the capital is covered by *HNP*, pp. 14–16; Hu Chün, 1:16–17.

9. Chang's summaries of the *Chiao-p'ing Yüeh-fei fang-lüeh* (Strategy in suppression of the Yüeh bandits) and *Chiao-p'ing Nien-fei fang-lüeh* (Strategy in suppression of the Nien bandits) appear in *CC,* 222:4–10b, 11–18. For a brief description of the two works, see Hummel, I, 383.

10. *CC*, 225:13–14.

took part in convivial gatherings with his friends, and made sightseeing tours of Peking and its vicinity.[11]

His next provincial assignment was announced on August 14, 1873, when Chang was directed to proceed to Szechwan to serve as an assistant examiner for a provincial test in Chengtu. After reaching Chengtu, he received instructions to remain there and become the provincial director of education for Szechwan.[12] He held that position until the beginning of 1877. Thus, excluding two brief jobs as an assistant examination officer and the period of waiting in the capital, Chang served between 1867 and 1877 as a *hsüeh-cheng*, sometimes translated as "director of studies" or "literary chancellor," as well as "director of education."[13]

General Duties

Under the Ch'ing government, directors of education were normally selected from the members of the Hanlin Academy. Appointed directly by the emperor, they had the right of memorializing the throne and enjoyed considerable jurisdictional independence of the governors or governors general of the provinces to which they were assigned. They were responsible for supervising the training, examination, and conduct of the provincial *sheng-yüan*. They had the power to degrade the *sheng-yüan*, bar them from higher examinations, suspend their allowances, and dismiss them from government schools. Local officials could not punish the *sheng-yüan* without first consulting the directors of education.[14]

There were financial advantages to serving as an examiner or education director. Localities where examinations were presented supplied the needs (lodging, board, wine, oil, and paper) of the directors administering the examinations, and it was customary for successful candidates to present gifts to their examiners, teachers, and sponsors. Furthermore, the directors of education were in a favorable position to form teacher-

11. Chang's friends during this period included Wang I-jung, P'an Tsu-yin, and Ch'en Pao-ch'en. On Wang I-jung and P'an Tsu-yin, see Hummel, II, 608–609, 826–827. For Ch'en Pao-ch'en, see Ch. 4.

12. *CC*, 71:1b–2.

13. The official designation of the office was *t'i-tu hsüeh-yüan*, or *hsüeh-yüan* for short. The colloquial designation was *hsüeh-t'ai*, and the director was known by several literary designations. Brunnert and Hagelstrom, p. 407. Prefectural examinations supervised by the director of education were known as *yüan* examinations, after the director's official title.

14. Hsieh Pao-chao, pp. 146, 151–152; Chang Chung-li, pp. 36–37; Esther Morrison, "The Modernization of the Confucian Bureaucracy: An Historical Study of Public Administration," unpub. diss., Harvard University, 1959, pp. 129–130, 743–744. For duties of the director of education, see *Ta-ch'ing hui-tien*, comp. K'un-kang et al (1899), ch. 10.

student cliques based on examination relationships and thus build up their own political power.[15]

The directors of education supervised a number of subordinate officials. Under them were the prefectural directors of schools (*chiao-shou*), the departmental directors of schools (*hsüeh-cheng*),[16] and the district directors of schools (*chiao-yü*), all of whom were assisted by subdirectors of schools (*hsün-tao*). Collectively, the director of education and his subordinates were known as education officials (*chiao-kuan*).[17]

During his three-year term of office, a director of education was obliged to tour his province twice to conduct examinations in the various prefectures and independent departments (*chih-li chou*).[18] The primary purpose of one tour was to give the *sui-k'ao*, which enabled the *sheng-yüan* to maintain their status. The main purpose of the other tour was to give the *k'o-k'ao*, which qualified the *sheng-yüan* for participation in the provincial examination. However, after each *sui* or *k'o* examination in a given locality, the director presided over a *t'ung-shih* (also called *yüan-k'ao*) to select new *sheng-yüan* from candidates who already had passed preliminary tests before the district and prefectural officials. The director of education also presided over *sui* and *t'ung* examinations for military candidates, who were exempted from the *k'o-k'ao*. In addition, he tested the education officials who were subordinate to him at each locality. The examination program at one prefecture required about three weeks, and a tour of all the prefectures of a province required about seven months. Periodically the director of education helped administer tests to select *pa-kung-sheng*, *yu-kung-sheng*, and *sui-kung-sheng*. Between tours of the province, he might give an extra examination in the provincial capital for men who had not attended or had failed the last *k'o-k'ao* held in their prefectures. He might also determine themes for use in various routine tests given by schools or academies of the province, administer tests at schools in the provincial capital, and lecture occasionally at the schools.[19]

15. Chang Chung-ju, pp. 6–7; Chang Chung-li, pp. 122, 194–196. While there is no evidence that Chang Chih-tung used his position as director of education for unfair financial profit, he did gain "disciples" during his tours in Hupeh and Szechwan. The best example was Yang Jui, who became attached to Chang in Szechwan and later joined his personal secretariat. See Ch. 6.

16. Not the same *cheng* as in *hsüeh-cheng* for provincial directors of education. See *Glossary*.

17. Brunnert and Hagelstrom, pp. 429, 432, 435. The position of prefectural director of schools was the lowest to which a *chin-shih* could be appointed. Positions as departmental and district directors were ordinarily filled by *chü-jen*, while subdirectors were drawn from the *kung-sheng*. Chang Chung-ju, p. 5.

18. For a detailed discussion of the frequency of these tours, see Chang Chung-li, pp. 74–75.

19. Zi, *Pratique des examens litteraires*, pp. 12–14, 57–60, 84–92; Chang Chung-ju, pp. 6–17.

This agenda meant that during his tenure as a director of education in Hupeh and Szechwan, Chang Chih-tung traveled frequently, gave scores of examinations, and checked thousands of examination essays. According to the *Pao-ping-t'ang ti-tzu chi* (Memoirs of the Pao-ping-t'ang disciples), when Chang was an assistant examiner, he personally scrutinized all of the essays submitted by candidates. When he was a director of education, he reviewed seven out of every ten essays. The account adds: "In the essays he passed, he looked only at the substance and for the attitudes and discernment (displayed). He did not limit himself to the style and form. Many (candidates) were passed even though their writings did not adhere to the examination regulations and writing rules. But those who violated righteousness or reason by even one or two words were failed. People revered him for his justice and wisdom, and there were no complaints about him."[20]

Although conducting examinations was an important part of his duties, Chang Chih-tung had a broader conception of his responsibilities as a director of education. He made this clear when informing the throne of his arrival at Wuchang in 1867: "An education director must not only judge and compare the good and bad (examination essays) of one day but must also nourish the roots (of learning) on ordinary days. His business is not merely promoting literature, for he should place first the whetting of moral integrity (*chih-li ming-chieh*)." Chang posted a notice before the Hupeh examination hall expressing the desire that all candidates should follow in the footsteps of the virtuous sages and not merely pass examinations. Upon taking over his seal in Chengtu in 1873, he asserted that he would direct his attention toward "conduct" (*p'in-hsing*) and "solid learning" (*shih-hsüeh*) in an attempt to stop educational decline and rectify corruption: "Your servant will first encourage a sense of shame and next urge the study of useful books."[21]

In carrying out his assigned tasks, Chang was operating in a scene of devastation. Although Hupeh had been cleared of rebels before his arrival in 1867, the newly appointed governor general of Hukwang, Li Hung-chang, was still directing a campaign against the Nien-fei in Shantung and did not assume his duties until 1869.[22] Warfare had disrupted the Hupeh educational system, causing the destruction of libraries and

20. *CC*, 228:2–2b.
21. *HNP*, pp. 12, 16. The similarity to Ku Yen-wu is apparent: "In your action be guided by a sense of shame, in your learning be comprehensive." Benjamin Schwartz, "Some Polarities in Confucian Thought," in *Confucianism in Action,* ed. D. S. Nivison and A. F. Wright (Stanford, 1959), p. 60.
22. For Li Hung-chang, see Hummel, I, 464–471. The governor of Hupeh during Chang's residency was Kuo Po-yin. *Ch'ing-shih,* 6:4854.

other facilities, the dispersal of population, and the lowering of morale among the gentry and scholars. In Szechwan, where Wu T'ang was governor general when Chang arrived in 1873, the remaining physical effects of the hostilities were not so pronounced as they had been in Hupeh.[23] Yet corruption had proliferated in that West China province during the long period of national disorder.

Against this background Chang Chih-tung was fairly successful in the tasks of restoration that he undertook. His accomplishments in Hupeh were so impressive as to earn him the praise of the most famous official of the empire, the Grand Secretary Tseng Kuo-fan (who died in 1872, the year before Chang was assigned to Szechwan). In a letter to a friend, Tseng commented that the Hupeh director of education had "satisfied the people's hopes."[24] In Szechwan, Chang Chih-tung was not able permanently to purify education or the examination system, for many years later a censor could still complain that the amount of corruption existing in the examination system of Szechwan "surpassed that of any other province in the empire."[25] Yet Chang was responsible for several notable achievements in Szechwan. The credit that he acquired in both provinces was won, first, by controlling the students and, second, by encouraging them.

Control of Examination Candidates

Many of the problems that confronted Chang Chih-tung in his efforts to control the scholar class of Hupeh and Szechwan derived from the intense competition for access to *sheng-yüan* rank, to gentry status, and ultimately to the closed circle of the bureaucracy. Personal ambition was not the only force driving young candidates toward these goals; they were also pushed on by strong pressures of family, clan, and even whole villages or districts, to which a scholar's success might bring honor, protection, or prosperity. Despite the high moral tone of their classical learning, the Chinese literati were sometimes most ungentlemanly in fighting for an entrée to privilege for themselves and their own.

Although later in life Chang Chih-tung would support a program for westernized mass education, at the outset of his career he was concerned with limiting the number of students competing for examination system degrees. The increase of *sheng-yüan* quotas during and immediately after

23. For Wu T'ang see *Ch'ing-shih*, 6:4841. Wu was succeeded by Li Han-chang in 1875, and Ting Pao-chen became governor general in 1876. *Ch'ing-shih*, 6:4952–4953; Hummel, II, pp. 723–725.
24. Letter from Tseng Kuo-fan to Hsü Hsien-p'ing, *HNP*, p. 14.
25. Quoted in R. K. Douglas, *Society in China* (London, 1894), p. 167.

the Taiping Rebellion had added greatly to the normal total of men started on the road to official position. The practice of increasing quotas in exchange for military contributions was begun in 1853. Imperial edicts provided that each subprefecture, department, and district of a province could temporarily increase its quotas for civil and military *sheng-yüan* by one for every Tls. 2,000 that its people contributed toward military expenses. One permanent increase in both the civil and military quotas was permitted for every contribution of Tls. 10,000. In 1868 an edict changed the figures to one temporary increase for Tls. 4,000 and one permanent increase for Tls. 40,000. Before 1871 the 1,810 government schools of the empire had raised their permanent *sheng-yüan* quotas by 4,648 (from 25,465 to 30,113). Among the individual provinces, Szechwan added 544 new permanent *sheng-yüan* positions, ranking second only to Kiangsi, for which 670 new positions were approved. Hupeh province was in third place with a total increase of 427.[26]

In 1871 the practice of granting permanent increases was stopped, but by then the damage had been done. Opponents of the increases pointed out that the practice favored wealthy localities. Furthermore, they "lamented the great ease of admission into government schools as a result of this change and denounced such measures as degrading the schools by using them as instruments of profit."[27] Among the opponents was Chang Chih-tung.

Chang reported in a memorial to the throne in 1868 that the quota for some schools in Hupeh was double the figure that had prevailed before the Taiping Rebellion. He feared that it would triple if increases continued. "Human talent has limits and does not depend upon an amount (of money) subscribed," Chang protested. The increases were encouraging coarse and shallow scholarship. "Moreover," he wrote, "when the number of men is too great, discipline becomes difficult for the officials and teachers to maintain; when the number of those selected is too liberal, then the scholars' social standing becomes unclear." He recommended changes in the regulations for the increase of quotas, as well as measures for a thorough investigation of all local claims based on wartime contributions.[28]

26. Chang Chung-li, pp. 83–92, 143 (Table 16). The 155 government schools of Szechwan had a regular quota of 1,374, which was increased permanently to 1,918. The 79 schools of Hupeh had a regular quota of 1,107, increased permanently to 1,535.
27. Chang Chung-li, p. 85.
28. *HNP*, p. 13, gives a digest of this memorial, not included in the *CC*. In response to the memorial, an edict ordered stricter maintenance of qualifying standards. Mary C. Wright, p. 81.

Szechwan was reputed to have a total of thirty thousand students.[29] Chang Chih-tung commented on the unfortunate economic consequences of this overproduction of *sheng-yüan*: "In recent years there have been too many students in Szechwan. The more numerous they are, the poorer they are. In seeking lodging, they cast themselves upon relatives. They scheme to eat what others save. They die in dire poverty. All of these are actual conditions."[30]

These actual conditions made harder for Chang one perennial problem of all directors of education—the prevention of cheating during civil service examinations. Government regulations designed to prevent examination abuses were numerous and precise. They were principally directed against illegal registration, dishonest guarantee, employment of substitutes to take examinations for unprepared or unqualified students, the smuggling and use of "cribs," and various forms of collusion between candidates and examiners, attendants, or outside parties.[31]

Methods for evading the regulations were many and resourceful. Colorful stories have been told of the cheating practiced at provincial and metropolitan examinations when candidates were confined to cells within a sealed compound. According to these tales, notes or prefabricated essays were wrapped around rocks and thrown in to candidates, flown in by carrier pigeon, sealed in wax and floated in by water pipes, or tunneled in through underground passages. At prefectural examinations unusual places were found, such as hollow table legs, for concealing notes, and devious ways were devised of shifting from assigned seats so that one candidate could aid another.

Justus Doolittle, in an 1865 account, tells of the education director who was determined that there should be no cheating in a prefectural examination over which he was presiding. He turned out all of his assistants and servants, trusting no one but himself. While he was shutting and sealing the door of the examination hall, however, a sheet of notes was attached to the back of his gown by his chief clerk. Unwittingly, the

29. *Ch'uang-chien Tsun-ching shu-yüan chi* (Memoirs on establishment of the Tsun-ching Academy), *CC*, 213:19.

30. *HNP*, p. 18.

31. A number of regulations from the *K'o-ch'ang t'iao-li* are translated in Robert Morrison, under the character for "learning" (*hsüeh*). Morrison commented: "The endless precautions to prevent fraud, in an examination of professed students of *moral* science; all of which, minute and often ingenious precautions, they contrive occasionally to evade, is one, among many other proofs, of the wickedness and deceitfulness of the human heart." See Chang Chung-li, p. 190 *n.*103, for a K'ang-hsi listing of ten "traditional" examination malpractices.

director carried the paper into the hall, where it was deftly plucked off by a waiting candidate.[32]

Expert conclusions on the seriousness and extent of corruption in the examination system have varied. Chang Chung-ju, Hsieh Pao-chao, and Chang Chung-li, for example, paint grim pictures, while Mary C. Wright is more charitable. Chang Chih-tung's experience suggests that actually there may have been significant regional differences, which would complicate generalizations: some corruption existed in Hupeh, but abuses were far worse in Szechwan.

In Hupeh, Chang noted the existence of both "inner" and "outer" corruption. The first involved the passing of messages to or between candidates being examined, with attendants acting as accessories. The second was the practice of substitution, with "salaried student" (*lin-sheng*) guarantors acting as accessories. To help control "inner" corruption, Chang reported to the throne in 1868 that he had forbidden servants a part in assigning the seats for examinations. To help control substitution, he appealed to the conscience of the candidates and at the same time announced increased punishments for guarantors found guilty of abetting deception. He also proclaimed that he would liberally reward informers.[33]

In 1870 Chang was instrumental in introducing a reexamination of candidates who had passed the first test of the prefectural examination— the reexamination being aimed at eliminating those who had passed the initial trial because of luck or dishonesty. This reexamination (called a *t'i-fu*) was approved by the emperor for general usage but was not instituted in all provinces.[34]

After Chang Chih-tung reached Szechwan, he reported that examination malpractices were much more widespread there than they had been in Hupeh. Students were constantly discussing deceitful practices and daily devising more clever schemes to evade regulations. In 1876 Chang submitted a long memorial describing some of the forms of corruption as well as his own efforts to prevent fraudulent substitution, punish those who had sold their services, prohibit cheating, and stop disturbances.[35]

Brawls, extortion, and kidnaping were peculiar outgrowths of the practice of illegal registration and substitution in Szechwan and constituted a

---

32. Justus Doolittle, *Social Life of the Chinese* (New York, 1865), p. 428.
33. For a digest of this memorial, see *HNP*, p. 13.
34. Zi, *Pratique des examens litteraires*, pp. 64–65, 251.
35. For digests of this memorial, see *HNP*, p. 18; *PG*, pp. 42, 48–49.

special problem for Chang Chih-tung. The people of Szechwan had become disgusted with the official unwillingness or inability to take legal action against substitutes. "Local villains" took advantage of this situation to form armed gangs who would wait outside the examination halls or courtyards. After the results of an examination had been announced, they would waylay and molest suspected substitutes and sometimes hold them for ransom. This form of retaliation was known as "seizing and striking" (*la-k'o*). When examination candidates began to hire bodyguards for protection, the brawls became more serious, resulting in cases of injury and death.

Chang Chih-tung attempted to prevent such battles of the literati. He threatened to call out troops to maintain order. He directed that all accusations concerning substitution be brought before him personally after each examination. He would promptly adjudicate the cases, make a public announcement of his findings, and mete out punishments whenever necessary. As a result of such measures, the people and students of Szechwan reportedly "submitted" and put away their weapons.[36]

When informing Peking about his methods of discipline, Chang Chih-tung would cite the importance of high standards among the students, who were the future officials of China. He would also appeal to the Confucian belief in the power of moral example: immorality would rule the masses unless morality ruled the educated classes. "Scholars are the people's hope, especially in the border provinces," he wrote on one occasion. If the scholars devoted themselves to crafty transgression of rules, resisted the officials, and created trouble, similar practices would become prevalent throughout the province and its subdivisions. After the students became officials, they would "follow in the old ruts." The common people would observe their habits and imitate them. "Consequently," Chang wrote, "if we wish to regulate the people of Szechwan, we must first regulate the scholars of Szechwan."[37]

While some of the problems that faced Chang Chih-tung derived from the bitter competition for the rank of *sheng-yüan*, other problems originated in the abuse of privilege by students who had already attained that rank. Not content with the legal and social advantages that accrued to them upon obtaining gentry or "blue gown" (*lan-shan*) status, many pressed for greater profit. Their rank gave them "a great opportunity to play the villain among the common people," Doolittle noted in 1865, and many "soon became hated and feared by shopkeepers and the common

36. *Pao-ping-t'ang ti-tzu chi, CC*, 228:3–3b. See also *HNP*, p. 16; *PG*, pp. 48–49.
37. *HNP*, p. 18.

people generally.''[38] Some of the *sheng-yüan* patronized underlings in the mandarin's office in order to obtain special favors. Others banded together to form political pressure groups. According to at least one source, the magistrates often feared the *sheng-yüan* because they "knew not when they (the *sheng-yüan*) would succeed in a future examination and secure appointments more influential than their own.''[39]

Government regulations existed to restrain the *sheng-yüan*. Illegal guarantee was prohibited. An ethical code stipulated that the *sheng-yüan* should not entreat or befriend officials for advancement, enter the offices of local authorities lightly, meddle in lawsuits, write on current affairs, or form cliques "to control the local authorities, or to settle matters by force in their localities.''[40] The evasion of such regulations contributed significantly to the worries of an educational director.

The matter of litigation proved one of Chang Chih-tung's most troublesome worries, especially in Szechwan. In almost every memorial dispatched to Peking from Chengtu, Chang commented on the Szechwan *sheng-yüan*'s fondness for litigation. According to his reports, the Szechwan *sheng-yüan* were addicted to fomenting lawsuits, supporting excessive and repeated charges, and offering their services in cases of appeal. They thus drew upon the people's wealth for litigation fees. They intimidated the rich by threatening to institute legal proceedings for various causes unless bought off with liberal presents. Departmental and district officials seemed incapable of deterring these activities. The *sheng-yüan* worked in many of their offices and pried into their business as well. If crossed or angered, the *sheng-yüan* might make accusations against the officials.

In order to enforce existing regulations against involvement in litigation, Chang Chih-tung repeatedly directed his subordinates to submit full reports on all *sheng-yüan* who participated in lawsuits. When not a single report was forthcoming, Chang appealed to the throne for support. He requested an imperial reprimand for his subordinates, as well as a command that they comply with laws pertaining to the exposure of irregularities. The throne sent his memorial to the Board of Rites for consideration.[41] The outcome of Chang's request is not recorded, but he undoubtedly continued his struggle against students who stirred up lit-

38. Doolittle, p. 394.
39. Hsieh Pao-chao, p. 153.
40. For a translation of the code from *Kuang-hsü Ta-ch'ing hui-tien*, 32:10b–11a, see Chang Chung-li, pp. 198–199. See also Hsieh Pao-chao, pp. 151–152; Esther Morrison, pp. 130–131.
41. *HNP*, p. 18.

igation. Probably he persisted in admonishing the *sheng-yüan* directly, as he had done earlier: "If Confucian scholars have roots, they will not be proud and peevish. It is especially unthinkable that they will become involved in angry disputes. . . . A hundred battles and a hundred victories are not as good as desisting from war and giving the people peace. A hundred lawsuits and a hundred awards are not as good as desisting from argument and causing the people to submit (by virtue)."[42]

Encouragement of Scholarship

Much of Chang Chih-tung's work in Hupeh and Szechwan had the object of controlling dishonest or factious scholars. Yet it would be misleading to suggest that repressive measures constituted the sum of his labors. Besides seeking obedience to the law through discipline, Chang undertook several activities that were designed to encourage the incorruptible students and to reform the others. He expanded educational facilities, offered incentives toward better scholarship, and through his own writings provided study aids and guidance on correct conduct for the *sheng-yüan*.

As one incentive to the scholars enrolled in his administrative areas, Chang publicly commended or rewarded the authors of outstanding writings and classical research. In 1870 in Hupeh he edited and published a collection called the *Chiang-Han ping-ling chi*.[43] This work brought together worthy essays and poetry written by examination candidates of Hupeh, as well as writings produced in the academies of the province. In Szechwan, Chang enlarged and expanded the activities of a publishing house that Governor General Wu T'ang had established to print classical, historical, and philosophical works.[44]

Among Chang's own writing that provided aid to students was the *Shu-mu ta-wen* (Answering questions on bibliography), an annotated bibliography compiled in 1875 for the guidance of Szechwan scholars.[45]

---

42. *CC*, 204:7.
43. See *Chiang-Han ping-ling chi hsü* (Preface to the Collected writings of the Chiang-Han geniuses), *CC*, 213:1–2b.
44. *HNP*, p. 17.
45. For text, see *CC*, ch. 206–209. These four chüan were first printed in 1878. Chang Chih-tung was assisted in the work by Miao Ch'üan-sun (1844–1919), one of his disciples and an indefatigable bibliophile. A *chin-shih* of 1876, Miao helped P'an Tsu-yin collect the bibliographical notes of Huang P'ei-lieh (1763–1825), published in 1883, to which Miao added four chüan in 1919. As director of the Nan-ch'ing Academy in Kiangsu, Miao helped the Kiangsu director of education, Wang Hsien-ch'ien, compile the *Nan-ch'ing shu-yüan tsung-shu*, 41 works by Ch'ing scholars, published in 1888. In 1909, when financial difficulties caused the family of Ting Ping (1832–1899) to dispose of his large and excellent book collection, Miao was instrumental in transferring it to the library of the Kiangsu government

This work went through many editions and even at the present time is considered the most important and most widely used bibliography compiled since the *Ssu-k'u ch'üan-shu tsung-mu* (Catalogue of the Complete library in the four branches of literature), finished in 1782.[46] In 1875, Chang finished the *Yu-hsüan yü* (Light carriage talk), a handbook on study and composition for Szechwan students.[47] This two-chüan text, essentially a "how-to-do-it" book, was divided into six main parts, with discourses on the conduct of *sheng-yüan*, study, composition, classical research, and the rules for elevation, tabooed characters, and grading examination papers. Many of the general ideas were repeated in the *Ch'uang-chien Tsun-ching shu-yüan chi* (Memoirs on the establishment of the Tsun-ching Academy), a 4,000-character essay in question and answer style that Chang wrote at the time of his transfer from Szechwan in 1877.[48]

Although most of the *Yu-hsüan yü* is technical, portions of it reveal the doctrines and methods instilled into the minds of a generation of Chinese students. Simultaneously, it offers additional insight into Chang Chih-tung's thinking at the time. The discourse on conduct, for example, is made up of nineteen brief paragraphs of injunction and admonition. Individual items urge students to avoid a premature commitment to writing essays or examinations, dependence on luck, careless recommendation, addiction to litigation, and opium smoking. The principal message of other paragraphs is that scholars, while holding themselves above the masses, should not allow their status to become a cause of self-pride nor take advantage of it for self-profit; rather, they should cultivate virtue, righteousness, courage, and frugality in emulation of the ancient worthies.

Chang balanced a series of "do not's" against a series of "do's."[49] He repeated injunctions against lawsuits, the formation of cliques, and participation in local governmental affairs, Students should not "scheme

---

at Nanking, where Tuan-fang was governor general. In recognition of the services of Miao and Tuan-fang, a library building was named the T'ao-Feng Lou, composed of parts of their two literary names. Miao was the first librarian in the new quarters. He compiled one supplement to the *Kuo-ch'ao pei-chuan chi*, a Ch'ing biographical collection, which was published in 88 chüan in 1910. For biography, see *Pei-chuan chi-pu*, 9:24b–30.

46. Teng Ssu-yü and Knight Biggerstaff, *An Annotated Bibliography of Selected Chinese Reference Works* (Cambridge, Mass., rev., 1950), p. 4. They describe the *Shu-mu ta-wen* as revised and enlarged by Fan Hsi-tseng during the 1930's.

47. For text, see *CC*, ch. 204–205. The preface appears in *CC*, 213:1–5b. Light carriages were formerly used by envoys of the Son of Heaven, and in time the name was applied to the officials themselves. The title apparently refers to Chang's position as an imperially appointed, touring director of education.

48. For text, see *CC*, 213:18b–29. This work was engraved on stone at the Tsun-ching Academy. *HNP*, p. 19.

49. *Yu-hsüan yü*, *CC*, 204:2–4b, 7b–8.

for the good fields and fine property of others," he warned. They should not consider their privileged status as a cause for complacency, nor an ability to write essays as a cause for self-satisfaction. In both study and action, they should compare themselves with men of the past, not with their contemporaries. They should avoid pledges in wine and licentious behavior. They should learn to "say what should be said and do what should be done," for "only by upholding the right and not toadying can one be unashamed as a scholar."

The discourse on study in the *Yu-hsüan yü* comprises sections on the classics, history, and philosophy, besides a general discussion of reading. In the reading section students are advised to read extensively, study good editions, make use of survey works, and continue reading after winning their degrees. They should not fear the difficult, excuse themselves on grounds of a bad memory, or allege that they have no books to read and no time for reading.

The section emphasizes "utility" (*yung*)—which is a recurrent theme throughout the *Yu-hsüan yü*. Chang Chih-tung warned the *sheng-yüan* against bogging down in detail. When studying books, they should strive to understand the general principles set forth, and upon understanding those principles, they should put them into practice. He wrote:

> Books are like grain. (Grain) is planted, reaped, threshed, steamed to make food, and eaten with all kinds of delicacies. It is good for the muscles and flesh and makes the sinews and bones strong. This is the effect of grain. If you diligently labor in a field all year or toil over a cook-stove but do not taste the grain, then why plant it? Today men often consider reading books and understanding principles as two separate matters, or knowing the classics and putting them into practice as absurd. Shallow persons (read) for the purpose of examinations; more serious ones (only) for the purpose of writing commentaries and achieving fame . . . This is like planting and not eating, or eating and not becoming fat.[50]

Chang Chih-tung's idea of utility did not refer at this time to science, technology, or the practical arts, which he later advocated. His definition of useful books, for instance, was limited to the following three classes: "those that can be used to investigate antiquity, used for statecraft (*ching-shih*), and used to regulate the individual mind." He denounced several literary forms of the previous thirteen centuries as "a waste of the people's genius"—for example, the creative writing of the T'ang dynasty

50. *Yu-hsüan yü, CC,* 204:36b–37.

had included many "trifling, empty and extravagant, and irrational books."[51]

According to Chang, the degree of utility in all literature except historical writing was directly proportional to its age. His formula ran as follows: "In general, in the pre-Ch'in books one character is worth a thousand pieces of gold. From the Han through the Sui, one can often find much that is precious . . . From the T'ang through the Northern Sung, eliminate half and retain half. From the Southern Sung through the Ming, select the good."[52]

In the case of history, Chang conceded that "the more recent a period is, the greater its relation to utility (*yung*)."[53] Presumably he had in mind the field of practical government administration—for which recent history would yield precedents better applicable to contemporary problems than examples drawn from earlier times, when institutions were far different.

Among the books of antiquity, Chang rated the classics as the most important. While Chang's comments in the *Yu-hsüan yü* are confined to specific problems of reading or research in the classics, the *Ch'uang-chien Tsun-ching shu-yüan chi* stresses the overall necessity of classical study: "The root of all knowledge is necessarily in the classics and histories. The root of reading all books is in understanding the classics. The root of historical study also is in understanding the classics. The root of understanding the classics is in understanding the etymology. This is a principle that is valid for all ages. If the etymology is not understood, one's exposition of the classics will be mere chatter."[54]

Although Chang Chih-tung thus emphasized classical study, he refused to be drawn into the conflict between the Ch'ing dynasty's two major schools of classical interpretation. He took a stand midway between the "Sung learning" and the "Han learning." Since the time of Ku Yen-wu (1613–1682), the advocates of Han learning had opposed the metaphysical, historical, and textual interpretations of Sung Neo-Confucianism and had promoted "inductive" methods of research that might uncover new evidence on the real meaning of the classics. Chang declined to argue minor differences between the two schools. He was impressed by the methodology of the Han learning, as applied to such matters as textual criticism, but admitted the validity of Neo-Confucianism as a satisfying personal philosophy. He advised students not to

51. *Yu-hsüan yü, CC,* 204:30–30b.
52. *Yu-hsüan yü, CC,* 204:28.
53. *Yu-hsüan yü, CC,* 204:19.
54. *Ch'uang-chien Tsun-ching shu-yüan chi, CC,* 213:21.

accept one and reject the other and to desist from wrangling:

> Han learning is learning; Sung learning is also learning . . .
> In general, for reading books, follow the Han learning. For reg-
> ulating action, follow the Sung learning. The Han learning is not
> without its deficiencies, but if you follow it, then you can eliminate
> the evils of empty discussion and contempt of antiquity. The Sung
> learning is not without its defects, but if you follow it, then you
> can lessen personal faults. We should be aware of the short-
> comings of each that have been attacked by men previously.
> Scholars value understanding. When they discuss facts and
> principles, they also value hearts at rest . . . I find something to
> admire in both schools and see no reason for cliques.[55]

Thoroughness, exactness, and objectivity were principles to which the
school of Han learning did homage. The same requirements were stressed
in the *Yu-hsüan yü* section on historical study, where Chang Chih-tung
cautioned against reckless criticism in efforts to distinguish good from
evil and success from failure.[56]

Establishment of Academies

Chang Chih-tung's compilations and writings were intended especially
to encourage students enrolled in the government-supported schools of
Hupeh and Szechwan provinces. Among those schools were two new
academies that Chang himself had founded as part of his effort to improve
educational facilities and standards in the provinces to which he was
assigned. Chang's interest in academies—an interest generated during
his tours as a director of education—remained active during later years.
He founded three other academies while serving as governor of Shansi,
governor general of Liangkwang and governor general of Hukwang.

---

55. *Ch'uang-chien Tsun-ching shu-yüan chi, CC,* 213:24–24b. Similar ideas, in greater
detail, appear in *Yu-hsüan yü, CC,* 204:31b–33. In adopting this conciliatory attitude,
Chang Chih-tung, consciously or not, was following the lead of Tseng Kuo-fan. Levenson
has suggested that the harmonizing of such peculiarly Chinese disputes was a first step
toward reorientating Chinese thought about the West. He wrote of Tseng Kuo-fan: "The
tendency to lose interest in purely Chinese intellectual disputes was characteristic of those
who recognized the fact of the Western intrusion . . . As a loyal Chinese, but a Chinese
among Westerners, he lost the will to dwell on intramural distinctions. An eclectic in the
larger sense, ready to infuse something of Western civilization into Chinese civilization, he
was catholic too, in the field of native Chinese choices and sought to impose a peace on traditional Chinese enemies . . . Tseng wrote approvingly, too, of both the 'Sung learning' and
the later 'Han learning' which attacked it . . . according to Tseng, the peacemaker, there was
little distinction between them, and he urged their adherents not to be inflexible." Joseph R.
Levenson, "'History' and 'Value': The Tensions of Intellectual Choice in Modern China,"
in *Studies in Chinese Thought,* ed. Arthur F. Wright, pp. 152–154.

56. *Yu-hsuan yü, CC,* 204:18–21.

When Chang Chih-tung arrived in Hupeh, the Chiang-Han Academy was already functioning as a state-sponsored institution. However, it was considered by Chang to be "old-fashioned" and not large enough to accommodate many students. He therefore established the Ching-hsin Academy in Wuchang during 1869.[57] He consulted on the project in an exchange of correspondence with the Hukwang governor general, Li Hung-chang, then acting concurrently as the governor of Hupeh. Li gave instructions for raising funds to build the academy on a site that Chang had selected. He suggested that Chang pattern the regulations of the new academy after those of the Ching-ku Academy in Soochow. Liu Kung-mien, an authority on the *Analects of Confucius*, became the president (*shan-chang*) of the Ching-hsin Academy.[58] Offering training in the classics, history, and ancient prose (*ku-wen*), the academy reportedly attracted much talent during its early years of operation. More than two hundred of the students who sought to register could not be accommodated in its quarters.[59]

The Ching-hsin Academy was still operating twenty years later when Chang Chih-tung returned to Wuchang as the Hukwang governor general. However, in an 1891 memorial to the throne, Chang indicated that the academy had not prospered in recent years.[60] He admitted that the location he had chosen for the academy was a poor one. The site on a lake shore was swampy and subject to inundation. Floods in 1887 and 1889 had damaged buildings of the academy and forced students to seek higher ground. The few roughly built "cottages" (dormitories) erected in the beginning had never been adequate. The academy lacked funds, student stipends were insufficient, and enrollment was dwindling. Chang cited these facts in trying to justify the establishment of a new institution, the Liang-Hu Academy.

57. Literally, the "Heart of the classics academy." The school was originally called the Wen-ch'ang (Literary improvement) Academy. *HNP*, p. 14. See also *Hu-pei t'ung-chih*, comp. Chang Chung-hsin (Shanghai, 1934), 59:1–2b, on the Chiang-Han and Ching-hsin Academies.

58. Liu Kung-mien had served on the staff of the Kiangnan Printing Office, established by Tseng Kuo-fan. In 1866 he completed and printed the *Lun-yü cheng-i*, an authoritative commentary begun by his father, Liu Pao-nan, a man "celebrated for his exact studies in the classics . . . free from partisan prejudice that marked either the followers of the School of Han Learning or the adherents of Sung philosophy." While directing the Ching-hsin Academy, Liu Kung-mien compiled several local gazetteers. Hummel, I, 529. Chang had invited Huang P'eng-nien to serve as director, but apparently the invitation was not accepted. Huang was in mourning from 1866 until late in 1868 and then returned to Peking. *HNP*, p. 14; Hummel, I, 341–342.

59. *CC*, 30:7b–8.

60. *CC*, 30:6b–12b.

While Chang Chih-tung was serving as director of education in Szech-wan, he founded the Tsun-ching Academy in cooperation with Governor General Wu T'ang.[61] Construction of this academy was begun in 1874 and completed the following year. The official Chin-chiang Academy already existed in Szechwan, but again Chang felt it was too old and small. He sought to pattern the new academy after two famous ones founded by Juan Yüan—the Ku-ching Academy, established in Hang-chow in 1801, and the Hsüeh-hai Academy, established in Canton in 1820.[62] Chang encouraged rich gentry and merchants of Szechwan to contribute land for the academy and to subscribe money, which was used to buy several thousand chüan of books for a library. He selected one hundred *sheng-yüan* of high standing to enter the academy. The chief members of the faculty were the president (*shan-chang*), the superinten-dent (*chien-yüan*) and the warden (*chai-chang*).[63]

Regulations of the Tsun-ching Academy specified that the director meet with the students in the lecture hall once every five days. The students would then submit their daily records of study (*jih-chi*) and undergo an oral examination on their reading. Questions, however, were not necessarily limited to matters covered in the students' notes. After the question period, the director would present a lecture. Students who failed to demonstrate "solid learning" or who could not answer questions for the director were punished. For first failures, the monthly stipend of the culprits was docked, but more serious offenders were caned. Formal written examinations were given twice a month, one test administered by visiting officials and the other by professors of the academy. There were four subjects for examination: explanation of the classics (*ching-chieh*), historical discussion (*shih-lun*), writing in miscellaneous prose styles (*tsa-wen*) and prose-poetry (*fu*), and composition of poetry (*shih*).[64]

Writing the eight-legged essay was a significant omission from the curriculum of the Tsun-ching Academy and an instance of radicalism in Chang Chih-tung's policy as a director of education. When students of the academy asked Chang why they were not tested in this kind of essay, he replied: "There is no need!" He then made a flank attack rather

61. Literally, the "Academy for reverence of the classics." See *HNP*, pp. 16, 17, 19; *Ch'uang-chien Tsun-ching shu-yüan chi, CC*, 213:18b–20.
62. Properly, the Ku-ching ching-she (Studio for explaining the classics) and Hsüeh-hai t'ang (Sea of learning hall). On Juan Yüan and these academies, see Hummel, I, 400–401.
63. *Ch'uang-chien Tsun-ching shu-yüan chi, CC*, 213:27.
64. *Ch'uang-chien Tsun-ching shu-yüan chi, CC*, 213:26–27.

than an all-out frontal assault upon the form—which in later years he denounced outright as artificial and intellecturally stultifying. Chang's chief argument was that eight-legged essays on the Four Books were a part of the examinations that the *sheng-yüan* had already taken to achieve their rank, as well as a part of the curriculum of the district schools. Students should by then be well-versed in the form. Further testing at the Tsun-ching Academy would be repetitious. Moreover, considering the time required and the demands on the students' energy, it would be impractical to add monthly tests in still another subject. The academy, therefore, was to concentrate on preparing the *sheng-yüan* to cope with problems of interpreting the Five Classics that they would encounter in the advanced civil service examinations. Already the throne had ordered that more attention be paid to classical dissertations (*ching-ts'e*) in the provincial and metropolitan examinations. The still higher examinations did not require the writing of eight-legged essays. If the students wished to practice the form on their own or take tests on it at other academies, they would be free to do so.[65]

At the end of Chang Chih-tung's term as a director of education, he wrote to a fellow-official that, although he was leaving Szechwan, he would find it hard to forget the Tsun-ching Academy. The academy lasted until Szechwan began establishing modern schools (*hsüeh-hsiao*), when its properties were turned over to the newer institutions.[66]

The experience that Chang gained in operating the Tsun-ching Academy in Szechwan and the Ching-hsin Academy in Hupeh proved valuable to him later in his career when he founded three additional academies, which represented his continuing effort to revive Chinese education by traditional means. In 1882, when serving as governor of Shansi, Chang Chih-tung established the Ling-te Academy in cooperation with two directors of education, one of whom was Wang Jen-k'an, later known as a "model official."[67] The new school was built on the ruins of a Ming academy in Taiyuan. Among the faculty members employed by Chang was Yang Shen-hsiu, destined to play a prominent role in the Reform Movement of 1898.[68] The Ling-te Academy originally had only thirty

65. *Ch'uang-chien Tsun-ching shu-yüan chi, CC,* 213:28–28b. Eight-legged essay exercises were also omitted from the curriculum of the Ching-hsin Academy in Hupeh and the Ling-te Academy that Chang later founded in Shansi. *Pao-ping-t'ang ti-tzu chi, CC,* 228: 3b–4.

66. *HNP,* pp. 17, 19.

67. *HNP,* p. 33. For Wang Jen-k'an, see *Ch'ing-shih,* 7:5137–5138; Hummel, II, 814. The name of the academy, Ling-te t'ang, means "Hall leading to virtue."

68. *HNP,* p. 33. See also Hummel, II, 705; and Ch. 5 below.

students, but the number eventually increased to fifty and then to seventy. After 1898 the academy was converted to a school, and under the Chinese Republic it became a normal school.[69]

When assigning Yang Tu, an assistant professor at the Ling-te Academy, to serve concurrently as superintendent of the school, Chang Chih-tung again revealed some of his ideas on the Han and the Sung learning. "The duty of an assistant professor is closely related to teaching the classics and has the Han learning as its basis," Chang wrote. "The duty of a superintendent is closely related to teaching men and has the Sung learning as its basis. The positions require that both the *t'i* and the *yung* be stimulated."[70]

In 1887, while serving as governor general of Liangkwang, Chang Chih-tung established the most famous of his academies, the Kuang-ya Academy. In a memorial to the throne announcing his plans, he stressed the deficiencies of six other Kwangtung academies.[71] The Hsüeh-hai Academy, for example, was adjudged good, but its funds were not great and its stipends were exceedingly small. Furthermore, it had a limited amount of land suitable for additional construction. It offered lessons but had no living quarters for students. Chang stated that in his opinion students should live close together for an extended period. This would help the teachers to enforce discipline and would inspire the students to compete with one another. In all of his experiments with educational institutions, Chang opposed the practice of laxly registering "day students," whose infrequent appearances at the academies had been condoned in the past.

To finance construction of the Kuang-ya Academy and provide for its annual operating expenses, Chang Chih-tung contributed from his own savings, solicited pledges from various associations of Canton, and received contributions from rich merchants. The total cost of building and equipping the academy was Tls. 138,866. Chang directed that Tls. 20,000 of the contributions and Tls. 100,000 taken from Canton customs revenue be deposited with the Hongkong and Shanghai Banking Corporation to draw an estimated annual interest of Tls. 6,600. The amount of the interest would be allocated to the Kuang-ya Academy from year to year.[72]

69. *HNP*, pp. 38–39.
70. *HNP*, p. 34.
71. The memorial appears in *CC*, 22:8–12. The name means roughly "Academy for the refinement of the Kwang provinces."
72. *CC*, 94:9–10b, 10b–11; *HNP*, p. 57. See also Liu Po-chi, *Kwang-tung shu-yüan chih-tu* (Hong Kong, 1958), pp. 124–128, 145.

With the funds obtained, Chang acquired a spacious and scenic site for the academy at Yüan-t'ou-hsiang, five li northwest of Canton. There he built a lecture hall, library, sacrificial temple, and quarters to accommodate two hundred students, one hundred each from Kwangtung and Kwangsi.[73] Foreign officers of the Imperial Maritime Customs described the main building as "an exceptionally fine edifice." The library halls and reception rooms were "imposing," and the accommodations for the students "almost luxurious."[74]

The academy was completed and opened to students in 1888. It was originally divided into four departments. Students could elect to study the classics, history, Neo-Confucianism (*li-hsüeh*), or government (*ching-chi*).[75] In defining the goals of these four departments, Chang explained that in classical studies the main emphasis would be placed upon understanding the general significance or broad meaning (*ta-i*) of the classics. Energy would not be dissipated over trifling and vexatious points of classical criticism. In historical studies emphasis would be placed on thorough knowledge of the past and present, while empty discussion was prohibited. Philosophical studies would stress sincerity and truth, rejecting pretense and falsehood. "In the study of government," Chang wrote, "knowledge of the present and concern with the useful will be the main points."[76]

After the Kuang-ya Academy had been in operation for about a year, Chang reported that the students were being taught to discriminate strictly between righteousness (*i*) and profit (*li*), to study both extensively and intensively without losing sight of the main purposes, to avoid the prejudices of either the Han or the Sung learning, and to guard against developing literary knowledge (*wen*) to the detriment of action (*hsing*).[77]

As another measure to encourage learning in Liangkwang, Chang Chih-tung established the Kuang-ya Printing Office in 1887 to publish

73. *CC*, 22:8–12, 94:6–7b; *HNP*, p. 57.
74. China, Imperial Maritime Customs, *Decennial Report*, 1882–1891, pp. 567–568. The report calls the academy's founding "a very notable event in the literary history of the province," although the date is in error. Students were not allowed to "sleep out" and were given leave only on "very special occasions." They received stipends of Tls. 5 a month and prizes of Tls. 1–3 in bimonthly examinations. The president at the time was Chu I-hsin.
75. *CC*, 26:20b–21b. Chang reorganized the Kuang-ya Academy in 1889, combining the departments of history and government and creating a new department of literature. A professor was given charge of each department so that the academy president was free for general supervisory duties. The academy was divided into two "schools," one for Kwangtung students and the other for Kwangsi students. *CC*, 95:38–40b.
76. *CC*, 22:10b.
77. *CC*, 26:20b.

classical commentaries and historical works.[78] The plant remained in operation until the end of the Kuang-hsü reign (1908) and issued about 176 works. Meribeth Cameron has written: "So spectacular were the achievements of the Academy and the Printing Office that Chang Chih-tung was often called Chang Kuang-ya in reference to his connection with these establishments."[79] During the Manchu Reform Movement at the turn of the century, Peking ordered that the academy be converted into a university (*ta hsüeh-t'ang*), but a shortage of funds prevented immediate fulfillment of the plan.[80]

In 1890, shortly after Chang Chih-tung had been transferred from Liangkwang to serve as governor general of Hukwang, he established the Liang-Hu Academy in Wuchang. This academy had no president, but professors were given charge of its six departments: classics, history, Neo-Confucianism, literature, mathematics, and government.[81] Students were to be tested in their subjects of study two times each month.[82] Some provisions were made for "day students," but the academy was to function mainly for the benefit of resident students, who would receive monthly stipends of Tls. 3 each. Chang ordered that two hundred *sheng-yüan* who had passed *sui* or *k'o* examinations be selected for admission to the academy. He enrolled a hundred students from Hupeh and another hundred from Hunan. In addition, forty students from the merchant class were admitted.[83]

The acceptance of these forty students from merchant families was related to Chang's method of financing the Liang-Hu Academy, being intended to make more palatable a levy imposed on tea merchants for support of the academy. When Chang reached Wuchang, he had noted that salt merchants were supporting most of the academies of Hunan and Hupeh, while tea merchants were getting off lightly in the matter of sub-

78. For basic documents on the Kuang-ya Printing Office (Kuang-ya shu-chü), see *CC*, 23:17–18, 93:2b–3b. Works published by the plant were collected and reprinted in 1920 under the title *Kuang-ya shu-chü ts'ung-shu*.

79. Hummel, I, 28. For three years after leaving Kwangtung, Chang continued to prepare the quarterly examinations for the Kuang-ya Academy and mail them to Canton. The students' essays were afterward sent to Wuchang to be read and graded by Chang. *HNP*, p. 71.

80. China, Imperial Maritime Customs, *Decennial Report*, 1892–1901, 2:190.

81. *CC*, 97:16–17. There were also three supervisory officials. On the Liang-Hu Academy, see also *Hu-pei t'ung-chih*, 59:2b–3; and Ch. 7 below.

82. These tests were also open to students of the Ching-hsin Academy. Testing in the eight-legged essay was continued at the Chiang-Han Academy. *CC*, 97:17–17b.

83. *CC*, 97:16–20b. However, the Imperial Maritime Customs' *Decennial Report*, 1882–1891, p. 182, indicated 480 students were enrolled at the academy—240 from Hupeh and 240 from Hunan. The report identified the six chairs as literary essays, rites, poetry, classics, mathematics, and chemistry, although it remarked the last two chairs were still vacant.

scriptions. In 1862 Hunan tea merchants had begun to make a special "contribution" to the Hankow defense forces. The amount contributed was two ch'ien, eight fen on every 100 catties of tea sold.[84] The amount was reduced by half in 1879, and the collection was halted altogether in 1886. Hupeh tea merchants were still making a contribution to Hankow defense, but it amounted to only seven fen on every 100 catties of tea. Chang Chih-tung sent emissaries to consult with leading tea merchants and found that they would be "pleased and happy" to submit to a new levy for the Liang-Hu Academy. Hunan merchants, therefore, were required to pay one ch'ien on every 100 catties of tea sold. Hupeh tea merchants were required to pay three fen in addition to the seven fen provided for Hankow defense, bringing their total contribution to one ch'ien, or the same as Hunan's. Chang estimated that the total tea trade of the two provinces amounted to about Tls. 10,000,000 a year. By means of the levy, he hoped to realize a thousandth of this total or about Tls. 10,000, most of which would be used for annual operating expenses of the Liang-Hu Academy.

After the levy had been in force for a year, Chang Chih-tung received an edict from the throne demanding an explanation. According to the edict, "someone" had memorialized that Hunan tea sales were declining and the tea merchants were losing money. They had repeatedly requested relief from the levy, but approval had been denied by Chang Chih-tung. In replying to the edict, Chang insisted that any protest came from one or two troublemakers and did not represent the view of the tea merchants' associations. The majority was still willing to contribute to the progress of Hukwang education. Nevertheless, in deference to the court's sympathy for the merchants, Chang announced that he would reduce the levy by one-third.[85] Despite this concession, objections continued. In 1892 the throne demanded another explanation of Chang. Although he still contended that the majority of the tea merchants was "pleased and happy," he admitted that tea crops had recently been damaged by excessive rainfall. He declared that he had been on the point of abolishing the levy when Peking inquired. Chang thereupon gave up his scheme and reported that he would "devise other means" for managing the Liang-Hu Academy.[86]

84. The tael was a weight of silver averaging about one and one-third ounces. The ch'ien (mace) was one-tenth of a tael, the fen one-hundredth, and the li one-thousandth.
85. *CC*, 30:6b–12b.
86. *CC*, 32:9–13. Although Chang originally stated that the merchants would pay about Tls. 10,000 a year, his opponent who reported to Peking in 1892 claimed they were actually paying about Tls. 20,000.

When founding the Liang-Hu Academy in 1890, Chang wrote: "The reason for establishing academies is to create and nourish worthy talent and obtain scholars understanding the *t'i* and comprehending the *yung* in order to prepare officials for the state."[87] Other documents dated about that time show signs of change in Chang's usage of the *t'i-yung* formula. As a director of education, Chang tended to equate *t'i* with literary knowledge (*wen*) and the Han learning. By associating Sung learning with moral action (*hsing*), he shaded it in favor of *yung*. However, his employment of *yung* appeared to denote more generally that which would be practical in Confucian statecraft (*ching-shih*). In his bibliography of recommended readings, he offered a long list of authors identified with what has been loosely called the School of Statecraft.[88] After Chang had become a governor general, he gradually applied *t'i* and *yung* to new factors. *T'i* was linked with the old (*chiu*), the inner (*nei*), and the Chinese (*Chung*). *Yung* was used in reference to the new (*hsin*), the outer (*wai*), and the Western (*hsi*). Before this change, however, Chang Chih-tung reached new heights as a conservative official, experienced failure, and was confronted with an acute need for reappraising his values. The period immediately following his service as a provincial director of education was in fact a crucial one in Chang's personal development.

87. *CC*, 97:16–16b.
88. *CC*, 209:48–49. By professional statecraft, scholars of this persuasion "meant primarily administrative and managerial expertise which were considered not contrary to, but still within the framework of, basic moral-political values of Confucianism." Chang Hao, "Liang Ch'i-ch'ao and Intellectual Changes in the Late Nineteenth Century," *Journal of Asian Studies*, 29.1 (November, 1969), p. 27. See also Benjamin Schwartz, *In Search of Wealth and Power, Yen Fu and the West* (Cambridge, Mass., 1964), pp. 6–15.

4 The Hanlin Academician
(1877–1882)

When Chang Chih-tung ended his tour of duty as director of education in Szechwan, he returned to Peking for new assignment as a Hanlin academician. He remained in the capital from the beginning of 1877 until early in 1882. Chang's activities during this five-year period were not directly related to Chinese education. Nevertheless, they were highly significant to his evolution as an educational reformer. Conclusions reached by Chang during this period and immediately afterward led him to modify his analysis of China's needs and alter his approach to Chinese educational problems. He arrived at a turning point in his official career. As a matter of secondary interest, his activities from 1877 to 1882 typified the interests and the ceremonial, editorial, and nominal teaching assignments of members of the Hanlin Academy.

The Chinese people regarded Hanlin members as "the flower of the intellectual aristocracy."[1] The duties of the academicians were varied. First of all, they functioned as aides to the emperor. Members were required to attend the emperor at audiences in Peking, at the outer palaces, or during imperial travels. They prepared prayers and sacrificial addresses for use in ceremonies at the Altars of Heaven and Earth, the imperial tombs, and the ancestral temple. The academy conducted its own sacrifices to Confucius and his disciples. Twice a year, in the second and eighth months, sixteen members of the academy formally expounded the classics to the emperor. In addition, "daily expositors" held sessions with the emperor during about five months of each year.

Academicians did the actual work on all "imperially-edited" books and collections. They drafted biographies of rulers, nobles, officials, scholars, virtuous women, and filial sons. As agents of the State Historiographer's Office (Kuo-shih kuan), they gathered material for the dynastic history. When assigned to the Office for Keeping a Diary of the Emperor's Activities (Ch'i-chu-chü kuan), they recorded words and deeds of the sovereign during audiences, ceremonies, and public appearances, and kept a record of petitions and memoranda addressed to the throne.

Academy members, in conjunction with the Board of Rites, also copied and published specimens of the best essays from the provincial and metropolitan examinations. They were responsible for proposing post-

1. Ku Hung-ming, *The Story of a Chinese Oxford Movement*, 2nd ed. (Shanghai, 1919), pp. 18–19.

humous and honorary titles, and preparing monumental inscriptions, patents of dignity, and patents of nobility.[2] They helped staff the Imperial Library, the Imperial College, and the Supervisorate of Imperial Instruction.[3] Serving in these capacities, they were sometimes called "literary ministers" (tz'u ch'en) to the throne.

This list of functions makes it clear that Hanlin academicians could not conscientiously perform their duties without deeply appreciating the state cult of Confucianism or the rituals and ceremonies through which it was expressed. In addition, through dealing constantly with archives and records, they could hardly avoid reinforcing the historical consciousness that had first been fostered in their minds when studying for the civil service examinations. Yet as court attendants, diarists, and recorders of history in the making, they were also obliged to keep themselves well informed of current political affairs. They were prevented from becoming detached or secluded scholars of "pure history"—but were able to present themselves as experts in "applied history," capable of founding arguments for modern programs on lessons drawn from the past. The members of the academy, who thus made their living by knowledge of Chinese tradition, tended to side with the conservatives in a political context where conservatism represented strong commitment to Confucian statecraft and liberalism favored increased borrowing from the West. Generally, the Hanlin Academy was regarded as a bastion of conservatism.

As a member of the academy, Chang Chih-tung received a number of metropolitan assignments between the time that he left Szechwan and his appointment as governor of Shansi in 1882. While en route to Peking early in 1877, he was designated a collator of the Imperial Library, an assistant compiler of the State Historiographer's Office, and an assistant reviser of the Office for Keeping a Diary of the Emperor's Activities.[4] In 1877 and again in 1880 he was reappointed a professor of the Hanlin

2. On the functions of the Hanlin Academy and related agencies, see the *Kuang-hsü hui-tien* (Collected statutes of the Kuang-hsü reign; 1899), 70:1–16; W. A. P. Martin, *Hanlin Papers, or, Essays on the Intellectual Life of the Chinese* (London, 1880), pp. 15–20; Brunnert and Hagelstrom, pp. 72–75; W. F. Mayers, *The Government of China, a Manual of Chinese Titles, Categorically Arranged and Explained,* 3rd ed., rev. G. M. H. Playfair (Shanghai, 1897), pp. 24–26.

3. The Supervisorate of Imperial Instruction was "an absolute sinecure." During the early Ch'ing period the office was charged with instructing the crown prince, but it had been an anachronism since the K'ang-hsi reign, when the emperor's sons quarreled over the right of succession and the practice of naming an heir-apparent during the lifetime of the the ruler was discontinued. Thereafter the emperor named his successor by will. The supervisorate continued merely "as a stepping stone for promotion of the members of the Academy of Letters." Brunnert and Hagelstrom, pp. 484–485.

4. *HNP*, p. 20.

Academy's Department of Study. Successive assignments in 1879 were as a tutor of the Imperial College, a secretary in the Supervisorate of Imperial Instruction, and Groom of the Library (Ssu-ching-chü hsi-ma), an office under the Supervisorate of Imperial Instruction. In 1880 Chang was promoted from compiler to subexpositor (*shih-chiang*) and then to reader (*shih-tu hsüeh-shih*) of the Hanlin Academy. During the same year he became Junior and then Senior Deputy Supervisor of Imperial Instruction. He was also appointed to serve as a diarist in the Office for Keeping a Diary of the Emperor's Activities. In 1881 Chang was made an expositor (*shih-chiang hsüeh-shih*) of the Hanlin Academy and appointed a subchancellor of the Grand Secretariat, with the brevet rank of a Board of Rites vice-president. During the 1877–1881 period he also served as chief editor of a gazetteer of the metropolitan prefecture, the *Shun-t'ien-fu chih*, published in 130 chüan.[5]

While holding these various jobs and titles, Chang Chih-tung acted as one of the most vocal conservatives of the Hanlin Academy. He attracted national attention and some international notice for the first time as a specialist in "straightforward speech and unflinching remonstrance." He dramatized himself as an alert watchman for the throne, the eyes and ears of the Son of Heaven. Some Peking officials began to find him useful, or admired his scholarly glitter. But others had cause to fear his skillfully inflammatory writings or were angered by his frenzied shrillness. Chang's exhortations and admonitions were uttered in alliance with a curious coterie of young Hanlin scholars, who made their influence felt in Peking for almost a decade while for the most part digging their own political graves.

The "Pure Group"

The circle of low- or middle-ranking Peking officials with whom Chang Chih-tung was associated became known as the "Pure Group"—the Ch'ing-liu or Ch'ing-liu Tang.[6] Demanding strict adherence to Confucian

5. *HNP*, pp. 20, 23–24; *CC*, 71:2–5b. For the table of contents of the *Shun-t'ien-fu chih*, see *CC*, 213:43–47b.

6. Lloyd E. Eastman ably related the Ch'ing-liu to the larger body of *ch'ing-i* or "literate opinion" of which it was a part. Eastman, "Ch'ing-i and Chinese Policy Formation during the Nineteenth Century," *Journal of Asian Studies*, 24:4 (August 1965), 595–611. See also Immanuel C. Y. Hsü, *China's Entrance into the Family of Nations: The Diplomatic Phase, 1858–1880* (Cambridge, Mass., 1960), p. 200 and passim; Hao Yen-p'ing, "T'ung-Kuang hsin-cheng-chung ti so-wei 'ch'ing-i'" (The so-called "ch'ing-i" during the reforms of the T'ung-chih and Kuang-hsü reigns), unpub. bachelor's thesis, National Taiwan University, 1958; Hao Yen-p'ing, "A Study of the Ch'ing-liu Tang: The 'Disinterested' Scholar-Official Group (1875–1884)," *Papers on China*, 16 (1962), 40–65 (East Asian Research

principles, the group claimed dedication to the cause of cleansing the Chinese government by restoring former so-called norms of excellence. In regard to domestic policy, its members sought the removal of officials who did not meet high standards of ability, integrity, and loyalty. Institutionally, they favored the improvement of government operations through a closer imitation of ancient models. Theoretically, they were prompted by lofty ideals without regard for private or partisan advantage. In foreign policy, like most officials, they opposed the alienation of Chinese territory or foreign aggression toward Chinese tributary states. But unlike many of the officials in actual charge of foreign affairs, they urged that Chinese diplomacy be backed by the threat or actual use of armed force. Proponents of a "positive" foreign policy, they fought the "appeasement" approach of Prince Kung and Li Hung-chang.[7] Pedantically inclined to accept a "golden age" of the past, they tended to overestimate China's strength in the present. They thus appeared immature beside certain older leaders who had been made more cautious by bitter experience with the West or who possessed more penetrating insight into the sources of Western strength.

At least eight men were identified with the Pure Group.[8] In addition to Chang Chih-tung (1837–1909) a native of Chihli and a *chin-shih* of 1863, they included Chang P'ei-lun (1848–1903), a native of Chihli and a *chin-shih* of 1871; Ch'en Pao-ch'en (1848–1935), a native of Fukien

---

Center, Harvard University); Ku Hung-ming, *The Story of a Chinese Oxford Movement.* Several sources, including the *Ch'ing-shih,* 6:4937, 4939, call the group the Ch'ing-liu tang, but as Eastman points out, the phrase is redundant since both *liu* and *tang* may mean "circle, group, coterie, etc." Besides being the most literal translation, "pure group" is the most accurate. Other translations are "purification clique," "pure current party," and "national purification party." Use of "party" seems misleading for this small amorphous group because of the word's Western connotations of organized political activity carried out by a structured membership.

7. The moderate Prince Kung (I-hsin), one of the great leaders of the T'ung-chih Restoration, headed the Tsungli Yamen from 1861 to 1884. He incurred the dislike of the Empress Dowager Tz'u-hsi, however, and after 1865 his authority gradually diminished, while Li Hung-chang became the de facto minister of foreign affairs. Li also became doyen of the bureaucracy in 1870 when he succeeded Tseng Kuo-fan as governor general of Chihli, the choicest provincial administrative post.

8. Hao Yen-p'ing, "A Study of the Ch'ing-liu Tang," p. 41, excludes Sheng-yü and Hsü Chih-hsiang and includes Wu Ta-ch'eng, Li Hung-tsao, and Liu En-p'u as members. The *Ch'ing-shih* biography of Chang P'ei-lun, 6:4937, mentions Wu as a member, but the biographies of Wu himself in the *Ch'ing-shih,* 6:4976–4977, and in Hummel, II, 880–882, do not similarly identify him. During the period of the of the Pure Group (1875–1885), Wu was engaged in practical affairs as a provincial director of education, circuit intendant, defense leader, and diplomatic envoy, teamed on occasion with Li Hung-chang, in dissimilar activities to those of other group members. Although Liu En-p'u is included in Tso Shun-sheng, *Chung-kuo chin-tai-shih tzu-liao chi-yao* (Shanghai, 1945), p. 333, other sources do not, to my knowledge, accord him prominence in the Pure Group. Li Hung-tsao's putative leadership role is discussed in Hummel, I, 472, which notes that Li was "sometimes referred

and a *chin-shih* of 1868; Hsü Chih-hsiang (1838–1899), a native of Kiangsu and a *chin-shih* of 1860; Huang T'i-fang (1832–1899), a native of Chekiang and a *chin-shih* of 1863; Pao-t'ing (1840–1890), an imperial clansman and a *chin-shih* of 1868; Sheng-yü (1850–1900), an imperial clansman and a *chin-shih* of 1877; and Teng Ch'eng-hsiu (1841–1891), a native of Kwangtung and a *chü-jen* of 1861.[9] This listing reveals no similarity of regional background, for the men were natives of north, east, and south China. However, they were all fairly young men during the period in which the Pure Group flourished, being mainly in their thirties or forties, with Sheng-yü the youngest member of the group and Huang T'i-fang the oldest. With the single exception of Teng Ch'eng-hsiu, all were *chin-shih*; and aside from Chang P'ei-lun and Sheng-yü, all obtained their degrees in the 1860's. Chang Chih-tung and Huang T'i-fang shared a common experience in having graduated the same year. Ch'en Pao-ch'en and Pao-t'ing were also graduates of the same year.[10] Again with the exception of Teng Ch'eng-hsiu, a censor, all were members of the Hanlin Academy and during this period held positions with the academy or its related agencies. The most articulate of the octet were Chang Chin-tung, Chang P'ei-lun, Huang T'i-fang, and Pao-t'ing, who became known collectively as the "four admonishing officials" (*ssu-chien-ch'en*) or the "four remonstrants of the Hanlin Academy" (*Han-lin ssu-chien*).[11]

All apparently were ambitious for advancement in the bureaucracy. A measure of opportunism was mixed with their professed Confucian altruism. They used the classics, for example, in repeatedly impressing

to as the leader of a group of officers who were natives of the northern provinces—among them Chang Chih-tung, Sheng-yü, Chang P'ei-lun and Pao-t'ing. As these same men were also members of the party known as Ch'ing-liu Tang . . . Li Hung-tsao was branded as leader of that party also." As Eastman points out, p. 601, confusion of the Ch'ing-liu and the Northern Party, a regional faction, "undoubtedly contributed to much misunderstanding concerning the Ch'ing-liu." Sheng-yü and Hsü Shih-hsiang are included on the basis of Hummel, I, 472, and statements of Ku Hung-ming; their grouping with other Pure Group members in chüan 445 of the *Ch'ing-shih*, 6:4934–4939; and the similarity of their activities and careers to other group members. My list includes only those regarded as the most important members. Others might be included. Ku Hung-ming, for example, referred to Ch'en Ch'i-tai as a "well known" member, and Sun I-yen referred to himself as Ch'ing-liu. Eastman, "Ch'ing-i and Chinese Policy Formation," p. 600 *n.*28. Additional names are given by Richard C. Howard in his introduction to "The Chinese Reform Movement of the 1890's; A Symposium," *Journal of Asian Studies*, 29.1 (November 1969), pp. 12–13.

9. For biographies of Chang P'ei-lun, Hsü Chih-hsiang, Huang T'i-fang, Pao-t'ing, Sheng-yü, and Teng Ch'eng-hsiu, see *Ch'ing-shih*, 6:4934–4939. For Ch'en Pao-ch'en (not to be confused with Ch'en Pao-chen, governor of Hunan during the 1898 reform movement), see *Chūgoku bunka-kai jimbutsu sōkan*, ed. Hashikawa Tokio (Peiping, 1940), p. 472. For Chang P'ei-lun, Huang T'i-fang, Pao-t'ing, and Sheng-yü, see Hummel, I, 48–49, 348–349; II, 611–612, 648–649.

10. See Fang Chao-ying and Tu Lien-che, pp. 193, 197.

11. *Ch'ing-shih kao*, 450:7b; *Ch'ing-shih*, 6:4939.

upon the throne the need for "men of talent"—then recommended one another. In 1882 Chang Chih-tung proposed higher offices for Chang P'ei-lun, "a leading man of the present age," Ch'en Pao-ch'en, called worthy of employment in the Tsungli Yamen, and Sheng-yü, "indeed a rare talent in respect to current affairs."[12] Members of the clique memorialized pertinaciously upon controversial issues, keeping their names before the court with labored literary offerings. They were generally obsequious in their approach to the empress dowager. But on one occasion in 1879 even Tz'u-hsi became so tired of their rehashing of traditional schemes for famine relief that she ordered a halt to "imitative and sycophantic verbiage."[13] In 1885 she took a more drastic step and closed "the road of speech" (yen-lu), withdrawing a traditional privilege that allowed the voicing of opinions by officials not directly concerned with the matter under discussion.[14]

Opponents of the clique accused its members of reckless character assassination and of fastening on popular causes for the primary purpose of ingratiating themselves with the throne and advancing their own careers.[15] Chang Chih-tung in this period has been likened to "a rat looking both ways," ready to turn in any direction that would mean better salary and rank for himself.[16] The judgment may be too harsh. Although members of the Pure Group were overeager to assume positions of higher leadership, they were probably honest in their basic conservative orientation.

Among the opponents of the group were the "Westernizers," represented near the beginning of the Kuang-hsü reign by men like Tung Hsün, Kuo Sung-tao, Ch'ung-hou, and Tseng Chi-tse, in addition to Prince Kung and Li Hung-chang.[17] Delivering the coup de grace to the

12. *CC*, 4:7–9. Teng Ch'eng-hsiu was also recommended for office by Chang P'ei-lun. Eastman, "Ch'ing-i and Chinese Policy Formation," p. 601.

13. *HNP*, p. 22.

14. The *yen-lu* was closed in immediate response to a memorial by Hsü Chih-hsiang that angered the empress dowager. See Eastman, "Ch'ing-i and Chinese Policy Formation," pp. 597, 607–609.

15. Li Tz'u-ming made charges of this kind against the Northern Party, which included Pure Group members. In his diary, *Yüeh-man-t'ang jih-chi* (Peking, 1922), he claimed the Northerners recommended each other for promotion, protected each other from deserved punishments, censured other officials as a means of revenge, and sought high office by interfering in the affairs of the court. Eastman, "Ch'ing-i and Chinese Policy Formation," p. 601.

16. Ch'en Kung-lu, *Chung-kuo chin-tai shih* (Shanghai, 1935), p. 244. See also Li Chien-nung, *The Political History of China, 1840–1928*, trans. and ed. Ssu-yu Teng and Jeremy Ingalls (Princeton, 1956), p. 123. Li speaks of the "so-called pure and honest censors" who "liked to be courageous in their criticism of the government in order to incur a good reputation and quick promotion."

17. For biographies of Ch'ung-hou, Kuo Sung-tao, Tseng Chi-tse, and Tung Hsün, see Hummel, I, 209–211, 438–439; II, 746–747, 789–791.

declining Prince Kung and defeating Li Hung-chang seemed to be two main objectives of the group. Ku Hung-ming, one of the disciples of Chang Chih-tung but a man who professed to even more conservatism than his master, described the clique's attitude toward Li Hung-chang:

> This Chinese Oxford Movement was chiefly directed against Li Hung-chang—the Lord Palmerston of the Chinese middle class liberalism . . . Li Hung-chang had attracted around him men of the rich, lower middle and compradore classes who had made money by foreign trade; and these men all showed an inclination to favour what they called progress in the direction of adopting foreign ways and methods. Their crude ideas of adopting foreign ways and methods however had all the vulgarity and hideousness which Matthew Arnold speaks of in the English middle class Liberalism. This vulgarity and hideousness of course shocked the flower of the intellectual aristocracy in the Hanlin Academy—the Oxford of China. In this way, the Oxford movement became intensely anti-foreign. It was anti-foreign, not because these scholars hated foreigners; it was anti-foreign because these scholars saw before their eyes that the foreign ways and methods of Li Hung-chang and his entourage were hideously vulgar and demoralizing.[18]

The Pure Group accused Li of preferring utility (*kung-li*) to moral fortitude (*ch'i-chieh*), ability (*ts'ai-neng*) to virtue (*jen-p'in*), and in general of "overlooking Confucianism" (*ch'ih-chiao*). They heaped abuse on him, particularly during the Annam crisis of the early 1880's.[19]

Officials who were sympathetic to the aims of the Pure Group included Li Hung-tsao, P'an Tsu-yin, and Li Wen-t'ien. Although Weng T'ung-ho, tutor to the Kuang-hsü emperor, later became a political rival of Chang Chih-tung, he and Hsü T'ung, who had been tutor to the T'ung-chih emperor, also sided with Chang and his cohorts upon occasion.[20]

18. Ku Hung-ming, *The Story of a Chinese Oxford Movement*, pp. 16, 18–19. According to Ku, competition between Li Hung-chang and Chang Chih-tung continued for years: "At the time of the Boxer troubles in 1900, when the Empress Dowager and the Emperor went to Hsi An, Li Hung-chang sent a telegram urging them not to listen to the advice of the bookworm, Chang Chih-tung. Some one reported what Li had said to Chang Chih-tung who exclaimed in fury: 'If I am a bookworm, he is a wily old rascal!' and even up to the present time whenever adherents of Chang Chih-tung discuss Li Hung-chang, they always roundly abuse him." Ardsheal, *Journal of the North China Branch of the Royal Asiatic Society*, 45 (1914), 98.

19. Hao Yen-p'ing, "A Study of the Ch'ing Liu Tang," p. 51. See also Eastman, "Ch'ing-i and Chinese Policy Formation," pp. 604–605.

20. For biographies of Li Hung-tsao, Li Wen-t'ien, P'an Tsu-yin, and Weng T'ung-ho, see Hummel, I, 471–472, 494–495; II, 608–609, 860–861. On the evolution of Weng T'ung-ho's relations with Chang Chih-tung, see Hsiao Kung-chuan, "Weng T'ung-ho and the Reform Movement of 1898," *Ch'ing-hua hsüeh-pao*, n.s., 1.2 (April 1957), 111–243. Weng may be classed as conservative and antiforeign in this period. He esteemed and was on cordial terms with Chang until at least 1884. However, unlike Chang, he sided with Prince Kung during the Ili crisis and advocated caution during the Annan crisis. Hsiao, pp. 116, 118ff, 134.

Li Hung-tsao, a member of the Grand Council, also served as a chancellor of the Hanlin Academy. He was sometimes referred to as leader of the clique, but such references may have been gratuitous. Li was in mourning from 1877 to 1880, in which period the clique flourished. High in rank, he possessed "great sweetness of temper and purity of character" and did not participate in the virulent attacks upon others that characterized the low and middle grade officials comprising the Pure Group.[21] While serving as a member of the Tsungli Yamen, he sided with the clique during the Ili crisis. Yet he also maintained close relations with Prince Kung, and he fell from power along with Prince Kung in 1884 as a result of the Annam crisis.[22]

P'an Tsu-yin, a vice-president and president of various boards between 1868 and 1895, was a conservative official zealous in reforming administrative corruption. He exerted a strong influence on Chang Chih-tung, his friend and occasionally his junior collaborator in the discussion for and preparation of memorials.[23] Li Wen-t'ien, who served in the Imperial Study (Nan shu-fang) was in retirement between 1874 and 1884, but after his return to Peking, he advised Chang Chih-tung on Sino-French relations during the Annam crisis.[24]

Aid for the Empress Dowager

Although the sympathy of these officials was helpful, members of the Pure Group probably derived their strongest support from the empress dowager and Prince Ch'un (I-huan), who rose in influence as Tz'u-hsi gradually withdrew her favor from Prince Kung.[25] The clique came to the aid of the empress dowager at a critical point in her career and consequently earned her gratitude.

When Tz'u-hsi's son, the T'ung-chih emperor, died without an heir on January 12, 1875, the empress dowager made her own choice of a new occupant for the throne and foisted her wishes upon a carefully staged court conference of nobles and high officials.[26] She selected as her candi-

21. Ku Hung-ming, *The Story of a Chinese Oxford Movement*, p. 19.

22. Li Chien-nung, p. 123.

23. *HNP*, p. 21.

24. Hummel, I, 495.

25. In 1865 the empress dowager stripped Prince Kung of the rank of Prince Counselor and conferred the title on his less liberal and less capable younger brother Prince Ch'un. In 1873 Prince Ch'un was raised to a princedom of the first degree, equal to Prince Kung. In 1884, when Prince Kung was discharged from all offices, it was announced the Prince Ch'un would be consulted on all important matters of state. Hummel, I, 384–385.

26. For other accounts of the problem, see Lo Tun-yung, "Te-tsung chi-t'ung ssu-chi" (A private account of the succession of Te-tsung), in Tso Shun-sheng, *Chung-kuo chin-pai-nien shih tzu-liao ch'u-pien* (Taipei, 1958), pp. 429–453; J. O. P. Bland and E. Back-house, *China under the Empress Dowager* (Philadelphia, 1910), pp. 117–147; Hummel, I, 296; II, 730–731.

date her three-year-old nephew, Tsai-t'ien, the son of Prince Ch'un and her own younger sister. Her announcement shocked the court. According to the dynastic law of succession, an adopted heir should have been selected from the generation below the deceased emperor, so that order could be preserved in the relative ranking of sovereigns. The T'ung-chih emperor and Tsai-t'ien were first cousins and of the same generation. For the sake of her own power, however, Tz'u-hsi could not allow a choice from a lower generation, which would have raised the late emperor's wife, the Empress Hsiao-che, to the rank of empress dowager and would have ended Tz'u-hsi's days of palace glory. Tz'u-hsi prevented any such development by hastily effecting the enthronement of Tsai-t'ien as the Kuang-hsü emperor. She announced his adoption as the heir of her own late husband, the Hsien-feng emperor, a device that made her the adoptive mother of the new ruler and permitted her to continue as regent. Seventy-four days later Peking was again shocked when the Empress Hsiao-che committed suicide.

Breaking the proper line of succession in this manner was tantamount to dispossessing Tz'u-hsi's own son, the T'ung-chih emperor. A most serious step in the view of good Confucians, the move left the T'ung-chih emperor without an heir to perform sacrifices in his behalf. In order to ward off objections on this score, Tz'u-hsi announced that when the Kuang-hsü emperor had a son, the boy would be named the adopted heir of the T'ung-chih emperor.

These maneuvers, which completely obfuscated the problem of imperial succession, aroused only a few courageous courtiers and censors to open protest. But they created an undercurrent of criticism that lasted for more than four years while the empress dowager was trying to consolidate her power anew and forestall the growth of opposition. Then in 1879, soon after the interment of the T'ung-chih emperor, the issue broke into the open once again. A former censor, Wu K'o-tu, committed suicide as a dramatic protest against Tz'u-hsi's actions. He left behind a memorial accusing the dowager of "compounding one mistake with another."[27] He also demanded a clear statement that the next occupant of the throne would be the same as the adopted heir of the T'ung-chih emperor. Wu K'o-tu's suicide unleashed an excitement long repressed, and Tz'u-hsi was required to recognize the existence of bureaucratic opinion. Perhaps she sought to control it through formalizing its expression, for she called on all princes, high officials, and Hanlin academicians to present their

---

27. For the Chinese text and a translation of Wu K'o-tu's memorial and will, see Evan Morgan, *A Guide to Wenli Styles and Chinese Ideals* (Shanghai, 1912), pp. 258–279.

views. Two court conferences on the subject were subsequently held, one on May 21 and the other on May 30, 1879.[28]

It was at this time that members of the Pure Group rallied to the aid of Tz'u-hsi. Chang Chih-tung, Pao-t'ing, and Huang T'i-fang were among those who came forward with memorials that provided the empress dowager with an "official line" on the Wu K'o-tu suicide. Tz'u-hsi commended all three by ordering that their memorials be copied and preserved in the Yü-ch'ing Palace, the emperor's study hall. The memorials of Chang and Pao-t'ing, together with a joint memorial participated in by P'an Tsu-yin, Hsü T'ung, and Weng T'ung-ho, were noted in Tz'u-hsi's final decree on the case.[29]

Chang Chih-tung supported Tz'u-hsi in this instance at the price of compromising a former friend. Just before poisoning himself, Wu K'o-tu wrote a farewell letter to his son containing the instruction: "Present my compliments to Chang Chih-tung and Chang P'ei-lun: I only wish that I could have had more of the old-time talks with them."[30] Chang was not unduly harsh in judging Wu K'o-tu and praised his "complete loyalty and high principle." Nevertheless, he depicted Wu's suicide as useless. There were no substantial grounds, he argued, for doubting the good intentions of T'zu-hsi or the wisdom of her decisions.

Chang's 2,500-word memorial on the case analyzed two matters over which Wu K'o-tu had displayed excessive anxiety and two matters over which his anxiety had been insufficient. Although the text is a fine example of historical argument applied by a Hanlin scholar to a contemporary problem, one is inclined to agree with the translators of the *Peking Gazette* that "it would be tedious to follow the memorialist through the complicated and apparently meaningless quotations in which he clothes his ideas."[31]

One of the key arguments revolved around a point of terminology. The empress dowager had stated that a son of the Kuang-hsü emperor would "succeed as the adopted heir" (*chi-ssu*) of the T'ung-chih emperor. Wu K'o-tu's memorial protested that the words did not necessarily mean that the adopted heir would "succeed to the imperial rule" (*chi-t'ung*). Chang Chih-tung tried to prove that, historically and etymologically, the terms *chi-ssu* and *chi-t'ung* were interchangeable. Starting with the Hsia dy-

28. *HNP*, p. 21.
29. *CSL*, 93:5–6. For an analysis of Tz'u-hsi's relations with *ch'ing-i* officials, see Eastman, "Ch'ing-i and Chinese Policy Formation," pp. 606–607.
30. Morgan, p. 276.
31. *PG*, 1879, pp. 76–77. For Chang's memorial, see *CC*, 1:1–7.

nasty, he worked forward to the Ming to show the similarity. In the Ming the two terms were distinguished, he said, because of the "distorted, reckless, and misleading dicta" of Chang Ts'ung and Kuei O.[32] However, the interpretations by these two men were fully refuted in a work called the *I-li i-shu* (Commentary on the decorum ritual), commissioned by the Ch'ien-lung emperor and printed in 1748.[33] When Tz'u-hsi had spoken of an "adopted heir," she naturally meant that he would be ruler after the Kuang-hsü emperor.

Wu K'o-tu apparently desired an announcement that the first son of the Kuang-hsü emperor should be named the heir apparent, Chang said, yet primogeniture had not been practiced for many years. The fulfillment of Wu's wish would therefore constitute a violation of imperial family law. It could also give rise to disputes among sons, should the Kuang-hsü emperor be blessed with more than one male child. Or it might preclude the choice of the best qualified successor by naming the first-born son as the heir apparent.

On such grounds as these Chang Chih-tung defended the empress dowager against the charge of "compounding one error with another." But he agreed with Wu K'o-tu that a second decree would be advisable. The question would be resolved, Chang argued, if only the empress dowager would announce that the next successor to the throne, whichever of the Kuang-hsü emperor's sons he might be, would also be the adopted heir of the T'ung-chih emperor. This course would result in five advantages: maintaining the dynastic regulations, providing against interruptions in the imperial line, preventing future jealousies among princes, forestalling further changes, and allowing for selection of the worthiest prince as the next emperor.

The final decree on the case, handed down by the empress dowager on May 30, 1879, closely resembled the recommendations of Chang Chih-tung. It stated in part:

> The request by Wu K'o-tu for a proclamation on the succession was actually contrary to the family law of this dynasty. The (Kuang-hsü) Emperor has received the heavy responsibility of government from the (T'ung-chih) Emperor Mu-tsung. In the future when imperial sons are born to him, he will of course care-

32. Chang Ts'ung and Kuei O supported the Ming Emperor Shih-tsung, a paternal second cousin of the preceding ruler, in his desire to have his own father canonized as an emperor. The general body of officials urged that Emperor Shih-tsung recognize his predecessor alone as his (adopted) father. Giles, pp. 46–47, 388–389.

33. Hummel, I, 236.

fully select the best one to become his successor to the throne. He who succeeds to the rule will become the adopted heir of the Emperor Mu-tsung.[34]

Chang Chih-tung and several other members of the Pure Group thus helped to supply Tz'u-hsi with the sanction and ratification that she badly needed in 1879. In return, for a time the group was permitted considerable liberty in airing its views on domestic and foreign policies. Moreover, Chang Chih-tung at least was marked for rapid promotion. He received five new appointments in 1880 alone and two in 1881, before being elevated to a position as governor of Shansi province and next as governor general of Kwangtung and Kwangsi.

Domestic Policy Proposals

Just as men identified with the Pure Group were in general agreement on the question of imperial succession, so were they in general accord in their approach to other domestic problems. A series of natural disasters and evil omens provided them with additional opportunities to make their views known. Between 1876 and 1879 large areas of North China were scourged each summer by drought and famine. While the suffering centered in Shansi, other disaster areas were Shensi, Honan, Chihli, and Shantung. One foreign chronicler described the misfortunes of 1877 as "by far the most important incident in Chinese domestic affairs."[35] Other writers have used other superlatives, such as "the worst famine on record."[36] Chang Chih-tung left his own description of people eating leaves and bark, beggars lining the sides of the roads and the Grand Canal, and villages depopulated by death and migration.[37] In 1879 an earthquake occurred in Kansu and Sinkiang, with tremors felt in Shensi and Szechwan. Among the evil omens was the daytime appearance of Venus, accompanied by "strange mists," first in 1879 and again in 1881. A comet was observed in the sky for ten successive days during the fifth month of 1881, and this phenomenon recurred in the seventh month of 1881.[38]

Politicians of many countries have blamed depression or disaster upon their opponents' ill-advised policies or failure to take preventive mea-

34. *CSL*, 93:5–6.
35. R. S. Gundry, ed., *A Retrospect of Political and Commercial Affairs in China and Japan during the Five Years 1873 to 1877* (Shanghai, 1878), p. 74.
36. E. W. Price Evans, *Timothy Richard* (London, 1945), p. 64.
37. *CC*, 1:25–26.
38. *CC*, 1:20, 3:28b–29; *PG*, 1879, pp. 127–128, 134–135; 1881, pp. 86–87; *HNP*, pp. 26–27.

sures. In imperial China, however, governmental theory on the inter-action between Heaven and Earth provided a unique cause for linking natural calamities and political issues. This theory placed upon the Chinese emperor one of the heaviest burdens ever conceived. Wedged between Heaven and humanity, the emperor was responsible to both. As evil action by mankind would incur the displeasure of Heaven, the Emperor through his own moral example was obligated to direct his people toward good. If he failed at times, Heaven's displeasure was expressed through omens and calamities. If he failed too often, Heaven would adopt a new son and pass its mandate to some deserving rebel. Where there was belief in these ideas, natural calamities raised questions transcending the immediate problems of relief and rehabilitation. Periods of disaster became periods for "self-cultivation and examination" (*hsiu-hsing*). Wherein had the emperor been morally remiss? What were the wrongs of his officials and people? At such times of introspection, the throne would appeal for honest advice and suggestions on reform. In response, officials would present pet schemes or private peeves, trade charges and countercharges. Omens and natural calamities thus catalyzed both political house-cleaning and political reprisal.

If the empress dowager felt insecure before mankind at the outset of the Kuang-hsü reign, perhaps she also trembled before Heaven. Members of the Pure Group were on her side and imputed to her no personal blame for the omens and disasters. But they seemed to play upon her fears in an effort to win the dismissal of corrupt officials and political rivals. They were also active in stressing the need for moral reform and suggesting relief programs rooted in Chinese antiquity. At least six memorials directly inspired by disasters of the period are included in the complete works of Chang Chih-tung. They may be taken as representative of Pure Group "policy" in regard to domestic affairs. Chang emphasized the following themes.

Self-cultivation and self-examination. Chang recommended that the throne call upon all people to "cleanse their hearts and fulfill their responsibilities in order that we may receive the blessings of Heaven." Without self-examination and self-cultivation, the people's suffering could not be relieved, nor could problems in foreign policy be overcome.[39]

Straightforward speech. Chang described imperial solicitation and toleration of straightforward speech as a primary duty of moral cultivation. Because the eyes and ears of the emperor could not encompass the

39. For memorial, see *CC*, 1:20–25.

nine divisions of the Celestial Empire, the throne should be willing to heed "public opinion" (*kung-i*) and accept ministerial advice. To drive his point home, Chang drew an analogy between the family and the state:

> I humbly state that ministers serving the sovereign are like sons serving the parents. The chief minister is like the household manager, and the other ministers are like the remaining sons. The chief minister plans, and the junior ministers assist. The junior ministers consult, and the chief minister decides. Outspoken disputes spring from common concern. If we believe that someone is making trouble for us, then even peaceful words may cause anger. But if we believe that we are being helped, then even unpleasant truths may be forgiven. If the family is harmonious, it will prosper; if the court is in agreement, the empire will be regulated.[40]

Men of talent. Chang repeatedly urged that more attention be paid to selecting respected men for the bureaucracy and removing incompetent officials. "Degrade those who neglect duty while taking pay," he said. "Eliminate those who pretend to play the pipes." Ministers should "store up men of talent in their bags beforehand" and constantly recommend the most capable ones, while the throne should "measure ability and then make appointments."[41]

Improvement of the people's livelihood. One of the most effective ways to improve their livelihood, Chang argued, would be to stamp out bureaucratic corruption. "There are many capable officials but few honest ones," he asserted. Officials at the lower levels of government were impoverishing the people and enriching themselves through exorbitant levies. Governors and governors general should be required to prohibit personal profit among their subordinates and provide special rewards for incorrupt officials.[42]

Attention to water control. To prevent further damage from floods, Chang proposed that secondary "moon-dikes" be built seven li from the main dikes at threatened places along the Yellow River. To prevent drought, he proposed a program of well-digging, presented as a plan superior to the construction of irrigation ditches leading from rivers.[43]

Equitable distribution of grain. Among other plans for securing an equitable distribution, Chang suggested a form of the "ever-normal granary." Four or five public granaries should be established in all de-

40. *CC*, 1:18–20.
41. *CC*, 2:15–16b. The expression "in their bags" refers to the story of a ruler who kept a notebook in his bag to record the characteristics of his visitors.
42. *CC*, 1:23–24.
43. *CC*, 1:24–24b. See also *CC*, 1:25–29b.

partments and districts. The gentry would be required to deliver to these public granaries 20 percent of their grain in excess of 100 piculs and 30 percent over 300 piculs. The local poor could then borrow from the granaries. As soon as the borrowers were able, they would make repayments, with interest, to the original lenders. Rich families without land would give money to buy grain and would be rewarded with hereditary titles or decorations. Chang explained, "The classics say that in times of disaster both relief and borrowing must be undertaken."[44]

All of these themes were sound, traditional ones, displaying Chang Chih-tung's indebtedness to the classics and histories. Yet the themes were perhaps too familiar, for memorials on these topics submitted by Chang and his Pure Group colleagues seem to have stirred little excitement in Peking. Two of Chang's memorials inspired imperial decrees ordering officials to be honest, recommend able men, submit "straightforward speech," consider tax reforms, and carry out dike repairs.[45] But most of his petitions did not even earn the imperial endorsement, "Noted."

The Pure Group was more successful in attracting attention through impeachments. Teng Ch'eng-hsiu belonged to the Censorate (Tu-ch'a yüan) in this period, and Chang P'ei-lun was acting vice-president of the Censorate during part of 1882. The Hanlin members of the clique freely infringed upon the functions of the Censorate.

Some of Chang Chih-tung's impeachments were directed against minor officials or were relatively mild. In 1879 he submitted four reports condemning district officials of Tung-hsiang, Szechwan, for corruption that led to a riot by the populace. The case already had been under trial for two years, but Chang brought new evidence to show that the officials had been collecting 500 mace for themselves for every tael of authorized taxation they levied.[46] In 1881 Chang protested against palace eunuchs who had been brawling with Peking gate guards.[47] During the same year he complained about newly-appointed governors and governors general who were procrastinating in departing for their posts. On these grounds he censured Tseng Kuo-ch'üan, P'eng Yü-lin, and others.[48] The first important case in which Chang participated, however, was a campaign against Tung Hsün, president of the Board of Revenue.

44. *CC*, 1:26–27b. See also *CC*, 1:29b–32b.
45. *PG*, 1879, pp. 127–128; 1881, pp. 86–87.
46. *CC*, 1:7b–18b.
47. *CC*, 3:27–28b.
48. *CC*, 3:31b–34.

In 1878 Chang drafted a memorial accusing Tung Hsün of maladministration of famine relief, and the document was submitted to the throne in the name of Huang T'i-fang. The throne judged the charges against Tung Hsün to be ill founded, and Huang was brought to trial before the Board of Civil Appointments. Chang Chih-tung escaped punishment, but according to his *nien-p'u*, Huang T'i-fang was sentenced to demotion by two grades. Other sources state that Huang finally escaped punishment because of a plea on his behalf by Pao-t'ing, one of the imperial clansmen associated with the Pure Group.[49] Chang P'ei-lun took up the attack against Tung Hsün, however, and in 1882 Tung was finally dismissed from the Board of Revenue. It was perhaps no coincidence that Tung, in addition to having headed the Board of Revenue, had been associated with Prince Kung in the Tsungli Yamen since the establishment of that office in 1862, had close contacts with the Peking College of Languages (T'ung-wen Kuan), and strongly favored Chinese diplomatic missions abroad.[50]

In 1882 bribery charges pressed by Chang P'ei-lun and Teng Ch'eng-hsiu resulted in the dismissal of another Board of Revenue president, Wang Wen-shao, regarded by some as a protégé of Li Hung-chang. Earlier Chang P'ei-lun and Huang T'i-fang had impeached Ho Shou-tz'u, who was removed as president of the Board of Works. Chang P'ei-lun also caused the downfall of Wan Ch'ing-li, president of the Board of Civil Appointments. And Sheng-yü was among those who criticized the Board of War president, P'eng Yü-lin, for having declined office too often.[51]

Teng Ch'eng-hsiu, the censor, was one of the busiest impeachers of all. His biography in the *Ch'ing-shih* cites his many memorials on corruption in the bureaucracy and examination system and lists by name a number of officials against whom he protested, including Li Han-chang, the brother of Li Hung-chang, and Tso Tsung-t'ang, who was criticized as being too old for office.[52]

Whereas many of the impeachments were directed against officials in charge of domestic affairs, they were in some cases aimed at the "Westernizers." The Pure Group often showered obloquy on men concerned with foreign relations or modernization projects. Sheng-yü protested against Wu Ch'ang-ch'ing, who in 1882 had forced the father of the Ko-

---

49. *HNP*, p. 21; Hummel, I, 349; *Ch'ing-shih*, 6:4934.

50. For Tung Hsün, see Hummel, II, 789–791.

51. *Ch'ing-shih*, 6:4935–4937; Hummel, I, 48.

52. *Ch'ing-shih*, 6:4937. For additional impeachments, see Hao Yen-p'ing, "A Study of the Ch'ing-liu Tang," passim.

rean king to accompany him to China after an attempted coup d'etat in the tributary state. And Sheng-yü's memorial helped provide the empress dowager with a needed pretext to deprive Prince Kung of all offices in 1884.[53] Hsü Chih-hsiang vehemently opposed the railroad building plans of Li Hung-chang.[54] Huang T'i-fang censured Minister Ts'ui Kuo-yin for harming China's prestige by attending sporting events in the United States; and in 1885 Huang unsuccessfully attacked Li Hung-chang's plans for development of the Chinese navy.[55] But by far the heaviest attack, led by Chang Chih-tung, Chang P'ei-lun, and Ch'en Pao-ch'en, was directed against Ch'ung-hou, who signed the Treaty of Livadia with Russia in 1879 and inflamed a dispute over Ili. More than any other factor, it was their interference in foreign affairs that brought about a reversal of fortunes and eventually the downfall of the Pure Group.

The Ili Crisis

The Pure Group flourished in a period when Western powers were changing their policies toward China. The end of China's war with Great Britain and France in 1860 had been followed by a relaxation of foreign pressures upon the Ch'ing empire. The Western powers temporarily substituted patient diplomacy for armed force as the instrument for upholding their treaty rights and gaining new commercial concessions in China. This program, which became known as the "cooperative policy," was initially carried out in Peking by ministers called the "Four B's"— Bruce of Britain, Berthemy of France, Balluseck of Russia, and Burlingame of the United States.[56] It allowed China a breathing spell for constructive reform and served to deter unilateral territorial acquisitions by any of the Western powers. The "cooperative policy" in its essentials outlasted the four originators' tours of duty in Peking. However, it was shaken by the Tientsin massacre of 1870 and was disintegrating by the time of the Margary murder and its sequel in 1876, the Chefoo Convention. Within the next few years a complete breakdown took place.

As the Western powers, now joined by Japan, resumed aggression, they no longer strove only for treaty ports and trade privileges in the Chinese heartland but engaged individually in an effort to absorb the tributary states of the Chinese empire. Between 1876 and 1885, Chinese

53. *Ch'ing-shih,* 6:4936. Hummel, I, 382.
54. *Ch'ing-shih,* 6:4938.
55. Hummel, I, 349; *Ch'ing-shih,* 6:4935.
56. On the "cooperative policy," see H. B. Morse, *The International Relations of the Chinese Empire* (London, 1918), II, 113–137; Mary C. Wright, pp. 21–47.

statesmen were forced to consider defense on four peripheral fronts. The Ili crisis occurred in the northwest, where Russia attempted to seize a large portion of Sinkiang. A controversy developed when Japan occupied the Liu-ch'iu Islands off the Southeast China coast. Troubles in the northeastern vassal state of Korea, which began when Japan opened that country to trade in 1876, culminated in Chinese and Japanese intervention in Korea during 1885. And the French occupation of Annam in the southwest led to war with China in 1884 and 1885.

Under these conditions foreign policy became one of the liveliest topics of debate in the Chinese government. Li Hung-chang and Prince Kung vacillated. Not wholly willing to accept Western concepts of international law and Chinese state responsibility for semidependencies, nor at all willing to risk war, they were yet unwilling to abandon the Chinese tributaries. As they worked for the best possible negotiated settlements, they were hampered by their political opponents in Peking. A "war party," with members of the Pure Group well in the lead, kept them under steady censure. Pure Group members submitted memorials on the Liu-ch'iu and Korean problems, but reached the height of their bellicosity with demands made during the Ili and Annam crises.

The Sino-Russian dispute over Ili was spawned in 1866 when Yakub Beg began setting up a rebel state in Central Asia.[57] He made himself master of Kashgar and several neighboring khanates and began to eye Ili, north of Kashgar across the T'ien-shan range, as another field for conquest. Russia felt that Yakub Beg endangered her commercial interests in the region, where trade had been developing steadily since 1851 when the Sino-Russian Treaty of Kuldja provided for a Russian consulate in Ili and Russian settlements in Ili and Tarbagatai. In the opinion of Governor General K. P. von Kaufman, appointed the proconsul of Russian Turkestan in 1867, there was another urgent consideration in addition to commerce. Kaufman stressed the necessity of keeping British influence out of Ili. Already the British, from their bases in India, were making overtures to Yakub Beg, and it was feared that they would follow him into Ili. Because of these factors, Kaufman independently ordered the occupation of the area and on July 4, 1871, captured Ili city.

The foreign office in St. Petersburg was said to be puzzled at first, realizing that Kaufman's action would not appear consistent with Russia's

---

57. For the Ili crisis, see Chu Djang, "War and Diplomacy over Ili," *Chinese Social and Political Science Review*, 20.3 (October 1936), 369–392; Immanuel C. Y. Hsü, *The Ili Crisis* (London, 1965).

traditionally friendly relations with China.[58] The Russian minister in Peking, General G. Vlangaly, was instructed to inform China that a high Chinese official should be sent to reclaim the region. The Chinese appointed General Jung-ch'üan for the task. But the Russian government then decided to uphold Kaufman and delayed the return of Ili, expressing fear that Jung-ch'üan's forces would be incapable of maintaining order there and that the region again would be menaced by Moslem rebels if reoccupied by China. The outcome of talks between Vlangaly and Prince Kung was an understanding that Russia would return Ili to China only after the rebels had been suppressed and the northwestern frontiers secured. In the meantime, Russia would protect Ili and hold it in trust for China.[59] Later the *North China Herald* reported that, while this assurance was given in Peking, a special proclamation by Tsar Alexander II declared that Russia would hold Ili "in perpetuity."[60] Whether or not there actually was such a proclamation, other governments suspected this was the real Russian intention.

By 1876 the time was obviously drawing near for Russia to redeem or renounce her promise. Tso Tsung-t'ang was then advancing victoriously through Sinkiang, and it appeared that the area would be tranquilized much more quickly than the Russians had anticipated. A secret conference was called in St. Petersburg in March 1876, presided over by the minister of war and attended by the governors general of Turkestan and Siberia and the head of the Asiatic Department. The conferees decided to return Ili to China if necessary—but only for a high price. Russia would keep the whole territory unless China would cede the fertile Tekkes River valley south of Ili city, grant further trade privileges, and pay an indemnity to cover Russian occupation costs. Basic Russian policy was thus apparently determined three years before the mission of Ch'ung-hou.[61]

However, this fact was carefully concealed, even after Tso Tsung-t'ang completed the reconquest of Kashgar in 1878 and began urging the throne to recover Ili. When Prince Kung took up the matter with Eugene K.

58. On Kaufman and the Russian foreign office response, see A. Lobanov-Rostovsky, *Russia and Asia* (New York, 1933), pp. 184–187.

59. See Prince Kung's review of the early negotiations in Henri Cordier, *Histoire des relations de la Chine avec les puissances occidentales* (Paris, 1901–1902), II, 172–176.

60. *North China Herald*, 1880, p. 534. Another account says G. A. Kolpakovskii, the general under Kaufman who led Russian troops into Ili, on his own authority declared the area annexed "in perpetuity." Hsü, *The Ili Crisis*, pp. 14, 31.

61. L. E. Frechtling, "Anglo-Russian Rivalry in East Turkestan," *Journal of the Royal Central Asian Society*, 26 (1939), 484–485. On Russian policy discussions early in 1878, see Hsü, *The Ili Crisis*, pp. 51–52.

Butzow, who had been the Russian minister in Peking since 1874, Butzow renewed Russia's delaying tactics. He insisted that before the retrocession of Ili there should be a settlement of accumulated "old cases," that is, alleged Chinese outrages against Russian merchants and subjects in the northwest and elsewhere. On March 3, 1878, Butzow informed the Tsungli Yamen that he was returning to Russia on leave and that his office would be managed by Chargé d'Affaires Koyander. Koyander subsequently pleaded a lack of authority to deviate from the position that Butzow had taken.[62]

Giving up hope that any settlement of the case could be achieved in Peking, the Tsungli Yamen recommended the dispatch of a Chinese envoy to St. Petersburg. Accordingly, an imperial edict of June 22, 1878, announced the appointment of Ch'ung-hou for the job. Although Ch'ung-hou was then serving as military governor of Mukden, he earlier had been chief of the Chinese diplomatic mission sent to France to apologize for the Tientsin massacre. When he was chosen for the mission to St. Petersburg, plenipotentiary powers were conferred upon him in order "to facilitate the conduct of affairs." In view of the mission's importance, the Tsungli Yamen also obtained permission to give Ch'ung-hou the rank and salary of a "first-class imperial commissioner" (*t'ou-teng shih-ch'en*).[63] Prince Kung later maintained that when Ch'ung-hou received his credentials and appeared at an imperial audience, he was instructed to exercise the greatest prudence while in Russia and to do nothing without consulting the court or the Tsungli Yamen in advance.[64] However, among foreign diplomats in Peking "it was taken for granted that the Yamen had been too slack to give him definite instructions."[65]

At this time Chang Chih-tung showed his first interest in the Ili issue, by drafting a memorial that was submitted in the name of Chang P'ei-lun. This document recommended that Ch'ung-hou visit Sinkiang before departing for Russia and acquaint himself with conditions there by consulting with Tso Tsung-t'ang. "If the minister is to discuss Sinkiang, he must first know Sinkiang," the memorial maintained. It also protested against giving Ch'ung-hou plenipotentiary powers, on the ground that Russian coercion could lead him to make damaging commitments. The memorial was submitted but did not receive an imperial endorsement.[66]

62. See memorials of the Tsungli Yamen in *WCSL*, 13:28, 15:16–17.
63. *WCSL*, 13:28b, 14:8–8b.
64. Cordier, II, 185.
65. E. V. G. Kiernan, *British Diplomacy in China, 1880 to 1885* (Cambridge, 1939), pp. 50–51.
66. *HNP*, p. 21. See also partial translation in Hsü, *The Ili Crisis*, pp. 49–50.

Ch'ung-hou presented his credentials to Tsar Alexander II in St. Petersburg on January 20, 1879.[67] He then began talks with Russian officials, mainly Nicholas de Giers, the assistant foreign minister, A. G. Jomini, senior counselor in the Foreign Office, and Butzow. The Russian strategy in the talks was threefold. First, the Russians wooed Ch'ung-hou personally through a great show of respect and friendship, which impressed other diplomats by its "caressing nature."[68] Next they ostensibly abandoned their procrastination, readily agreed to restore Ili, and began putting forth innocuous requests to which China could easily consent. Finally, they revealed their important demands bit by bit, apparently to test the Chinese reaction. Response was so slow in coming from Peking that no great deterrent to the Russian schemes appeared obvious. At precisely the proper moment, when Ch'ung-hou's faith in the Russians seemed secure and his wisdom had not yet been seriously challenged by Peking, Butzow disclosed the Russian demands in full, obtained Ch'ung-hou's approval of practically everything requested, and sped the ambassador to a treaty-signing ceremony on the Black Sea.[69]

On October 2, 1879, Ch'ung-hou committed China to the Treaty of Livadia, consisting of eighteen articles, a trade agreement with seventeen articles, and two special protocols. The treaty provided essentially all that the Russians had asked.[70] It permitted Russia to retain the western portion of Ili and the Tekkes River valley, constituting seven-tenths of the region in question. Boundaries in the vicinity of Tarbagatai and between Kashgar and Fergana were modified in Russia's favor. Russia was allowed to establish seven new consulates in the northwest; buy land and build shops, houses, and warehouses where the consulates were located; and carry on duty-free trade in Sinkiang. The Russians also were permitted to trade along overland routes from Kalgan to Tientsin and from Chia-yü-kuan to Hankow. Within a year China was to pay Russia an indemnity of five million rubles. One of the protocols was a total surprise to Peking. By this agreement, Ch'ung-hou conceded to Russia the rights of navigation and trade on the Sungari River as far as Petuné (Pa-tu-na) in northwestern Kirin.

After Ch'ung-hou had signed the Treaty of Livadia, he returned to St. Petersburg. There he handed his funds, records, and seal to his first sec-

67. *WCSL*, 15:5–6b.
68. Kiernan, p. 41 *n*.2.
69. For key documents on Ch'ung-hou's negotiations, see *WCSL*, 15:6–6b, 16–17, 32–32b, 34b–36, 16:2–10.
70. For Chinese text of the treaty, trade agreement, and protocols, see *WCSL*, 19:23b–48b.

retary, Shao Yu-lien. On October 11 he began his homeward journey, without first obtaining imperial permission to depart. He explained this step in a memorial to the throne: "It is noted that in the treaty-making of all countries, once a minister has signed a treaty, he personally carries back to his own country the signed text of the treaty, leaving an assistant in temporary charge to cement friendly relations."[71] Ch'ung-hou left Russia unaware of the storm that was brewing in China. His memorial on the end of his mission reflected nothing but placidity and satisfaction.[72] Yet Henri Cordier remarked that Ch'ung-hou must have been out of his mind at the time, because his treaty granted terms that might have followed a defeat in war but should never have resulted from peaceful negotiations.[73] Cordier's evaluation was mild compared with the expletives of some of Ch'ung-hou's fellow officials.

When Prince Kung learned of the signature of the Treaty of Livadia, he denounced Ch'ung-hou's inexplicable capitulation to the Russians. However, the Tsungli Yamen was uncertain how to remedy the situation.[74] The Yamen realized that China might refuse to ratify the treaty but felt that would be a risky course. China's plenipotentiary already had agreed to the terms and "to first approve and later reject" would place China in the wrong and anger the Russians. Prince Kung sighed: "The more foreign affairs are managed, the harder they become; the harder they become, the more unmanageable they are." He recommended that Shen Pao-chen, Li Hung-chang, Tso Tsung-t'ang, and others be called to consider the problem.

In reply, Shen Pao-chen objected to the "irresolute" stand of the Tsungli Yamen and its argument that nonratification of the treaty would place China in the wrong. He cited international law to demonstrate that China would be fully within its rights to refuse approval of the treaty.[75]

---

71. See *WCSL*, 17:19b–20.
72. See *WCSL*, 17:20–24b.
73. Cordier, II, 191. Kuo Sung-tao, who was Chinese minister to England and France when Ch'ung-hou traveled to Russia in 1878, charged four mistakes to Ch'ung-hou in negotiating the treaty. First, not knowing geography, he had to rely on the misleading maps of the Russians. Second, in fixing his mind only on the city of Ili, he became so anxious for the Russians not to change their minds about returning the city that he underestimated their many extraneous demands. His third mistake was an awe of Western might. Finally, Ch'ung-hou followed a slovenly plan and was overly sanguine. *WCSL*, 20:15b–22b. Similar ideas were expressed in an evaluation of Ch'ung-hou by S. Wells Williams: "To the seemingly apparent defect of an unusually Boeotian temperament was added a profound ignorance of any European language, of modern methods of diplomacy, or of the topography of the territory in question." Williams, *A History of China* (New York, 1897), p. 379.
74. *WCSL*, 16:25–28b. See partial translation in Hsü, *The Ili Crisis*, pp. 59–60.
75. *WCSL*, 17:6b–8. For Shen Pao-chen, a senior official, see Hummel, II, 642–644.

Li Hung-chang agreed that China could rightfully refuse to ratify the treaty, but he feared that such a step would lead to war with Russia, encourage Japanese encroachments in case of such a war, and arouse England and France to anxiety over their own diplomatic relations with China. Li counseled against any hasty action and urged that China attempt to reopen the negotiations with the Russians. If it finally became necessary to make commercial concessions, China should "establish controls in the midst of no controls." Russian traders might be admitted to China but then restrained by "establishing laws" and "using men." The establishment of laws would mean instituting local regulations for the control of foreign trade, and the use of men would mean employment of officials familiar with foreign affairs to enforce the local regulations strictly.[76] Tso Tsung-t'ang's reply was the simplest of all: decide which articles of the treaty should be accepted and which rejected, prepare for war, gird for endurance, and strive for victory. It was Tso's advice that the throne accepted initially. An imperial edict of December 17, 1879, ordered that military preparations be made along the entire northern frontier, from Sinkiang to Heilungkiang.[77]

At this point Chang Chih-tung and other members of the Pure Group clamorously entered the controversy. The clique became the self-appointed Peking agents of Tso Tsung-t'ang and the cadre of a "war party" that also included Prince Ch'un and Prince Li (Shih-to). Chang Chih-tung was so vociferous that he gave a later writer the impression that his efforts "practically decided the course of events."[78] Of the fifty memorials on the Ili crisis selected for the *Ch'ing-chi wai-chiao shih-liao*, a collection of documents on foreign affairs, thirteen were submitted by Chang, more than double the six of Tso Tsung-t'ang, his nearest contender in the volume. Chang's collected works contain nineteen memorials pertaining to the Sino-Russian dispute. During the crisis he often teamed with Chang P'ei-lun and Ch'en Pao-ch'en. One would dictate a memorial, another make the rough draft, and the third prepare the final copy and submit it to the throne.[79]

Huang T'i-fang was the first member of the Pure Group to enter the fray. In a memorial of January 2, 1880, Huang recommended that Ch'ung-hou be punished for "acting on his own authority to deceive the country" and for having left his post without permission. Huang also suggested that

76. *WCSL*, 17:16–19; Hsü, *The Ili Crisis*, pp. 63–65.
77. *WCSL*, 18:1b–8; Hsü, *The Ili Crisis*, pp. 60–63.
78. Bland and Backhouse, p. 502.
79. *HNP*, p. 23.

a court conference be called to consider the case. The throne thereupon ordered the Tsungli Yamen to make available to high Peking officials and members of the Hanlin Academy all documents pertaining to the crisis. The officials should study the documents and then submit a joint report.[80]

This edict provided Chang Chih-tung with the opportunity to set forth his own ideas, in a memorial that became the basic platform of the "war party" and that has been called "by far the most remarkable" of all the petitions submitted during the crisis.[81] Chang's 2,500-word memorial, dated January 16, 1880, took the position that China would not be worthy to call herself a nation if the Treaty of Livadia were accepted.[82] Point by point, Chang presented his arguments on ten concessions that should be rejected, the most important being concession of the Tekkes River valley, granting of a trade route to Hankow, permitting duty-free trade by Russians in the northwest, and opening the Sungari River to navigation as far as Petuné. Throughout the Ili crisis Chang remained firm on these major points.

His memorial presented four other arguments. First, Ch'ung-hou should be executed at once. "His fellow countrymen, with one voice, say let him be killed," Chang declared. Second, China should adopt a bold attitude, reject the treaty, and make Russian injustice known to all the world. The Chinese position should be: "The Russians deceived our unprotected and imbecile Ambassador, and browbeat him into signing a treaty by which, for every penny they spent, they got back a hundred and yet were not satisfied. The Russians, in a loutish way, are a great nation, and one does not expect them to act in this manner." Third, China should consistently maintain that right was on her side in rejecting the treaty. The Chinese stand should be: "Our Ambassador certainly signed the treaty, but he never had Your Majesty's permission to do so, and the instrument itself, not having been sealed with the Imperial seal, is in the position of a document (in the olden days) unattested by the oath of blood." Finally, China should mobilize for warfare, proceed apace with defense preparations, and try to enlist Britain as an ally against Russia. Chang recommended that Li Hung-chang be placed in charge of mobilization and ordered to accept the responsibility. Chang doubted that

80. *WCSL*, 18:9b–10. See partial translation in Hsü, *The Ili Crisis*, p. 78.
81. Chu Djang, p. 381.
82. For memorial, see *CC*, 2:1–6b. Translations appear in the *North China Herald*, June 1, 1880, pp. 480–482; *Papers Relating to Foreign Relations of the United States, 1880* (Washington, 1880), pp. 267–271. While the second translation is annotated, it is inferior to the first. For accounts of how the memorial reached the foreign legations and the press, see *HNP*, p. 22; *North China Herald*, 1880, pp. 460, 493.

Russia would fight: her troops were still tired from their recent war with Turkey; her resources were exhausted; and her rulers were estranged from the people. Chang recognized that if conflict should follow, Russia might win a limited victory, but he was confident that the Russians could never penetrate far enough into China "to disturb the general prosperity of our country."[83]

Chang's memorial resulted in a decree appointing him a special adviser on Sino-Russian relations and entitling him to consult at any time with the Tsungli Yamen.[84] His arguments evoked varied responses from his Western contemporaries. Sir Thomas Wade, the British minister to Peking, called Chang "the ablest pen in the Empire" but ridiculed his memorial as "a sadly bombastic and puerile state paper."[85] The editors of the *North China Herald* thought otherwise:

> No doubt the memorial is intemperate in language, but there are occasions when intemperance is demanded . . . taking it as a whole, and bearing in mind that it is a Chinese state paper, certain characteristics stand out in bold and very notable relief. First of all, there is no nonsense about it. We read nothing about the Son of Heaven bearing with the feeble and fantastic vagaries of despicable barbarian vermin. The honor of the country is set forward in a thoroughly manly and businesslike way as something likely to be assailed, and therefore as something to be eagerly defended.[86]

At the Chinese court and among Chang's fellow officials in Peking, the memorial had great influence. It created a sensation among the literati, catapulting Chang to fame as "the hero of the hour."[87] The day after the memorial was submitted, Ch'ung-hou was dismissed from office and handed over to the Board of Punishments.[88] On February 19, 1880, Prince Li publicly recognized the contributions of Chang Chih-tung to the deliberations of the officials who had been conferring on the case. Prince Li reported that the conferees had reached general agreement on three points: the treaty and special agreements that Ch'ung-hou had signed should be rejected; Ch'ung-hou should be punished; and the preparations for war should proceed. However, the memorialists also suggested that another minister be sent to St. Petersburg to reopen negotiations with the Russians.[89] The throne accepted these suggestions and

83. From translation by the *North China Herald*, 1880, p. 481.
84. *HNP*, p. 22; *WCSL*, 18:32.
85. Kiernan, pp. 53–54.
86. *North China Herald*, 1880, pp. 421–422.
87. See comments by Hsü, *The Ili Crisis*, pp. 72, 74–75.
88. *WCSL*, 18:22b–23.
89. See memorial of Prince Li and others, *WCSL*, 19:1–3.

appointed Tseng Chi-tse to serve as the new minister to Russia. Tseng had been the minister to England and France since 1878. The throne later endorsed recommendations by Chang Chih-tung that Tseng proceed directly to St. Petersburg, without visiting China first, but that he be given explicit instructions and careful guidance.[90]

The appointment of Tseng Chi-tse represented a gain for the "peace party" led by Prince Kung, Li Hung-chang, Governor General Liu K'un-i of Liangkiang, and others. Prince Kung and Li Hung-chang had cited and continued to make good use of foreign reaction to the treatment being accorded Ch'ung-hou. On January 4, Koyander had protested that negotiations with Ch'ung-hou were carried out in good faith and that his arrest represented an insult to the Russian empire.[91] Ministers of England, France, Germany, and the United States also expressed concern to the Tsungli Yamen. They resented "the treatment accorded to an ambassador who had tried to solve an international difficulty by the accepted rules of diplomacy, and who was charged not with treason, but with failure."[92]

Despite such pleas, the Chinese government renounced the Treaty of Livadia on February 19, and on March 3 it sentenced Ch'ung-hou to imprisonment pending decapitation.[93] Foreign and "peace party" pressures for Ch'ung-hou's pardon or the mitigation of his sentence were applied. The British and French ministers provided the "peace party" with valuable support when they intimated that their governments would intercede to try to persuade the Russians to reopen negotiations if Ch'ung-hou were released.[94] Pao-t'ing and Huang T'i-fang, members of the Pure Group, were implacably opposed to the pardon of Ch'ung-hou. Chang Chih-tung also was opposed, but indicated his willingness to accept a pardon providing war preparations continued. Without a show of force, Chang argued, the pardon of Ch'ung-hou would be interpreted as another sign of Chinese weakness and would therefore undermine any negotiations by Tseng Chi-tse. Prince Ch'un recommended that Ch'ung-hou's sentence be reduced, but suggested that he be held as a hostage and executed if Tseng's negotiations failed or if war broke out.[95]

90. *WCSL*, 19:3–3b, 7–8, 22b–23b.

91. *WCSL*, 18:10–13.

92. H. B. Morse, p. 333. See also memorial of the Tsungli Yamen on the foreign ministers' notes in *WCSL*, 21:2–4; Cordier, II, 192–196; *Papers Relating to Foreign Relations of the United States, 1880*, pp. 221–223.

93. See *WCSL*, 19:3–3b, 11b.

94. See memorial of the Tsungli Yamen, *WCSL*, 21:4–5b; Hsü, *The Ili Crisis*, p. 90.

95. See memorial of Huang T'i-fang, *WCSL*, 21:5b–6b, and memorial by Prince Li and others, *WCSL*, 21:11b–12b; *CC*, 2:21–24; *WCSL*, 21:8–10b.

The empress dowager ordered Chang Chih-tung to prepare a report summarizing these and other views for the guidance of the Grand Council. The Grand Council then recommended the lightening of Ch'ung-hou's sentence in order to encourage British and French intercession. On June 26, 1880, the throne reduced the sentence from execution to imprisonment. A decree to Tseng Chi-tse, apparently intended for Russian eyes, explained that a desire for peace and friendship motivated the change of sentence, which unfortunately had been misinterpreted as an insult to Russia. At the same time, however, an order to Li Hung-chang and others explained that the reduction of sentence had been granted because China was not yet ready to fight; border and sea defenses should be quickly strengthened.[96] Russia, too, seemed to be preparing for war. She concentrated at Vladivostok "the greatest naval force which up to that time had ever been assembled in Far Eastern waters."[97]

Chang Chih-tung still felt that the risk of war was justified. In his memorials he harped upon a major theme: unless China demonstrated a willingness to fight, Russia would not renegotiate the Treaty of Livadia to China's advantage. In one of his memorials Chang attacked Prince Kung personally. Airing a personal grievance, he complained that Prince Kung "always feels that the views of scholars should not become policy." Nor could Prince Kung make up his mind: "Although he does not favor war, neither does he dare set forth trenchantly and firmly a plan for approving the treaty and withdrawing the troops."[98]

Chang Chih-tung's own ideas on war and the treaty negotiations became well known in Peking. He submitted numerous suggestions for the guidance of Tseng Chi-tse, who presented his credentials in St. Petersburg on August 22, 1880, and began talks on a new agreement with Russia.[99] Chang also made numerous proposals on defense measures, the assignment of generals, and the training and disposition of troops.[100] Some of his ideas seemed sound, but others were too fanciful for serious consideration. In the latter category, for example, was Chang's scheme

96. *WCSL*, 21:11b–12b, 15–16b; Hsü, *The Ili Crisis*, pp. 92–93. On August 12, 1880, as a result of intercession by Tseng Chi-tse, Ch'ung-hou was fully pardoned and released.

97. Lobanov-Rostovsky, p. 190. On the Chinese concern over Russian naval operations, see *WCSL*, 21:27–28, 28–31.

98. See Chang's review of the crisis, *CC*, 3:9b–12b, esp. p. 12. He also criticized Li Hung-chang and Liu K'un-i, for being fearful of war. Li counterattacked by accusing Chang and Pao-t'ing of irresponsibly inflaming public opinion. Hsü, *The Ili Crisis*, pp. 92, 104.

99. Chang's memorials on diplomacy are in *CC*, 2:16b–17b, 20b–21, 29b–31b, 3:1–3b, 14b–20.

100. Chang's memorials on the military are in *CC*, 2:6b–16b, 17b–19b, 24–29b, 3:4b–9b, 12b–14b, 20–22b.

for draining the Sungari River: "There are many shallow places west of the Ussuri River. If we make breaches at several places on the south bank of the Sungari River and release water to enter the shallows, on the pretext of undertaking irrigation projects, the main stream will become so shallow that steamships will naturally be obstructed."[101]

While Chang Chih-tung memorialized, Tseng Chi-tse advised Peking to be calm and reminded the throne that the nineteenth century was not like the Warring States period.[102] To facilitate his negotiations, Tseng also entered a plea that finally resulted in the pardon of Ch'ung-hou, announced by an edict of August 12, 1880.[103] Tseng afterwards negotiated patiently with the Russians, and on February 24, 1881, he was able to sign the Treaty of St. Petersburg that finally brought the Ili crisis to a close. By this treaty China paid Russia a larger indemnity, nine million rubles instead of five million, but China was released from the most objectionable terms of the Treaty of Livadia. The western portion of Ili was kept by Russia, but the Tekkes River valley was returned to China. The two governments agreed to appoint commissioners to investigate other boundary questions. Russian traders could carry on their business in Sinkiang without paying duties only until the two governments agreed on tariff rates. Russian merchants could travel as far as the caravan terminus at Chia-yü-kuan but could not proceed to Hankow. Russian trade on the Sungari River was left a matter for future discussion.[104]

Lord Dufferin, the British ambassador at St. Petersburg, remarked, "China has compelled Russia to do what she has never done before, disgorge territory that she had once absorbed."[105] The conclusion of the Treaty of St. Petersburg was hailed as a great diplomatic victory in China.[106] The victory was partly attributed to Tseng Chi-tse's skillful negotiations and partly to the support he received from the "peace party" in Peking. However, members of the Pure Group and other advocates of

101. *CC*, 3:22.
102. *WCSL*, 21:18–23.
103. *WCSL*, 22:7b.
104. For text of the treaty and special agreements, see *WCSL*, 25:30b–42b.
105. D. C. Boulger, *The Life of Sir Halliday Macartney* (London, 1908), p. 351.
106. L. E. Frechtling, p. 488, however, takes exception to describing the treaty as a Chinese victory: "Granting that this retrocession is without parallel in the history of Russian expansion, it is still unusual to ascribe the action either to the astuteness of the Chinese envoy or to the belligerent attitude of the Chinese patriots. The Russian government always had the situation in hand and dictated the final settlement. That she was so lenient in the territorial arrangement was due in a small part to pressure by Britain, but more to considerations of commerce and finance. The commercial privileges obtained as a ransom for Kuldja were more valuable than a few thousand square miles of Central Asian mountain and desert."

military preparedness or war also claimed a substantial share of the credit. The moral they drew from the Ili crisis was that Chinese diplomacy, in order to be effective, must be backed by force. Victory could not have been achieved without efforts like those of Chang Chih-tung. H. B. Morse described the attitude well:

> In her history of many centuries, China was accustomed to military victories, but a bloodless diplomatic triumph such as that of the Marquis Tseng was new in her experience. The masters of the empire were learning their lesson. The country was ready for war—as ready as her rival, on a frontier which was equally distant for both; and being ready, found that diplomacy was after all the better weapon. But diplomacy had scored its triumph only because the empire was ready to use armed force effectively.[107]

Another consequence of the Chinese diplomatic victory was noted by Cordier: "The treaty signed by Marquis Tseng resulted in making China arrogant. Russia's backward step had astonished the Chinese; they attributed to intimidation what was only self-interest and foresight, and they jumped from panic to the most outrageous boasting."[108]

Chang Chih-tung was among those whose confidence was bolstered by the successful outcome of the Ili negotiations. An overweening attitude was reflected in his memorial of August 29, 1881, proposing that Tseng Chi-tse be sent on another mission to St. Petersburg. Chang noted that since the assassination of Tsar Alexander II on March 13, 1881, the new ruler, Alexander III, had been surrounded by troops and was living in dread of terrorists who wished to establish a populist government. This state of affairs had come about, Chang argued, because of the Russian government's harshness and severity, heavy taxation, annoying labor services, and love of ceaseless warfare. Chang proposed the following scheme:

> The best thing that China could do would be to issue credentials to Tseng Chi-tse to go to Russia. He should first pay condolences and then explain a plan for relieving distress and achieving harmony. He should say that the Chinese court, with regard for alliance and friendship, is concerned and anxious over the harm represented by Russia's rebellious people. However, defensive measures taken in fear are not, after all, the best tactics. He should urge them to eliminate harsh government and be liberal (k'uan-ta), lighten punishments, reduce taxes . . . If the government is liberal, the people will be happy and naturally will not have rebellious

107. Morse, pp. 338–339.
108. Translated by Morse, p. 339, from Cordier, II, 240.

> hearts. (Tseng) should say that since antiquity this has been
> China's method for pacifying the people and preventing rebellion,
> and it is desired that the Russian ruler follow it.[109]

If China could end the threat of Russian revolution, Chang wrote, all countries of the world, large or small, would laud and honor China's great majesty. Confucius was correct in saying: "Cherish the princes and the whole world will stand in awe."

The Annam Crisis

Referring to the Chinese success in concluding the Treaty of St. Petersburg, W. A. P. Martin observed: "This result had the effect of inspiring the Chinese with confidence in their ability to resist aggression (as the French found to their cost)."[110] Members of the Pure Group continued their bellicosity and applied it to France between 1882 and 1885, during the crisis over the status of Annam.[111]

French encroachments in Annam had been developing since 1862 when France seized Saigon and three provinces of Cochin China. In 1874 the king of Annam was forced to sign a treaty of "peace and alliance" with France, which ceded to France the right to navigate the Red River and to help Annam put down internal disorders. Although the treaty recognized the Chinese vassal state as an independent country, it made Annam virtually a protectorate of France. China protested the treaty but took no further positive action at the time, and the French disregarded the Chinese objections. The French began to establish military posts along the Red River, on the pretext of providing protection against the Black Flag bandits of Liu Yung-fu, a former Taiping rebel operating in Annam. Clashes occurred between the French and Liu's forces, which the Chinese secretly began to reinforce. In March and April 1884, the French defeated contingents of Chinese troops in Annam. Angered by this de-

---

109. *CC*, 3:34–35b.
110. W. A. P. Martin, *A Cycle of Cathay, or China, South and North, with Personal Reminiscences* (Edinburgh, 1897), p. 389.
111. The following brief sketch of the Sino-French War is drawn mainly from Li Chien-nung, pp. 115–123, with additional data from biographies of the Chinese principals in Hummel. For a complete study, see Lloyd E. Eastman, *Throne and Mandarins: China's Search for a Policy During the Sino-French Controversy, 1880–1885* (Cambridge, Mass., 1967). To accord with original Chinese sources, the name Annam is used herein for Viet Nam. Douglas Pike, *Viet Cong* (Cambridge, Mass.: M.I.T. Press, 1966), p. *5n*, points out: "After the tenth century the Chinese referred to all of Vietnam as An Nam, a humiliating term meaning 'pacified south.' For their part the Vietnamese used the term Dai Co Viet, or Greater Viet State. In 1802, under Emperor Gia Long, the term Viet Nam came into official as well as wide usage."

velopment, the empress dowager dismissed Prince Kung and the entire Grand Council for mismanaging the Annam affair. Prince Li was given charge of the Grand Council and I-k'uang (later Prince Ch'ing) succeeded as head of the Tsungli Yamen.

While leaders of the earlier "war party" were now resurgent, the empress dowager still hoped for a peaceful settlement and supported the cautious policy of Li Hung-chang. On May 11, 1884, Li signed a convention with a French envoy, Commander François-Ernest Fournier. According to the terms of this agreement, China would recognize all treaties between France and Annam, immediately withdraw her forces from Annam, and permit trade with France over the border with Tonkin. When the terms of the convention became known, memorial after memorial was submitted to the throne attacking Li Hung-chang. The empress dowager also expressed her displeasure.

On May 17 Fournier presented Li a memorandum specifying that Chinese troops would withdraw from areas of Tonkin bordering Kwangtung and Kwangsi on June 5, and those opposite Yunnan by July 1. Evidence indicates that Li accepted these terms but failed to convey precise orders for evacuation to China's frontier commanders.[112] On June 23 a French force, marching northward with instructions to reoccupy Langson, encountered a strongly fortified Chinese outpost at the village of Baclé. When the Chinese refused to withdraw, a clash occurred and the French were defeated.

Upon reaching Paris, news of the Baclé incident incensed the French government. Jules Patenôtre, newly appointed minister to China, was instructed to demand that China conform to the Li-Fournier convention and, in addition, pay an indemnity for its "bad faith." Still displeased with Li Hung-chang, the empress dowager on July 19 appointed Tseng Kuoch'üan to negotiate with Patenôtre in Shanghai. After China refused to agree to an indemnity, the French bombarded Keelung in Formosa on August 5. They attacked Foochow on the China coast on August 23 and destroyed the small Chinese navy there.

For at least three months after the humiliating setback at Foochow, Tz'u-hsi seemed to support the war effort with resolution. But fighting in Annam and Taiwan had been indecisive; hopes that Britain or Germany would join China in the war against France had been dashed; and fears had grown that Russia and Japan would take advantage of China's troubles to advance their own interests. By early December 1884, these

---

112. Eastman, *Throne and Mandarins*, p. 127.

mounting complications caused a change in Tz'u-hsi's attitude. She determined on peace and closed the "road of speech" to militant spokesmen.[113]

In Annam during February 1885, the French occupied Langson and pursued Chinese troops to Chen-nan-kuan on the Kwangsi border. However, the Chinese forces, under the leadership of General Feng Tzu-ts'ai, counterattacked and recaptured Langson on March 29. But at this point, just as a military victory in Annam seemed within sight, a conclusion was reached in quiet negotiations with the French in Paris which had been carried out by agents of Sir Robert Hart, inspector general of the Chinese customs. To the chagrin of forces in the field, Peking agreed on April 4, 1885, to ratify the Li-Fournier convention. Li Hung-chang, recalled to diplomatic service, signed the Treaty of Tientsin on June 9. By the terms of the treaty, China paid no indemnity to France but renounced her suzerainty over Annam, thus suffering the final defeat. According to the Chinese historian Li Chien-nung, "The success of France was due to sheer luck, while the failure of China was brought about by indecision." Tz'u-hsi had wavered too long between the two viewpoints represented by Li Hung-chang, on the one hand, and the scholars who clamored for war but were "ignorant of domestic and foreign conditions."[114]

Members of the Pure Group were in the thick of the debate over Annam and the war with France. Chang P'ei-lun demanded decisive action against the French as early as 1882.[115] Chang Chih-tung assumed his duties as governor of Shansi on February 4, 1882, and thus was remote from the center of the controversy in Peking. However, in June 1882, he memorialized from Taiyuan and presented plans calculated to stop French encroachments and strengthen China's ability to resist. In November 1883, Chang presented still more detailed plans in three memorials, one of which proposed seventeen different defense measures, including the use of Liu Yung-fu's Black Flag forces.[116] Other memorials on the crisis were submitted by Huang T'i-fang, Teng Ch'eng-hsiu, and Hsü Chih-hsiang, while Sheng-yü helped to bring about the dismissal of Prince Kung.

Two trends of opinion were discernible among the war advocates.[117] They were split between those who believed that China's military capac-

---

113. Eastman, "Ch'ing-i and Chinese Policy Formation," pp. 605–606.
114. Li Chien-nung, pp. 121, 122.
115. Hummel, I, 48.
116. CC, 4:1–1b, 4:3b–19, 7:9–23b.
117. Eastman, Throne and Mandarins, p. 98.

ity was incontestably superior to the French and that success in war was inevitable, and those who were realistically aware of the difficulties confronting China but who felt that China must nevertheless fight or resign herself forever to foreign domination. Chang Chih-tung belonged to the latter group. He differed with those who asserted that "the French need not be feared, and that we can easily defeat them." He recognized that China would suffer initial defeats, but believed that combat experience would quickly provide the Chinese forces with the skills and fortitude required to attain ultimate victory.[118]

Chang remained firm in this view to the bitter end. On the very day that he learned of the April 4 peace protocol, he dispatched a protest to Peking, and from then until the signing of the final treaty, "he kept the telegraph wires to the north singing with his condemnations of the 'wolf-hearted,' 'insatiable' and 'unscrupulous' French."[119]

As the controversy with France developed, leading members of the Pure Group were placed in positions of greater responsibility and were called upon to support their ideas with action. Their influence grew until the defeat at Foochow, but in the end, as Ku Hung-ming remarked, these "young, hot-headed scholars without any experience of affairs, of course, made a mess of things."[120] A similar judgment was voiced as early as December 1883 by the diarist Li Tz'u-ming, who commented that Tz'u-hsi had "committed her affairs to two or three green youths who then called their buddies (p'eng-t'u). They have since frivolously and dangerously ruined things. It is lamentable!"[121]

Chang P'ei-lun was promoted to the Tsungli Yamen late in 1883 and in May 1884 was made commander in chief of the Fukien naval squadron. In August 1884, from a hilltop near Foochow, he watched French ships sink the Chinese fleet in less than an hour. After fleeing the scene, Chang dispatched a falsified battle report to Peking. He was dismissed from office and banished to the northwest, where he remained until 1888. Chang then suffered what Ku Hung-ming considered a fate worse than banishment: he married the daughter of Li Hung-chang. For a while he subsisted under the patronage of Li, but in 1894 he was driven from Tientsin on the ground that he was an evil influence in the office of his

118. See letter from Chang Chih-tung to Chang P'ei-lun in *Chung-Fa Chan-cheng* (Shanghai, 1957), ed. Shao Hsün-cheng et al. See also Eastman, "Ch'ing-i and Chinese Policy Formation," p. 605; Hao Yen-p'ing, "A Study of the Ch'ing-liu Tang," p. 54.

119. Eastman, *Throne and Mandarins*, p. 195.

120. Ku Hung-ming, *The Story of a Chinese Oxford Movement*, p. 20.

121. Li Tz'u-ming, *Yüeh-man-t'ang jih-chi*, 41:56a, cited by Eastman, "Ch'ing-i and Chinese Policy Formation," p. 604.

father-in-law. In his declining years even Chang Chih-tung is said to have turned against him.[122]

Ch'en Pao-ch'en was made the acting Southern Trade Commissioner (Nan-yang ta-ch'en) during the Annam crisis and was sent to Shanghai to participate in negotiations with Patenôtre. When Li Hung-chang returned to favor in 1885, Ch'en was dismissed from the bureaucracy and did not return to office until the Hsüan-t'ung reign. Teng Ch'eng-hsiu was also promoted to the Tsungli Yamen and later assisted Li Hung-chang in concluding the peace treaty with France. Teng was then sent on an independent mission to Kwangsi to delimit the Sino-Annamese border. Upon completing this frustrating assignment, which was replete with additional disputes with the French, Teng retired from the bureaucracy in 1887 on the basis of illness. He died in 1891.[123] Huang T'i-fang, who became a senior vice-president of the Board of War in 1885, criticized the naval program that Li Hung-chang promoted after the hostilities, but Li was strong enough by that time to have Huang demoted to a commissionership in the Transmission Office (T'ung-cheng ssu). Huang never succeeded in making a political comeback.[124]

Nemesis overtook other members of the Pure Group. Pao-t'ing had a weakness for women, his household including a wife and three concubines. In 1882 he was sent to Fukien as a chief examiner and returned to Peking with another concubine, a girl taken from a pleasure boat on the Ch'ien-t'ang River in Chekiang. As an ironic twist in the history of the Confucian purists, Pao-t'ing denounced himself in a memorial to the throne and was dismissed from office.[125] Hsü Chih-hsiang was permanently shelved in the Hanlin Academy, where he was allowed to continue his fulminations, which later included a scathing condemnation of Chang Chih-tung for betraying Confucian principles. But no one took Hsü seriously. According to the *Ch'ing-shih*, he became a bureaucratic joke, an object of ridicule.[126] Sheng-yü, not having advanced in his career since 1884, in 1889 resigned from the bureaucracy to devote the rest of his life to scholarship.[127]

---

122. Hummel, I, pp. 48–49; Ku Hung-ming, *The Story of a Chinese Oxford Movement*, p. 20; John L. Rawlinson, *China's Struggle for Naval Development* (Cambridge, Mass., 1967), pp. 117–120.
123. Ku Hung-ming, *The Story of a Chinese Oxford Movement*, p. 20.
124. Hummel, I, 349.
125. Hummel, II, 611–612.
126. Ku Hung-ming, *The Story of a Chinese Oxford Movement*, pp. 20–21; *Ch'ing-shih*, 6:4938, 4939.
127. Hummel, II, 648–649.

Of all the leaders of the Pure Group, only Chang Chih-tung survived for long politically. Several reasons for his hardiness can be surmised. Chang did not make as many political enemies as did some of his friends through rash impeachments. He entrenched himself more firmly in the good graces of the empress dowager and secured promotion ahead of his colleagues. Because he was sent to serve as governor of Shansi in 1882, he became dissociated to some extent from the Pure Group in the minds of other officials. On May 2, 1884, he left Shansi to take up a new assignment as governor general of Liangkwang.[128] He was thus given charge of a key region (Kwangtung) for coastal defense and an important staging area (Kwangsi) for the military operations in Annam. Chang was fortunate in that the French did not attack Canton, for otherwise his fate might have resembled that of Chang P'ei-lun.

The throne recognized Chang's magnificent efforts in rear support of the Chinese troops. During the war Chang worked indefatigably in supervising Kwangtung defenses; raising money, supplies, and reinforcements for the troops in Annam; conducting a communications relay center; serving as a liaison between Peking and Chinese officers in the field; and freely offering advice on diplomatic and military tactics. He did the best he could to impede a negotiated settlement of the troubles with France. Although he was held partly responsible for military failures of the governor of Kwangsi in 1885 and narrowly escaped punishment, he was awarded a peacock feather and promoted one rank after the victory at Langson, so that he emerged from the war in a comparatively strong political position.[129]

Influence of the War on Educational Reform

Chang Chih-tung also emerged from the war with a new approach to the problems that beset China. The traditional approach was not working, at least insofar as staving off foreign aggression was concerned. The Ili crisis convinced Chang that China could not succeed in negotiations with foreign powers unless she was willing and prepared to bolster her diplomacy with force. The final Chinese defeat in the Sino-French War brought Chang face to face with the fact that China lacked adequate might to support her diplomacy successfully and press on to military victory if her bluff were called. Chinese unity born of strength was deficient. And the debacle at Foochow clearly demonstrated that Chinese weapons for

128. See his memorial, *CC*, 8:39–39b.
129. *Ch'ing-shih kao* biography of Chang in *CC, chüan-shou shang*, p. 24b; *Ch'ing-shih,* 6:4906, Chüan 9–12 of Chang's complete works contain his memorials on the war effort.

applying force were still woefully inadequate. Despite the victory at Langson, Chang Chih-tung's confidence was shaken. He became convinced that China must increase her strength by adopting Western weapons. As a result of these conclusions, Chang was converted into a latter-day leader of the Self-Strengthening (*tzu-ch'iang*) Movement. This movement had developed before the Sino-French War, with Prince Kung and Li Hung-chang among its leaders. The term "self-strengthening" was applied to officials and political commentators who urged, primarily, that China develop its defenses by means of Western technology. Following the Sino-French War, Chang Chih-tung embraced similar views and turned to Westernization with a vengeance.

An initial interest in Western arms led Chang to an interest in Western education. During the Ili crisis he admitted the superiority of Western arms, and during the Sino-French War he recommended their purchase from abroad.[130] He soon became an advocate of China's manufacturing her own weapons, as well as of improved troop training, modern communications, and enlargement of the small corps of "foreign affairs" experts capable of representing China in dealings with the West. To manufacture weapons and achieve other desired ends, China must provide a new kind of training for her students. New educational facilities had to be established to teach Western skills. Gradually, Chang developed an interest in Western learning as a key to general Chinese economic prosperity and popular well-being, and in this he advanced beyond the original self-strengtheners. But his initial interest was in Westernization as a technique of military and diplomatic power.

Earlier generations had reached conclusions similar to Chang Chih-tung's. The Opium War of 1840 awakened Lin Tse-hsü to an interest in Chinese military modernization; Prince Kung became an advocate of borrowing from the West after the crises in foreign relations between 1858 and 1860; and the Taiping Rebellion made men like Tseng Kuo-fan, Tso Tsung-t'ang, and Li Hung-chang aware of the efficacy of Western arms and industry. Despite his historical consciousness, Chang Chih-tung did not immediately profit from the experience of these men. Influences from much earlier Chinese history dominated his thought before 1885. It was necessary for Chang to make his own mistakes, develop his own awareness of China's weaknesses in his time, and reach his own conclusions before evincing a willingness to amend his dependence upon traditional formulas. He then sold out the purists, as Hsü Chih-hsiang and

130. For one of Chang's earliest comments on the superiority of Western arms, see *CC*, 3:30–30b.

Ku Hung-ming lamented. But even so, he was unprepared to imitate fully the "vulgarity and hideousness" of Li Hung-chang's methods. He sought instead the Sino-Western compromise represented by his *t'i-yung* formula.

When Chang Chih-tung turned to the problems of reform through the application of Western means, he was in a position to act as well as to advocate. By espousing tradition, using Confucianism, winning the confidence of the empress dowager, and clamoring for war, he had risen from the Hanlin Academy to a high position in the Chinese bureaucracy. When his "sell-out" occurred, he was the governor general of Liang-kwang, wielding authority in one of China's most advanced and progressive regions and enjoying the semi-independence from the throne that had accrued to viceroys since the Taiping Rebellion. Of course, the throne, too, had altered its views, and after the Sino-French War the empress dowager, temporarily at least, was more amenable to borrowing from the West. This factor augured well for Chang's success in his new role as a self-strengthening reformer.

5 The Self-Strengthening Reformer (1885–1898)

When Chang Chih-tung undertook the role of a self-strengthening reformer, he had much to learn about the West. Naïveté and bumbling characterized many of his initial efforts to introduce new methods. In 1889, for example, he launched his iron and steel works from Kwangtung with a message to Germany that said in effect: "Please send one complete smelting plant."

Chang had little knowledge of the processes involved in mining or smelting, and no definite plans for obtaining iron ore and coking coal. Conscientious German engineers refused to fill his order without precise information, but the English were less scrupulous:

> The manufacturers called for a sample of the ore. . . . The Viceroy declined to send a sample. They explained that there were two varieties of ore, which needed different plants. His Excellency kept to his point, "Send a plant." Eventually a plant was sent, the sellers sending that required for the more common form of ore, but pointing out it might be useless for the actual ore in sight. The reason for refusing to send the samples as requested was that no ore had been discovered; its future discovery was merely taken for granted.[1]

The English shipped a Bessemer plant, which caused innumerable difficulties when Chang erected it at Hanyang after becoming the governor general of Hukwang. Two blast furnaces were put into operation in 1894, but the iron produced was expensive and poor in quality. Facing bankruptcy in 1896, Chang turned the plant over to Sheng Hsüan-huai, making it an "officially supervised, merchant managed" (*kuan-tu shang-pan*) enterprise. Sheng thereupon set about developing new coal supplies and installing Siemens-Martin open hearth equipment.

A report of the British-administered maritime customs pointed to Chang's experience as "a good lesson to China as to what not to do."[2] A

---

1. China, Imperial Maritime Customs, *Decennial Reports*, 1902–1911, pp. 357–358. See also William Ayers, "Chang Chih-tung and the Hanyang Iron and Steel Works, 1890–1896," unpub. seminar paper, Harvard University, 1952, and three works by Albert Feuerwerker: "A Draft History of Sheng Hsüan-huai, Official and Industrialist (1844–1916)," *Papers on China*, 8 (1954), 13–15 (East Asian Research Center, Harvard University); *China's Early Industrialization*, pp. 67–68; "China's Nineteenth-Century Industrialization: The Case of the Hanyehping Coal and Iron Company, Limited," Reprint No. 5, Center for Chinese Studies, The University of Michigan.

2. China, Imperial Maritime Customs, *Decennial Reports*, 1902–1911, p. 357.

different point of view was taken by another contemporary source, a Western resident of the Wuhan area: "These iron works are hardly a means of making money—that is the task of the mint over at Wuchang. But as they do make iron ore out of iron-stone, and set a fine example for future enterprise on more commercial lines, let us take our hats off to a prominent pioneer in the land of the Dragon, and give him a hearty three cheers."[3]

Chang Chih-tung, who was about fifty years old when he became seriously interested in borrowing from the West, profited from his early mistakes and demonstrated a remarkable ability to learn as he exhorted others to learn. His approach to Western-style reforms showed a steady gain in confidence and sophistication with the passage of time. Aside from the insight he gleaned from bitter personal experience, he drew upon the knowledge of a previous generation of self-strengtheners. It is reasonable to surmise that Chang was impressed by Feng Kuei-fen's *Chiao-pin-lu k'ang-i* (Protests from the study of Chiao-pin). This work, which first popularized the term "self-strengthening" (*tzu-ch'iang*), was written in 1861 and distributed informally before its publication in 1884. The work anticipated Chang's own ideas on the Chinese *t'i* and the Western *yung*.[4]

Chang was also familiar with the self-strengthening activities carried out before 1885 by such men as Prince Kung, Wen-hsiang, Tseng Kuo-fan, Tso Tsung-t'ang, and Li Hung-chang. After 1885 Chang frequently cited the experiences of those leaders as precedents to draw support for his own undertakings. He knew the background of their enterprises, including the Peking College of Languages, the Kiangnan Arsenal at Shanghai, and the Foochow Shipyard. In Kwangtung he had the opportunity to observe personally the Canton College of Languages, which had operated since 1864.[5] His immediate predecessor as governor general in Canton, Chang Shu-sheng, had been active in the field of self-strengthening and also helped provide Chang Chih-tung with a foundation on which to build.[6]

Translated works were another inspiration to Chang. As early as the Ili crisis, he recommended that the government give wide distribution

3. W. Arthur Cornaby, "Morning Walks around Hanyang," *The East of Asia Magazine*, 2:3 (1903), 282.

4. Teng Ssu-yü and John K. Fairbank, *China's Response to the West; A Documentary Survey, 1839–1923* (Cambridge, Mass., 1954), p. 50; Teng and Fairbank, *Research Guide for "China's Response to the West"* (Cambridge, Mass., 1954), p. 7 *n*.3.

5. On these institutions, see Knight Biggerstaff, *The Earliest Modern Government Schools in China* (Ithaca, N.Y., 1961).

6. For Chang Shu-sheng, see *Ch'ing-shih*, 6:4954–4955; *Yang-wu yün-tung* (Shanghai, 1959), 2:130–135, 3:419–421, 607–609, 5:494–495, 6:474–478.

to a Western book recently translated and published under the title of *Fang-hai hsin-lun* (New discussion of coastal defense).[7] He later recommended other works and commissioned translations himself.

Western advisers also helped to broaden Chang's knowledge of the West. One of the earliest of these was the English Baptist missionary Timothy Richard, a man with an imagination almost as fertile as Chang's own. In 1877 Richard went to Shansi for famine relief work and, while there, submitted a number of proposals to the governor, Tseng Kuo-ch'üan, on opening mines, building railroads, and constructing industries. When Chang became the governor of Shansi in 1882, he discovered Richard's proposals in the provincial archives. Richard related in his memoirs: "[Chang] called together the leading officials and laid the suggestions before them, and afterwards sent me a deputation of three officials, asking me to give up the missionary work and enter the Chinese service for the purpose of carrying out my ideas. I replied that although I knew the value of these reforms, I was not an expert, and it would be necessary for a number of foreigners to be engaged who were experts in their respective lines of work."[8] Chang eventually accepted Richard's suggestion on hiring experts and engaged French, German, English, American, and Japanese military men, technicians, and teachers to assist him in his various programs of modernization. He learned from all these specialists. In later years he also continued to turn to Richard for informal advice.

Chang also learned from his Chinese subordinates. Among the government promoters of Westernized reforms between 1885 and 1898 there was keen competition for the services of qualified Chinese "foreign affairs" (*yang-wu*) experts. Chang Chih-tung, Li Hung-chang, and Weng T'ung-ho were among those who bid against one another.[9] Chang succeeded in building up a small corps of capable and knowledgeable aides.

7. *CC,* 2:27. Probably Von Scheila's *Coast Defense* (1871), tr. John Fryer (6 vols.), with Hua Heng-fang as Chinese writer. See Nathan Sivin, "The Translation Bureau of the Kiangnan Arsenal," unpub. seminar paper, Harvard University (1959), Appendix B, citing John Fryer, *An Account of the Department for the Translation of Foreign Books at the Kiangnan Arsenal* (Shanghai, American Presbyterian Mission Press, 1880), p. 24.

8. Timothy Richard, *Forty-five Years in China* (New York, 1916), p. 172. What influence, if any, missionaries and their schools in the Wuhan area had upon Chang is not clear. In later years, he by-passed the missionary example to follow Japanese patterns. In this respect he was representative of the general trend described by Robert K. Sakai, "Politics and Education in Modern China," unpub. diss., Harvard University, 1953, pp. 19–26. Missionary institutions in Wuchang, where Chang governed for many years, included Hua-chung University, founded by American Episcopalians in 1871.

9. On the competition of Chang, Li, and Weng, see Hsiao Kung-chuan, "Weng T'ung-ho and the Reform Movement of 1898," *Ch'ing-hua hsüeh-pao* (April 1957), passim.

They included graduates of the older self-strengthening institutions, such as Ts'ai Hsi-yung, who attended the Peking College of Languages and then, until his death in 1898, helped Chang execute reforms in Kwangtung and Hupeh.[10] They also included Chinese students returned from foreign schools, such as Yung Wing, the first Chinese to graduate from an American university.[11]

During the Ili crisis, Chang Chih-tung expressed disappointment over previous self-strengthening results. He wrote that "from the Hsien-feng reign onwards, not a year has passed without management of *yang-wu*, not a day without talk about self-strengthening." Yet the *yang-wu* experts who had been put to use numbered only a few hundred, while millions of taels had been wasted on *yang-wu* schemes.[12] Chang did not mean to imply that self-strengthening was wrong. Rather, he criticized the effort for having been inadequate and badly managed. He was then beginning to change his approach to China's problems, and in Shansi a few years later would commence his own self-strengthening activities to learn more of the secrets of Western power.

Early in 1884, near the end of his term as governor of Shansi, Chang established an Office of Foreign Affairs (Yang-wu chü) at Taiyuan. This was conceived of as a research institute where *yang-wu* experts could gather to conduct inquiries into such Western subjects as "astronomy, mathematics, navigation, surveying, physics, manufacturing, international law, treaties, spoken languages, written languages, armaments, ships and guns, mining, and electricity." Chang thought of this ambitious program as a long-range plan for "knowing others and knowing ourselves" (*chih-pi chih-chi*), for "developing resources and succeeding in affairs" (*k'ai-wu ch'eng-wu*) in order to enrich the people, for "understanding the *t'i* and comprehending the *yung*" in order to stand on one's own feet, for storing up ample talent to benefit the country, and for reviving old standards and planning new achievements. Shansi, Chang wrote, was ignorant of the strange *yang-wu*. But it should not take comfort in its distance from the seacoast or its rustic seclusion among mountains, for the problems of foreign relations were becoming so many and so complex that in time they would inevitably affect the inland province.[13]

10. See the memorial by Chang upon Ts'ai Hsi-yung's death, *CC*, 47:22b–24b. See also *CC*, 28:32b–34.
11. For Jung Hung (Yung Wing), see Hummel, I, 402–405; Yung Wing, *My Life in China and America* (New York, 1909).
12. *CC*, 2:14b.
13. *CC*, 89:22b–24.

In issuing a call for *yang-wu* experts from all parts of the country to join his staff, Chang justified the Office of Foreign Affairs on the following grounds:

> Self-strengthening is fundamental to controlling the empire. Gathering talent is the first essential of self-strengthening. Today when the affairs of international intercourse are constantly increasing, *yang-wu* are of the utmost urgency. Coastal provinces have established bureaus to investigate them and are showing results. In relations between China and the outside world, commercial affairs are the *t'i* and armed force is the *yung*. Understanding regulations embodied in treaties and having a thorough knowledge of various countries' mining production, trade conditions, border defenses, administrative orders, schools, military equipment, public laws and statutes are fundamental. The gateway is an understanding of the languages of other nations.[14]

Such ideas and phrases, first expressed in Shansi, were to be repeated over and over again in Chang Chih-tung's writings after the Sino-French War. Following that war, Chang entered upon his most creative period as a promoter of projects based on Western models. Between 1885 and the end of his term as governor general of Liangkwang in 1889, he planned or inaugurated most of the major programs that were to occupy him for the remainder of his life. While in Canton, he took the first steps toward establishing the iron and steel works that was later erected in Hanyang. Also in Canton he founded an arsenal, mint, and other industries which he later duplicated elsewhere. He planned the Peking-Hankow Railroad within this period, and he worked toward construction of rail lines until his death in 1909.[15] In Canton, Chang also founded his first Western-style military academy, the prototype for similar institutions that he later established in central China.

In undertaking the creation of Western-style schools, Chang did not at once present a systematic statement of his "educational philosophy." Such a statement was not made until he published the *Ch'üan-hsüeh p'ien* (Exhortation to learning) in 1898. However, references scattered through his memorials and correspondence before 1898 reveal some of his motivations and present in rudimentary form a number of the principles later elaborated in the *Ch'üan-hsüeh p'ien*. These references make

---

14. *CC*, 89:24–25.
15. A number of Chang's documents on these specific projects are arranged topically in the collection *Yang-wu yün-tung*. See sections on coastal defense and the navy, manufacturing, railroad building, mining and textile industries.

it clear that Chang was concerned with education primarily as a means of stabilizing the Ch'ing dynasty and enhancing Chinese power. The way of self-strengthening, he wrote, was to distinguish between what was good and bad for China and to select men according to their abilities. Neither China nor the West had a monopoly on truth. The Chinese should not "value the new and attack all else," nor should they make the mistake of "being limited to what is already known." The purpose of education should be to "blend the Chinese and Western with thorough understanding and discrimination, in the hope that education will create talent and prepare responsible officials for the Empire." In the process of borrowing from the West, Chang stated, "we must accept and popularize that which is of practical value, in order to meet the needs of the times." Chinese men of talent should be led to a mastery of the practical arts and to an understanding of current events, which are requisite for good government. By exercising discrimination, educators should "choose the strong points of various nations but not copy their evil customs." "All men of talent emerge from learning," Chang wrote, "and learning is a combination of investigation and study." "Training men of talent cannot be delayed," he emphasized. Elsewhere he added, "If we wish to control the changing times, we must (first) establish schools."[16]

Acting upon these principles, Chang personally established a number of training centers. He founded schools at each of the major posts to which he was assigned as governor general from the end of the Sino-French War in 1885 to the beginning of the Reform Movement of 1898. Schools were opened in Liangkwang, where Chang remained until 1889; in Hukwang, where he served from 1889 to 1894, and then returned from 1896 to 1898; and in Liangkiang, where he was established from 1894 to 1896. The main schools that Chang planned or founded during these years were as follows, with the addition of one school founded in 1899:

1886—Torpedo School (Yü-lei hsüeh-t'ang), founded in Canton.[17]
1887—School of Telegraphy (Tien-pao hsüeh-t'ang) and Naval and

16. *CC*, ch. 21–25, 28:7, 34:5–5b, 120:20b–21b.
17. Establishment of the Torpedo School is briefly mentioned in *HNP*. *The Chronicle and Directory for China, Corea, Japan, etc.* (Hong Kong, 1889), listed the Imperial Torpedo and Seamine Departments at Whampoa under the direction of Wong Pan Cheng and Tsai Sih-yung (Ts'ai Hsi-yung), with "Pr. Trop. Lieut. E. Kretschmar" as an instructor. Later issues identified Kretschmar as a member of the I.G.N.R. (Imperial German Naval Reserve?). In 1893 Capt. G. L. Hummel was listed as the teacher of navigation. By 1898 the institute was being called the Imperial Torpedo Department and School, with Hummel the only foreigner mentioned. By 1906 the torpedo school apparently had been combined with the Whampoa Naval Academy.

Military Officers' School (Shui-lu-shih hsüeh-t'ang), founded in Canton.[18]

1889—School of Western Arts (Hsi-i hsüeh-t'ang), planned for Canton shortly before Chang's transfer to Wuchang.

1890—School of Mining (K'uang-wu hsüeh-t'ang), established in connection with the Hanyang Iron and Steel Works.

1893—Self-Strengthening School (Tzu-ch'iang hsüeh-t'ang), founded in Wuchang.

1896—School for Gathering Talent (Ch'u-ts'ai hsüeh-t'ang), Military Academy (Lu-chün hsüeh-t'ang), Railroad School (T'ieh-lu hsüeh-t'ang, and School of Chemistry (Hua-hsüeh hsüeh-t'ang), established in Nanking. Military Preparatory School (Wu-pei hsüeh-t'ang), founded in Wuchang.

1898—School of Agriculture (Nung-wu hsüeh-t'ang) and School of Industrial Arts (Kung-i hsüeh-t'ang), established in Wuchang.

1899—Noncommissioned Officers' School (Chiang-pien hsüeh-t'ang), established in Wuchang.

Institutions established by Chang in later years included a Commercial Affairs School (Shang-wu hsüeh-t'ang), opened in Wuchang during 1902, and the San-chiang Normal School (San-chiang shih-fan hsüeh-t'ang), which Chang founded while on duty in Nanking during 1903. Brief case studies of selected institutions will illustrate the founder's methods, the problems he encountered, and the results he achieved.

Promotion of Military Schools

With Chang Chih-tung's developing concern over effective resistance to foreign incursions and his growing consciousness of the need for greater Chinese strength, it was natural that promotion of foreign-style military training should constitute his first interest when considering the adoption of Western educational methods. Teaching troops to use modern weapons and training officers to provide better leadership for China's armed forces were the most obvious needs for national defense and the development of national power.

Before the onset of Chang Chih-tung's interest, foreign drill and weapons had already been adopted by a few Chinese military units, and

---

18. The School of Telegraphy is mentioned in *HNP*. Its curriculum included Chinese classical studies and French. On other early schools of telegraphy, see Biggerstaff, *The Earliest Modern Government Schools in China*, pp. 65–68. Canton was connected by telegraph with Kowloon in 1883, and another overland line, connecting with Lung-chou in western Kwangsi, was completed in June 1884. *Chronicle and Directory*, 1889, p. 373.

several arsenals had been established. A naval and shipbuilding school was opened at the Foochow Shipyard in 1867, and another naval school was set up in Tientsin in 1881. In 1885, on the recommendation of General Charles C. Gordon, a military preparatory school was opened in Tientsin by Li Hung-chang.[19] Yet so little had been accomplished that Chang Chih-tung was pioneering in this field when he established the first of his military academies, the Kwangtung Naval and Military Officers' School, in Canton during 1887.

Chang's experiments in the operation of military academies were closely coordinated with his creation of modernized defense forces. In Canton during 1885 Chang began to train the Kwangtung Victorious Army (Kuang-sheng chün) in foreign drill taught by German instructors.[20] He also established the Kwangtung Pacification Naval Force (Kuang-an shui-chün) to man a fleet of one hundred small vessels that he planned to construct.[21] In Nanking during 1895 Chang organized the Self-Strengthening Army (Tzu-ch'iang chün), composed of infantry, cavalry, artillery, and engineering units.[22] In Wuchang during 1896 he began to organize the Hupeh Defense Force (Hu-pei hu-chün), consisting originally of two battalions of foreign-trained troops and one detachment of engineers.[23] Chang's military academies were designed primarily to provide qualified officers and petty officers for the new provincial forces he was forming.

In organizing this training, Chang stressed the need for raising the status of the Chinese soldier and heightening the prestige of a military career. He pointed out that for centuries the Chinese educational system had emphasized refining youth through literary studies, while army recruits generally were poor, illiterate men of low social origins. A wide disparity between the civil (*wen*) and the military (*wu*) had developed in the unfolding of Chinese history. That such a disparity should exist was not the intent of China's ancient sages, he argued. The military classics recorded that in the olden days all ministers and high officials received a certain amount of military training. These former leaders had been able to achieve outstanding results because they practiced both the *wen* and the *wu*. This was made clear in the classical commentaries. Even among the disciples of Confucius there were capable warriors who took up the

19. Ralph L. Powell, *The Rise of Chinese Military Power, 1895–1912* (Princeton, 1955), p. 41; Teng and Fairbank, *China's Response to the West*, p. 111; Hummel, II, 643; Biggerstaff, *The Earliest Modern Government Schools in China*, pp. 43–46, 52–54, 61–64.

20. See memorials, *CC*, 11:24b–26, 26–28.

21. See memorial, *CC*, 12:1–3b.

22. For the Self-Strengthening Army, see Powell, pp. 60–71; *CC*, 40:1–5b.

23. *CC*, 44:13b–17.

sword to defend the state. After the T'ang and Sung dynasties, according to Chang's interpretation, the gulf between the civil and the military began to widen, and the practice of the ancients was forgotten.[24]

Chang maintained that the Western approach of "citizens serving as soldiers and officers attending schools" was more in harmony with the intentions of the ancients than was contemporary Chinese practice. To minimize the differences between the civil and the military, he believed, the training of a literate officer corps was an absolute necessity. However, he maintained it would take too long and cost too much to raise illiterate men from the ranks and convert them into literate officers. It would be preferable to take literate civilians and give them military training. Unless army officers were literate, Chang stated, they could scarcely master the superior methods of those Western nations that had made military studies into an "exact science."[25]

"To train troops," Chang wrote, "we must also train officers, and to train officers, we must rely entirely upon schools."[26] The highest military school in the West was the *a-k'o-t'e-mi* (academy) for general officers. Below it were schools for training lower grade officers and schools for training noncommissioned officers. Chang attempted to model his own academies after the last two types of Western military schools—without losing sight of the Chinese heritage in the process.

The Kwangtung Naval and Military Officers' School. In a memorial on coastal defense submitted to the throne in the spring of 1885, Chang Chih-tung first revealed his plan to establish the Kwangtung Naval and Military Officers' School. If China were to defend her southern shoreline adequately, Chang explained, Kwangtung province should exploit its natural resources and manufacture modern weapons. However, Chang argued, "the need for military men is more urgent than that for military equipment." Ships and guns would be of little use without troops trained to handle them.[27]

Although Chang outlined his plan for the new academy in 1885, the school was not established until 1887. Chang built it upon a foundation laid by governors general who had preceded him in Liangkwang. In 1877 Governor General Liu K'un-i had contributed Tls. 150,000 for use as an

24. *CC*, 45:13b–14, 120:11b–15b.
25. *CC*, 100:28.
26. *CC*, 100:27b.
27. *CC*, 11:16–24b. Unless otherwise specified data in this subsection are drawn from *CC*, 21:25–28b, 28:2b–7.

endowment "to gather and nourish talent in foreign affairs."[28] The money was later loaned to Shansi, Shensi, and Honan provinces for relief. In 1880 Shansi still owed Tls. 50,000, but Shensi and Honan had repaid Tls. 100,000. Using these funds, Governor General Chang Shu-sheng established the College of Solid Learning (Shih-hsüeh kuan) at Whampoa.[29] Nearly Tls. 20,000 were spent to build the new school, and the balance was invested to draw interest and provide for the annual operating expenses of the college. Work was begun in January 1881 and completed a year later.[30] Fifty students were enrolled in the first class, which opened in the summer of 1882.[31] The curriculum included mathematics, English, and Chinese literature. After Chang Chih-tung became governor general in 1884, he changed the name of the institution to the College of Extensive Learning (Po-hsüeh kuan). The college was then expanded in 1887 to form the Kwangtung Naval and Military Officers' School.

In organizing the new academy, Chang declared that naval and military training should go hand in hand. Neither should be undertaken at the expense of neglecting the other. But in practice, because of Kwangtung's location on the coast, he placed more emphasis on naval training from the outset of this experiment. The naval school of the Foochow Shipyard and the naval academy at Tientsin were the acknowledged models for Chang's project and, incidentally, the chief sources of supply for his faculty and student body, a factor that gave his academy the aspect of a "graduate school."

Chang enlarged the College of Extensive Learning by acquiring 47 mou of additional land at a price of Tls. 4,592. On the new site, he constructed five courts, which included lecture halls, staff and student residences, and miscellaneous buildings. Outside of the courtyards he built a machine shop and a cast iron plant that by 1891 were "well provided with modern mechanical appliances worked by steam power."[32] Drill grounds were prepared, and a wooden dock was built. Chang reported that the total cost of labor and materials was Tls. 59,200. However, he did not include

28. *Liu K'un-i i-chi* (Peking, 1959), 1:429–431. Pao Tsun-p'eng, *Chung-kuo hai-chün shih* (Taipei, 1953), p. 227, asserts that Liu appropriated the funds from customs revenue.

29. Biggerstaff, *The Earliest Modern Government Schools in China*, pp. 28, 30, 48–49, calls this institution the School of Western Studies (Hsi-hsüeh Kuan). On final selection of the name, see Chang Shu-sheng memorial in *Yang-wu yün-tung*, 2:127.

30. *Yang-wu yün-tung*, 2:124–127, 130–135.

31. Pao Tsun-p'eng, pp. 227–230. On the curriculum and organization of the school, see Biggerstaff, *The Earliest Modern Government Schools in China*, pp. 48–49.

32. China, Imperial Maritime Customs, *Decennial Reports*, 1882–1891, p. 575.

in this accounting 2,500 pounds sterling worth of equipment he had ordered from England, including a 12-horsepower steam engine, machines for drilling, boring and cutting metal, and various hand tools.

Chang estimated that a training ship for use by the school could be provisioned, fueled, and maintained for an annual cost of Tls. 40,000. The ship to be assigned to the school was the torpedo cruiser *Kuang-chia,* "a handsome corvette . . . well armed with Krupp and Hotchkiss guns and fitted with boilers of French make."[33] The vessel was one of sixteen craft planned or completed in a shipbuilding program that Chang carried out between 1886 and 1888. The *Kuang-chia* was constructed at the Foochow Shipyard at a cost variously estimated at between Tls. 220,000 and Tls. 360,000. Chang described it as a 1,296-ton vessel, having 1,600 horsepower, a length of 221 English feet, breadth of 33 feet, draught of 13 feet, and speed of 47 li an hour.[34]

Estimated operating costs of the school, including faculty salaries, student stipends, and the wages of laborers, were set at about Tls. 80,000 a year. To meet these needs, Chang proposed to supplement the income of the old College of Extensive Learning with an allotment from a special Kwangtung coastal defense fund. Arrangements for books, instruments, and other supplies would be made as the occasion arose.

In a memorial of August 3, 1887, submitted jointly with Wu Ta-ch'eng, who had become governor of Kwangtung, Chang indicated that the enrollment of the school would not exceed 140 students, or 70 each in the naval and military divisions. Naval students, who were to be trained in the departments of marine engineering and navigation, would study the English language. Military students, who were to study German, would be enrolled in the three departments of cavalry and infantry, artillery, and military engineering.[35]

In a later memorial Chang explained that the program was intended to balance "principle" and "practice." After principles had been learned in the classrooms, they would be put into practice aboard the training

---

33. China, Imperial Maritime Customs, *Decennial Reports, 1882–1891,* p. 574.

34. For the shipbuilding program, see *CC,* 17:18–20; 21:28b–32b, 24:13b–17, 28:9b–11.

35. *CC,* 21:26. The marine engineering department was not opened at once, for on November 10, 1889, Chang reported that it was just being organized. With the addition of this department, the enrollment quota of the school was raised to 210—70 students each in the department of navigation, the department of marine engineering, and the military division. Chang's memorials are not clear on the length of the course, but apparently he planned a three-year program for the military students and six years for the naval students, the latter spending three years each in classroom study and on the training ship. In addition to Chang's memorials on the school, see China, Imperial Maritime Customs, *Decennial Reports, 1882–1891,* p. 575; Biggerstaff, *The Earliest Modern Government Schools in China,* pp. 54–55, 64–65.

ship and on the drill grounds. After one year of training aboard the ship, the best students of a class would be sent to foreign naval academies. After three years of army training, the best students would be sent to foreign military academies. Abroad, the students would spend nine months in the classroom and three months at sea or in the ranks. If war broke out in the foreign countries while the students were there, Chang observed, they would be sent to the front as observers to acquire first-hand experience, "in accordance with the general custom of Western nations."

Although the curriculum of the Kwangtung school was to include Western subjects, the students would not be allowed to forget Chinese studies. Chang explained that at dawn each day the students would be required to read passages from the Four Books and the Five Classics "in order to strengthen the root." When the foreign instructors gave them a holiday, they would attend lectures and be tested on Chinese history and military affairs. They would also be permitted to take part in military and civil service examinations. "In progressing from the coarse to the refined, they shall not be allowed to pursue the end by abandoning the beginning," Chang explained.

The school opened in 1887 with 70 student transfers from the College of Extensive Learning. Two years later the enrollment was 115 students. Only 38 of the students from the old college remained, the others having been eliminated by examinations. Twenty of the total enrollment were military students transferred from Tientsin in 1888. Another 20 were civilian students transferred from Tientsin in 1889 to study English and mathematics preparatory to more advanced work. The remaining 37 students had already trained for three or four years at the naval school of the Foochow Shipyard. Their transfer to Kwangtung was arranged in 1889 after Chang Chih-tung learned that the school in Foochow was being forced to dismiss students as an economy measure.[36]

The students were under the general supervision of Wu Chung-hsiang, recommended by Chang Chih-tung to head the Naval and Military Officers' School and ordered by the throne to proceed to Kwangtung in 1887. Wu previously had been employed for more than ten years at the naval school in Foochow and then had been transferred at Li Hung-chang's request to manage the naval academy in Tientsin. Ts'ai Hsi-yung was the managing director of the Kwangtung school, and Liu En-jung, ordered from Tientsin, was placed in command of the training ship.[37] Liu

36. *CC*, 132:20b–27b.
37. For Ts'ai Hsi-yung, see *Chronicle and Directory*, 1889, p. 371.

was assisted by Ch'en Pi-kuang, a lieutenant who had completed his studies at Foochow. Chang likewise drew upon the Foochow Shipyard for his chief foreign naval instructor, an Englishman named F. T. Richards, whose contract in Fukien had expired. Richards, who taught theoretical navigation, nautical astronomy and English, was soon joined by J. C. Edmonds, who had been an engineer in the British Royal Navy.[38] Chang reported that a German, "Ou-p'i-tz'u," would be the first army instructor assigned to the school, but either this plan did not materialize or "Ou-p'i-t'zu" had a short tenure, for other sources state that Captain A. Tenckhoff of the German Army gave language instruction to the military students and taught them military science and fortifications.[39]

According to the original plan, the Chinese faculty of the school was to consist of eleven members: one naval instructor, one military instructor, three instructors of Chinese studies, two assistants for English, one assistant for German, and three assistants for Chinese.[40] Chang planned to staff the training ship with three foreigners: a chief instructor, a gunnery officer, and one instructor in seamanship. Negotiations for the hiring of English experts were begun through Liu Jui-fen, the Chinese minister to London. But none of these foreign instructors had arrived before Chang Chih-tung was transferred to become the governor general of Hukwang at the end of 1889.

Chang planned the Naval and Military Officers' School, built the plant, mustered the faculty, and enrolled the students. Shortly before his transfer to Wuhan, he reported to Peking that fourteen students of the advanced navigation class were almost ready for assignment to the training ship and nineteen military students were ready for assignment to the army, where they could pass their knowledge on to others. The school seemed to be getting well under way, but it suffered a setback with Chang's departure from Kwangtung.

One of the weaknesses of the Ch'ing system of frequently transferring officials was that a successor often failed to follow up the projects initiated by his predecessor. Chang was succeeded as the Liangkwang governor general by Li Han-chang, a more cautious man than his younger

38. For Richards and Edmonds, see *Chronicle and Directory*, 1889, p. 371; 1891, p. 188; 1892, p. 191; 1893, p. 192; China, Imperial Maritime Customs, *Decennial Reports*, 1882–1891, p. 575.

39. For Captain A. Tenckhoff, see *Chronicle and Directory*, 1889, p. 371; 1891, p. 188; 1892, p. 191; 1893, p. 192; China, Imperial Maritime Customs, *Decennial Reports*, 1882–1891, pp. 575–576.

40. The *Chronicle and Directory*, 1889, p. 371, lists only four Chinese faculty members in addition to Wu Chung-hsiang and Ts'ai Hsi-yung: "Jeme Tien-yow, Fong-kai, Tong Kam-ming, Chow-king Lam."

brother, Li Hung-chang, Li, who evinced little enthusiasm for Chang's industrial and educational schemes, thwarted the plans that Chang had made for expanding the Naval and Military Officers' School.[41] Li's lack of fervor was shared by Kang-i, the reactionary Manchu official who served as governor of Kwangtung from May 1892 to November 1894. According to one source, Kang-i "completely wrecked" the Kwangtung naval development program by closing the school in Whampoa and ordering 29 gunboats and 19 torpedo boats to be docked and all hands to be dismissed, "thus allowing these fine vessels to become utterly ruined through sheer neglect."[42]

The Nanking Military Academy. Chang Chih-tung did not immediately establish new military schools after his transfer to Wuchang. Between 1890 and 1894 he devoted most of his attention to setting up the Hanyang Iron and Steel Works. It is also possible that he was lulled into feelings of false security by the relative quiet then prevailing in foreign relations. Any complacency upon his part was shattered by the outbreak of the Sino-Japanese War in 1894. The hostilities, which resulted in another Chinese defeat, highlighted military reform once again as a matter of the utmost urgency. In November 1894, Chang was shifted to Nanking to serve temporarily as governor general of Liangkiang and supervise the defense of that area, in place of Liu K'un-i, who was sent to command troops at Shanhaikuan. Chang remained in Nanking through February 1896.[43] Shortly before leaving, he created the Self-Strengthening Army and organized a new military academy to train officers for that force.

In memorializing upon the academy, Chang expressed admiration for the military prowess of Germany: "The reason that the German army

41. For a report by Li Han-chang on the school in 1892, see *Yang-wu yün-tung*, 2:622–623. A telegram from Chang Chih-tung to Li in 1889 suggests that Li had urged that the school be transferred to Hupeh along with Chang, just as the machinery for the Iron and Steel Works was moved. *CC*, 133:34.

42. Wen Ching, *The Chinese Crisis from Within* (London, 1901), p. 161. According to China, Imperial Maritime Customs, *Decennial Reports*, 1892–1901, 2:195, the school was closed and the foreign staff was discharged "chiefly because there was no navy on which to employ the students." Pao Tsun-p'eng, p. 228, reports the joint academy was reorganized as a naval school by T'an Chung-lin, governor general of Liangkwang, in 1893. Although T'an did not become governor general until 1895, a reorganization of 1893 is mentioned in the military monograph of the *Ch'ing-shih*, 3:1675. Pao traces the evolution of the school into the Whampoa Naval Academy in 1930. See also Biggerstaff, *The Earliest Modern Government Schools in China*, pp. 54–57; Rawlinson, *China's Struggle for Naval Development*, pp. 155–156; Roderick L. MacFarquhar, "The Whampoa Military Academy," *Papers on China*, 9 (1955), 152 (East Asian Research Center, Harvard University). In 1896 graduates of the school were selected to serve as officers of Chang's Self-Strengthening Army, and he engaged instructors from the Canton Academy to teach at the Hupeh Military Preparatory School. *CC*, 41:8b, 45:15b.

43. *CC*, 36:1–2, 44:1–2.

stands first among those of Western nations is that all men of the country, of high or low origin, serve as soldiers, and, more important, all troop commanders are graduates of military schools." Chang reported that he had cabled Hsü Ching-ch'eng, the Chinese minister to Germany, to hire five German specialists in military affairs as instructors at the Nanking Military Academy. Chang proposed selecting 150 literate youths between the ages of thirteen and twenty to become students of the school. They would be given three years of training in infantry, cavalry, field artillery, engineering, and fortress artillery methods. Study of surveying, mathematics, and the German language would also be included in their course. Chang estimated that the cost of constructing and equipping the school would be about Tls. 40,000, with annual operating expenses to total Tls. 40,000 as well.[44]

Less than a month after Chang had memorialized on the Nanking Military Academy, he was ordered to return to his original post at Wuchang. The academy, therefore, had no chance to prosper under his aegis. When Liu K'un-i returned to Nanking, he assumed control of the military organizations that Chang had left behind. Jealousy became apparent between Liu's own Hunanese troops and the men of the Self-Strengthening Army. In June 1896 a clash occurred between the Hunan soldiers and a detachment of the foreign-trained troops. The clash led to the wounding of a German corporal, and two German gunboats were ordered to Nanking. To avoid further incidents, Liu transferred the Self-Strengthening Army to Woosung and did not renew the contracts of the German instructors when their terms expired in 1898.[45]

At the time of the transfer, the army employed more than thirty foreign training officers. The number had declined to twenty-three by 1898 at the termination of their contracts. Liu K'un-i requested decorations and awards for them, sent them home, and placed the Chiang-nan circuit intendant Li Chan-chuang in charge of the force. The Self-Strengthening Army did not prosper thereafter. Liu K'un-i denied reports in 1899 that it was troubled by desertions, but in 1901 he complied with an order from Peking to transfer the army to Shantung and place it under the command of Yüan Shih-k'ai. At the time of the move, the army consisted of 2,540 men organized into eleven battalions.[46]

At Nanking, meanwhile, the army school continued in operation under the supervision of Intendant Ch'ien Te-p'ei. When Chang Chih-tung

44. *CC*, 41:8–10b, 150:19b–20.
45. *Liu K'un-i i-chi*, 2:935.
46. *Liu K'un-i i-chi*, 3:1015–1016, 1150, 1305.

returned to Hukwang, Liu K'un-i retained three German instructors for the school. The chief instructor was Captain C. Loebbecke, who had arrived in October 1895 and served until November 1898. He was assisted by Lieutenant E. Toepffer and Baron von Tettenborn.[47] When the first class was graduated near the end of 1899 and Liu K'un-i assigned the superior cadets to the army, he noted that the students had received an education which took the classics and histories as the *t'i* and military subjects as the *yung*. He reported also that admiring visitors to the school had included Prince Henry of Germany, Lord Beresford of England, and the American Minister to China, Edwin H. Conger.[48] Lord Beresford, who was in Nanking during December 9–12, 1898, on behalf of the Associated Chambers of Commerce, penned a matter-of-fact report on his visit to the school:

> I visited the Military College. It was started in the year 1895. There is room for one hundred and twenty students; there were only seventy three at the time of my inspection. They are divided into three classes, according to the status of their knowledge. The first class gets six taels, the second four taels, and the third two taels per month, together with their food and clothes. They are all the sons of gentlemen. They remain there three years, and are then liable to be drafted to different armies about the Empire, but most of them go into the Liang Kiang provinces—i.e., those provinces under the administration of Viceroy Liu Kwen Yi.
>
> I asked to have them put through company formation and other drill—they were very good indeed. They had been instructed by a Chinese officer, who had originally been taught by a German officer.
>
> They had modern Mauser rifles, bought in Germany. They were a remarkably fine, smart lot of young men, aged between sixteen and twenty. Most of them came from Hunan.
>
> It is another instance of what may be done by the Chinese, if properly organized.[49]

Though the Nanking Military Academy could thus impress "men from afar," it had little impact upon the Chinese army in the long run. None of the graduates were used in Liu K'un-i's personal bodyguard, and only a few were scattered through other units under Liu.[50]

---

47. *Liu K'un-i i-chi*, 3:1068; *Chronicle and Directory*, 1898, p. 186. According to later editions of the *Chronicle and Directory*, the instructors in 1906 were Von Tettenborn and Count Praschma. An instructor named Blyhofer was listed in 1907.

48. *Liu K'un-i i-chi*, 3:1189–1190.

49. Lord Charles Beresford, *The Break-up of China* (New York, 1899), pp. 112–113.

50. Powell, pp. 66, 68–69.

Hupeh Military Preparatory School. In 1895, during the aftershock of the Sino-Japanese War, Chang Chih-tung received an edict demanding a general intensification of army training. The following year he was ordered specifically to consider and memorialize upon the advisability of creating additional provincial military schools. Chang, of course, was in favor of founding new academies, and after returning to Wuchang in 1896, he at once organized the Hupeh Military Preparatory School. He informed the throne of this accomplishment at the beginning of 1897.[51] The Hupeh Military Preparatory School could accomplish two objectives, he reported. It could raise the status of the Chinese soldier by helping to eradicate the disparity between the civil and military officials, and it could make the Chinese soldier more efficient by training officers in Western techniques, the knowledge of which could then be passed down through the ranks.

Chang planned that the Hupeh Military Preparatory School would produce low grade commissioned officers.[52] As in the former case of the Kwangtung Naval and Military Officers' School, work in the classrooms would be aimed at "understanding its principles" (*ming ch'i-li*), while that on the drill grounds would be intended for "mastering it in practice" (*chin ch'i-yung*). The curriculum would be composed of infantry, artillery, and cavalry studies, military engineering, mathematics, cartography, geography, and a number of related subjects. Like the cadets of Kwangtung, the Hupeh students would be expected to devote a part of each day to Chinese classical and historical studies. Graduates of the school would receive commissions, enter the public service, and become a part of the "family of officials." The best graduates would be given troop commands, while those lower in achievement would be given garrison commands or used for such tasks as recruiting and examining troops, planning and modernizing arsenals, and inspecting fortifications.[53]

Chang bought land for the Military Preparatory School at Huang-t'u-p'o in the eastern part of Wuchang. But while construction of the school was under way, he temporarily located the academy in buildings of the Iron Administration Bureau (T'ieh-cheng chü). Originally Wang Ping-en was referred to as "general manager" of the school, but Chang later addressed Ts'ai Hsi-yung, his chief lieutenant for *yang-wu*, by that title.[54] These men were assisted by a staff of about twenty Chinese supervisors from

51. For Chang's basic memorial on this school, see *CC*, 45:13–16b.
52. *CC*, 100:27b–28.
53. *CC*, 45:14–15b.
54. *CC*, 100:29b, 45:16.

Tientsin and Canton and by several German officers. Two of the Germans were hired after negotiations with the Berlin War Office conducted through Minister Hsü Ching-ch'eng. The negotiations were protracted. The high salaries demanded by the Germans were one obstacle. Command responsibility was another. Probably mindful of unfortunate Chinese experiences with foreign military advisers extending back at least to the incident of the Lay-Osborne flotilla, Chang demanded a clear understanding that any Germans employed would be subject to regulation by the Liangkwang governor general, would be instructors only, and would have no right to command troops.[55]

The two Germans finally sent to Hupeh were a Captain von Falkenheyn and Lieutenant R. Genz. Upon their arrival, they were given brevet ranks as colonel (*fu-chiang*) and major (*yu-chi*) in order to increase their prestige. Later a third German officer, Lieutenant E. von Strauch, was transferred to the academy from the Self-Strengthening Army in Nanking.[56] Chang informed the throne that he would pay the Germans' salaries and build and operate the Military Preparatory School with money from a special rehabilitation fund, salt taxes, and surpluses of the mint he had established in Wuchang.

By the fall of 1896, Chang Chih-tung was prepared to announce an entrance examination for the Military Preparatory School.[57] Application was permitted to all expectant civil or military officials, men with civil or military degrees, students of the classics, and the sons of reputable gentry or official families from any province. From those persons applying, 120 men were to be chosen to enter the school. An applicant would first be examined on the styles of composition (*wen-li*), which men with a civil background would be expected to understand thoroughly and men with a military background to understand roughly. After a one-day test for each group, 240 men would be selected to present themselves for an examination to determine the state of their health and character. From this test, the final 120 students would be selected, with another 30 to 40 men designated as reserve students. After three months of study, the 120 finalists would be given a third examination, and those who failed would be replaced from the list of reserves.

All students chosen would receive a stipend of four taels a month. They would graduate after three years and then be given military rank.

---

55. For telegrams exchanged with Minister Hsü, see *CC*, 151:5–5b, 6b–7, 15b, 16–16b.
56. *Chronicle and Directory*, 1898, p. 199. According to the 1900 edition, p. 235, the foreign staff then consisted of F. W. Hoffman, A. Welzel, and C. Fuchs.
57. *CC*, 120:11b–15b.

After the selection of the students and alternates, the first registration for the Military Preparatory School would be closed. Chang was groping toward a regularized "school term" in the Western sense. The continual arrival of students at the academy would, he explained, make it impossible to form "classes," handicap instruction, and cause confusion by mixing new and old students. If students withdrew during a school term, the vacancy created could not be filled immediately by other applicants. Such applicants would have to await the announcement of a new registration and the formation of a new class in the future.

The response to Chang's announcement of the initial entrance examination was overwhelming. Within a month 4,000 men had applied for inclusion in the 120-man student body. Chang exclaimed that this was evidence of the abundance of men "determined to resist the foe and defend the besieged." But he was forced to issue a second proclamation to discourage further applications. He suggested that the 4,000 might include idle impostors and schemers for stipends who would do well to withdraw their applications. He reminded the applicants that the military school would require eight hours of hard work every day—four hours in the lecture halls and four on the drill grounds. He would have to exclude men over forty years of age, for they would not be equal to the rigorous program. Others who failed to meet the specified requirements on education or to come from reputable families would not be permitted to take the entrance examination. Those who hoped to pursue other occupations concurrently with their studies should also withdraw. Chang also tried to steer applicants to the other military schools then in operation in Tientsin, Canton, and Nanking. He apologized for his strictness in limiting the enrollment of the Military Preparatory School but emphasized that careful consideration had to be given to quality because "today's students will be tomorrow's officers."[58]

The Hupeh Military Preparatory School was subsequently opened, presumably with only the 120 students finally selected from the 4,000 applicants. How successfully the academy operated is another matter. It eventually supplied some officers for service with the Hupeh troops, but a brief letter written by Chang Chih-tung in the summer of 1898 stated that little progress had been made until that time. Apparently the governor of Shensi had requested that Chang send him graduates of the school to use in training troops in the Northwest. Chang replied that his students were not yet qualified to serve as instructors; they were still "too shal-

58. See Chang's announcement, CC, 120:17–18.

low." Construction of the school buildings had just begun, and regulations had not yet been drawn up for the academy. "The complications have been too many, and the time taken has been altogether too long," Chang reported. Pessimistically but significantly, he concluded: "If we wish military preparedness, we must either send men to Japan or hire Japanese instructors before there will be real results. This is my humble advice based upon experience."[59]

Noncommissioned Officers' School. Chang Chih-tung soon acted upon his opinion that effective results in military training could be achieved through the employment of Japanese instructors. His view perhaps reflected in part the troubles that had been experienced with his German staff. Upon one occasion he had discharged a German officer on the grounds that he was too domineering.[60] However, Chang's belief also reflected a growing tendency throughout China in favor of employing Japanese officers. Commenting on this trend, Ralph L. Powell stated:

> This shift demonstrated a growing conviction that Japanese problems in the modern world and her solutions to them were more closely related to China's conditions than were those of the Western powers. There were also specific advantages in using Japanese advisers. The employment of Japanese reduced the language problem, for they were more willing than most foreigners to speak Chinese. Japanese officers were less expensive to employ; they would accept poorer treatment than Occidental officers; and they more readily adapted themselves to Chinese realities. The Japanese had modeled their army on that of Germany; so the transition from German to Japanese instructors did not necessitate a major change in training methods or techniques . . . Finally, the shift to Japanese advisers was indicative of growing belief that Orientals could match the prowess of the West.[61]

Chang did not dismiss his German officers at the Hupeh Military Preparatory School, but in 1899 he first revealed plans to by-pass them to an extent, as well as the British instructors. During 1898 Lord Beresford also visited Wuchang. In the course of his conversations with Chang Chih-tung, he proposed a scheme whereby Britain would reorganize and provide Western training for the entire Chinese army. The Tsungli Yamen seemingly had concurred in the plan to the extent of approving the training of 2,000 men in Hupeh. Lord Beresford received the impression that Chang Chih-tung was "entirely in sympathy with the proposal" and

59. *CC*, 156:30b.
60. Powell, p. 69.
61. Powell, p. 162.

strongly in favor of the reorganization.[62] After Lord Beresford's visit, however, at the beginning of 1899, Chang privately expressed reservations to the Tsungli Yamen and hoped that the British would not press the scheme, so that it could be quietly dropped. Yet in case the British intended to carry through their idea, Chang proposed that he employ Japanese instructors at once. He could then, if necessary, present the British with a *fait accompli* and point out that there was no longer any need for their services in Hupeh. At the same time the number of German instructors in Hupeh would be held steady and not be allowed to exceed the number of Japanese employed. Among the reasons for desiring the Japanese, Chang mentioned lower salaries. Furthermore, Japan had provided him with several hundred books on military topics. As these were in the Japanese language, Japanese readers were needed to make them useful. Chang also commented that "recently the Japanese have been very peaceful in their attitude toward China and have carried on trade quietly."[63]

Chang's ideas on employing Japanese instructors apparently met with the approval of the Tsungli Yamen. Later in 1899 Chang received a small Japanese military mission headed by a major and including an engineer, a cavalry officer, a surgeon, and three noncommissioned officers. He used the Japanese to staff a new Noncommissioned Officers' School.[64] Chang's collected works contain relatively little information on the new institution. They suggest, however, that initially noncommissioned officers from all of Chang's defense battalions were ordered to rotate in attending classes at the school. They received instruction in military methods, geography, surveying, mathematics, and cartography. However, the Boxer Uprising intervened, and some of Chang's battalions were transferred to help suppress the rebels. The noncommissioned officers remaining behind were given increased patrol and security duties. Rotating attendance at the school proved impractical under these circumstances, and in the summer of 1901 Chang decided to regularize the student body. He ordered that one hundred selected representatives from his battalions be chosen on the basis of an examination and be transferred to the school, to give it a more stable enrollment.[65] A European observer felt that the equipment and facilities of the Noncommissioned Officers' School were inferior to those of the Military Preparatory School

62. Beresford, pp. 157–161.
63. See telegrams to Tsungli Yamen, *CC*, 158:9b–11, 11–11b, 11b–12.
64. Powell, pp. 120–121.
65. *CC*, 104:21b–23b.

and that the Japanese instructors commanded less respect than did the Germans.[66] However, Chang claimed that the two schools cooperated closely with each other.

Chang Chih-tung's experiments with military schools do not appear to have been strikingly successful in quickly providing an effective officer corps. However, the schools were only one part of his military modernization program. Equipping his forces with better arms and conducting training within the ranks (as well as within the schools) were other parts of the program. Chang insisted on higher regard for his troops and stressed the importance of literacy. He also selected his enlisted personnel carefully, paid them regularly, and provided them with food, uniforms, and quarters far above the average. By 1902 certain military observers believed that the Hupeh troops were the best in all of China. The nucleus of the troops, a 7,750-man, German-trained bodyguard commanded by General Chang Piao, "was a fine body of men to whom Chang Chih-tung showed partiality." One foreign observer, Captain Gadoffre, reported that the close order drill and manual of arms of the foreign-trained battalions were comparable to the best in Germany, while the physical training of the Wuchang troops was superior to that of the French army. However, he remarked, once the officers were no longer directly under the critical eye of Chang, they tended to neglect the foreign principles they had been taught. Citing Gadoffre's observations, Powell later concluded: "The greatest weakness of Chang's troops, as of the older Chinese armies, was mediocrity and lack of initiative among the officers. It was a case of good troops commanded by unqualified leaders."[67] Chang tried to overcome this weakness through his military academies, but he met with only limited success.

Promotion of Western Language and Technical Training

When Chang Chih-tung became generally aware of China's need for borrowing from the West, he soon perceived that Western strength was founded upon more than weapons and a knowledge of their use. The development of Chinese industry and communications and the improvement of agriculture and commerce through the application of Western methods began to rank high among his interests.

As Chang was founding industries, exploiting mines, encouraging railroad building, and seeking to strengthen commerce and agriculture in the

66. Powell, p. 151, citing Captain Gadoffre, "Vallée du Yang-Tse: les troupes chinoises et elurs instructeurs," *Revue des troupes coloniales*, 2nd year, 1 (January 1903), 6–8, 22.
67. Powell, pp. 147–150, 152.

provinces under his control, he was also establishing schools of a non-military character. His schools of foreign languages, technology, commerce, and agriculture were intended primarily to supply engineers and managers to carry on his projects for industrial and economic development. In setting up the language and technological schools, Chang was able to follow such pre-existing models as the Peking College of Languages, founded in 1862 to train interpreters and expanded in 1866 to become a college of science and law.[68] In establishing the schools of agriculture and commerce, however, he was more of a pioneer. He made his first attempt to open a general school of Western learning while still serving as governor general of Liangkwang.

The School of Western Arts. A short time before his transfer from Kwangtung, Chang Chih-tung revealed that his interests in Western education were beginning to extend well beyond the single field of military training. In the summer and fall of 1889 he planned a School of Western Arts that would have five courses, all of which he related to "self-strengthening" and foreign affairs. Chang proposed building this school next to the Naval and Military Officers' School and intended that its curriculum should complement the military academy's. The School of Western Arts was to offer instruction in mining, chemistry, electricity, botany, and international law—the last being the only nonscientific course but one closely related to foreign affairs. Each of the five departments would have thirty students, drawn from Foochow and from two interpreters' colleges—the Canton College of Languages and the Shanghai College to Increase Language Knowledge (Kuang fang-yen kuan), the latter established by Li Hung-chang in 1863. Negotiations with Minister Liu Jui-fen in London were begun for the employment of five English instructors.[69]

Chang Chih-tung's transfer to Wuchang ended action on the School of Western Arts. His successor, Li Han-chang, was unwilling to follow through. On the grounds of insufficient funds, Li was able to prevent the hiring of English instructors in mining and electricity, but he was not in time to stop the employment of three others: "Ha-erh-p'o" (Harper?), signed at the London School of Law to a three-year contract providing a monthly salary of £71; Percy Groom, a Cambridge botanist; and H. H. Robinson, an Oxford graduate with an M.A. in chemistry. Groom and Robinson were to draw monthly salaries of £41 13s. 4d.

68. Knight Biggerstaff, "The Tung Wen Kuan," *Chinese Social and Political Science Review*, 18.3 (October 1934), 307–340.
69. *CC*, 132:27b–28, 133:8b, 16–16b.

Robinson, upon arrival, was sent immediately to work with Chang Chih-tung in Hupeh. "Ha-erh-p'o," who arrived with Groom in January 1890, was discharged less than six months later in a salary dispute involving exchange rates. Groom, the botanist, was assigned to the Naval and Military Officers' School until the spring of 1892, when he was sent home with six months' pay and ship fare. Li Han-chang reported that Groom had been unable to achieve results because "seeds and plants were not suitable." A customs report added that the botanist's services were "exceedingly small, and their utility altogether doubtful."[70]

Thus, plans for the School of Western Arts came to naught. In originating the plans, however, Chang Chih-tung laid the basis for his later educational projects, most notably the Self-Strengthening School that was to open soon after his arrival in Hupeh. As one of his first comprehensive statements on the value of Western technological training, the memorial he submitted in 1889 to justify the School of Western Arts is particularly revealing of the scope of Chang's interests at the time. One by one, he treated his proposed five courses of study as follows.

Mining. Foreign countries gave high priority to mining as a means of enriching the nation (*fu-kuo*). China had abundant mineral resources but still imported most of her metals, which could not always be obtained immediately when needed. Merchants who operated mines did not understand the underlying principles or use the best methods; they frequently went bankrupt and achieved no results. In the future when railroads were built, the need for iron would increase; when steamships increased in number, the need for coal would grow. In general, Chinese resources should be used to fill Chinese needs. This was why the study of mining should be undertaken.

Chemistry. Refining the five metals, making good arms, and manufacturing sundry products all depended on chemistry. Manufacturing was extremely complex, and its materials involved chemistry. If the Chinese could not make things themselves and repair them themselves, they must depend on foreigners, as before. Moreover, if the Chinese did not understand the underlying principles, they could not put them to use. This was why the study of chemistry should be undertaken.

Electricity. The uses of electricity in such devices as the telegraph, electric lights, and electrically-fired torpedoes and guns were of great advantage militarily. Electricity was used extensively in the various provinces, but China still looked to foreign countries for the machines

70. *Yang-wu yün-tung*, 2:623–624; *Chronicle and Directory*, 1893, p. 158; China, Imperial Maritime Customs, *Decennial Reports*, 1882–1891, p. 576.

and materials needed to generate and employ it. This was why the study of electricity should be undertaken.

Botany. The sages had taught the people the art of planting, yet later generations were held down as farmers. Westerners took up the clue of planting and developed it. The study of botany, which was subsequently established, distinguished the types and characteristics of plants and determined their soil and water requirements. It described how deficiencies of climate could be made up by manpower, and how deficiencies of manpower could be supplemented by machines. Because of botany, a nation could eliminate waste of land and energy. Agriculture and sericulture were the basic industries of the people. Natural calamities were increasing day by day, which China could not afford to let go uncontrolled. This was why the study of botany should be undertaken.

International Law. Among the various nations of the West, international relations were established on the basis of international law. Only in relations with China was there a regular tendency to put aside and disregard international law, and China's knowledge of international law was not deep enough to allow her to combat this tendency. Furthermore, when Chinese went to a foreign country, they were made subject to the laws of that country; but when foreigners came to China, Chinese laws could not be used to restrain them. For a long time this had been a source of vexation and trouble. The emphasis in Chinese law and foreign law was different. In China, criminal law was first and civil law second. Since Western nations were so constituted that they favored business enterprise, their civil law was much more detailed. Even in criminal law, the use of the five punishments and the degrees of leniency and severity were different. Chinese should clearly understand Chinese law, compare it with Western international law, and examine the differences and similarities. They should set forth commercial laws, and inform all nations that if there were problems in foreign affairs, not only Chinese but all foreigners on Chinese soil would be judged by Chinese law uniformly. It would be impossible to accomplish this without men who were thoroughly familiar with both Chinese and foreign law. This was why the study of international law should be undertaken.[71]

The Self-Strengthening School. In 1893 when Chang Chih-tung informed the throne that the Self-Strengthening School had been opened in Wuchang, he justified the establishment in broad terms. Because Hupeh province, on the Yangtze River, occupied a strategic position

71. *CC*, 28:7–9b.

between North and South China, besides including the treaty ports of Hankow and Ichang, foreign affairs were daily becoming more complex and critical, to the extent that "one move could affect the whole situation." Training "human talent" in foreign affairs could therefore no longer be delayed.[72]

Although Chang thus spoke in generalities, one specific impulse seemed to lie behind the Self-Strengthening School. In the spring of 1891 Chang had received a petition from a district magistrate named Tseng Kuang-fu asking that courses in foreign languages and commerce be added to the curriculum of the Liang-Hu Academy as a measure to strengthen the tea trade of Hunan and Hupeh.[73] Local merchants were finding it difficult to compete in the market without a knowledge of foreign languages and business practices. Tseng believed that their ability to compete would be improved by a two- or three-year course in Western practical studies.

Chang Chih-tung endorsed this idea but suggested that instead of adding new courses at the Liang-Hu Academy, it would be more effective to found a special school for foreign studies, with provisions made for enrolling the sons of tea merchants. As requested by Tseng, the new school would provide training in Western languages and commerce, with emphasis on "the arts of increasing resources, stopping leakage [i.e., dissipation of Chinese wealth in foreign purchases], extending the sale of native goods, and enhancing the wealth of the people." Chang began dispatching orders to his subordinates, which two years later resulted in the opening of the Self-Strengthening School.[74] In 1893 when he reported that the school was in operation, he stated that the initial funds had been supplied from "the outside." While exact financial data are lacking, it is probable that the school was partially supported by contributions from the tea merchants of Hunan and Hupeh.

As originally organized, the Self-Strengthening School had four departments: Western languages, natural sciences, mathematics, and commercial affairs. "The study of Western spoken and written languages is essential for controlling the foreigners," Chang wrote. "Natural sciences, including chemistry, mechanics, electricity and optics (*kuang-hsüeh*) are gateways to the various branches of learning. Mathematics is the basis of manufacturing. Commercial affairs are related to the great plan for wealth and strength."[75]

72. *CC*, 34:5–6.
73. *CC*, 97:23b–25.
74. *CC*, 97:23b–25, 98:23b–24.
75. *CC*, 34:5b.

Chang's program called for one instructor and twenty students for each of the four departments. Language students were to be chosen on the basis of recommendations, but students for the other three departments were to be selected by competitive written examinations. The school was established in Wuchang next to the Iron Administration Bureau, the office that supervised Chang's Hanyang Iron and Steel Works. It was initially placed under the general control of Ts'ai Hsi-yung, who again proved himself one of Chang's most loyal disciples and chief assistants in the sphere of Westernization.[76]

The Self-Strengthening School's operations in the first years after its establishment were disappointing to Chang Chih-tung. He was forced to admit that he had failed to place first things first when founding the school. Although there was slight progress, the students were guilty of "much empty talk and little practicality." Their studies were not deep. Chang decided that it would be impossible for the students to master natural sciences and commerce without a foundation in Western languages firmer than that which the Self-Strengthening School had originally envisaged. "Today when Western books with new principles and new learning are coming out unceasingly," Chang wrote, "we still have no way to gain information about the splendors (they describe) or investigate their benefits and faults . . . If we do not have men who fully understand foreign languages, we cannot obtain the true import of the new principles and new learning." Elsewhere he presented the axiom: "If one does not have a thorough knowledge of foreign languages, one cannot read Western books. If one does not read Western books extensively, one cannot attain thorough knowledge."[77]

Chang decided to convert the Self-Strengthening School into an institution primarily for language study. However, he was mindful of the disrespect with which Chinese officials had regarded interpreters as early as the days of Feng Kuei-fen, who in 1860 had denounced "stupid and silly 'linguists'" for being men of shallow knowledge or frivolous rascals caring only for material profit.[78] Chang made it clear that his desire was not merely to train students for service as interpreters; his deeper purpose was to encourage determined scholars to investigate the systems of other countries and understand the learning of other lands so that they might contribute substantially to overcoming the difficulties of

76. In 1896 Ts'ai was ordered to revise regulations of the school. *CC*, 100:24b–27; *Chronicle and Directory*, 1898, p. 199. The 1900 and 1906 editions of the *Chronicle and Directory* listed the intendant Chang S. Ting-fan as director.
77. *CC*, 47:20b–21, 100:24b–27.
78. Teng and Fairbank, *China's Response to the West*, pp. 50–52.

the times. He provided penalties for students who withdrew from the Self-Strengthening School with covetous motives of serving foreign business firms as interpreters.[79]

In pursuit of his purpose, Chang moved mathematical studies from the Self-Strengthening School to the Liang-Hu Academy in 1896.[80] He pointed out that mathematics was an ancient Chinese discipline described in many available Chinese books. Works on Western mathematics were also available in a comparatively large number of translations. China was better off in this field than in natural sciences and commerce, for which concentrated preparatory work was still necessary. Mathematics could be offered in a traditional-type academy just as well as in a specialized, Westernized school.

Chang maintained that the situation differed with respect to natural sciences and commerce. Neither Chinese professors nor students had the means of delving deeply into these subjects. Neither subject was highly developed in Chinese literature, and the few works that had been reproduced in Chinese by translation bureaus at Shanghai and Tientsin were "mere outlines."[81] Natural sciences and commerce were therefore dropped as individual courses for study and examination at the Self-Strengthening School. Chang planned instead that they would be approached indirectly and inductively through language study. During the course of language study, materials on science and commerce would be read as texts, but more intensive work would be postponed until the students had gained language proficiency.

When these revisions of the curriculum were ordered in 1896, the Self-Strengthening School also established four new departments—in English, French, German, and Russian. Japanese was added in 1897 or early 1898.[82] Chang Chih-tung especially emphasized study of the Russian language, probably because of the strong Russian interest in the Hankow tea market. In giving instructions to Ts'ai Hsi-yung, Chang explained that Russian constituted a special problem because, he claimed, the language was derived from Greek, whereas English, French, and German were derived from Latin. But the need for Russian was especially great, since China and Russia were close neighbors.[83] Chang employed a foreign instructor to teach Russian at the Self-Strengthening School. Japanese and German instruction was also initially entrusted to foreign-

79. *CC*, 120:23b–24.
80. *CC*, 100:24b–25, 152:30b.
81. *CC*, 120:21.
82. *CC*, 47:20b–21b.
83. *CC*, 100:35–35b.

ers, but Chinese teachers were used for English and French, to which Chinese scholars had been longer exposed.[84]

An enrollment quota of 30 students was established for each of the language courses offered by the Self-Strengthening School, making a total allowable enrollment of 120 students before the addition of Japanese language studies, or 150 after the addition of Japanese. The enrollment was opened to all men of upright and loyal character who came from honorable families—or specifically, to minor officials, persons with the rank of *sheng-yüan* or above, and the sons of officials and gentry who had previously studied the classics and knew the principles of righteousness (*i*) and propriety (*li*). In 1897 after the Self-Strengthening School had been reformed, Chang publicly announced that an entrance examination would be given. His proclamation set forth requirements and regulations of the school, the most important of which are summarized as follows.

1. Students must be between the ages of fifteen and twenty-four. Others need not apply.

2. Students must be well-grounded in Chinese learning and accept the Way of the Sage as the general rule of conduct. If the Confucian classics were understood, the teaching of Western literature would be twice as easy.

3. Opium smokers would not be registered. They need not apply.

4. Applicants would first be tested in Chinese, and a selection would be made according to the quota. They would then be given an oral examination to judge their deportment, integrity, age, respect for etiquette, and bearing.

5. Students whose age was advanced or who had taken civil service examinations were already proficient in the Confucian classics. Aside from their Western lessons, they must only review the old learning daily. Students who were young or whose knowledge of Chinese was shallow must enroll in Chinese courses, study the Chinese classics and composition, and write discussion essays.

6. Students must devote all of their attention and energy to lessons given in the school. They would not be allowed to write eight-legged examination themes at the school; nor would they be allowed to take

---

84. In 1900 the foreign teaching staff consisted of Count W. Bernstorff for German (then in at least his third year as instructor), S. T. Bolschacoff for Russian, and M. Yanizahara for Japanese. Yang Pen Kua assisted in German, with Cheng Yü Ying and Hsü Shou Jen teaching English and French, respectively. By 1906 Count Bernstorff had been dropped and Yang Pen Kua promoted to principal teacher of German. *Chronicle and Directory*, 1898, p. 199; 1900, p. 235; 1906, p. 778.

examinations at the various old-style academies lest they harm both types of study.

7. After students had already entered the school, they would be permitted to request leave for provincial examinations but would not be granted leave for lower examinations.

8. Students would graduate from the school after five years, following which they would become "official students" (*kuan hsüeh-sheng*). Before graduation, students could not request leave except for urgent and proper business. If they created pretexts to withdraw for the purpose of entering base professions or covetously taking employment as interpreters for foreign firms, they must repay all funds spent by the school for their food, upkeep, and personal allowances. The school would investigate and determine the reputation of a student's family and require that an official of his native place verify the student's dependability and post security for him.

9. In teaching Western languages, it was feared that continually adding students would confuse the new and the old and make it impossible to form classes. After the initial selection had been made, registration would cease. If students withdrew because of urgent business, the vacancy would remain and would not be filled immediately by alternate candidates. Men who came seeking entrance to the school must await the call for a new registration; at that time they would be ordered to report for an entrance examination and make up a new class. Teachers would not be permitted to add new students to an old class midway.

10. All students must submit to the discipline of Chinese and foreign instructors in the recitation halls and should obey the officials in charge of the quarters and refectory. If there were infractions of the rules, punishment would be decided by the instructors and officials in charge, and those students who did not comply would be expelled.[85]

With the rules against practice of the eight-legged essay, in favor of a regular "school term," and in favor of a stricter and more formal academic environment than that prevailing in the traditional academies, Chang Chih-tung seemed to be following Western patterns in school organization as well as in curriculum. He moved even further in that direction when he proclaimed that the Self-Strengthening School would abolish the payment of stipends to its students. When the entrance examination for the school was announced early in 1897, Chang stated that the school would pay for the food, books, paper, brushes, and other supplies

85. *CC*, 120:20b–24b.

of all students accepted, and in addition, each man would receive a
monthly stipend of five silver dollars (yuan) "to put his mind at ease
while studying."[86]

A month after this announcement, Chang revised the plan and issued
a long proclamation that he claimed had been composed after thorough
investigation of Western methods and Chinese scholarly opinion.[87] In the
West, Chang noted, officialdom allocated large sums for education, but
aside from poor students who received scholarships mainly in the lower
schools, all others "from the age of seven until graduation" were required to pay tuition fees. Such fees were paid in "upper, middle, and
lower schools, as well as in special schools and normal schools." While
he did not advocate an outright tuition system for the Self-Strengthening
School, he argued that the abolition of stipends would be a step in that
direction, which would reduce the financial problems of the school and
raise the level of scholarship. He placed more emphasis upon the second
point and stressed the need for discouraging students who were more interested in daily necessities than in receiving an education. If stipends
were abolished, the Self-Strengthening School would no longer be attrac-
tive to such students, he claimed. Only sincere and ambitious scholars
would register. The state would not be reckless in the expenditure of its
funds, and the integrity of students would not be impaired. Chang decided that the Self-Strengthening School would continue to pay for the
student's room, board, and supplies, but the personal allowance of five
yuan a month would be cut off. As one compensation, however, and as a
means of further encouraging high scholarship, awards would be given to
the most worthy students selected after monthly examinations.

The School for Gathering Talent. Like the Nanking Military Academy,
the School for Gathering Talent was one of Chang Chih-tung's final cre-
ations when serving as the acting governor general of Liangkiang in 1896.
Both schools were in a sense Chang's response to the Chinese defeat in
the Sino-Japanese War. In 1895 Chang had drawn up what was one of the
longest memorials of his career—an 8,000-word document recommending
a sweeping reform program designed to provide for recovery from the
disgrace of the Treaty of Shimonoseki and prevent China's extinction as
a nation. In the various points of the memorial, Chang called for intensi-
fied training of a modern army, the building of a navy, construction of
railroads, establishment of more arsenals, promotion of schools, en-

86. *CC*, 120:22.
87. *CC*, 120:24–26b.

couragement of commerce, development of industry, and assistance for Chinese students in studying abroad.[88] Both the Nanking Military Academy and the School for Gathering Talent were among Chang's first attempts to push reform more vigorously after presenting these recommendations.

The School for Gathering Talent was designed to provide training in four fields: international affairs, agriculture, industry, and commerce.[89] Four subjects were to be covered within each field: law, taxation, geography, and translation in international affairs; cultivation, irrigation, animal husbandry, and agricultural implements in agriculture; chemistry, steam engines, mining, and engineering in industry; and foreign demand, Chinese products, currency values, and the state of foreign production in commerce. Chang intended to employ a total of seven foreign professors. French and German instructors would conduct the courses in law and agriculture, and English instructors would be responsible for the courses in commerce and industry. Students would also receive language training in French, German, and English.[90] The students were to be divided into an "upper class," consisting at the outset of 40 men, and a "beginning class," consisting of 120 men. The upper class members must be intelligent and "able to read Chinese books," but also familiar with a Western language. The beginners would concentrate on language study until qualified for promotion to the higher class. Chang planned for the Nanking College of Languages to train the beginners. He reported that at the time of his writing, only thirty men were studying English and French at the local interpreters' college.

Chang informed the throne of the new school only a month before returning to Wuchang. He was ordered to hand the institution over to the management of Liu K'un-i.[91] Liu later made it exclusively a school of languages for training translators, changed the name to the Chiang-nan High School (Chiang-nan kao-teng hsüeh-t'ang) in 1898, and in 1899 converted it to the Natural Sciences Academy (Ko-chih shu-yüan). Chang administered examinations at the academy in 1903 after he had returned to Nanking as acting governor general of Liangkiang following the death of Liu K'un-i.[92] In general, however, Chang's experience with the school

88. *CC*, 37:17b–36b.
89. For memorial on this school, see *CC*, 40:33b–36b.
90. According to the *Chronicle and Directory*, 1898, p. 187, the staff then included Yang Chao-yuen, commissioner; J. R. Barclay, headmaster and professor of English; A. Lam, professor of French; and Sen Chang-sang, professor of German.
91. *CC*, 40:36b.
92. *Liu K'un-i i-chi*, 3:1044–1046; *HNP*, p. 169.

was so brief that it did little more than provide him with ideas for similar schools that he initiated in Hupeh.

Schools of Agriculture and Industry. Early in 1898 Chang informed the throne that he was establishing a school of agriculture and a school of industry in Wuchang.[93] The purpose, he stated, was to enrich the nation, relieve the people's suffering, and reduce reliance on others. China had been founded upon agriculture and had been the first country of the world to develop industrial production. The country was still rich in human and natural resources, Chang stated, but had lost its ancient advantages through neglect of scientific studies. Few farmers or merchants had time for concentrated study, and officials paid little attention to agriculture or industry. However, officialdom should change its ways, for unless the government took the lead in improving agriculture and industry, there would be no means of developing the people's knowledge.

Chang noted that "America is the most advanced country in agricultural management."[94] In 1897 he had engaged two American specialists to make a survey of Hupeh agricultural conditions. New-style American farm tools had been ordered, and new varieties of seed had been procured for experimental planting. He then decided to establish the School of Agricultural Affairs with American instructors.[95]

A few weeks after Chang memorialized on this decision, he asked for applications from sons of the gentry, merchants, or officials.[96] The school opened in rented quarters, and for several years its students were confined to classrooms. In 1902, however, Chang reported that 2,000 mou of uncultivated public land outside Wuchang had been made available to the school for use as an experimental farm, and the school was ordered to move to the new site.[97]

The School of Industrial Arts, established in 1898, was similar to a Western trade school. Instruction was in the charge of two Japanese teachers, with Chinese assistants. Training was offered in arithmetic, physics, chemistry, and mechanics. The school was opened to sixty boys between the ages of twelve and sixteen. Applicants were required to know 2,000 characters and to be familiar with the Four Books. The stu-

93. *CC*, 47:9–11b.
94. *CC*, 47:9b.
95. Later the faculty included "Chang H. S. Taotai," director; G. D. Brill, B.S., and J. W. Gilmore, B.S., professors; and T. Nakamsli (?) and K. Minemura, instructors in silk culture. *Chronicle and Directory*, 1900, p. 235. The same staff is listed in editions for 1906, 1907, and 1909.
96. *CC*, 121:1–1b.
97. *CC*, 185:35b–36.

dents would study mathematics and science four hours a day and work at crafts for another four hours, with their performance graded monthly.[98] A significant departure from the traditions of Chinese classical scholarship was the following school regulation: "Each industrial art must be practiced with one's own hands before thorough understanding can be achieved. All students must listen to the instructions of the foremen and teachers of each department and take part in actual practice. They will not be allowed to look on with their hands in their sleeves."[99]

Another significant departure, attempted at least, was the charging of student fees. Early in 1898 when entrance examinations for the agricultural and industrial schools were first announced, Chang Chih-tung's proclamation stated that the government would provide funds for building the schools, renting land, buying supplies, and paying faculty salaries. But four yuan a month would be collected from each student to pay for his fuel, food, oil, candles, brushes, and ink. The innovation may have been too radical. At the end of 1898 a new call was issued for students to enroll at the School of Industrial Arts, and this announcement stated that the school would not pay stipends but would provide for the students' food, books, paper, and brushes.[100]

The School of Industrial Arts was set up within Chang Chih-tung's Bureau of Foreign Affairs (Yang-wu chü). Both that bureau and the Iron Administration Bureau were two of Chang's offices which shared in the execution of educational reforms. In 1898 in Hankow, Chang also established a Commercial Affairs Bureau (Shang-wu chü), which was the forerunner of the Commercial Affairs School that he organized in 1902.[101]

Sending Students Abroad

The schools that Chang Chih-tung established in Canton, Nanking, and Wuchang were conceived on a small scale and progressed haltingly, but they provided an introduction to topics of study in which China was indisputably weak. To a certain extent, they supplied Chang with the specialists he wanted for his defense forces and industries. Through the schools, new principles and methods of education were publicized and brought to the attention of scholars and officials elsewhere. Chang's founding of the schools helped inspire others to espouse reforms of a

98. *CC*, 47:10, 121:2-5b.
99. *CC*, 121:4b.
100. *CC*, 121:2b–4b.
101. *CC*, 47:10. Chang created the Foreign Affairs Bureau in 1897 in a reorganization of the Iron Administration Bureau. *HNP*, p. 108. On the Commercial Affairs Bureau, see *CC*, 49:4b–9b; on the Commercial Affairs School, see *CC*, 105:7b–8b.

similar nature. His example was influential in arousing demands for more comprehensive educational change, which were voiced insistently during 1898 and later years. When an empire-wide program of school construction was decreed, Chang already had an institutional framework upon which to build. His area was one of the few prepared to enact the program and work conscientiously toward achieving further results.

Yet Chang Chih-tung was impatient over the shortcomings of his early schools and anxious about the slowness of school expansion in China as a whole. In a memorial at the beginning of 1896, he stated that England, France, and Germany, with less than half the total area of China, had 200,000 primary, middle, and higher schools with an enrollment in excess of 17,800,000 persons. In comparison, China had hardly begun the task of training talent as a method of self-strengthening. Since China still had such a long way to go, Chang concluded, training men in her own self-strengthening schools should be supplemented by the sponsorship of studies abroad. He became an ardent advocate of sending Chinese students to foreign schools, just as Tseng Kuo-fan had sent students to America in 1872 and the Foochow Shipyard had sent them to England and France. "If we study only in Chinese schools," Chang wrote, "since observations and contacts are inadequate, the results will be too slow." While China was developing her new-style education, Chinese students should also be undergoing training in schools already established in the West. When they returned home, they could be put to work as teachers.[102]

Chang was instrumental in having many students sent abroad after 1898, especially after the Boxer Uprising of 1900.[103] Before 1898 he recommended the practice but did little about it himself. In 1892 he sent ten artisans to Belgium for training at the Cockerill Company, which had supplied much of the equipment for the Hanyang Iron and Steel Works.[104] In 1896, on the eve of his departure from Nanking, he drafted another of his plans which he had no opportunity to execute personally. According to this plan, Liangkiang would try to maintain sixty students abroad constantly for about twenty years. Each student would receive three years of middle school education and three years of college. The first group would consist of forty students with knowledge of a Western language. Chang estimated that the group and its accompanying supervisors could be

102. The memorial appears in *CC*, 43:10b–13. Among accounts of the first educational missions to the United States is Thomas E. LaFargue, *China's First Hundred* (Pullman, Wash., 1942), p. 176.
103. On Chang's later promotion of studies abroad, see *CC*, 59:29–30b, 67:16b–17b, 104:39–40, 186:6–6b, 7b, 10–10b, 13b–14.
104. *CC*, 137:4b.

maintained abroad for Tls. 64,000 a year, exclusive of travel expenses. He allocated Tls. 200,000 for the project, which he recommended that Liu K'un-i carry out upon his return to Nanking.[105]

When proposing this plan, Chang Chih-tung expressed a special interest in sending students to Germany. "The teaching methods of German schools are better and more advanced than those of England and France," he noted.[106] He urged that study of the German language be increased in order to prepare Chinese students for entering German schools. By 1898, however, Chang had begun to place his major emphasis on studies in Japan. At the beginning of the year, two Japanese emissaries, Kamio Mitsuomi and Utsunomiya Taro, visited Wuchang and discussed, among other topics, the dispatch of Chinese students to Japan. A short time later Chang sent a mission headed by Yao Hsi-kuang to inspect Japanese educational facilities, particularly the military schools.[107]

Studying in Japan was also under discussion with Japanese diplomats in Peking early in 1898. During the spring the Tsungli Yamen telegraphed Chang Chih-tung that Japan, as a gesture of friendship, had signified its willingness to receive Chinese students in groups of not more than two hundred and was prepared to discuss aid in payment of their expenses. Chang was asked how many students he could provide. Enthusiastically, he planned to send one hundred men from Hupeh and another hundred from Hunan. However, his enthusiasm was dampened several months later when the Tsungli Yamen informed him that the Japanese aid would consist only of paying the salaries of the teachers assigned to the Chinese students. Each student would be expected to pay for his own food, clothing, and supplies at a cost of about 300 yuan a year. It was thereupon decided that Hupeh and Hunan would send only fifty students each. This was in the midst of the Hundred Days' Reform, when the Hupeh governorship and the office of the revenue commissioner were abolished. Chang intended to use funds previously allotted to those two offices to finance the Chinese students in Japan. But when the reform movement failed, the two Hupeh offices were restored and Chang was suddenly without funds for the educational project. However, he finally succeeded in sending twenty men to attend Japanese military schools.[108]

Later, Hupeh students traveled to Japan in increasingly large numbers, and they did so with the continuing encouragement of Chang Chih-tung.

105. *CC*, 43:10b–13.
106. *CC*, 43:11.
107. *HNP*, pp. 110, 112.
108. *CC*, 155:9–10, 31b–33b; 156:21b–22b, 35b–36; 157:2–2b; 159:3b; *HNP*, pp. 122–123.

Chang favored study in Japan instead of Europe for at least four reasons: because Japan was nearer to China, more men could be sent there for the same amount of money required to train fewer men in Europe; officials could be sent more easily to inspect Chinese student activities in Japan; the Japanese language was related to the Chinese and easier for students to master than European languages; and in making translations, Japan had already distilled the essence from many Western books and discarded many worthless volumes. Chang presented these views in a chapter of the *Ch'üan-hsüeh p'ien* published during the early phase of the Reform Movement of 1898.[109] His book as well as his activities during the reform movement made known throughout the empire Chang's ideas on educational reform.

---

109. *CC*, 203:6–7b.

6 The Advocate of Moderation (1898–1900)

Chang Chih-tung's efforts on behalf of educational reform acquired new scope during 1898. Until that year Chang had been essentially a regional reformer in the field of education. The Self-Strengthening School, the military academies, and the other institutions he had organized in Liangkwang, Hukwang, and Liangkiang were largely undertaken on his own initiative and were not closely related to or integrated with an effective, centralized, imperial program for educational reform. Until 1898 Chang's school policies stood as somewhat isolated, local examples of modernization, on a national scene still overwhelmingly dominated by support for the traditional academy and the old examination system.

In 1898 Chang drew on his previous provincial experience and on his growing knowledge of Western systems to outline an educational program that could be applied to the empire as a whole. While effecting a personal transition from regional to national educational reformer, he brought forward proposals on reorganizing the old-style academies, constructing a network of new schools throughout the provinces, amending the civil service examinations, and radically altering the military examinations.

During the aftermath of the Sino-Japanese War and this period in which foreign powers were renewing their contests for concessions in China, Chang Chih-tung was by no means the only statesman or reformer advocating changes in education that might lead to greater state strength. Between 1895 and the fall of 1898, many others published or presented to the throne their own recommendations for educational reform.[1] Chang's proposals, however, were among the more influential, coming as they did from an official who governed one of China's most important areas and

1. According to a count by Cyrus Peake, the *Kuang-hsü Tung-hua hsü-lu* (Continued Tung-hua records of the Kuang-hsü reign) gives about 25 of the more important memorials on educational reform for the period 1895–1898, including the Hundred Days. Peake, *Nationalism and Education in Modern China* (New York, 1932), p. 20. The *Wu-hsü pien-fa*, Chien Po-tsan et al (Shanghai, 1953), reprints 109 memorials of the reform era, with about 47 related to educational reform, and only one of these written by Chang Chih-tung. About 250 of the 316 edicts given in the *Wu-hsü pien-fa* fall within the period August 4, 1894 (date of the first edict included)–September 21, 1898 (end of the Hundred Days' Reform). Of these, more than 60 are related to educational reform, most of them originally inspired by memorials or audiences with the emperor. See *Wu-hsü pien-fa*, II, 1–121 (edicts) and 123–512 (memorials). Some of the more significant memorials and writings on education, including work done by K'ang Yu-wei, Liang Ch'i-ch'ao, and Li Tuan-fen, are summarized in Franke, pp. 32–40.

who was widely known for both scholarship and political acumen. Chang's proposals were an integral part of the over-all Reform Movement of 1898 (*Wu-hsü pien-fa*), which culminated in the Hundred Days' Reform led by K'ang Yu-wei and Liang Ch'i-ch'ao. Yet Chang was by no means a reformer in the same sense as were K'ang Yu-wei and Liang Ch'i-ch'ao.

Relations with the K'ang-Liang Party

The Hundred Days' Reform, extending from June 11 to September 21, 1898, developed with confusing rapidity after K'ang Yu-wei, Liang Ch'i-ch'ao, and their followers gained the confidence of the Kuang-hsü emperor, who had ruled independently since the retirement of the Empress Dowager Tz'u-hsi in 1889. Developments portending the Hundred Days' Reform included the Ten Thousand Word Memorial signed by K'ang, Liang, and about 1,200 other *chü-jen* in Peking during 1895, protesting the Treaty of Shimonoseki and demanding numerous changes in the Ch'ing government; the establishment of reform clubs or "study societies," notably the Strength Study Society (Ch'iang-hsüeh hui), also known in English as the Society for the Study of National Rejuvenation or the Society for the Diffusion of Enlightenment, founded in 1895, and the Southern Study Society (Nan-hsüeh hui), founded in March 1898; K'ang Yu-wei's book *K'ung-tzu kai-chih-k'ao,* depicting Confucius as a reformer; and the opening of reform newspapers such as the *Shih-wu pao* (Current Affairs News) in Shanghai and the *Hsiang hsüeh-pao* (Hunan Journal) in Changsha. The events terminating the Hundred Days' Reform represented a conservative reaction, in which Tz'u-hsi resumed her personal rule, confined the Kuang-hsü emperor, put K'ang Yu-wei and Liang Ch'i-ch'ao to flight, and executed the "Six Martyrs" of 1898.[2]

Although Chang Chih-tung was a participant in the Reform Movement of 1898, he was not considered to be an affiliate of "the K'ang-Liang party" (*K'ang-Liang tang*) that briefly dominated the Chinese political scene. Chang saw merit in and was sympathetic to some specific reform ideas advanced by K'ang, Liang, and their coterie, but he also disagreed with elements of their philosophy and method. During the actual Hundred Days, he remained relatively aloof from the activities of the party, although he did not strenuously protest those activities and made at least

2. A brief bibliography on the Reform Movement of 1898 may be found in Teng and Fairbank, *Research Guide,* pp. 17–18. See also Hsiao Kung-chuan, "Weng T'ung-ho and the Reform Movement of 1898," pp. 111–243.

a token effort to comply with imperial edicts instigated by the party. Gradually Chang turned against the party. In the end he sided with the forces of Tz'u-hsi and proved to be one of the empress dowager's leading aides in a campaign to destroy the vestiges of the K'ang-Liang influence.

However, there is no gainsaying the fact that Chang Chih-tung helped inspire the Hundred Days' Reform and functioned as a senior patron and adviser of K'ang Yu-wei's followers during the initial phases of the movement. The reformers looked upon Chang "as one of their best advocates, and perhaps as their staunchest friend."[3] In 1897 they refused to cooperate with the revolutionary Sun Yat-sen, on grounds that they were committed to peaceful change and were counting on the support of officials like Chang Chih-tung.[4] As late as September 22, 1898, one prominent reformer, Ch'en Pao-chen, apparently not yet apprised of the empress dowager's coup d'état of the previous day, recommended that Chang Chih-tung be sent to Peking as an adviser on the "new policies" (*hsin-cheng*).[5]

Chang Chih-tung's inspiration to the reformers was both direct and indirect. Indirectly, the K'ang-Liang party derived encouragement from Chang's example, as a progressive governor general, who had himself initiated reforms in the provinces during the years preceding 1898. Directly, and somewhat ironically, Chang's *Ch'üan-hsüeh p'ien* (Exhortation to learning), written early in 1898, proved a powerful incentive to the younger generation of reformers. Chang also provided financial aid to members of the K'ang-Liang party, recommended their services to the throne and encouraged their activities in the territory that he governed. Several of Chang's friends, protégés, or subordinates were intimately associated with the K'ang-Liang party.

When the Strength Study Society was founded by a small group of officials in Peking during 1895, it included among its charter members at least one of Chang Chih-tung's disciples, Huang Shao-chi.[6] When K'ang

3. Wen Ching, p. 215.

4. Joseph R. Levenson, *Liang Ch'i-ch'ao and the Mind of Modern China* (Cambridge, Mass., 1953), pp. 58–59, citing Feng Tzu-yu, *Chung-hua min-kuo k'ai-kuo-ch'ien ko-ming shih* (History of the revolution prior to the establishment of the Chinese Republic; Chungking, 1944), 1:38.

5. *HNP*, p. 122.

6. Huang Shao-chi (1854–1908) was the son of Huang T'i-fang, a former Pure Group associate of Chang Chih-tung. He studied Sung philosophy and the methods of the Han school of learning in his youth but later was much influenced by the pragmatism of Chang Chih-tung. After receiving his *chin-shih* degree in 1880, he spent a long period with the Hanlin Academy. During the Reform Movement of 1898 he was appointed chancellor of Peking Imperial University. He was closely associated with Chang in carrying out reforms after 1898. From 1900 to 1904 he headed the Liang-Hu Academy in Wuchang. After two years in Peking with different compilation and translating offices, he returned to Hupeh in 1907 to become provincial director of education. Hummel, I, 343–344.

Yu-wei, who resided in South China, proceeded to Peking to assume leadership of the society, he reportedly traveled with the monetary assistance from Chang Chih-tung.[7] Chang also contributed Tls. 5,000 to the society and enrolled as a member.[8] When the reformers were forced to move their headquarters from Peking to Shanghai in 1896, Chang allegedly promised them further "hearty cooperation."[9] He had already been one of the contributors of Tls. 1,500 to the *Ch'iang hsüeh-pao* (Strength Journal), published by the Shanghai branch of the society.[10] In Shanghai during August 1896, Wang K'ang-nien, a former subordinate of Chang Chih-tung, and Liang Ch'i-ch'ao reorganized the *Ch'iang hsüeh-pao* as the *Shih-wu pao,* and the new journal also received "heavy financial aid" from Chang Chih-tung.[11] Chang is said to have submitted a memorial in behalf of the paper, and he ordered all Hupeh departmental and district officials to buy and read it.[12]

In the fall of 1897, after declining an offer of direct employment by Chang Chih-tung,[13] Liang Ch'i-ch'ao moved from Shanghai to Changsha and left Wang K'ang-nien in sole charge of the *Shih-wu pao.* Hunan, one of the two provinces under Chang Chih-tung's jurisdiction, had by that time become the chief provincial center of agitation for reform. In addition to Liang Ch'i-ch'ao, leaders of the movement there included the Hunan governor, Ch'en Pao-chen, and his son, Ch'en San-li; the judicial commissioner, Huang Tsun-hsien; the education director, Chiang Piao (succeeded by Hsü Jen-chu); and the gentry members T'an Ssu-t'ung and Hsiung Hsi-ling.[14] Chang Chih-tung maintained close contact with

7. Wen Ching, p. 42. Chang Chih-tung and K'ang Yu-wei had met in Canton as early as 1886. When he served as the Liangkwang governor general, Chang invited K'ang to take part in founding a book translation bureau and in teaching at the San-hu Academy in Nan-hai. Neither plan materialized. Lo Jung-pang, *K'ang Yu-wei: A Biography and a Symposium* (Tuscon, Ariz., 1967), p. 43.

8. Lo Jung-pang, p. 72; Levenson, *Liang Ch'i-ch'ao,* p. 20, citing the *North China Herald,* Nov. 22, 1895, p. 851.

9. Wen Ching, p. 43. Chang himself is listed as a member in *JWCK,* pp. 248, 340.

10. Roswell S. Britton, *The Chinese Periodical Press, 1800–1912* (Shanghai, 1933), p. 91; Hu Ssu-ching, *Wu-hsü lü-shuang lu,* in *Wu-hsü pien-fa,* 1:372.

11. Levenson, *Liang Ch'i-ch'ao,* p. 24. Wang was the general manager and Liang the chief editor. Before 1896 Wang had served as a tutor in Chang Chih-tung's household. He was also an editor at the Self-Strengthening School and a teacher at the Liang-Hu Academy. *JWCK,* pp. 90, 355.

12. Levenson, *Liang Ch'i-ch'ao,* p. 24, attributes the statement about Chang's memorial to Liang Ch'i-ch'ao, "San-shih tzu-shu" (Autobiography at the age of thirty), *Yin-ping-shih wen-chi* (Writings of the Ice-drinker's studio), 44:25. The memorial does not appear in Chang's complete works. On the order to local officials, see Hu Ssu-ching in *Wu-hsü pien-fa,* 1:366. Chang ordered 288 copies for provincial offices, academies, and schools. *JWCK,* p. 248.

13. Teng and Fairbank, *China's Response to the West,* p. 154.

14. Liang Ch'i-ch'ao, *Wu-hsü pien chi* (Record of the 1898 reforms), *Wu-hsü pien-fa,* 1:270.

Ch'en Pao-chen and consulted him frequently on reform projects in 1898.[15] Chang also was on intimate terms with Huang Tsun-hsien. In 1894 Chang had secured Huang's transfer from the post of Chinese consul general in Singapore to Wuchang, where Huang settled a number of "church cases" (*chiao-an*) for Chang before being assigned to Hunan.[16] Chang's connection with T'an Ssu-t'ung was through T'an's father, T'an Chi-hsün, who served in Wuchang from 1890 to 1898 as the governor of Hupeh.[17] When these reformers in Hunan established the Southern Study Society and the *Hsiang hsüeh-pao* under the direction of T'an Ssu-t'ung, and the Current Affairs School (Shih-wu hsüeh-t'ang) with Liang Ch'i-ch'ao as chief instructor, Chang Chih-tung ordered the Hupeh Reconstruction Bureau to provide a subsidy for the newspaper. Furthermore, he directed that the paper be circulated to all officials and academies in Hupeh.[18]

The center of the reform movement shifted from Hunan back to Peking in June 1898. Ushering in the Hundred Days' Reform on June 11, the emperor issued a sweeping decree recognizing the need for general reforms.[19] Also on June 11 the Hanlin reader Hsü Chih-ching recommended that K'ang Yu-wei, Liang Ch'i-ch'ao, T'an Ssu-t'ung, Huang Tsun-hsien, and others be summoned as reform advisers to the emperor.[20] On June 13 an edict ordered K'ang Yu-wei and Chang Yüan-chi to an imperial audience, directed that Huang Tsun-hsien and T'an Ssu-t'ung be sent to Peking, and told the Tsungli Yamen to examine Liang Ch'i-ch'ao with a view to his employment.[21] Chang Chih-tung relayed the imperial orders to T'an Ssu-t'ung, who was in Wuchang at the time, and to Huang Tsun-hsien, who was ill in Hunan.[22]

15. See correspondence between Chang Chih-tung and Ch'en Pao-chen in *CC*, esp. telegrams in chüan 154–156.

16. Huang Tsun-hsien (1848–1905) had served as counselor of the Chinese legations in Tokyo and London and as consul general in San Francisco and Singapore before 1894. During the Hundred Days' Reform he was appointed minister to Japan, but retired from public life before the empress dowager's coup d'état. Hummel, I, 350–351. While serving as judicial commissioner of Hunan, Huang established a modern police bureau (*pao-wei chü*), which Chang was ordered by the empress dowager to abolish when she resumed control of the government. However, Chang circumvented the order by reorganizing the *pao-wei chü* as a *pao-chia chü*. See *CC*, 49:22b–24, 156:33–35b.

17. T'an Chi-hsün lost his position as governor of Hupeh during the Hundred Days, when on August 30 an imperial edict abolished the post. Although T'an was a conservative, cautious official who did not understand the vagaries of his son, T'an Ssu-t'ung, he too was punished during the suppression of the 1898 movement, being expelled from the bureaucracy on October 2. *CSL:KH*, 424:6b–8, 427:11b; *HNP*, pp. 107, 122; Hummel, II, 702.

18. *CC*, 155:21–21b; *JWCK*, p. 249.

19. *CSL:KH*, 418:15–15b.

20. Hummel, II, 704. Hsü Chih-ching was the father of Hsü Jen-chu, who served as Hunan director of education in 1898.

21. *CSL:KH*, 418:17–17b.

22. *HNP*, p. 119.

Chang himself recommended reformers to the throne during the Hundred Days. When the emperor ordered high provincial officials to propose "upright men accomplished in scholarship and conversant with current affairs," Chang memorialized suggesting the names of Huang Tsun-hsien, Ch'en Pao-ch'en, Fu Yün-lung, Ch'ien Hsün, and Cheng Hsiao-hsü.[23] The emperor, furthermore, called upon provincial officials to recommend candidates for a "special examination in public administration" (*ching-chi t'e-k'o*). Prominent reformers on a list said to have been submitted by Chang Chih-tung were Liang Ch'i-ch'ao, Huang Shao-chi, and Yang Jui.[24]

Yang Jui was especially close to Chang Chih-tung.[25] Born in Szechwan in 1857, Yang had been selected for training and virtually adopted by Chang when the latter served as the Szechwan director of education. Yang was a member of Chang's secretariat for more than ten years. A *chü-jen* of 1885, he received assignment in 1889 as a secretary of the Grand Secretariat in Peking. His lodging and expenses were reportedly paid by Chang. Although Chang Chih-tung's own son was in Peking at the same time, Chang depended upon Yang to keep him informed of affairs in the capital. As the reform movement developed, Yang joined the Strength Study Society and established the Szechwan Study Society (Shu-hsüeh hui) in his native province.

---

23. For Chang's memorial, see *CC*, 48:20b–22b. See also *Wu-hsü pien-fa*, 1:396. Ch'en Pao-ch'en had been one of the leaders of the Pure Group. Ch'ien Hsün, a prefect in Hupeh when recommended by Chang, was a native of Chekiang. During later years of the Ch'ing dynasty, he served as counselor of the Chinese legation in Japan, supervisor of Chinese students in Japan, and minister to Italy. He died in 1922. He was the father of Ch'ien Tao-sun, who served as president of Peking University under the Japanese puppet regime of the Sino-Japanese War (1937–1945). *Chūgoku bunka-kai jimbutsu sōkan*, p. 733. In 1897 Cheng Hsiao-hsü (1860–1938), a native of Fukien and a *chü-jen*, became judicial commissioner of Anhwei and then was transferred to a similar position in Kwangtung. He soon resigned to devote himself to publicizing modernization and constitutional thought. He later served as Hunan provincial treasurer and became a director of the Commercial Press after the Chinese Republic was founded. In March 1933 he was appointed premier of Manchukuo by the Japanese. *Chūgoku bunka-kai jimbutsu sōkan*, p. 713.

24. According to Liang Ch'i-ch'ao, high officials procrastinated after the emperor's first call for recommendations, hoping secretly to obstruct the plan for a special examination. Hsü Chih-ching and Sung Po-lu asked the emperor to issue an edict urging haste, which he did on July 13, 1898. *CSL:KH*, 420:12–12b. Chang Chih-tung and Li Tuan-fen thereupon recommended about ten men, and other recommendations followed rapidly. *Wu-hsü pien-fa*, 2:36–37. Although it has been stated that at the beginning of 1898 Chang recommended some thirty "progressives," including Liang Ch'i-ch'ao and Yang Jui, documentation is lacking. Bland and Backhouse, pp. 220, 505. For lists of persons recommended by Chang, see *Wu-hsü pien-fa*, 1:391–392, 395–396.

25. For Yang Jui, see *Wu-hsü pien-fa*, 4:54–68; *Ch'ing-shih kao*, 470:404b; *Ch'ing-shih*, 7:5054; *JWCK*, pp. 49–50.

On September 5, on the immediate recommendation of Ch'en Pao-chen, Yang Jui was appointed one of four special secretaries to the Grand Council, who were placed in strategic positions for controlling documents that reached the emperor.[26] On September 28 he was executed by order of the empress dowager and became one of the Six Martyrs of the reform movement.[27] Another of the martyrs, Yang Shen-hsiu, a censor who had been an indefatigable memorialist during the Hundred Days, also was an early associate of Chang Chih-tung. While serving as governor of Shansi, Chang had appointed Yang to the faculty of the Ling-te Academy, the school that Chang had founded to teach classical and historical interpretation to the gentry of the province.[28]

Such examples illustrate ways in which Chang Chih-tung abetted the Reform Movement of 1898 during its initial stage and show the closeness of his relationship with several of the reformers. During the Hundred Days, Chang did not resort to outright obstructionism when decree after decree was passed down by the emperor. Hsü Ying-k'uei, president of the Board of Rites, Liu K'un-i, the governor general of Liangkiang, T'an Chung-lin, the governor general of Liangkwang, and Jung-lu, the governor general of Chihli, all received imperial rebukes for their efforts to sabotage the reform movement. Hsü Ying-k'uei was relieved of his position and T'an Chung-lin's dismissal seemed imminent by mid-September 1898.[29] However, no censure was directed toward Chang Chih-tung in Hukwang, and his opposition to the reform movement did not become militant until the Hundred Days were ended.

Chang acquiesced in the empress dowager's resumption of the regency on September 21. On September 22 the Shanghai Telegraph Bureau relayed an edict to Chang: "The Empress Dowager from behind the screen is listening to reports on government. She sternly orders the arrest of K'ang Yu-wei." On September 25 Chang was informed by telegram of the arrest of the six reform leaders who subsequently were executed. On October 7 the empress dowager ordered Chang to dissolve the Southern Study Society and destroy its books and documents. Chang consulted with Ch'en Pao-chen and on October 10 notified the Tsungli Yamen that

---

26. *CSL:KH*, 424:20b. The other secretaries were T'an Ssu-t'ung; Lin Hsü, a former student of K'ang Yu-wei and chairman of the Fukien Reform Society; and Liu Kuang-ti, a former secretary of the Board of Punishments for over ten years. Liu also "had connections" with Chang Chih-tung, *JWCK*, p. 258.
27. *CSL:KH*, 427:4b. In addition to Yang, the Six Martyrs were T'an Ssu-t'ung, Lin Hsü, Liu Kuang-ti, Yang Shen-hsiu, and K'ang Kuang-jen.
28. For Yang Shen-hsiu, see *Wu-hsü pien-fa*, 4:58–61.
29. *CSL:KH*, 419:2b; 424:4–4b, 15; 425:3b, 19b–20b.

Tzu-hsi's directive had been carried out. Next, taking steps of his own against the K'ang-Liang party, Chang protested to Liu K'un-i over a letter from K'ang Yu-wei printed in the foreign press of Shanghai. Chang suggested that pressure be applied to that press and to foreign consuls in Shanghai to deny publicity to the exiled reformers. Chang also protested to the Japanese consul in Hankow against the political asylum that the "rebels" had found in Japan.[30] Chang's efforts to eradicate "rebellious" influences of the K'ang-Liang party in Hupeh continued after 1898 and reached a climax on August 7, 1900, when Chang discovered a plot for an uprising in Wuchang to be led by T'ang Ts'ai-ch'ang. T'ang was formerly a student of the Liang-Hu Academy, a close friend of T'an Ssu-t'ung, and one of the leaders of the Hunan reform movement in 1898. Chang executed him and nineteen of his associates.[31]

The Uneasy Alliance

Survivors of the K'ang-Liang party were outraged by Chang Chih-tung's actions after the Hundred Days were over. They denounced him as an opportunist, a traitor to the sovereign, and a murderer.[32] Certainly Chang's support of the empress dowager was hard to reconcile with the Confucian ideal of ministerial loyalty to the emperor. It also contrasted with the reaction of Liu K'un-i, who pleaded on behalf of the confined Kuang-hsü emperor.[33] But the charge that Chang clamored for the

30. *CC*, 80:7b–8, 13b–15; 156:29b–30, 33b–35b; 157:1–2.
31. For Chang's side of this story, see his memorial "on capturing and executing a leader of the Independence Society and seeking out, arresting, and dispersing other bandits," *CC*, 51:9b–17b; his memorial "on proclaiming the K'ang Yu-wei party to be treasonous and arresting a leader of the Independence Society," *CC*, 51:24–26; and his letter on the T'ang Ts'ai-ch'ang plot to Ch'ien Hsün in Tokyo, *CC*, 166:9–10. A useful study of the abortive uprising is E. Joan Smythe, "The Tzu-li Hui: Some Chinese and Their Rebellion," *Papers on China*, 12 (1958), 51–68 (East Asian Research Center, Harvard University). See also sketches of T'ang Ts'ai-chang in *Wu-hsü pien-fa*, 4:89–91, and *JWCK*, p. 189.
32. For one of the strongest denunciations of Chang, see the letter to him by K'ang Yu-wei, *Wu-hsü pien-fa*, 2:522–529. An English-language account reflecting the views of K'ang and Liang is Wen Ching, *The Chinese Crisis from Within*. Calling Chang a "weathercock mandarin" (p. 45), Wen Ching wrote (p. 22): "Recent events have confirmed the opinion that Chang Chih-tung is not a man to be depended upon to act straightforwardly when placed between conflicting interests." He observed (pp. 212–213): "He is not to be blamed, perhaps, for his position is exceedingly difficult. It is only by chicanery, lying, hypocrisy, and subterfuges that any man can hold office in China. Let us do the old man the justice to admit that he, perhaps, loves his work better than his reputation, and like Brutus, he kills his friends not because he loves them less, but because he loves his country more . . . At any rate, he is quite sixty-five years old, and cannot be expected to be the same strong individual he was when a young man. It is perhaps only natural that he seeks to avoid difficulties, and to throw in his lot with the strongest party at Court."
33. Wen Ching, pp. 216–217; Bland and Backhouse, p. 220.

execution of the Six Martyrs is hard to substantiate.[34] Especially in the case of Yang Jui is there conflicting evidence. K'ang Yu-wei claimed that Chang demanded the execution of Yang Jui.[35] However, the collected works of Chang include a telegram interceding on behalf of Yang Jui and pleading for his freedom on the grounds that he was not truly sympathetic with the aims of K'ang Yu-wei. Other sources, casting further doubt on the allegation of K'ang, likewise maintain that Chang sought Yang Jui's release.[36]

On the charge of opportunism against Chang, it can be demonstrated that the break with the reformers was not altogether a matter of expediency. Behind the break lay honest differences of philosophy and variant diagnoses of China's ills and how to remedy them. Notably, Chang differed with K'ang Yu-wei on interpretation of the classics and opposed K'ang's reform group in its plans for instituting a constitutional monarchy. Chang felt that K'ang was distorting China's past in an effort to justify changes that would surrender too much to Western culture. The differences between Chang Chih-tung and K'ang's group became increasingly obvious between 1895 and 1898. As friction developed in the relationship of Chang and the younger reformers, an astute reading of the facts might have shown a break impending long before the end of the Hundred Days. However, the K'ang-Liang party either failed to perceive, underestimated, or chose to ignore the strength of Chang's devotion to ideals more conservative than those to which they themselves adhered.

34. After the empress dowager's coup d'état, "the first thing he [Chang] did was to telegraph Peking that these men should be beheaded." Wen Ching, (p. 215). Meribeth Cameron also stated, "Chang telegraphed the Empress urging the punishment of the reformers, despite the fact that he had associated personally with many of them." Hummel, I, 30.

35. See letter of K'ang to Chang, cited above.

36. On September 26 Chang telegraphed the Hupeh provincial judge in Peking: "Yang Jui (Shu-ch'iao) is upright and careful. He has always disliked K'ang's theories, and he decidedly does not belong to the K'ang party. In ordinary discussions he has been extremely critical of K'ang's falsehoods, not one of which has satisfied him. I am fully aware of this, you are fully aware of this, and every reputable man and well-known scholar in the empire is fully aware of this. His summons to court to receive the imperial favor was upon the recommendation of Governor Ch'en Yu-ming (Pao-chen) and had nothing to do with K'ang. Moreover he (Yang) was in the service of the Grand Council only a little more than ten days and was not consulted about important affairs. His arrest truly represents the implication of an innocent (man). I pray that you will quickly beseech Generals K'uei and Shou to devise means to set him free, so that distinction can be made between the good and the disloyal. Good people of the empire will be grateful to the two officials for their great kindness." CC, 156:31–31b. Chang also telegraphed Jung-lu to intercede for Yang Jui, but Jung-lu, having already left Tientsin for the capital, did not receive the message. Wu-hsü pien-fa, 4:66. Hu Ssu-ching stated that when Chang heard of Yang's execution, he telegraphed the Grand Secretary Hsü T'ung, blaming him for not saving Yang and decrying the lack of action, Wu-hsü pien-fa, 4:65. Chang also reportedly made representations on behalf of Yang through Sheng Hsüan-huai. JWCK, pp. 49–50.

Several instances of disagreement were evident in Chang's dealings with reform societies and the reform press.

K'ang Yu-wei recounted in his chronological autobiography that he had arrived in Nanking on November 1, 1895, and stayed there twenty days to consult Chang Chih-tung on establishing a branch of the Strength Study Society. K'ang wrote of Chang: "He appeared to be very much interested. We met every day and each time our conversation lasted until late at night. He would not, however, subscribe to the view Confucius was an advocate of reform. He tried to persuade me to refrain from preaching this view; if I did he would give me support." K'ang refused to refrain and went on to Shanghai to have regulations for a branch society printed. Chang telegraphed him, asking him not to form the society. When K'ang refused, he received no further financial support from Chang. He accused Chang of breaking a promise to help because of "our differences in scholarly matters."[37]

Chang also disagreed with K'ang Yu-wei and Liang ch'i-ch'ao over policies of the *Ch'iang hsüeh-pao* and *Shih-wu pao* in 1896 and 1897. When the *Ch'iang hsüeh-pao* first appeared on January 12, 1896, it bore a double dating: first, "K'ung-tzu chiang-sheng" (the number of years since the birth of Confucius), and then, "Ta-Ch'ing Kuang-hsü" (the reign year).[38] The dating of Chinese history from the birth of Confucius offended Chang Chih-tung as a needless imitation of the Western system commemorating the birth of Christ and as one part of K'ang's scheme for converting Confucianism into a well-defined religion. It is recorded that Chang was displeased and upbraided K'ang Yu-wei.[39]

When the *Shih-wu pao* was begun, Chang, as a financial contributor, felt free to interfere with the editorial policy of the paper, managed by Wang K'ang-nien and edited by Liang Ch'i-ch'ao. Chang was especially offended by what he considered the paper's excessive emphasis on the concept of *min-ch'üan*, the "people's rights." An article written by Wang K'ang-nien on this subject in 1896 drew a sharp protest from Chang. Liang Ch'i-ch'ao also had trouble with Chang—on one occasion over an article criticizing foreign instructors of the Self-Strengthening Army. Another article by Liang, containing "false" ideas, caused Chang to ban an issue of the *Shih-wu pao* in Hunan and Hupeh. Liang became increasingly restless under Chang's pressure and came to consider his status vis-à-vis Chang as "that of laborer in relation to capitalist."[40]

37. Lo Jung-pang, p. 74.
38. Britton, p. 151; Levenson, *Liang Ch'i-ch'ao,* p. 22.
39. *Wu-hsü pien-fa,* 1:372.
40. Levenson, *Liang Ch'i-ch'ao,* 24–25; *JWCK,* pp. 20–21, 90–92, 249.

Chang also attempted to control the policies of the *Hsiang hsüeh-pao*, edited by T'an Ssu-t'ung in Hunan. In the seventh lunar month of 1897 (July 29–August 27), Chang strenuously objected to an article published in the paper on Confucius as a reformer. The article apparently reflected K'ang Yu-wei's thoughts on this subject, on Confucius as the author of the Six Classics, and on the superiority of the *Kung-yang chuan* (Kung-yang Commentary) to other commentaries on the *Ch'un-Ch'iu* (Spring and Autumn Annals). Chang denounced the article as "new talk by the present-day *Kung-yang* school." The talk, he charged, was spread by Liao P'ing of Szechwan and K'ang Yu-wei of Kwangtung and was most strange and startling for people to hear. Ideas on Confucius reforming the state of Lu, Chang believed, were first introduced in classical glosses written by Han dynasty scholars. The *Tso-chuan* (Commentary of Tso) had nothing to report on the subject. And to describe Confucius as the author of the Six Classics was to deny the actuality of governments by Yao and Shun and the houses of Hsia, Shang, and Chou. To accept the classics as an invention by Confucius intended to support his own political philosophy was to accept falsehood and to blaspheme the Two Emperors, the Three Kings, and the Holy Sage.[41]

Despite this protest, Chang's troubles with the *Hsiang hsüeh-pao* did not cease. When Hsü Jen-chu passed through Wuchang en route to Changsha to relieve Chiang Piao as the Hunan director of education, Chang Chih-tung discussed the *Hsiang hsüeh-pao* with Hsü and elicited a promise from him to restrain the paper after arriving at his post. However, later issues still failed to satisfy Chang. His dissatisfaction turned to anger during the intercalary third month of 1898 (April 21–May 19) when the paper printed a "false" essay by I Nai, one of the Hunan reformers. Chang declared the essay could stir up so much trouble that "evil men and heterodox scholars" might raise a cry for rebellion. Calling upon Hunan officials to be loyal to the empire and to pacify the people, he ordered Huang Tsun-hsien to rectify the *Hsiang hsüeh-pao*.[42] At the same time, Chang rebuked Hsü Jen-chu for failing to suppress articles in the paper that toadied to the West, advocated "people's rights," or compared international law with the *Ch'un-ch'iu*. Chang informed

41. Chang's telegram with these views is not included in his complete works but appears in *HNP*, p. 116. Chang had long been an opponent of the *Kung-yang* commentary. *Pao-ping-t'ang ti-tzu chi, CC*, 228:27b. For the views of K'ang Yu-wei, T'an Ssu-t'ung, and Liao P'ing, see Fung Yu-lan, *A History of Chinese Philosophy*, II (Princeton, 1953), 673–721. When Chang had been director of education in Szechwan, he selected Liao P'ing to study at the Tsun-ching Academy. *JWCK*, p. 77.

42. *CC*, 155:20–20b. For Governor Ch'en's reply, see *CC*, 155:20b.

Hsü that he was cutting off the Hupeh subsidy for the *Hsiang hsüeh-pao* and told him that no further copies need be mailed to Hupeh.[43]

About the same time that Chang Chih-tung withdrew his support from the *Hsiang hsüeh-pao*, he endorsed a new journal that was to reflect more faithfully his own ideas. Edited by Liang Ting-fen, the president of the Liang-Hu Academy, this newspaper was entitled the *Cheng hsüeh-pao*, a title heavy with Confucian connotations, since *cheng* stood for "right, truth, orthodoxy, and rectification."[44] Chang Chih-tung himself wrote a preface for the *Cheng hsüeh-pao*, in which he related *cheng* (the right) to *chung* (the mean) in a plea for a middle course between reaction and radicalism.[45] Both stubborn adherence to the old and mistaken delight in the new were neither *cheng* nor *chung*. Conservatives who refused to recognize change were deceiving themselves, whereas radicals who forgot the Chinese root were inviting misfortune. Among those whom the new journal hoped to *cheng*, or put on the right path, were men who sought to abolish the classics, promoted "people's rights," maintained that prince, minister, father, and son were equal (*p'ing-teng*), held that all have the right of self-rule (*tzu-chu chih ch'üan*), claimed that Confucius was a religious pope (*chiao-wang*), or refused to use the proper reign years. The preface to the *Cheng hsüeh-pao* was no gentle criticism of the political philosophy of K'ang Yu-wei and Liang Ch'i-ch'ao.

During the actual Hundred Days' Reform, Chang sided against K'ang Yu-wei in a dispute over the ownership of the *Shih-wu pao*. On July 17 the censor Sung Po-lu suggested that the Shanghai newspaper be transformed into an official organ, and the emperor ordered Sun Chia-nai to consider the memorial. Sun recommended in favor of the proposal, and on July 26 the emperor ordered that K'ang Yu-wei become the director

43. *CC*, 155:21–21b. The Hupeh subsidy reportedly began with the tenth issue and stopped with the thirty-third issue after the articles became "too wild." *HNP*, p. 115.

44. Chang left Wuchang on May 7, 1898, en route to Peking for an audience with the emperor. At Shanghai, he was directed to return to Wuchang to settle an incident involving the burning of foreign residences at Sha-shih. While absent from the Hupeh capital, Chang telegraphed to Liang Ting-fen to take charge of the newspaper, in accordance with earlier plans, and to approve all articles selected for publication. *CC*, 47:24b–25, 48:1–2, 155:22b. Evidently Liang had visited Hunan before this date. Hu Ssu-ching related that when Liang Ch'i-ch'ao lectured at the Current Affairs School in Changsha, Liang Ting-fen was among those who debated with him. *Wu-hsü pien-fa*, 1:373.

45. The preface appears in *CC*, 213:11b–15b, without a date. *HNP*, p. 113, dates it in the fifth lunar month of 1898 (June 19–July 18). In the preface, Chang remarked that the paper was not an "official" organ. Appended to the preface is a list of names, including Liang Ting-fen, Wu Chao-tai, Shen Tseng-chih, Chou Shu-mo, Yao Chin-ch'i, Ts'ao Yüan-pi, Wang Jen-chün, Hu Yüan-i, Ch'en Yen, Ch'en Ch'ing-nien, Chi Chü-wei, and Chu K'o-jou, who presumably were sponsors, editors, or contributors. How long the paper lasted, or how long Liang Ting-fen continued as editor, is problematical.

of a state-owned *Shih-wu pao*. Wang K'ang-nien, who had been publishing the paper, resented this attempted expropriation and refused to turn the property over to the state. Instead, he began issuing a new paper under the title *Ch'ang-yen pao* (Straight Talk News), with Liang Ting-fen as his editor. K'ang Yu-wei thereupon telegraphed Chang Chih-tung and Liu K'un-i asking that they prevent publication of the *Ch'ang-yen pao*. The emperor took cognizance of the dispute and on August 22 ordered Huang Tsun-hsien to proceed to Shanghai to investigate Wang K'ang-nien's claim to have founded the *Shih-wu pao*. At this point Chang Chih-tung telegraphed Sun Chia-nai protesting K'ang Yu-wei's demand that the *Ch'ang-yen pao* be proscribed. Chang took the position that, because Wang K'ang-nien had raised private funds and had not used official funds in launching the *Shih-wu pao,* the paper was like any other commercial enterprise, and Wang should therefore have the right to continue it under another name if he wished. Chang wrote: "K'ang will manage an official paper, and Wang will manage a private paper; naturally they should have separate names." Since state funds were available to finance the *Shih-wu pao* under the new management, there was no reason to seize the private property of Wang K'ang-nien. Sun Chia-nai replied that he agreed with Chang's views, which were just and reasonable, and did not agree with K'ang Yu-wei's demand that the *Ch'ang-yen pao* be discontinued. In the end, Wang K'ang-nien continued to publish his paper, while K'ang Yu-wei, reluctant to leave the center of power, delayed his departure from Peking to assume management of the *Shih-wu pao*. On September 17 the emperor handed down an edict ordering K'ang to stop procrastinating and proceed at once to Shanghai to take up his duties as director of the *Shih-wu pao*.[46] Four days later the Hundred Days ended.

While these examples from the history of the reform press illustrate several points at which Chang Chih-tung's views diverged from those of the K'ang-Liang party, the major statement of Chang's position was contained in his *Ch'üan-hsüeh p'ien*, a series of eloquent essays on reform.[47] Chang Chih-tung completed the *Ch'üan-hsüeh p'ien* in the third

---

46. *CSL-KH,* 420:17b, 421:7b–8, 423:9, 426:2b; Britton, pp. 103–107; Levenson, *Liang Ch'i-ch'ao,* p. 29; *CC,* 126:22b–23b. The *Ch'ang-yen pao* first appeared on August 17, 1898. It ceased publication after ten issues. *JWCK,* pp. 90–91.

47. For text, see *CC,* 202; 1–4 (Preface), 202:1–40 (*Nei-p'ien*), 203:1–53 (*Wai-p'ien*). This version includes several lines on marriage customs that by an imperial decree of August 22, 1898, were ordered deleted from an edition for official distribution. *CSL:KH,* 423:7b–8. A partial and inferior translation, by Samuel I. Woodbridge, is *China's Only Hope* (New York, 1900). A better translation is by Jerome Tobar, *K'iuen-hio p'ien: exhortations à l'étude,* in *Variétés sinologiques* no. 26 (Chang-hai, 1909). Translated excerpts appear in Teng and Fairbank, *China's Response to the West,* pp. 166–174.

lunar month of 1898 (March 22–April 20), about two months before the beginning of the Hundred Days' Reform.[48] Wood blocks were cut, the work was printed, and the book soon became a "best-seller." In the fifth lunar month of 1898 (June 19–July 18), a new edition, revised by Chang, was brought out in Wuhu by Yüan Ch'ang, then serving as intendant of the South Anhwei Circuit. This edition became the "authorized version" (*ting-pen*).[49] During the Hundred Days' Reform, Huang Shao-chi presented the book to the emperor, who read it and was pleased.[50] On July 25 an imperial edict was handed down ordering the Grand Council to distribute forty copies to provincial governors general, governors, and directors of education.[51] A later decree ordered the Tsung-li Yamen to print three hundred copies. The only other work similarly honored by the emperor during the Hundred Days was the *Chiao-pin-lu k'ang-i* (Protests from the study of Chiao-pin) by Feng Kuei-fen (1809–1874).[52] After the imperial recommendation of the *Ch'üan-hsüeh p'ien*, scholars in the capital eagerly sought the work, and those who could not obtain it passed manuscript copies from hand to hand. In Shanghai, Western lithographic methods were used to reproduce the book, and "in less than ten days there were three different editions."[53] According to one source, a million copies of the *Ch'üan-hsüeh p'ien* were sold.[54]

It has been claimed that the 1898 reformers immediately seized on the *Ch'üan-hsüeh p'ien* "as a sort of party platform."[55] However, if that was the case, they perceived but half of Chang Chih-tung's purpose in

48. Chang's authorship is questioned by Cyrus Peake, p. 24: "In 1898 Chang Chih-tung collected a number of the better essays by students at modern schools already established in Shanghai, and published them in his own name under the title of *An Exhortation to Learning*." In a footnote (p. 219), Peake states: "Dr. John C. Ferguson, who was associated with Chang's yamen in those years, confirms my statement that Chang was the editor and not the author of these essays." The chronological biography by Hsü T'ung-hsin, which gives the completion date of the work, depicts Chang as the actual author. According to the *HNP*, p. 113, Chang wrote one section of the book a day, generally working in the evening and finishing at dawn. He revised the following day, and rewrote some parts as many as six or seven times. While Chang could have referred to student papers in this process, and did receive assistance from Wang Luan-hsing and others, the work shows a distinctive style that appears to be Chang's own, with favorite phrases, ideas, and illustrations common to his other writings.

49. *HNP*, p. 113.

50. *Wu-hsü pien-fa*, 1:361.

51. *CSL:KH*, 421:6. The edict also precedes the text of the *Ch'üan-hsüeh p'ien* in *CC*, 202.

52. For the imperial edict on Feng's work, see *CSL:KH*, 420:17–17b. On Feng and his essays, see Teng and Fairbank, *China's Response to the West*, pp. 50–55; Hummel, I, 241–243.

53. *Wu-hsü pien-fa*, 1:361.

54. Chang Chih-tang, *China's Only Hope*, Translator's Note, p. 6.

55. Hummel, I, 30.

writing the book. The *Ch'üan-hsüeh p'ien*, a definition of the proper limits of reform as conceived by the author, was Chang's foremost plea for the mean and his most eloquent appeal for a balance of the Chinese *t'i* and the Western *yung*. The famous slogan commonly attributed to Chang—*Chung-hsüeh wei t'i, hsi-hsüeh wei yung* (Chinese learning for the foundation, Western learning for practical use)—does not appear with this exact wording in Chang's work.[56] But the basic *t'i-yung* dualism or dichotomy was utilized, and a harmony of Sino-Western learning and institutions, if not a thoroughgoing synthesis, was prescribed by Chang for the reform movement.

In the preface to the *Ch'üan-hsüeh p'ien*, Chang depicted China's intelligentsia as drawn up into two hostile camps. On one hand, there were the advocates of old learning (*chiu-hsüeh*), defending the *tao* and "refusing to swallow food because of a fear of choking." On the other hand, there were the advocates of new learning (*hsin-hsüeh*), proposing various schemes for national salvation but acting "like sheep lost because of many forks in the road."[57] The defenders of the old did not understand the need for broad, general knowledge (*t'ung*).[58] The proponents of the new did not understand their Chinese root (*pen*). With the forces thus opposed, Chang stated, the more the advocates of the old disparaged the new, the more the advocates of the new detested the old. There should be a compromise. If those who were devoid of *t'ung* would not oppose reforms, those who were ignorant of *pen* would develop a more generous appreciation of Confucianism. To further such a compromise, Chang had written the *Ch'üan-hsüeh p'ien* in two parts. The *nei-p'ien* ("inner essays," chiefly on the Chinese heritage and stressing moral cultivation) would draw attention to *pen* in order to rectify men's hearts (*cheng jen-hsin*). The *wai-p'ien* ("outer essays," chiefly on Western methods and stressing national power) would draw attention to *t'ung* in order to extend enlightenment (*k'ai feng-ch'i*). The *nei-p'ien* would speak of goodness (*jen*), and the *wai-p'ien* would speak of seeking wisdom (*chih*) and

56. A fact pointed out to me by Dr. P'u Yu-shu, formerly of the University of Michigan. To my knowledge, neither does the slogan appear elsewhere in Chang's works in the precise wording usually quoted.

57. *CC*, 202:1–1b (Preface).

58. The word *t'ung* can mean "to go through, to succeed, thoroughly, to understand, and to circulate." Chang frequently used the word in connection with learning and seemed to denote by it, variously, a thorough knowledge of a given subject or broad knowledge covering a number of subjects. Advocates of the old are here being criticized for restricting their learning to the classics and not being *t'ung* or well-versed in Western learning. In his *Ch'üan-hsüeh p'ien* essay on thorough understanding (*Hui-t'ung*), *CC*, 203:45–48b, Chang equated the word with "love of learning, deep thought, and penetrating knowledge." The opposite of *t'ung*, he wrote, is to limit one's experience and be poorly informed.

courage (*yung*) necessary for the gaining of strength (*ch'iang*).[59] In the various essays of these two parts, Chang Chih-tung set forth the elements of Chinese tradition that should be fostered and those that should be discarded, the elements of Western culture that should be adopted and those that should be avoided. He made skillful use of quotations from the Chinese classics and histories in order to arouse the recalcitrant ultra-conservatives of his time to a measure of reform. He also interpreted Western history in an effort to convince naïve idealists that they were misjudging Western liberality, and to deter them from too rapid or radical change.

The *nei-p'ien* rather than the *wai-p'ien* was designed especially for the reading of such men as K'ang Yu-wei and Liang Ch'i-ch'ao. It stressed, among other topics, the need for loyalty to the emperor and the imperial form of government as already constituted and the need for respect of the classics as guides to personal and government morality. Chang took particular issue with the ideas of K'ang and Liang in the *nei-p'ien* essays entitled "Understanding the Obligations" (*Ming-kang*) and "Rectifying Political Rights" (*Cheng-ch'üan*). The latter essay was a strong attack upon parliamentary government.[60] In the former essay, Chang discussed the "three bonds" (*san-kang*) of Confucianism. He maintained that the prescribed bond between sovereign and minister was incompatible with the theory of "people's rights"; the bond between father and son was incompatible with theories of equal individual responsibilities and rights, or of the unimportance of sacrificial ceremonies; and the bond between husband and wife was incompatible with ideas of equality of the sexes. He argued that, in truth, the West also recognized the "three bonds" and did not live faithfully according to the contrary theories attributed to it.[61] In short, Chang Chih-tung specifically recorded his major ideological differences with K'ang Yu-wei and Liang Ch'i-ch'ao not only before the coup d'état of the empress dowager in September 1898, but even before the onset of the Hundred Days' Reform in June 1898.

Education in the Ch'üan-hsüeh p'ien

In the years following 1898, many of Chang Chih-tung's ideas and actions on educational reform represented an elaboration of themes formulated in the *Ch'üan-hsüeh p'ien*. Whereas Chang's book was an

59. *CC*, 202:2, 3b (Preface).
60. *CC*, 202:23–26b. For a partial translation of this essay, see Teng and Fairbank, *China's Response to the West*, pp. 166–169.
61. *CC*, 202:13–15.

indictment of both those who demanded too little and those who demanded too much in reform, its primary purpose was exhortation to learning. It was Chang's vehicle for conveying his ideas on education. Even the essays on such topics as railroad building or tolerance of Western missionary activity represented appeals for the study of new methods and the learning of new viewpoints. A majority of the essays was more closely and obviously connected with problems of education. Fourteen of the twenty-four essays in the *Ch'üan-hsüeh p'ien* can be classified as directly concerned with the principles, methods, and institutions of education. A summary of the dominant ideas from the most pertinent essays, partly from the *nei-p'ien* but chiefly from the *wai-p'ien*, will reveal Chang's position on the aims of education, his interpretation of Chinese educational history, his general formula for change of existing conditions, his recommendations on Western educational practices that should be accepted, and his proposals for revision of the old Chinese educational system.

Chang opened the *wai-p'ien* with a statement that related education to strength:

> Self-strength (*tzu-ch'iang*) is born of power; power is born of knowledge; and knowledge is born of learning. Confucius said: "Though dull, he will surely become intelligent; though weak, he will surely become strong."[62] There has never been an unintelligent man who was able to become strong. A man is not strong enough to oppose a tiger or a leopard, but by knowledge he can trap them. A man is not strong enough to resist a flood or topple a tall mountain, but by knowledge he can control one and develop the other.[63]

After declaring that "knowledge is for the purpose of saving us from destruction, and learning is for the purpose of increasing knowledge,[64] Chang added, "A country's knowledge is its power."

In the past China had been both knowledgeable and strong, Chang maintained. Chinese civilization had reached its height during the disturbed years of the late Chou dynasty and, in fact, had shown great vitality during periods of disorder. Men of talent were exceedingly abundant during the Spring and Autumn period and the Warring States period, as well as during the later period of the Three Kingdoms. However, under dynasties that provided unity and peace, Chinese civilization became

62. Translation by Legge, *Chung-yung*, 20:21.
63. *CC*, 203:1.
64. *CC*, 203:2b–3.

stagnant or declined. There were no strong neighbors to whet Chinese strength. China had contact only with isolated barbarians of the south or with tribes of the northwestern deserts, both groups being inferior to the Chinese in learning and government. Therefore, Chinese civilization turned in upon itself. China followed her old laws, which were embellished from time to time, and preserved her old learning, without exceeding its bounds. The old laws and learning were sufficient to perpetuate peace and order until "ancient advantages were eliminated, corruption multiplied, and the fine meaning of the old laws and old learning was lost." During the later dynasties, China emphasized literary accomplishments to the exclusion of practically all else in education. This literary emphasis created emptiness, and emptiness created weakness.[65]

In the meantime, as China declined, Western countries began to rise and grow strong: "They flourished late, issued forth suddenly to tests of strength, and became skilled in competition. Each strove to perfect itself in order to avoid destruction." In the interest of self-preservation, Western countries "taught and developed a polity of wealth and strength, and the skills to survey heaven and earth, to investigate things, and to benefit the people." Their fear led to determination, and determination led to strength.[66]

The fact that China had waned, while Western countries flourished, could not be attributed to negligence on the part of successive emperors, Chang argued. Throughout history the rulers of China had fought against public ignorance and had fostered learning—practical knowledge as well as literary knowledge. The Han dynasty sought out books that had been handed down by earlier generations, encouraged scholars of the classics (po-shih), selected good and worthy men, and made use of varied talents. The T'ang offered public examinations in more than fifty categories. The Sung established a number of schools and founded military academies. In the Ming dynasty, during the third year of the Hung-wu reign (1370), examinations were offered in writing, mathematics, horsemanship, archery, and law, as well as in the customary classical subjects.

The rulers of the Ch'ing dynasty had also exhibited abundant concern with enlightening the people. As examples, Chang cited early Ch'ing sponsorship of Western astronomical, calendrical, surveying, cartographical, and geographical studies. The dynasty had published modern gazetteers and encouraged agricultural studies. The Imperial Manuscript

65. *CC*, 202:16b, 203:1b.
66. *CC*, 202:16b–17, 203:1–1b.

Library had been established; the Thirteen Classics, Twenty-four Histories, and Nine Encyclopedias had been re-issued; and classical commentaries had been published. Following the restoration of internal peace during the T'ung-chih reign, language institutes had been opened to train interpreters; manufacturing bureaus had been set up to foster mechanized industry; and the Board of Admiralty had been created to promote naval development. On several occasions students had been sent to America, England, France, and Germany for training in international law, mining, navigation, military matters, and railroad engineering. The Tsungli Yamen had published books on law, natural sciences, and chemistry, while the Shanghai Arsenal had translated more than seventy Western works.[67]

These accomplishments would not have been possible without the good faith of successive rulers, Chang Chih-tung stated. The blame for China's weakness lay not with the throne but with a mass of "common scholars and vulgar officials." Too many scholars were interested only in memorizing the classics in order to pass the civil service examinations. They avoided and vilified the new learning and impeded reform with their erroneous, absurd, and narrow-minded ideas. Translated works were not widely read, and students sent abroad were not sufficiently serious about acquiring knowledge. Reform demanded hard thinking and hard work and was therefore distasteful to any officials who were lax, lazy, or dependent on favoritism. Such men were content to cover their neglect and sham with bookish talk about "following the ancients." Officials unduly esteeming the past and scholars satisfied with aping the work of earlier generations were turning their backs on the throne and refusing to learn.

At the other extreme was a minority of students who had wholly and uncritically embraced Western studies. They looked upon China's court, government, peoples, and customs with contempt. They derogated their ancestors and could not find a single praiseworthy ruler or scholar in all of Chinese history.[68]

Given this dismal set of circumstances, Chang continued, China must strive to learn. Specifically, she must learn to become strong again. The prerequisites for success were new attitudes. Initially, Chinese scholars and officials should awaken to the danger that their country faced:

---

67. *CC*, 203:3–4.
68. *CC*, 203:4–5. See also Chang's essay on reform, *CC*, 203:19–22, or the translation in Teng and Fairbank, *China's Response to the West*, pp. 170–173.

"Only if we know the threat of destruction can we know the meaning of strength."[69] Warnings of China's impending destruction by the strong powers of the world had already been given: "The first warning was in the Taiwan rebellion, the next in the Liu-ch'iu Islands, the third in Ili, the fourth in Korea, the fifth in Annam and Burma, and the sixth was served by Japan."[70] China was on the verge of being swallowed. The warnings so far received should result in "knowing fear" (*chih-chü*) and "knowing shame" (*chih-ch'ih*). China should cringe before the fear of vassalage—"the fear of being like India, the fear of being like Annam, Burma, or Korea, the fear of being like Egypt, the fear of being like Poland." She should feel mortified by her lack of strength and realize "the shame of not being like Japan, the shame of not being like Turkey, the shame of not being like Siam, the shame of not being like Cuba."[71]

Confucius had said: "To know shame is to be near to courage."[72] The realization of shame and fear should lead China to a determined effort to overcome her weakness. Resolute action would presuppose "the elimination of foolishness" (*ch'ü wang*) and "the elimination of carelessness" (*ch'ü-kou*). Chang described "vulgarity, emptiness, and pride" as the gateways to foolishness, and "dependence upon luck and laziness" as the roots of carelessness. Unless the two deceits were eliminated, the Chinese people would become "as insignificant as cows and horses."[73] Resolute action would also denote a disposition for change. "Knowing how to change" (*chih-pien*) therefore was also required to overcome weakness. However, knowing how to change should include a knowledge of the proper limits of change. Chang advocated modernizing Chinese laws and methods without displacing Confucianism as the fundamental state philosophy. In the preface to the *Ch'üan-hsüeh p'ien*, he wrote: "Those who do not change their practices cannot change their laws; those who do not change their laws cannot change their instruments."[74] In the essay entitled "Reform" (*Pien-fa*), he explained further: "In general, that which should not be changed is our human relationships and fundamental principles, not the system of laws; it is our sage's way, not instruments; it is the principle of mind, not technology." He cited

69. *CC*, 202:4 (Preface).
70. *CC*, 202:2b (Preface).
71. *CC*, 202:3 (Preface). Cuba's inclusion here was explained by Chang elsewhere in the *Ch'üan-hsüeh p'ien:* "Cuba belongs to Spain, (but) not being completely ignorant, she still strives (for freedom)."
72. Quoted in *CC*, 202:3b (Preface), from the *Chung-yung,* 20:11. Legge, *The Four Books,* translates the passage: "To possess the feeling of shame is to be near to energy."
73. *CC*, 203:3.
74. *CC*, 202:3 (Preface).

the following "evidence" from the classics to support these conclusions on change:

> When all alternatives are exhausted, one has to make a change —change and accommodation to make the most of an advantage; change and accommodation to suit the time. The method of diminution and increase [of the statutes] should be used to keep abreast of the times. That is the idea of the *Book of Changes*.
> "In instruments we do not seek old ones but new." That is the idea in the *Book of History*. "Knowledge exists among the four barbarians." That is the idea in the *Commentary on the Ch'un-ch'iu*. The Five Emperors did not follow the old music and the Three Kings did not copy the old ceremony. "The timely ceremony is the most important." That is the idea of the *Book of Rites*.
> "He cherishes his old knowledge and is continually acquiring new . . . When I walk with two persons, they may serve as my teachers; I select their good qualities and follow them." That is the idea of the *Confucian Analects*.[75]

Chang Chih-tung maintained that the manifest Chinese reluctance to accept change derived partly from a misconception of Confucianism's true nature or distortion of the idea of "knowing the root" (*chih-pen*). In his essay on "Following the Proper Order" (*Hsün-hsü*), Chang described what he took to be the real nature of Confucianism:

> Shallow and vulgar expositions, worthless and obsolete eight-legged essays, abstract and contemplative metaphysics, complex and learned studies, frivolous and extravagant poetry are not Confucian learning . . . Confucianism means broad learning and strict propriety, reviewing the old and knowing the new, being an equal of Heaven and giving full development to the creatures and things of Earth. Confucian government means honoring those to whom honor is due, and loving those to whom love is due, first enriching the people and later instructing them, having civil (administration) but being prepared militarily, and doing the right thing at the right time.[76]

Those who resisted reform also failed to distinguish adequately between literary knowledge and functional knowledge, or knowledge of practical benefit. "Increasing knowledge" (*i-chih*) demanded that scholars know about "government, punishments, troops, food, national conditions, and international relations." Farmers required more knowledge of

75. Teng and Fairbank, *China's Response to the West*, pp. 170–173.
76. *CC*, 202:27–27b. Chang's definition is compounded largely of quotations from the classics, notably the *Lun-yü* and the *Chung-yung*.

seeds, soils, tools, and fertilizers. Artisans needed knowledge of machines and manufacturing methods. The information sought by merchants should embrace new lands, new products, domestic economic requirements, and international economies. Soldiers should know more about ships, arms, fortifications, surveying, and engineering. The time had come for the Chinese literati to cease looking upon these subjects as "strange abilities and obscene skills." The time also had come for the literati to show greater appreciation of China's farmers, workers, merchants, and soldiers. If they did not develop an understanding of agricultural, industrial, commercial, and military needs, they could not call themselves educated.[77]

Furthermore, the time had come for general acceptance of the fact that Western countries were superior to China in many of these fields. When this fact had been accepted, there should be a great increase in borrowing from the West—but the borrowing should be eclectic. Selectivity, indeed, should characterize the approach to both Chinese and Western learning. To the requirements of knowing fear, knowing shame, knowing how to change, and knowing one's roots, Chang added the requirement of discrimination or "knowing the important" (*chih-yao*). In Chinese studies, for instance, research into antiquity was not as important as applying the useful. In Western studies, Western crafts were not as important as Western government.[78]

Up to the present, Chang felt that imbalance had been the chief characteristic of China's response to the West. Three different reactions were represented by those who despised Western methods, by those who knew a little about them, and by those who were immersed in Western methods. In his essay on "Understanding" (*Hui-t'ung*), Chang wrote:

> Today those who despise Western methods see that they are not explicitly stated in the Six Classics and ancient histories. They do not examine whether they [the Western methods] are right or wrong, beneficial or harmful, but reject them all. For example, they say disparagingly that foreign drill is wrong, but they are unable to use ancient methods to train troops who can win. They say disparagingly that ironclad ships are wasteful, but they are unable to use native boats as a means for coastal defense. This is self-obstruction (*tzu-sai*). Self-obstruction causes men to be stubborn, blind, haughty, and slow, and to betray themselves to great danger.
>
> Those who know a little about Western methods generally cite a classical quotation for their statements and give a forced

77. *CC*, 203:2b–3.
78. *CC*, 202:3 (Preface).

interpretation. They think: "All of this is included in the Chinese classics already."[79] For example, they only boast that square root came from the East, and they do not study mathematics. They only brag that firearms were handed down from (the time of) Yüan T'ai-tsu's [Genghis Khan's] conquest of the Western frontiers, and they do not study manufacturing of guns and cannons. This is self-deception (*tzu-ch'i*). Self-deception causes men to contend with empty words and fail to attain practicality.

Those who are immersed in Western methods—even worse—take Chinese and Western learning and make a hodgepodge of them. They think there is no difference between the Chinese and the Western. For example, they say that the *Ch'un-ch'iu* is international law, or the teachings of Confucius agree with those of Jesus. This is self-vexation (*tzu-jao*). Those guilty of self-vexation cause others to feel confused and demented and to destroy that to which they have held.[80]

According to Chang Chih-tung, it was necessary that these conflicting groups harmonize their differences tolerantly and achieve a balance of Sino-Western learning to displace the obvious imbalance. He further pointed to the irrationality of the existing deadlock:

Today the new learning and the old learning are mutually maligned. If what each has to offer is not thoroughly understood, the old learning will loathe the new learning, but meanwhile will have no alternative to using it. The new learning will make light of the old learning, but meanwhile will have to endure it, since it cannot be completely eradicated at once.[81]

An equalized appreciation of the new and the old learning would solve this dilemma, Chang thought. The new and the old should coexist, and each should be fostered in its separate sphere—Chinese learning predominantly in the sphere of *t'i*, and Western learning in the sphere of *yung*. Chang recognized a possibility that the Western *yung* might begin to impinge on the Chinese *t'i*, and eventually overshadow or absorb it, reversing the existing dominance of *t'i* over *yung*. However, he seemed confident of the state's ability to control change and prevent such an occurrence through constant vigilance and cautious action. The Chinese

79. Chang's criticism on this count followed a long passage in which he himself found a link between Chinese classical ideas and Western natural sciences, chemistry, agriculture, mining, forestry, industry, trade, machines, factories, exhibits and fairs, concern for public welfare, railroads, commercial studies, tariffs, military academies, study abroad, physical education, schools, prison systems, representative government, the ruler's right to dissolve parliament, and newspapers. However, he conceded that the West had developed many ideas similar to those found in rudimentary form in the classics and had thus advanced far beyond China.

80. *CC*, 203:47b–48.

81. *CC*, 203:45.

and the Western reposing in equilibrium was his formula for the immediate crisis. Chang stated the formula most succinctly in three *Ch'üan-hsüeh p'ien* passages on the peaceful juxtaposition of the old (*chiu*) and the new (*hsin*), the substance (*t'i*) and the function (*yung*), the inner (*nei*) and the outer (*wai*):

> Wang Chung-jen said: "To know the past and not know the present is to be buried alive; to know the present and not know the past is to be deaf and blind." I would like to amend this and say: "To know foreign countries and not know China is to lose one's conscience: to know China and not know foreign countries is to be deaf and blind."[82]

> Study both the old and the new. The Four Books, Five Classics, Chinese history, government, and geography are old learning. Western government, crafts, and history are new learning. The old learning is the fundamental thing; the new learning is for practical use (*chiu-hsüeh wei t'i; hsin-hsüeh wei yung*). We must not neglect either because of prejudice.[83]

> Chinese learning is inner learning, Western learning is outer learning. Chinese learning is for regulating the body and mind. Western learning is for managing the affairs of the world. It is not necessary to seek for everything in the idea of the classics. But it is not necessary to contravene the meaning of the classics. If one's heart is the heart of the sages and one's actions are the actions of the sages, with filial piety, brotherly love, loyalty, and sincerity accepted as virtue, and respect for the ruler and concern for the people accepted as (principles of) government, then no harm will befall the disciples of Confucius even though they use machines and speed over railroads.[84]

A Tide of Schools

If Chang Chih-tung's principles of education were to be accepted on a national scale, a natural corollary would be reform of those educational institutions that concentrated solely upon the *t'i*, the *chiu*, and the *nei*. Adequate institutional means would have to be provided for the transmission of Western learning—the *yung*, the *hsin*, and the *wai*. In the second chapter of the *wai-p'ien* in the *Ch'üan-hsüeh p'ien*, Chang discussed study abroad as a means of acquiring Western learning. He recognized that "going abroad for one year is superior to studying Western

82. *CC*, 203:16.
83. *CC*, 203:9b.
84. *CC*, 203:48–48b.

books for five years" and that "attending a foreign school for one year is superior to attending a Chinese school for three years."[85] He dwelt especially on the advantages of study in Japan. However, while study abroad should be encouraged and carried out whenever practical, Chang concluded that it was too expensive a method for training large numbers of men. There could be no good substitute for establishing a network of modern schools in China itself. In the third essay of the *wai-p'ien*, therefore, Chang discussed his plan for schools at three different administrative levels.[86]

He proposed that colleges (*ta hsüeh-t'ang*) be opened in Peking and at each provincial capital. All circuits and prefectures would have middle schools (*chung hsüeh-t'ang*), and all departments and districts would have primary schools (*hsiao hsüeh-t'ang*). The curriculum of the primary schools would include the Four Books, outlines of Chinese geography and history, and elementary arithmetic, map-drawing, and natural sciences. The middle schools would offer "more advanced and useful" courses in the same subjects and would introduce study of the Five Classics; the *T'ung-chien* (Comprehensive Mirror), the historical work by Ssu-ma Kuang (1019–1086) and his successors; political science; and foreign languages. Of the college curriculum, Chang stated merely that it would be still deeper and broader than that of the middle schools.

As a means of starting and financing this new system of schools, Chang proposed that the *shu-yüan,* or traditional academies, be reorganized as *hsüeh-t'ang,* or modern schools, and that resources of the traditional academies be made available to the new institutions. "What is the use of having both *shu-yüan* and *hsüeh-t'ang?*" he asked. He further proposed that income from the land of benevolent institutions be devoted to education instead of being used for idol processions and theatricals, and that various clans contribute to the schools the funds spent on ancestral temples.

If a shortage of money still existed, Chang stated, then Buddhist and Taoist temples and monasteries, together with their lands, should be expropriated for school buildings and school support. Chang suggested limiting this confiscation to 70 percent of the religious properties. Thirty percent of the buildings and land would be left in the hands of the Buddhist priests and Taoist monks. To make this discriminatory recommendation seem more palatable, Chang suggested that awards be bestowed

85. *CC*, 203:6.
86. Data in the following paragraphs come from Chang's essay on establishing schools, *CC*, 203:8–11b.

on the priests and monks or that official positions be given their relatives at the time of settling the value of the religious properties. He also advanced the specious argument that the expropriation would in the long run redound to the benefit of the religious orders, because Buddhism and Taoism were currently in a state of decline and could not under existing circumstances be expected to endure for long. "Buddhism is already halfway down the path of hopelessness," Chang wrote, "and Taoism also experiences the grief of its devils not being supernatural." However, if Confucianism could recover its vitality through educational reform, and if its representatives could then restore Chinese peace and order, Buddhism and Taoism would naturally receive the benevolent protection of Confucianism and would flourish again themselves.

On the foundations of the traditional academies and the religious orders, Chang Chih-tung wrote, ten thousand schools would rise like a tide. After their establishment, the gentry and the rich would be urged to maintain and expand them through contributions. For operating the new schools, Chang listed six points that should be observed. The first, quoted above, called for the study of both the new and the old, with a curriculum composed of Western as well as Chinese learning. The remaining five points are paraphrased as follows.

Study both government (cheng) and arts (i). Education, geography, budgeting, taxation, military preparedness, law, industry, and commerce are the components of Western government. Mathematics, surveying, mining, medicine, physics, chemistry, and electricity constitute Western arts. Those advanced in learning and mature in years should study Western government. Those quick of mind but young in age should study Western arts. In the primary schools, Western arts should be studied before Western government. In the colleges and middle schools, Western government should be studied before Western arts. Western arts are specialized and cannot be mastered in less than ten years. In Western government several subjects can be learned concurrently and the essentials can be mastered in three years. In general, from the viewpoint of plans to meet current crises and national needs, government is more important than the arts. However, for those who study Western government to know how to utilize their knowledge, they must also acquire some knowledge of Western arts.

Teach the young. The study of mathematics requires acute students. The study of drawing requires adept ones. The study of natural science, chemistry, and manufacturing requires versatile and clever ones. The study of languages requires pupils with clear enunciation. The study of athletics requires students of strong vigor and healthy physiques. Men of middle age who have followed the path of scholarship have already weakened their spirits and strength and would often be unable to measure up to the standards in such courses. Furthermore, as their ideas are well-formed, it would be hard for them to receive learning with open minds. Not only would they be slow in accomplishment, but it is feared they would not investigate matters deeply and would become but half-accomplished.

Do not give eight-legged essay examinations. The new learning can be used for examinations just as well as the eight-legged essay. Those who wish to practice the formal style may do so at home. But do not trouble the school teachers and cause them to divide their minds (between teaching the eight-legged essays and their specialties) and waste their special proficiency gained through time and effort.

Do not allow contention for profit. All higher and lower foreign schools collect fees for board and tuition. They never pay stipends. The practice in Chinese academies of paying stipends is intended as an aid for poor scholars. However, many students come solely for the stipends and awards, so that the original intention has been repeatedly dragged in the dust, attended by petty discussions of trifling amounts, wrangling and accusations, decadence and lack of purpose, the disruption of school regulations, plagiarism, and dishonesty in examinations. While we cannot completely follow the Western system today, we should consider changing our old regulations so that the schools will provide fuel and food without charge but pay no stipends. We can use the Northern Sung method of percentile grades and compare the students' achievement each month. Those with high marks will be given awards. After a number of years, when our successors see the advantages of tuition payments, the collection of fees can be instituted, to the benefit of the schools and the encouragement of talent.

Do not worry about finding teachers. During the first years of school operation there will not be thousands of brilliant teachers In recent years, Shanghai has published many books on Western learning, covering the essentials of government and the arts. In general, any scholar who has already demonstrated high intellectual ability should be able to study these books for three months and then teach primary school. After two years, graduates of the colleges in the provincial capitals can teach in the middle schools. These products of the colleges will be shallow in learning for the first few years, but still a few qualified men can be found in each province. After three years, when the publication of new books has increased and normal school training has developed, the colleges need not be without teachers.

After dismissing the problem of teachers quite lightly—a problem to which he was forced to return more seriously in later years—Chang Chih-tung described other features that should characterize the new Chinese school system. In the fourth essay of the *wai-p'ien*, entitled "School Systems" (*Hsüeh-chih*), he outlined Western educational methods and forms of school organization that he felt China could easily accept in planning a new system of her own. The major part of this essay was devoted to additional remarks on the collection of tuition and fees by schools in the West, a system contrasted further with the Chinese payment of stipends. However, Chang also commented on the large enrollment of Western schools, their precision of school administration, and their teaching methods that emphasized explanation, understanding, and utility. Although Chang did not point out the contrast in this particular essay, he undoubtedly saw these factors in opposition to Chinese education, which in practice was open almost solely to the sons of the gentry, was loosely administered, stressed memorization and learning by rote, and overvalued literary accomplishment.

In the West, Chang noted, schools provided education for civil and military officials, the four classes of the people, and the hundred kinds of artisans. "You can ask a man what school he attended and know what he studied; you can ask how many years he was in school and know what grade he attained." One country might have primary schools in the tens of thousands, several thousand middle schools, and several hundred colleges. In Western public schools (*kung-kung chih hsüeh*), Chang explained, "there are definite books to be read, definite matters to be studied, definite principles to be learned, fixed standards for daily lessons, and fixed periods for graduation (three to five years)." He added: "For every matter and every school there is planning. All teachers expound upon books, and all students explain meanings. The professors teach books they already have studied; therefore, they are not overworked. The students take the ability to explain as (the basis of) learning; therefore, they do not suffer." Students who earned good grades, passed examinations, and were graduated received diplomas as evidence of their achievement. If Western governments needed talented men, they made a selection from the school graduates. "Upon examining the evidence of school diplomas, they know what government position (a student) should receive." This was not greatly unlike the Chinese system of selecting educated men for office, Chang observed, but it was possible in the West, because of the different subjects of Western education, to obtain officials "all of whom have studied (practical) affairs and not one of whom has acquired useless learning."[87]

In this essay Chang made a distinction for China between public schools and specialized or technical schools that would emphasize specific fields of Western government and arts. Subsequent essays of the *Ch'üan-hsüeh p'ien* recommended that attention be paid especially to military training and education in the fields of agriculture, industry, mining, and commerce.[88]

In regard to military education, Chang Chih-tung proposed that training be integrated with a system of universal military service. In his *Ch'üan-hsüeh p'ien* essay on the subject, he outlined a system as "originated in Germany, imitated in Europe, and followed by Japan." As he described it, the system called for three categories of troops. The first category consisted of the regular standing army. The second included men who became active reserves after three years of military service and drew no pay except when they assembled once a year for exercises. The third group consisted of inactive and unpaid reserves who had been discharged after three years of army service but were subject to recall as active reserves in case of large-scale war. Each year a percentage of the regular army was retired to the reserve lists and replaced by new recruits, with the whole army eventually "changing its skin." Under this system, all able-bodied men received military training, there was a great saving in military expenditures, the troop potential was large, and the martial spirit was constantly renewed. Chang urged that China adopt the system with minor modifications. With the traditional Chinese view of the soldier in mind, he wrote: "The reason that this system can be carried out (in the West) is that foreign countries respect the military. Their people consider it an honor to serve as soldiers and put forth effort in behalf of the country. They are not concerned only with making a living for themselves. Moreover, there are many artisans and merchants (in the army) and few loafers. Their troops all have skills, and when they are discharged from the army, they can engage in their professions as before."

In adopting the Western system of universal military service, Chang pointed out, China should also adopt Western methods of military training. In his essay on military education, he described the Western methods

87. *CC*, 203:12–13b.
88. See essays on military studies, *CC*, 203:35–39b; schools of agriculture, industry, and commerce, *CC*, 203:30–34b; and schools of mining, *CC*, 203:40–43. Data in the following paragraphs come from these sources.

under various categorical headings, several of which are paraphrased below.

There are three programs for military students: schools, drill, and field exercises. In the schools, the students study the principles of weapons, geography, surveying, methods of war and defense, and military history. On the drill ground there is the practice of calisthenics, marching, and firing. Field exercises include the practice of attack, defense, and reconnaissance.

There are two methods of teaching strategy to commanders: military chess (*ping-ch'i*) and war maps (*chan-t'u*). In military chess, the officers select maps that show in detail the mountains, rivers, roads, forests, and villages. They take wooden chess men representing units such as cavalry and infantry, sit in a circle, and then analyze the best methods of attack and defense, advance and retreat. In using war maps, they take charts of great Western battles of the past and study the causes of victory and defeat.

There are three terms of instruction. For the common soldiers trained only on the drill ground, the slowest students require a year of work and the quickest six months before they are useful. For petty officers there are schools, which require fourteen months of training for infantry and supply troops, sixteen months for cavalry troops, and eighteen months for artillery and engineering troops. Concurrently the petty officers participate in the drills and exercises of their army units. The officers have five years of schooling and two years of drill and exercises with army units. The general officers have five years of schooling, two years of drill and exercises with army units, and another two years in a college. From generals down to petty officers, all are literate and know mathematics, all have received physical training, and all are able to understand and draw maps.

There are two duties taught to officers: loyalty and love of country, and honesty and a sense of shame. Western officers in teaching Chinese military students say: "You must realize that you yourselves are Chinese. In the future when you have completed your training, you will repay your country. If there is war and you do not fight bravely, this is the shame of the country and also your personal shame. Without this spirit of patriotism, even though you have finished training and have the same ability as Western troops, it will be useless." The same ideas are expressed in military books by Westerners.

In regard to agricultural education, Chang Chih-tung stated that whereas farmers in former times had suffered because of laziness, in recent times they suffered because of ignorance. He gave ignorance as the cause of China's loss of the tea market to India and Ceylon and the silk market to Japan and Italy, and the cause of China's dependence on cotton imports and her poor utilization of domestic hemp. Ignorance was also the cause of low agricultural yields for home consumption: "Westerners say that one mou of land planted to the best advantage can support three persons; in China if the produce from one mou of land can support one person, this is said to be richness."

Chang defined the most important requirements for overcoming ignorance in agriculture as a knowledge of chemistry in order to improve land usage and a knowledge of machinery in order to improve farm tools. "Nourishing the soil, distinguishing different grains and seeds, fertilizing, irrigating, and introducing sunlight all require chemistry," he observed. "For obtaining water, killing insects, ploughing, weeding, and milling, there are new (mechanized) methods, no matter whether wind or water power is used." However, Chang did not feel that China's farmers, alone and unaided, were prepared to acquire the requisite knowledge of chemistry and machinery. Therefore, he recommended leadership by the scholars and the gentry. "We should establish schools of agriculture. The scholars of the outer districts should investigate the products of their villages and report to the schools, which will study new methods and new equipment on their behalf. Then the local gentry who are well known and the rich households with large amounts of land should try (the new improvements) so as to lead others. When there is achievement, the people will follow naturally."

Chang described industry as the pivot of agriculture and commerce, since creating prosperous farms and increasing foreign trade could not be accomplished without industry (*fei-kung pu-wei-kung*). He particularly stressed the close relationship of commerce to industry: "Industry is the *t'i* and commerce is the *yung*. . . . Commerce is the master and industry is the servant."[89] There were two ways to offer industrial education, Chang noted. The first consisted of converting scholars into engineers, conversant with the principles underlying industry. The second was to present practical, on-the-job training to artisans. Chang wrote: "In general, the most important principle in all matters of Western method is first to learn the art and later begin the work. First learn to be an officer and then train troops; first learn to be a seaman and then buy ships; first learn to be an industrial engineer and then manufacture; first learn to be a mining engi-

---

89. *CC*, 203:33. This passage suggests that Chang sometimes used the *t'i-yung* dichotomy as a mere literary device. If the two sentences are taken together, *t'i* is associated in this instance with "the servant," and *yung* with "the master," a reversal of the customary order.

neer and then open mines. The beginning seems slow, but the latter part is fast."

However, when the need for strength was so urgent, could China afford to await the perfection of learning before undertaking industrial development? Fortunately, Chang Chih-tung stated, it was unnecessary to wait, as his experience at the Hanyang Iron and Steel Works had shown. At that plant and its mines, Hupeh had employed Western engineers. Other provinces could do the same—placing qualified Westerners under contract to recruit personnel, buy machinery, and start production. "Listen to their directions and do not hinder them," Chang advised. But at the same time, Chinese employees and workers should observe the methods of the Western engineers and participate in schools of mining, which could be established at various sites. In time, the Chinese students, mine officials, and artisans would "educate themselves." This was the method of "using a mining mountain for a mining school."

Nevertheless, Chang did not believe that in this area China should concentrate exclusively on learning through doing. Since the method tended to create mechanics or technicians who could operate and maintain machines without really understanding the basic mechanical or scientific principles involved, he felt that it would inevitably limit industrial growth and affect the quality of industrial output. China should also educate genuine engineers and give them special status recognition, Chang maintained. He proposed that men be sent to study in foreign factories and that China establish special industrial schools. Scholars were to be selected for this training at home or abroad, and they would be called "industrial students" (*kung hsüeh-sheng*). After their training had been completed, they would be called "industrial officers (*kung-hsüeh jen-yüan*) and would be assigned to teach artisans and thereby encourage the establishment of more Chinese factories.

While Chang was in favor of Chinese workers learning what they could from Western engineers on the job, he was skeptical about using foreign teachers in the regular school system. During the preceding ten years, he wrote in an essay on increasing the translation of Western books, Chinese schools had employed a number of foreigners to transmit Western learning. The main defects of this employment had proved to be inferior and limited instruction for the Chinese students. High salaries were paid to foreigners who could speak no Chinese and were therefore obliged to depend on interpreters. Unfortunately, the interpreters were men of little learning. Even if they knew the foreign language of instruction, they were not likely to know the subject matter. Truth would be lost in matters where the least divergence could lead one miles astray. What they could not explain, the interpreters tended to abridge or alter. Even if the interpreters were good, Chang complained, the foreign teachers were slow. They taught only one or two things for two or three hours a day and might spend a whole year on addition and subtraction alone. Chang felt that they were sometimes guilty of deliberate delay in order to prolong their period of employment.

These Western teachers were nevertheless the custodians of the Western knowledge to which China must gain access. To bypass them, China must develop means of going directly to the Western books from which these middlemen derived their own knowledge. Because training a first-class interpreter required ten years, Chang noted, this was not the answer. Instead, the answer was to translate numerous Western books and use them extensively to teach men who lacked knowledge of Western languages. In order to increase translations, Chang suggested a three-fold program: all of the provinces should establish translation bureaus; Chinese diplomats abroad should seek out important books in the foreign countries where they were stationed and make a selection for translation; and influential Shanghai publishers should be encouraged to commission scholars to make translations for wide distribution and sale.[90]

Chang recognized that the increase of translations and the extension of Western learning in general could impose a serious hardship on Chinese students. How could the students hope to acquire Western learning and Chinese learning at the same time, when Chinese learning alone was so rich? Chinese books by themselves were so many "as to make the oxen bearing them perspire and to fill the house to the rafters."[91] In order to qualify for public office, students were already devoting thirty years or more to Chinese studies. Some were devoting a whole lifetime to the pursuit of Chinese scholarship and still not mastering or depleting the subjects of study. Chang Chih-tung did not envisage that the public school system would create two separate categories of student, one skilled only in Chinese studies and the other only in "foreign affairs" (yang-wu). Rather, a general knowledge of both China and the West should be sought by public school students. Chang admitted the need for specialists in both the fields of sinology and Western arts, but he felt that priority in the schools should be given to creating the "generalist." He believed that it would be possible for the student to cope with both Chinese and Western studies, despite the burdens of each, if the approach to Chinese studies

90. *CC*, 203:14–16b.
91. *CC*, 202:29b.

were altered. There was no question of the need for preserving Chinese studies; they must never be abandoned. But selectivity should be the method and utility the criterion in undertaking Chinese studies.

Chang discussed the problem in a chapter of the *Ch'üan-hsüeh p'ien* entitled *Shou-yüeh*, meaning "to preserve economy, maintain conciseness, or attend to that of the greatest importance."[92] In a key passage he declared: "Today if we wish to preserve Chinese learning, we must first attend to that of the greatest importance (*shou-yüeh*)." Chang added that China's salvation would depend upon "valuing usefulness in the management of affairs" and overcoming the existing reverence for exhaustiveness in Chinese scholarship. He outlined a revised program of Chinese studies and suggested shortcuts and aids that students might adopt in acquiring an adequate knowledge of Chinese learning. Chang's revised program, like the traditional educational program, was based on the primacy of the classics. However, it recommended more diversified learning, shorter periods of study, and above all, greater emphasis on explanation and understanding in contrast to mechanical repetition.

Before the age of fifteen, Chang recommended, students should study texts and explanations of the *Hsiao-ching* (Classic of Filial Piety), the Four Books, and the Five Classics. In addition, they should study Chinese history in outline, astronomy, geography, music, and drawing. They should furthermore become familiar with outstanding examples of Han, T'ang, and Sung literature that might prove beneficial in "present-day composition."

After the age of fifteen, students should study the chief Chinese "disciplines" according to specified methods. For classical studies, Chang's plan was for students to concentrate on learning the main idea or principal meaning (*ta-i*) of the classical works. The classics as a whole were concerned with regulating the body and mind (*chih shen hsin*) and regulating the empire (*chih t'ien-hsia*), he argued. In studying them, students should watch for wisdom that could be brought to bear on current problems ("In each classic, matters especially useful today may be as few as ten and not more than one hundred"). Students should reduce the material to be memorized to the absolute minimum ("Select the best sayings, master them, do not study further, and avoid waste of time and effort"). In all of their work they should "omit the doubtful" ("Do not worry about obscure and hard-to-understand fragments; put them aside and do not study them"). To make their study simpler and more meaningful, they should make use

---

92. *CC*, 202:30. Data in following paragraphs are drawn from *CC*, 202:30–37b.

of existing charts and tables, distinguish among various classical schools, and employ classical commentaries.

With regard to the commentaries, however, Chang Chih-tung recommended, with three exceptions, the use of only one expository work for each of the classics. He laid down a general rule that preference should be given to the ideas of the Ch'ing classical scholars. For the five classics in general, he recommended the *Tung-shu tu-shu chi* of Ch'en Li (1810–1882) and the *Ching-i shu-wen* of Wang Yin-chih (1766–1834). While Chang thus reduced the number of commentaries that should be studied to a small list, he admitted that a detailed, verse-by-verse study of even these few works would require at least five years. Therefore, he proposed that digests of the commentaries be prepared. Significant passages could be marked, extracted, and collected into one chüan for the commentaries on the small classics and not more than two chüan for the commentaries on the large classics. The digests could be used as school textbooks or exercise books, upon which teachers could base their lectures or students their practice. If this method of abbreviation were followed, Chang estimated, the study of the selected classical commentaries could be reduced to one year or one and one-half years. Chang concluded his remarks on the classics by stating: "Study of the classics in this manner will be simplified but not erroneous, brief but not crude. Even if one stops halfway, there will not be a complete loss. He will (still) have several thousand classical items to use in developing his nature and knowledge and nourishing his roots, and all his life there will not be the calamity of departing from the Way."

Chang Chih-tung divided historical studies into two categories: facts (*shih-shih*) and statutes (*tien-chih*). Those facts that elucidated good government or the causes of disorder should be selected for scrutiny. If factual accounts constituted "warning examples" applicable to the present day, they should be studied. Similarly, laws and statutes should be perused with contemporary needs in mind. The study of facts should be based on the histories entitled *T'ung-chien* but should be confined to the basic annals (*chi-shih pen-mo*). The study of laws and statutes should be based on the dynastic histories and the encyclopedias entitled *T'ung-tien* and *T'ung-k'ao*, but attention should be confined to memorials appearing in the essays (*chih*) and biographies (*chuan*) of the dynastic histories and to the introduction of each section of the *T'ung-tien* and *T'ung-k'ao*. For those encyclopedias entitled *T'ung-chih*, students should merely become familiar with the general scope of the monographic sections (*lüeh*).[93] A

93. On the scope and organization of the *t'ung* encyclopedias, see Teng and Biggerstaff, *An Annotated Bibliography*, pp. 147–158.

general history recommended for inclusion in the curriculum was the *Nien-erh-shih cha-chi* of Chao I (1727–1814). For historical criticism, students were urged to read the *Yü-p'i t'ung-chien chi-lan* of the Ch'ien-lung emperor (1711–1799), which Chang described as representing the mean between Ssu-ma Kuang's *Tzu-chih t'ung-chien* and the *Tu T'ung-chien lun* of Wang Fu-chih (1619–1692).

Study of the various philosophers, according to Chang Chih-tung, should be based on rigid selection and rejection—by which he meant the rejection of Taoist, Legalist, and all other non-Confucian philosophers "Select those whose ideas are not contrary to the classics," he wrote, "and reject those who are clearly opposed to Confucius and Mencius." Chang developed this theme in an earlier essay of the *Ch'üan-hsüeh p'ien* entitled "Respect the Classics" (*Tsung-ching*).[94] Therein he argued that during the Chou dynasty all of the good points of the Nine Schools of Philosophy had been incorporated into Confucianism and all of the bad points had been excluded.

Although Chang did not rule out the study of Chu Hsi's writings, he suggested an approach to later Neo-Confucianism through secondary works rather than through the original texts. The many philosophers of the Sung and Ming who sided with Chu Hsi or his opponent, Lu Chiu-yüan (1139–1193), had produced works that were vast and subtle, Chang noted, but their ideas were also characterized by a great deal of obscurity taken over from Buddhism and Taoism. Nor were many of the works distinguished by outstanding literary style. Unfortunately, the greatest of the Neo-Confucians were the most fatiguing to read. Deep study of Neo-Confucianism could be postponed, Chang maintained, and an adequate introduction obtained through three or four surveys of Neo-Confucian schools. Particularly recommended were the *Ming-ju hsüeh-an* of Huang Tsung-hsi (1610–1695) and the *Sung-Yüan hsüeh-an* of Ch'üan Tsu-wang (1705–1755).

Chang's pragmatic approach extended to creative writing or belles lettres, a field in which he recommended the study of realistic literature that might be "useful in memorials, official correspondence, and the recording of events." All creative writing could be eliminated from study except that which "relates affairs and describes principles." If students felt impelled to engage in creative writing themselves, they should avoid extravagant prose and poetic styles that would "tire their spirits and weaken their wills."

94. *CC*, 202:19–22.

Utility and recency were further emphasized in Chang's comments on the study of government ("The political events of the past century and the memorials of the past fifty years are the most useful"), of geography ("One may await a day of leisure to investigate the ancient evidence of the Han monograph or the broad learning of the *Shui-ching chu*"), and of mathematics ("Each should consider the profession he will study, learn sufficient mathematics for the practice of that profession, and stop there").

If some men found that even the recommended books were too many or too hard, Chang suggested, they could still acquire substantial Chinese learning by studying only four works: the *Chin-ssu lu*, the canon of Neo-Confucianism by Chu Hsi; the *Tung-shu tu-shu chi* of Ch'en Li; the *Yü-p'i t'ung-chien chi-lan*; and the *Wen-hsien t'ung-k'ao*, compiled by Ma Tuan-lin (ca. 1250–1319).

By attempting to modify the Chinese scholar's fondness for antiquity and love of detail, Chang Chih-tung hoped not only to combat pedantry but also to make room for Western studies in a reformed Chinese educational structure. In the *Ch'üan-hsüeh p'ien*, however, he did not cope manfully with the problem of meshing the proposed new school system, based on a Sino-Western curriculum, with the old examination system by which scholars were chosen for public office. This problem was reserved for later years. However, Chang did propose in the *Ch'üan-hsüeh p'ien* that the examination system be modernized. As he planned the introduction of Chinese studies into schools patterned after Western models, he also advocated that Western studies be tested in the Chinese civil service examinations. Chang's proposals on revision of the civil service examinations were accepted during the Hundred Days' Reform and represented his major contribution to change within that period. The enactment of his ideas was the only educational reform of the Hundred Days that could be traced exclusively to his efforts.

Education in the Hundred Days' Reform

The writings of Chang Chih-tung and others, the memorials of progressive officials, and the agitation of dissatisfied *chü-jen* sympathetic with the ideas of K'ang Yu-wei and Liang Ch'i-ch'ao all helped to establish the mood for the educational reforms decreed in 1898. Several broad changes were ordered by the throne in the early months of the year, even before the start of the Hundred Days' Reform on June 11. From June 11 to September 21, the pace of reform quickened. Action was taken toward founding schools and a metropolitan university, revising the civil service examination system, amending the military examinations, encouraging study abroad, and increasing the translation of Western books.

The year began with an imperial edict on instituting a "special examination in public administration" (*ching-chi t'e-k'o*), one of the first significant attempts to breach the civil service testing system at the end of the Ch'ing dynasty. This edict was issued on January 27, 1898, in response to an 1897 memorial by the Kweichow director of education, Yen Hsiu, and following deliberation of the plan by the Board of Rites and the Tsungli Yamen.[95] The special examination was to be held once every ten or twenty years and to cover six topics: government, foreign relations, economics, military affairs, science, and engineering. Ch'ing precedents for special examinations were found in the *po-hsüeh hung-tz'u k'o* of 1679 and 1736, but the purpose of reviving the method in the Kuang-hsü reign was to introduce practical topics into the examination system and to introduce *yang-wu* experts into the bureaucracy. The emperor told provincial and capital officials to start recommending candidates considered qualified to take the special examination. At a time to be announced later, the candidates would be sent to Peking. There five examiners would oversee a test to be written as dissertation essays (*ts'e*) and discussion essays (*lun*) rather than as the abhorrent eight-legged essay. Those who passed would be reexamined by the emperor and then ordered to await official assignment. Details of the special examination were discussed further during the Hundred Days, and the plan encountered opposition from conservative officials.[96] On July 13 six rules to govern the test were promulgated in Peking, and the demand that provincial officials make prompt recommendations was revived. The officials were given three months in which to reply.[97] The time limit had not expired before the end of the Hundred Days. The examination was not held, therefore, because after the empress dowager resumed the regency, she expressly ordered that the scheme be abandoned.[98]

Also on January 27, 1898, the throne directed the acceptance of Yen Hsiu's plan for a triennial examination on public administration (*ching-chi sui-chü*), constituting a special category (*k'o*) to parallel the literary category (*wen-k'o*) of the examination system.[99] Provincial directors of education were to select superior *sheng-yüan* who had received training

---

95. *CSL:KH*, 414:4–5b. For Yen Hsiu's memorials on the special examination, see *Wu-hsü pien-fa*, 2:329–332.

96. *CSL:KH*, 414:15–15b, 18, 419:10, 421:14, 21–21b.

97. *CSL:KH*, 421:12–12b.

98. *CSL:KH*, 428:7–8.

99. *CSL:KH*, 414:4–5b.

in "mathematics and the arts" at academies or new schools. The candidates would take a provincial examination consisting of writing dissertations and discussions. They would be tested on their specialty during the first session, on "current affairs" (*shih-wu*) during the second session, and on the Four Books during the third session. Those passing would become *ching-chi k'o chü-jen* and could go on to take a metropolitan examination in public administration for a *ching-chi k'o chin-shih* degree. Detailed regulations for this triennial examination were drawn up during the Hundred Days, but an effort to nullify the plan was made by the Board of Rites president, Hsü Ying-k'uei. Hsü arbitrarily revised the regulations to make the test an eight-legged essay examination and to limit the quota of persons who could receive degrees to one out of fifty candidates. This action caused the censor, Sung Po-lu, to impeach Hsü in a memorial of June 20, and it was reported that the emperor would have dismissed him save for the intervention of the Manchu statesman Kang-i.[100] Later during the Hundred Days, on September 1, Hsü was actually dismissed and replaced by Li Tuan-fen, who was sympathetic to educational reform.[101]

Other educational reforms announced before the Hundred Days included the establishment of a metropolitan university (*ching-shih ta-hsüeh-t'ang*) on the foundations of the College of Languages and known to foreigners as Peking Imperial University. One of the few innovations that survived the repression of the 1898 movement, this school was the forerunner of National Peking University under the Republic of China and Peking University during the Chinese Communist regime.[102] An edict of February 15, 1898, ordering the Tsungli Yamen to draw up regulations for the school, noted that the request for the university had just been made in a memorial by the censor Wang P'eng-yün but that the same request had been submitted earlier by many other memorialists.[103] On July 3 Sun Chia-nai was appointed superintendent of the university and Liang Ch'i-ch'ao was made director of a Translation Bureau (I-shu chü) subordinate to the university.[104] Prince Ch'ing and Hsü Ying-k'uei were placed in charge of construction work by an edict on the following day.[105] Later Dr. W. A. P. Martin of the College of Languages was appointed general instructor in Western studies (*hsi-hsüeh tsung-chiao-hsi*) and given the

100. Liang Ch'i-ch'ao, *Wu-hsü cheng-pien chi-shih pen-mo* (Complete record of events during the 1898 reform movement), *Wu-hsü pien-fa*, 1:315–316.
101. *CSL:KH*, 425:3b.
102. For a study of the school, see Renville C. Lund, *The Imperial University of Peking*, unpub. diss., University of Washington, 1956.
103. *CSL:KH*, 414:17b.
104. *CSL:KH*, 419:13b–14, 14b.
105. *CSL:KH*, 420:1b–2.

formal rank of a second class official. The university opened in Peking on August 9.[106]

A third significant edict before the Hundred Days' Reform, issued on March 18, approved reform of the outmoded military examination system. On January 17 the Grand Secretary Jung-lu had memorialized recommending that a new military category be added to the examination system to test candidates on a combination of Chinese and Western military subjects.[107] The throne forwarded this document and other memorials on the military examinations to the Grand Council and the Board of War for consideration. Accepting the final recommendations of the Board of War on March 18, the emperor vetoed Jung-lu's suggestion of a new category but nevertheless proclaimed a radical change in the established military examinations. All military examinations, according to the imperial edict, were to be based on the use of firearms.[108] This meant, in effect, abandoning the anachronistic tests in archery, swordsmanship, and stone-lifting. Also abolished was the examination session in which portions of a military classic were written from memory. The new system was to take effect at the next scheduled examination in the prefectures, in 1900 for the provincial examinations, and in 1901 for the metropolitan examinations. In the meantime, the Board of War was to work out details and decide how military schools could best be established in each province to provide the training necessary for candidates to pass examinations based on the use of firearms. Furthermore, high provincial officials were directed to submit their views on additional reforms needed for the military examinations.

During the three months following the emperor's June 11 invitation for further reforms, two more noteworthy educational measures were adopted. On June 23 an edict ordered that the eight-legged essay be purged from the examination system.[109] Beginning with the next tests, the prefectural, provincial, and metropolitan examinations were all to employ dissertations and discussions based on the text of the Four Books. Chang Chih-tung had called for such a reform in the Ch'uan-hsüeh p'ien, but his voice was only one of many raised against the eight-legged essay. Liang Ch'i-ch'ao credited the immediate inspiration of the edict to the efforts of K'ang Yu-wei. In the third lunar month of 1898 (March 22–April 20),

106. Tuan Chang-t'ung, Wu-hsü pai-jih wei-hsin yün-tung ta-shih piao (Table of important events during the hundred days' reform movement of 1898), Wu-hsü pien-fa, 4:65.
107. CSL:KH, 413:18.
108. CSL:KH, 416:16b–17.
109. CSL:KH, 419:5b–6.

K'ang Yu-wei and the censor Yang Shen-hsiu had submitted memorials urging that the eight-legged essay be abolished, but their plan was not endorsed because of obstruction by Hsü Ying-k'uei. During the fourth lunar month (May 20–June 18), Liang Ch'i-ch'ao and over one hundred other *chü-jen* had drawn up a petition opposing the eight-legged essay, but their request did not reach the throne. On June 16, K'ang Yu-wei and Chang Yüan-chi were received in audience by the emperor, and K'ang acquired the emperor's verbal assent to abolish the form. Following the audience, Sung Po-lu submitted a memorial in K'ang Yu-wei's behalf, and the formal edict doing away with the essay was issued on June 23.[110] A week later, on June 30, the throne accepted another memorial by Sung Po-lu, recommending that the previously approved triennial examination on public administration, which was to have employed dissertation and discussion essays, be "merged" with the regular examinations since the eight-legged essay had been overthrown in the established system. Officials were also ordered to eliminate the eight-legged essay from the routine *sui* and *k'o* examinations in the provinces.[111] And on July 6 the dissertation and discussion forms were adopted for the court examination and the reexamination of "tribute students by virtue of special selection" (*pa-kung-sheng*).[112]

In a second important reform of the Hundred Days, the establishment of schools below the university level was ordered by a series of edicts from July to September. On July 10 the emperor directed that all large and small academies in the provincial capitals, prefectures, departments, and districts be converted to "schools of Sino-Western learning" (*Chung-hsüeh hsi-hsüeh chih hsüeh-hsiao*).[113] Large academies in the provincial capitals would become high schools (*kao-teng hsüeh-t'ang*). The academies of the prefectures would become middle schools, and those in the departments and districts would become primary schools. It was further decreed that all ancestral shrines and temples not being used for sacrifice or rites should be converted to schools, as Chang Chih-tung had suggested, among others. All free schools (*i-hsüeh*) and village schools (*she-hsüeh*) were to adopt a Sino-Western curriculum. The goal of this reform, according to the edict, was to create a condition of "no one without learning, and no learning that is insubstantial" (*jen wu pu-hsüeh, hsüeh wu pu-shih*). Provincial officials were given a mere two months to effect

110. *Wu-hsü pien-fa,* 1:316, 2:24–25.
111. *CSL:KH,* 419:10.
112. *CSL:KH,* 420:4.
113. *CSL:KH,* 420:9–9b.

and report on these changes, and the failure of some of the most prominent officials to comply quickly elicited several imperial reprimands.[114]

Following up the decision to establish schools, an edict of July 29, in response to a memorial by Li Tuan-fen, called upon governors general and governors to select and assign members of the gentry to manage schools in their home localities.[115] Liang Ch'i-ch'ao interpreted this as granting a right of "local self-government," inasmuch as it represented, in his estimation, a reversal of the previous rule forbidding officials to serve in their native provinces.[116] In September the capital was discussing a plan whereby provincial officials who held educational assignments under the old system would be required to become middle or primary school teachers.[117] In addition to these changes, a number of special schools were approved during the Hundred Days. In response to a memorial by K'ang Yu-wei, an edict of August 21 ordered that agricultural schools whould be founded in all provinces, prefectures, departments, and districts.[118] Plans for specific primary and middle schools, a medical college in Peking, schools in overseas Chinese communities, schools of sericulture, a translation college in Shanghai, and other institutions were endorsed by the emperor.[119]

Chang on Military Examinations

Although Chang Chih-tung's efforts were not directly or immediately responsible for these educational reforms, he had in the past stood for new schools, abolishing the eight-legged essay, and eliminating the feats of strength that had constituted the military examinations. Chang himself made only two major reform proposals during the Hundred Days. One was in a 4,000-character memorial submitted to the throne on July 4, calling for additional changes in the military examination system.[120] Chang's memorial, drawn up several months after the edict of March 18 ordering the use of firearms in all military examinations, strenuously objected to that plan.

First, Chang felt that danger was inherent in any scheme that necessitated the distribution of firearms among the people. If examinations were to be based on firearms, candidates would have to learn to use these

114. *CSL:KH*, 423:2, 14b–15b; 424:15.
115. *CSL:KH*, 421:12–12b.
116. *Wu-hsü pien-fa*, 2:46.
117. *Wu-hsü pien-fa*, 2:87.
118. *CSL:KH*, 423:3–4.
119. *CSL:KH*, 422:1b–2, 423:4, 5b, 16, 425:3, 5b, 16b, 426:6b.
120. *CC*, 48:10b–20b.

weapons. And if large numbers of weapons were made available to the trainees, there would be no guarantee that the weapons would not be used for illegal or rebellious purposes. The dynasty had suppressed the Taiping and Nien rebellions in earlier decades precisely because government troops had maintained superiority in firepower, Chang argued. Although there had been no large rebellions in recent years, the "shoots" of rebellion had sprung up in several "nooks and corners." Recently there had been seditious movements in Jehol and Kansu; in 1891 the secret society Ko-lao-hui had planned to seize Chinkiang and attack Nanking with arms secured through the British subject Charles Welsh Mason; and in 1896 Sun Yat-sen had transported arms into Canton in an effort to seize the city. There had been a similar attempt in Canton during the very year in which Chang was writing. Too often in the past, Chang complained, military examination candidates had proved to be notorious troublemakers. Given arms for training, they might band together with rebels or brigands for "outrageous conduct." If arms were distributed widely, the responsibility for preventing their concealment or misuse would fall on local officials who were either overburdened or lazy. Could those officials enforce arms controls any better than they had the laws against private coinage, ox slaughter, or gambling? Chang did not think they could, without door-to-door searches that would merely stir up fresh trouble.

Second, Chang protested that the arms and ammunition available in China were too varied in make and size to be used for a competitive examination based on comparison. If each candidate shot a different kind of rifle, how could performance be graded justly? It seemed impractical to Chang to establish a government monopoly on the sale of weapons of a uniform type or an official inspection of retail purchases by private parties merely to standardize arms for use in preparation for the military examinations.

Finally, Chang pointed out, in an examination consisting only of firing at a target, too many candidates would hit the bull's-eye. Such tests would be far too easy to serve as a dependable means of securing qualified army officers. More comprehensive examinations were needed, although of course they would have to be preceded by the proper training. Chang cited the difficulties that stood in the way of training all military examination candidates in military preparatory schools established as academies separate from the army. There were only four or five military preparatory schools already open in all of China. Their operating expenses were great, they had trouble in finding good instructors, and they were able to enroll only a handful of students. Any plan to establish military academies in every prefecture and district would encounter similar troubles. For teachers, the academies would be unable to depend upon men who already held military commissions, since only a few had any knowledge of firearms, surveying, cartography, engineering, manufacturing, geography, foreign languages, or other subjects necessary to modernize military training. Those who did possess extraordinary knowledge of such subjects were desperately needed for training assignments in the army itself and could not be detached to teach military students all over the country.

In view of these objections, Chang Chih-tung had decided that the optimum reform must be based on a concept of the army, military training, and the military examinations as a unity. The basic principle should be: no one outside the army should be admitted to the military examinations. The bulk of military training should take place within or under the direction of the army. Chang proposed, however, that only militia (*fang-ying pien-yung*) be asked to the military examinations based on firearms. He made a special plea that these provincial defense forces, which had arisen since the Taiping Rebellion, should be admitted to the examinations.[121] They were far more familiar with modern weapons, he argued, than were the Banner Forces or the Army of the Green Standard whose members previously had been eligible for the tests.

Under such a system, Chang maintained, there would be controlled training in the use of firearms, without anxiety over abetting bandits and outlaws. Furthermore, uniformity of arms for training would be easier to achieve within the army. During examinations under this arrangement, it would be simple to verify the names and native places of the candidates, and discipline could easily be maintained. However, he listed three main advantages of his plan.

First, the plan would prevent waste. The cost of foreign weapons was great, and large amounts of ammunition would be required for training purposes. As many potential examination candidates would begrudge making the necessary expenditures if left to their own devices, they would be without tools for training, and the result would be such light registration for the examinations that the quotas could not be filled. If each province tried to make its own purchases in a haphazard manner, without any over-all plan, the costs would not be lessened. However, if the ex-

121. On the rise of the militia and its implications, see Franz Michael, "Military Organization and Power Structure of China during the Taiping Rebellion," *Pacific Historical Review*, 18 (November 1949), 469–483.

amination candidates were also troops of the army, they would be able to train with the arms and ammunition acquired for or already possessed by the army. The military *sheng-yüan* and *chü-jen* not already in the army who would enlist or enter military schools would be comparatively few, and they would use government-owned weapons, while paying for their own ammunition.

Second, the plan would "subdue violence." Chang roundly condemned candidates under the existing military examination system, whom he described as "dressed-up tigers," who regarded the people as "fish and flesh." Whenever there was an examination, they created trouble—cheating and intimidating shopkeepers, who could only pray for the examination to end, and abusing the people, who were afraid to come into the streets. They were merely rough blusterers and men of muscle. Nine out of ten were illiterate. They had no experience with firearms and even less understanding of military strategy. After taking the examinations in archery, swordsmanship, and weight-lifting, they quickly abandoned the practice of those skills. In sum, there was no relationship between such candidates and the talent capable of resisting national insult. Under the new plan, all candidates would be trained in useful military skills and in military disciplines. After the examinations, they would return to their army assignments, in which they would be subject to further discipline and would continue to practice their skills, instead of letting them fall into disuse.

The third principal advantage of Chang's plan was that it would encourage the army. Since the Taiping and Nien rebellions, Chang argued, conditions had been relatively peaceful in China, with the result that earning military promotions had become difficult, especially for the militia. Capable men were finding that they had no way of attaining "an officer's rations and pay." The troops had therefore begun to look on themselves as coolies and corvée laborers, making a living by the sweat of their brows. Disillusion turned many into local villains or bandits. "People slight the soldiers, and because of this the soldiers slight themselves," Chang said. If the troops were provided adequate means for advance, their morale and effectiveness would improve to such an extent that "admonition by the Court and exhortation by the generals" would become unnecessary.

At this point in his memorial Chang entered another long plea that military men (*wu*) be granted respect equal to that accorded civil officials (*wen*), and that China overcome the view that good men do not become soldiers, just as good iron is not used for nails. He concluded his memorial with suggestions on new content for the military examinations. Chang proposed that the military examinations remain divided into three sessions. The first session would consist of drills and target-firing with rifles and guns. The second session would test rifle firing from horseback and bayonet use afoot. The third session would be an examination on subjects such as surveying, engineering, fortification, railroads, land and water mines, geography, and military strategy. Chang proposed that from the time of enlistment until advancement to a military school, soldiers should not exceed twenty years of age, so that they would be physically and mentally capable of undergoing the new-style training. Candidates for the first degree should not be over twenty-five years of age, and age limits should also be fixed for the second and third degrees. Firearms to be used in the examinations should be the single-shot Mauser rifle, single-shot 7.5 centimeter guns, and six centimeter artillery pieces. Either these weapons could be obtained readily in China, Chang stated, or Chinese arsenals were capable of manufacturing ammunition for them. The use of rapid-firing rifles and guns would have to await the further development of Chinese military industry.

Chang's memorial mainly illustrated the kind of discontent with the military examinations expressed during the Hundred Days' Reform. The emperor did not approve the memorial, but forwarded it to the Board of War and the Tsungli Yamen for further consideration. It was one of about twenty memorials on the military examinations submitted to ministerial discussion during the Hundred Days. According to Hu Ssuching, the Board of War finally made a selection from the best memorials and recommended that the military examinations be opened only to men who had received army training or military schooling (as others besides Chang had proposed), and that the three sessions consist of mounted firing, dismounted firing, and dissertation and discussion essays on "military methods" (an order somewhat like that suggested by Chang but, according to Hu, closer to the plans proposed by Liu K'un-i and others).[122] However, the throne rejected the Board of War's recommendations and called for further discussion of the military examinations, which was still under way at the end of the Hundred Days.

Chang on Civil Service Examinations

A more encouraging imperial response met Chang Chih-tung's proposals on reform of the civil service examinations. A chapter of the

122. *Wu-hsü pien-fa*, 1:369–370.

Ch'üan-hsüeh p'ien briefly became the law of the land during the Hundred Days. Two months before the beginning of the Hundred Days, Chang telegraphed Ch'en Pao-chen, the governor of Hunan, saying that he hoped to incorporate ideas of the *Ch'üan-hsüeh p'ien* essay entitled "Reform the Examination System" (*Pien k'o-chü*) into a memorial for formal presentation to the throne.[123] He invited Ch'en to submit the memorial jointly. However, neither official acted at once, and not until June 26 did Chang repeat the idea in a telegram to Ch'en. Ch'en replied that the recent change of court administration augured well for a memorial on the examination system and urged Chang to forward a document to the capital speedily. Chang and Ch'en exchanged additional telegrams discussing the project. Chang completed drafting the document on July 4, and on July 6 he informed Ch'en Pao-chen that it had been forwarded to Peking. The memorial, consisting of over 3,000 characters, was presented to the emperor on July 19. In one of the telegrams to Ch'en, Chang correctly described the memorial as closely resembling the *Ch'üan-hsüeh p'ien* essay, except for a new introduction, a new conclusion, and changes of wording to correct the original hasty writing.[124]

In both the *Ch'üan-hsüeh p'ien* essay and the joint memorial, Chang proceeded from the premise that China's salvation depended on acquiring talented men for the government, which in turn necessitated reform of the examination system by which officials were recruited. Criticizing the system as it had stood until recently, he complained of the imitative nature of the work by candidates, who depended on commentaries and aped the writings of others, without knowing intimately the meaning of the original classics on which the tests were based, and without understanding the great philosphers of the past or possessing adequate knowledge of public administration (*ching-chi*). Furthermore, Chang regretted that the eight-legged essay had killed good style and that examination essays had grown more and more worthless in form. Candidates were adhering nearsightedly to the rules of the system, when they should instead be able to say: "We practice the fine principles of Confucius and Mencius and the governmental methods of Yao and Shun." Chang also complained that the three sessions of the metropolitan and provincial examinations had become in effect only one session.[125] The metropolitan

---

123. The *Ch'üan-hsüeh p'ien* essay appears in *CC*, 203:23–28b. For Chang's telegram to Ch'en, see *CC*, 155:16–16b.

124. *CC*, 156:3–3b, 5b–6b, 9b–10; *CSL:KH*, 421:1–2. For text of the memorial and edict, see *CC*, 48:2–10b.

125. *CC*, 203:23–23b.

and provincial examining officers placed emphasis only on the first session, in which the eight-legged essay was written. If a candidate succeeded in the first session, his work of the second and third sessions would be checked for stylistic or syntactical errors only. If there were no flaws in the writing of characters or sentences, the candidate would be passed. Thus, the second and third sessions of the examinations had become superfluous.

Chang conceded that some improvement in the examination system had been achieved through recently ordered changes. In the *Ch'üan-hsüeh p'ien* essay, he took cognizance of the imperial edict ordering a special examination in public administration (*ching-chi t'e-k'o*). This was a step in the right direction, Chang asserted, but not many men trained in current affairs (*shih-wu*) could be obtained if the special test was given only once every twenty years. Between the special examinations, the eight-legged essay, poetry of the *shih* and *fu* forms, and formal small calligraphy (*hsiao-k'ai*) would remain as fixtures of the regular examination system and would continue to dominate civil service selection. The imperial edict that schools be established to train men in current affairs was fine, Chang admitted, but unless some means of advance into the bureaucracy were provided for the school graduates in current affairs, students would not be attracted to the schools. The "superior talent of the clans" would continue to sit for the traditional examinations, while those who enrolled in the schools would be the "dull scholars from thatched huts" who could not write eight-legged essays.

By the time that Chang and Ch'en Pao-chen submitted their joint memorial, the eight-legged essay had been ordered out of the examination system, to be replaced by dissertation and discussion essays. Chang welcomed the scrapping of the "cramping and outmoded" eight-legged form but argued that its elimination created a need for new controls and regulations. Freedom from the eight-legged essay might lead to license, Chang warned, to selecting themes from "miscellaneous commentaries" or an unlimited range of works. Such a trend in the examinations could eventually result in no restrictions whatsoever, with abandonment of the Four Books and Five Classics—those works emphasizing the Five Relationships and the methods of government that had formerly made the Middle Kingdom the center of civilization (*Chung-hua chih so-i wei chung*). The eight-legged essay, *shih* and *fu* poetry, and formal small calligraphy could go; but study of the classics must remain. Chang and Ch'en, therefore, opened their joint memorial with a five-point program for preserving the classics in the examination system.

Rectify names (cheng-ming). The classical tests of the examination system should be called "interpretation of the Four Books" (*Ssu-shu i*) and "interpretation of the Five Classics" (*Wu-ching i*) to suggest a return to ancient prose (*ku-wen*) standards and such methods as exposition (*chiang-i*), classical discussion (*ching-lun*), and classical explanation (*ching-shuo*).

Fix themes (ting-t'i). Topics assigned for the classical portion of examinations should be drawn from the original texts of the Four Books and the Five Classics. "No matter whether a whole chapter or several chapters, a whole verse or several verses, one sentence or several sentences [are used], not a single character should be deleted, changed, added or subtracted; and use of the meaning but change of the wording should not be permitted."

Rectify form (cheng-t'i). Since sincere discussion and clear understanding should be emphasized and demonstrated in the examinations, candidates should be forbidden to use frivolous parallelisms or couplets. Nor should they be allowed to use marks of emphasis that would give their papers a strange and uneven appearance.

Present evidence (cheng-shih). Candidates should be granted relief from the pointless restrictions that had circumscribed the writing of eight-legged essays and should be permitted to present examples from history and cite any work not contrary to the spirit of the classics.

Bar heterodoxy (hsien-hsieh). The reasoning of fallacious philosophers of the Chou and Ch'in dynasties, the misleading ideas of the Taoists and Buddhists, troublesome talk from the foreign-language press, and all words that "departed from the classics and contravened the *tao*" should be strictly prohibited in examination essays.

If these five suggestions were accepted, Chang Chih-tung believed, the principles governing examination essays would remain in harmony with "pure and right sacred precepts." Having thus stated a plan for preserving the classics in the examination system, Chang proceeded to outline a plan that would reduce testing on the classics from two sessions to one during the metropolitan and provincial examinations—thereby opening one session to more practical and modern topics. The change would require that all candidates possess some knowledge of current affairs and would provide a better opportunity for school graduates to advance into the bureaucracy through the examination system. "If we do not consider the examinations, public administration, and schools as one matter," Chang wrote, "then those who advance by obtaining degrees will overvalue polished writing, and, as before, there will be the distress caused by an inability to overcome ignorance and uselessness." A plan was needed to provide for representation of both the *t'i* and the *yung* in the examination system, Chang declared. As a precedent for the specific plan which he would present, Chang referred to a proposal made in 1044 by Ou-yang Hsiu, who called for an elimination of candidates after each session of an examination and championed the dissertation and discussion essays over the *shih* and *fu* forms of poetry so prominent in the Sung examination system. Chang stated: "Ou-yang's desire to use the dissertation and discussion for relief from the *shih* and *fu* is like the present-day desire to use Chinese and foreign public administration for relief from the eight-legged essay." Chang's own plan for the three sessions of the provincial and metropolitan examinations was as follows.

The first session (formerly devoted to eight-legged essays on topics from the Four Books) would consist of a test on Chinese public administration (*Chung-hsüeh ching-chi*). Candidates would answer five questions with discussions (*lun*) on Chinese history and on government of the Ch'ing dynasty. Those passed from this session would number ten times more than the established quota for degrees. Thus, if the quota specified that eighty candidates could be chosen for the *chü-jen* degree following a provincial examination, eight hundred candidates would be selected following the first session. Results would be announced immediately after the session. Those selected could sit for the second session, but all others would be eliminated.

The second session (formerly devoted to essays on topics from the Five Classics) would consist of tests on Western public administration (*hsi-hsüeh ching-chi*), "the government of various countries of the Five Continents," and "specialized arts." Five questions would be answered with dissertations (*ts'e*) on current affairs (*shih-wu*). For example, questions on foreign government might call for dissertations on geography, schools, taxation, the military system, commerce, or the judicial system. Dissertations on the specialized arts might discuss natural sciences, manufacturing, chemistry, or physics. A candidate would be eliminated if he made irrelevant or wild attacks on Confucianism when explaining Western methods. In the second session, the number of candidates chosen would be three times more than the quota, and again results would be announced immediately after the session. If the quota were eighty degrees, two hundred forty candidates would be advanced to the third session.

The third session (formerly devoted to questions on Chinese government and history) would consist of two essays of interpretation (*i*) based on passages from the Four Books and one essay of interpretation based on passages from the Five Classics. When the papers were graded, the final results of the examination would be announced, and degrees would be awarded according to the quota.

Chang Chih-tung maintained that his plan would inject greater realism and a measure of Western learning into the examination system. By being liberal in selection at the outset and strict at the end, the existing emphasis on the first session of the examinations would be shifted to the last session, with redundancy being eliminated and no session being superfluous. Elimination of candidates after the first and second sessions would reduce the burden on examining officers. The copyists, who transcribed papers to prevent examiners from identifying the candidates' handwriting, and the essay readers would have fewer manuscripts to deal with; they would therefore commit fewer errors through carelessness or haste. The announcement of results after each session would mean less hardship upon poor scholars who in the past had been "haltered" for a long wait to learn the examination outcome. Summing up, Chang Chih-tung wrote of his plan: "In general, the first session will select those of broad learning; in the second session, those conversant with [practical] affairs will be selected from those of broad learning; and in the third session, the pure and upright will be selected from those able to manage affairs."

In neither the *Ch'üan-hsüeh p'ien* essay nor in the joint memorial with Ch'en Pao-chen did Chang Chih-tung give detailed attention to the regular, routine, or qualifying examinations below the provincial level. However, he did suggest that discussions of history (*shih-lun*) and dissertations on current affairs (*shih-wu ts'e*) be required and that interpretation (*i*) of the Four Books and Five Classics take the place of essays (*wen*) for the *sui-k'ao, k'o-k'ao,* and the *t'ung-shih.*

Chang ended both the *Ch'üan-hsüeh p'ien* essay and the joint memorial with an appeal that *shih* and *fu* poetry and formal small calligraphy be eliminated from the higher examinations. He argued that calligraphic skill was overemphasized in the palace examination, the court examinations, Hanlin Academy tests, and court examinations for the *yu-kung-sheng* and *pa-kung-sheng. Chin-shih* who had just begun to escape the rigors of the eight-legged essay were forced to suffer the difficulties of formal small calligraphy. Calling for a freer style of writing, Chang denounced the small calligraphy as damaging to ambition, wasteful of time and effort, and destructive of the scholarly spirit. In the palace examination it was especially undesirable that the small calligraphy be used as the basis of selection or rejection, for in this examination it was most important that the emperor seek men who were upright and knowledgeable of right (*tao*), who were straightforward in speech and honest in remonstrance. If these criteria were used, Chang suggested, the palace examination could be depended on to determine official rank and the court examination could possibly be discarded.

Chang's proposals on reform of the civil service examination system were less radical than plans presented by K'ang Yu-wei and Liang Ch'i-ch'ao in 1895 and 1896. In 1895 K'ang had suggested establishing different categories (*k'o*) of examinations in addition to the literary category (*wen-k'o*), advocating the re-introduction of diversity like that of the T'ang and early Sung examination systems. K'ang recommended the addition of an arts category (*i-k'o*) for subjects such as astronomy, geography, medicine, chemistry, and foreign languages, and a religious category (*tao-k'o*), whose graduates would become Confucian evangelists and ritual experts with official rank.[126] In 1896 Liang Ch'i-ch'ao proposed complete integration of the school and examination systems, with the conferral of *sheng-yüan*, *chü-jen*, and *chin-shih* titles on the graduates of the schools. Liang said the second best method would be to establish new categories (as K'ang Yu-wei had proposed), and the third best method would be to leave the system as it was except for adding new practical subjects.[127]

Chang Chih-tung's plan most closely resembled Liang Ch'i-ch'ao's third best method. Nevertheless, despite the political ascendancy of K'ang and Liang in 1898, it was Chang's plan that won imperial endorsement during the Hundred Days. An edict of July 19, 1898, accepted Chang's scheme for revising the three sessions of the examination system and ordered the Board of Rites to institute it in all the provinces.[128] Exactly one month later, on August 19, another edict abolished the court examination and directed that *shih* and *fu* poetry, and formal small calligraphy be eliminated from all examinations.[129] A provincial examination in accordance with Chang Chih-tung's plan was conducted in Shensi province before the end of the Hundred Days.[130] But other provinces

126. For K'ang's memorial, see *Wu-hsü pien-fa*, 2:131–154; summarized in Franke, pp. 33–35.
127. Liang Ch'i-ch'ao, "Lun K'o-chü" (On the examination system), part of the *Pien-fa t'ung-lun* (General discussion of reform), in the *Yin-ping-shih wen-chi*, summarized by Franke, pp. 40–41.
128. *CC*, 48:9b–10b; *CSL:KH*, 421:1–2; *Wu-hsü pien-fa*, 2:41.
129. *CSL:KH*, 423:1b–2.
130. *CC*, 83:7.

had no opportunity to comply with the imperial edict before the empress dowager resumed control of the government. On October 9 she issued an edict: the examination system would revert to its old form, with eight-legged essays on the Four Books for the first session, essays on the classics (*ching-wen*) for the second session, and answers to questions on history and government (*ts'e-wen*) for the third session.[131] Chang Chih-tung, however, did not forget his plan or its brief victory. Several years later, when conditions were ripe for the Manchu reform movement, he revived and once more began to promote the plan.

The Problem of Student Discipline

In his own domain of Hupeh and Hunan, Chang Chih-tung made an effort to comply with imperial edicts on the establishment of schools during the 1898 reform movement. Early in the year he revised the courses of study at the Liang-Hu and Ching-hsin Academies and ordered that academies at Hanyang and Te-an-fu abolish practice of the eight-legged essay and institute instruction in mathematics and current affairs. He later directed that all academies under his jurisdiction be converted to schools, as demanded by the throne. He opened schools in the ten prefectures and in one directly governed department of Hupeh, although each school had only two teachers. Chang also ordered that surpluses from the Hupeh land tax be applied to support the various schools, one-half to be used for institutions in the provincial capital and one-half for those in the eleven subordinate administrative areas.[132]

As Chang was attempting to increase the schools of Hupeh and Hunan in 1898 and the years thereafter, a serious problem confronted him: the question of student discipline. The start of the 1898 reform movement, insofar as it featured petitions and an organized protest by large numbers of *chü-jen*, represented a "student movement," forerunner of the nationalistic student movements of 1919, 1925, and 1935 under the Chinese Republic. The center of student protest began shifting from the old examination halls to the new schools, with restlessness among the new-school students (*hsüeh-sheng*), those studying abroad as well as those at home, beginning to overshadow discontent of the *chü-jen*. After 1898, K'ang Yu-wei, Liang Ch'i-ch'ao, and their followers, although divested of political power, continued to agitate for constitutional government and other reforms, and Chang Chih-tung correctly saw the "young and

131. *CSL:KH*, 428:7–8.
132. *HNP*, pp. 114, 121.

innocent students" as especially susceptible to their influence. In addition, Sun Yat-sen began to bid more actively for support from the growing student class. How to limit the developing political consciousness of students exposed to Western ideas, how to keep "rebellious" thoughts from their minds, how to encourage loyalty to prince, parents, and the Holy Sage became ever more serious concerns for Chang Chih-tung in the years following 1898. Exhortation or moral suasion continued to be his chief method of coping with the problem, but he also tried to establish rules and regulations, punishments and rewards.

The collected works of Chang merely suggest the scope of the problem in Hupeh and Hunan from 1898 until Chang's transfer to Peking in 1907, and the available documents provide more data on disciplinary measures promulgated than on the student incidents that inspired the measures. Chang's papers, however, do make it clear that discipline was flouted on several occasions, mainly at the Self-Strengthening School and the Hupeh Military Preparatory School. In the fall of 1898, soon after the close of the Hundred Days, one Chang Ying, a student at the military academy, "collected a mob and incited it to evil." About the same time two students of the Self-Strengthening School, Liu Wen-yao and Kuan Ts'un-yüan, got drunk and committed a similar offense, inciting a crowd to brawling and destruction.[133] By 1901 students who had "repeatedly stirred up trouble" were tearing down and destroying official notices and proclamations, and two were expelled from the Self-Strengthening School on these charges.[134] In 1905 Chang was forced to order Hunan officials to restore order among students who, incited by "outlaws," were demonstrating and seeking to intimidate the authorities because their demands had not been met. Their illegal demands should be rejected, Chang ordered, but a compromise settlement of the legal demands should be effected.[135]

In 1898 Chang merely protested against contraventions of custom (*kuei-chü*) and propriety (*li*) at the schools, but he later began to describe the situation as "frightful." More and more students were degenerating to "stupidity" and "senselessness," and their disregard of law as well as of school rules could easily lead to rebellion if carried much further.[136] To combat this trend, Chang initially ordered firmer faculty control over the students of his provinces. In the fall of 1898 he handed down direc-

133. *CC*, 102:23–25.
134. *CC*, 118:25–25b.
135. *CC*, 118:39b–40.
136. *CC*, 118:25–25b.

tions to instructors of the Self-Strengthening School and the military academy, advising them that they were responsible for more than the specialized subjects which they taught, and that their responsibility extended into the field of moral education. They were charged with giving the students additional instruction in methods of self-cultivation (*hsiu-shen*), character formation (*li-p'in*), perfecting talent (*ch'eng-ts'ai*), and building patriotism (*pao-kuo*). The instructors were to help the students develop loyalty, love, honesty, and a sense of shame. They were to devote at least six hours a day to Chinese studies, remain in attendance during all military and Western language classes to see that directions were obeyed and carried out diligently, and inspect the students' quarters daily.[137] In 1901 Chang assigned to the military academy two new proctors named Li Chung-chüeh and Chiang Chieh. The two men were ordered to make regular and thorough inspection of the students' quarters and to watch for "disorderly pastimes, neglect of study, scornful words and jeering smiles, wrangling and fighting, fondness for gambling, and all that is against the rules of the school." Chang added: "Inspect their doings in order to verify their diligence in studies. Investigate what they discuss in order to observe their heterodoxy or orthodoxy. Stimulate them to loyalty and filial piety in order to cultivate their base. Encourage them to modesty and shame in order to correct their tendencies."[138]

In addition, Chang called for tightening the regulations of the Self-Strengthening School and a revision of the entrance requirements. Rules about expelling disobedient students were to be enforced more strictly. Entrance examinations should be made harder. They had been too loosely administered, Chang complained, with the result that many "ignorant, unambitious pretenders" had crept into the student body. On the theory that discipline of a smaller group would be easier, he reduced the four classes of the school from thirty to twenty students each in 1898. In 1899 he revised the age limits. Previously the school had been open to men between the ages of fifteen and twenty-four. By the new regulations, Chang lowered the upper age limit to eighteen years. Only *sheng-yüan* of Hupeh who were eighteen or below would be admitted to the Self-Strengthening School. Such youths were mentally vigorous and acute, could progress rapidly, and were willing to receive instruction with "empty hearts" (*hsü-hsin*).[139]

137. *CC*, 102:24–25b.
138. *CC*, 104:19–20.
139. *CC*, 103:8b–9b.

If the students in Hupeh and Hunan created troubles for Chang Chih-tung, even greater worries were caused him by students native to the two provinces who were attending schools in Japan.[140] These students, remote from the personal surveillance of Chang, were exposed more directly to radical or "seditious" ideas. Chang's worries over their behavior became acute after the attempted uprising in Hupeh by the returned K'ang-Liang follower, T'ang Ts'ai-ch'ang, who sought to overthrow Manchu power and establish an independent constitutional regime in Southeast China. Soon after August 23, 1900, when T'ang and his main fellow-plotters were executed, Chang Chih-tung learned that Hupeh students in Japan had organized or were participating in an association allegedly inspired by K'ang Yu-wei and having similar aims to those of T'ang Ts'ai-ch'ang's Independence Society. Hupeh students had become members of the Society to Encourage Determination (Li-chih hui) and were meeting frequently to hear lectures and engage in "false and perverse" discussions. Chang cabled the Chinese minister in Japan to urge him to awaken the students to the danger of associating with rebels.[141] He also dispatched several cables to Ch'ien Hsün, who had been sent to Japan in 1899 to supervise the Hupeh students.[142] He upbraided Ch'ien for having been too lenient in dealing with the students and too irresponsible in his conversations with them. He directed Ch'ien to be stricter and more cautious.[143] In an appeal to filial piety, Chang ordered Ch'ien to bring the students to their senses and make them repent their wrongs so that they would not "give their parents cause for worry."[144]

In 1901 the governor general of Liangkwang heard that Chang was planning to recall all Hupeh and Hunan students abroad. He urged Chang to reconsider, lest the recalled students "act like wounded deer who do not choose the best place to shelter." Chang replied that although many students were agitating for revolution, he wished to give the majority of them a chance for self-reform. He had no intention of recalling them all, although as a warning to the others, he was directing that three

140. See Roger Hackett, "Chinese Students in Japan, 1900–1910," *Papers on China*, 3 (1948), 134–169 (East Asian Research Center, Harvard University); Marius B. Jansen, *The Japanese and Sun Yat-sen* (Cambridge, Mass.: Harvard University Press, 1954), pp. 112–115. By 1906 there were more than 5,400 Chinese students in Japan, 1,360 of them from Hupeh. Ch'en Ch'ing-chih, *Chung-kuo chiao-yü shih* (Shanghai, 1936), p. 634.
141. *CC*, 166:10–10b.
142. *HNP*, p. 128.
143. *CC*, 166:10b–11.
144. *CC*, 166:9–10, 34–34b.

of the most infamous "rebel followers" be denied scholarships and withdrawn from their schools abroad.[145]

In 1902 Chang sent a personal appeal to be circulated among Hupeh students in Japan. He admonished the students not to forget their ruler, their parents, or the Holy Sage; to obey the Chinese minister, the supervisor of Chinese students in Japan, and their Japanese teachers; and to stand firm and upright, having nothing to do with "rascals" and "heterodox theories."[146] On December 30, 1902, he ordered Chinese officials in Japan to suppress a newspaper that was being published under the title of *Hu-pei hsüeh-sheng lüeh* (Hupeh Student Summary). Until then, Chang admitted, the paper had not spread misleading ideas or given offense, but it might do so, and should therefore be closed as a precautionary measure. Furthermore, he asked why the students of Hupeh had presumed to start this paper on their own responsibility, without asking the permission of Chinese authorities. The students should stick to their studies and use their abilities in mastering knowledge that could be applied when they returned home. If they still felt the need of an outlet for feelings of patriotism, they should spend their spare time in translating useful Japanese books on government and education. Any student resisting the order to close the newspaper was to have his monetary subsidy cut off and the Japanese school he attended would be asked to expel him.[147]

In 1903 the empress dowager called Chang to Peking for an audience, and knowing his keen interest in students abroad, she gave him, among other tasks, the job of drafting a set of regulations to reduce "corrupt practices" among the Chinese students in Japan. While in Peking, Chang negotiated with the Japanese minister, Uchida Yasuda, on those regulations that would require commitments by the Japanese government or Japanese school authorities. After receiving a promise of cooperation from the Japanese, Chang formally presented the regulations to the throne on October 6, 1903. The nine most important provisions on the discipline of Chinese students in Japan are summarized as follows.[148]

All students going abroad at their own expense would be required to undergo a "security clearance" before departure. Their families or clans

145. *CC*, 171:10.
146. *CC*, 104:36b–37.
147. *CC*, 185:19–19b. For other incidents involving Chinese students in Japan, see Li Chien-nung, pp. 192–194.
148. *CC*, 61:1–10.

would report their names to local officials, who would investigate their reputations and make recommendations to the provincial authorities.

Only a limited number of Chinese students would be admitted to Japanese schools each year for the study of government, law, or military matters. No privately supported students would be permitted to receive military training in Japan, and Chinese government-supported students would be given first consideration for enrollment in government and law courses. There would be no restriction on the number of Chinese students admitted to Japanese technical schools.

All Chinese government and privately supported students, regardless of whether they planned to attend Japanese government or private schools, would be required to register with the Chinese minister to Japan and the Chinese general supervisor of students in Japan before their enrollment.

Students could enter only those private schools recognized by the Japanese Department of Education as maintaining standards equal to those of government schools. They could, however, enter special preparatory schools established for Chinese students, providing these, too, were recognized by the Japanese Department of Education.

Japanese school authorities would be responsible for grading the conduct of Chinese students within the schools. However, if evidence were obtained showing that the students' deportment outside the schools was incorrect, the Chinese minister and supervisor of students could at any time consult with the Japanese school authorities on reducing the students' grades for conduct.

In cases of proven serious offense, the Japanese school authorities would honor requests from the Chinese minister or supervisor to expel guilty governmental or privately supported Chinese students. Any student expelled would be deported from Japan, and reports on his case would be submitted to the Chinese Ministry of Foreign Affairs (Wai-wu pu) and the authorities of his home province.

Chinese students should regard study as their sole duty. Writing reckless essays, issuing newspapers, or meddling in politics would be considered as turning their backs on their duty. If the Japanese school authorities or Chinese officials in Japan discovered such activities, they would warn the Chinese students involved to desist. All not obeying would be expelled. If the Chinese officials had proof that inflammatory writings were printed or reprinted by students in Japan, they would consult with Japanese government authorities on means of effective prohibition. Charges of slander or libel brought against Chinese students would be dealt with according to Japanese law.

All Chinese students who were graduated or withdrew from schools in Japan would be prohibited from engaging in any activities disruptive of peace and order. If investigation showed that they had unpeaceful intentions, they would be deported.

And finally, all Chinese government-supported graduates of Japanese schools, upon returning home, would be required to serve for five years in the provinces that had subsidized them.

Chang's regulations were accepted by the throne, and according to the chronological biography by Hsü T'ung-hsin, additional items were added later in 1903 at the suggestion of the Japanese. Largely upon the insistence of the Japanese, the original regulations included a set of rules for the encouragement of Chinese students who were graduated from Japanese schools, as well as the rules for their discipline.[149] The method of encouragement specified was the conferral of Chinese civil service degrees on graduates returning from Japan. Before the court entertained this idea, however, numerous changes had occurred in the school and examination systems within China. Those changes were a part of the late Ch'ing reform movement, in which Chang Chih-tung, after emerging unscathed from the Reform Movement of 1898, functioned as China's foremost promoter of "general education."

149. *CC*, 61:1b; *HNP*, pp. 175–176.

7 The Promoter of General Education (1900–1905)

Chang Chih-tung renewed his zeal as a reformer after the Boxer Uprising of 1900. For the third time in his career a crisis in foreign relations had impressed him with the need for internal change. In general, his response to the uprising was similar to his reaction following the Sino-French War of 1884 and the Sino-Japanese War of 1894. However, Chang perceived that the need for reform had now become more urgent than ever. The dismemberment of China by foreign powers had not slackened as a result of reforms prior to the Boxer Uprising. Indeed, it had increased and greatly accelerated between 1894 and 1900. Within the same period, popular discontent had grown, as evidenced by the Boxer movement itself. Furthermore, among the intelligentsia, "heterodox ideas" had spread steadily, partly as a by-product of previous reforms. The influence of K'ang Yu-wei and Liang Ch'i-ch'ao had not been altogether eradicated, and the influence of Sun Yat-sen was developing. Problems of discipline in the "student class" were increasing. At the end of the Boxer Uprising, dynastic downfall seemed imminent to many. But some, including Chang Chih-tung, felt that collapse could still be avoided through more sweeping reforms than the dynasty had effected in the past.

Chang Chih-tung publicly professed confidence in the dynasty's continuing ability to control and channel reform and prevent it from further weakening the state. Recovery of strength and prosperity under an authoritarian system was still his basic purpose in advocating reform, and he remained opposed to "constitutional government." Yet it was obvious that forty years of piecemeal self-strengthening reform had failed to achieve the basic goal of the past effort. As self-strengtheners, the generation of Chang Chih-tung had progressed beyond the generation of Tseng Kuo-fan in the number and variety of reforms undertaken, but the scope of reform had never been truly empire-wide, and the procedures had not been altered much during four decades. Any specific reform was usually the innovation of one official, who carried out the project in his own administrative domain; he did the best he could with the means at his disposal, after receiving a vague directive from the court. Only during the unsuccessful Hundred Days' Reform led by K'ang Yu-wei and Liang Ch'i-ch'ao had there been a stronger effort at centralization. Chang could not condone the K'ang-Liang party tampering with the classics nor their promotion of "people's rights." The leaders of the 1898 movement, who were as much as twenty to thirty-five years younger than Chang, appeared to him as political upstarts and ingrates, despite the fact that he had helped advance some of them to positions of prominence. Yet by 1901 Chang was prepared to renew advocacy of certain of the 1898 reform plans that had been jettisoned. Mature and experienced officials were ready to provide leadership for a new reform movement under the empress dowager. Progress without the precipitate haste of 1898 was demanded, and blending of the Chinese and Western had become a byword.

As a result of the Boxer Uprising, Chang doubled his endeavor in behalf of an imperial reform program and came forward with concrete proposals that would alter important institutions of the country as a whole, require better planned and firmer central direction of reform, and demand more coordinated action by provincial officials. In the field of educational reform, Chang's proposals were especially broad. He called for a system of "general education" (*p'u-chi chiao-yü*) to be based upon a network of new schools and accompanied by abolition of the ancient examination system. After the Boxer Uprising a frightened court was prepared to heed the counsel of its Hukwang governor general, for Chang Chih-tung had emerged from the uprising in a strong political position, with his own prestige considerably enhanced.

The Boxer movement, in its origins, was an outpouring of resentment by the lower classes, expressing themselves against foreign incursion and indirectly against domestic depression. The Boxers were soon joined by conservative elements of the bureaucracy and the court in attacks upon foreigners as well as their establishments and legations. To end the Boxer Uprising, an expeditionary force organized by the Allied Powers occupied Peking on August 14, 1900. The empress dowager, the emperor, and the court fled to Sian in the Northwest. A year later, on September 7, 1901, the Allied Powers imposed upon China a severe settlement of the uprising. The weakness and humiliation of the Ch'ing dynasty were starkly evident to all, foreigners and restive Chinese alike.

During the Boxer crisis Chang Chih-tung turned an act of insubordination into an act of loyalty.[1] Chang's initial demand was that "the Boxer bandits" be suppressed by force. He telegraphed Peking that all "who resist government troops, kill military officers, stir up riots at the gate of the capital, and destroy railroads built by the country" should be exe-

---

1. Able use of Chang Chih-tung's numerous documents on the Boxer crisis is made in Chester C. Tan, *The Boxer Catastrophe* (New York, 1955), 276 pp. The quotations and citations of Chang's writings immediately following are drawn mainly from Tan's study, pp. 66–70, 76–88, 91–92, 131.

cuted in accordance with law.[2] The court refused to use forcible measures as recommended by Chang and other responsible officials. The court instead determined on a policy of appeasement. As the Boxer depredations continued and the Allies organized their expeditionary force to march on Peking, the court's policy of appeasement was converted into a policy of cooperation with the Boxers, through the influence of Prince Tuan, the Grand Councillors Kang-i and Chao Shu-ch'iao, and other "reactionaries." Chang Chih-tung opposed the policies of both appeasement and cooperation. On June 14, 1900, he and Liu K'un-i, the governor general of Liangkiang, sent a joint memorial to the throne urging that the Boxers be "suppressed first and pacified afterwards."[3] On June 20 he drafted and dispatched to Peking a similar telegraphic memorial signed by eight governors general and governors of the Yangtze provinces.[4] Further emphasizing the need for suppressing the Boxers as a means to forestall Allied military intervention, he and Liu K'un-i sent telegrams to the Grand Councillor Jung-lu, an intimate of the empress dowager and the most important minister at the court.[5] Despite such pleas, war was declared on the Allied Powers by an imperial edict of June 21, 1900.

Chang Chih-tung and other high officials in the southern and eastern provinces chose to ignore the declaration of war and preserve peace within their own jurisdictions. A decree of June 20 had ordered that the various provincial officials "should be united together to protect their territories." The throne intended that the officials should cooperate in defense against any foreign attacks, but Chang Chih-tung elected to interpret the order as empowering the governors general to use their own discretion in saving their territories from peril. He suggested to his colleagues that they comply with the decree by protecting the foreigners and suppressing seditious societies.[6] Chang gained the support of Liu K'un-i; Li Hung-chang, the governor general of Liangkwang; Yüan Shih-k'ai, the governor general of Shantung; and Sheng Hsüan-huai, the director of railroads and telegraphs (who originally recommended to Chang that the declaration of war be ignored). The governor general of Fukien also undertook to preserve order in his province. Chester C. Tan has written that "the contributions of the southern viceroys in maintaining peace in the southeastern provinces can hardly be exaggerated."

2. *CC*, 160:2; Tan, p. 65.
3. *CC*, 160:7b–8b.
4. *CC*, 80:22–23, 160:23.
5. *CC*, 160:9–10.
6. *CC*, 160:39b; Hummel, I, 30.

He further stated: "The decision [of the officials] was a bold and wise one, for it not only saved the southern and eastern provinces from the devastation of war but also made the war look like something beyond the control of the Throne, thus leaving the door for peace open and incidentally strengthening the position of the southern viceroys in the future negotiations."[7]

Once the decision was made, Chang Chih-tung actively attempted to eradicate Boxer influence in Hukwang. He also deterred Li Ping-heng, imperial inspector of the Yangtze Naval Forces, from impetuous action at Shanghai; helped direct local negotiations with foreign consuls on the protection of aliens; urged that Chinese diplomats remain at their posts abroad; advised against stopping payments on foreign loans; urged rescue of foreign ministers beseiged in their legations at Peking; and corresponded with Marquis Ito of Japan on settlement of the Boxer troubles.[8]

However, Chang Chih-tung did not push his insubordination to a reckless extreme. While maintaining peace in his own area, he complied with a decree to transfer troops to the north. Chang sent five thousand men from Hukwang on the grounds that it was required by the "loyalty of a minister."[9] Throughout the crisis, he showed great concern for the empress dowager and the emperor and urged foreign powers to guarantee their personal safety.[10]

When it became obvious that imperial policy had led to disaster, the negotiation of peace was entrusted to Li Hung-chang and Prince Ch'ing, with Chang Chih-tung and Liu K'un-i serving as advisers. Throughout the complex process, Chang more accurately reflected the viewpoints of the court than did Li Hung-chang. Chang was "always cautious, sometimes to the extent of timidity," while Li Hung-chang "boldly advocated actions which the Court would not like."[11] When the Allied Powers demanded the execution of eleven princes and ministers who had been implicated in the uprising, Li Hung-chang and Liu K'un-i were prepared to agree, but Chang Chih-tung flatly refused: "How can three Chinese ministers request the execution of so many Manchu princes?"[12] On December 24, 1900, foreign envoys presented to the Chinese government a

7. Tan, pp. 78, 239.
8. *CC*, 80:24–26, 29, 160:39–39b, 161:1–2, 6b, 24–24b, 29–29b.
9. *CC*, 160:30.
10. *CC*, 161:24, 29, 164:26.
11. Tan, pp. 142–143.
12. *CC*, 167:30.

joint note of twelve articles, setting forth terms demanded for settlement of the Boxer Uprising. Chang Chih-tung objected to a number of the terms he considered too harsh, and the empress dowager, feeling that Li Hung-chang was "too ready to counsel acceptance of the foreign demands," initially endorsed Chang's ideas. Li rebutted Chang's objections and countered with a personal attack on Chang's "academic way of thinking."[13] Li's views finally prevailed with the empress dowager, and on January 16, 1901, Li was given permission to accept the terms of the allied joint note, incorporated into the final Boxer protocol that was signed eight months later. Yet the empress dowager probably held Chang in higher personal esteem when the Boxer crisis ended.

Li Hung-chang died on November 7, 1901, a few months after the Boxer protocol had been signed. This was followed by the deaths of Liu K'un-i on October 6, 1902, and Jung-lu on April 11, 1903. Chang Chih-tung and Yüan Shih-k'ai remained as senior Chinese advisers of the empress dowager, both regarded well by Tz'u-hsi until the end of the Kuang-hsü reign in 1908. Both were in positions to make important contributions to the late Manchu reform movement.

Preparations for Reform

Chang Chih-tung, Li Hung-chang, Liu K'un-i, Yüan Shih-k'ai and their associates had preserved peace in large areas of China during the Boxer Uprising. A court that at first had spurned their counsel of moderation was compelled to rely heavily upon them in achieving a final settlement of the uprising. By their theory that the Boxer Uprising was a "rebellion," they had facilitated the settlement and perhaps had spared the empress dowager from being held personally responsible for the Boxer episode and being forced to abdicate.[14] The empress dowager acknowledged her gratitude to these officials, even if she was inclined to take unto herself credit for inspiring their actions. "If the Southern and Eastern parts of our Empire enjoyed full protection from disorders," one imperial pronouncement read, "the fact was solely due to our Decrees, which insisted upon the rigid maintenance of peace."[15]

The empress dowager also signified her willingness to accept the leadership of Chang Chih-tung and his colleagues when planning the

13. Tan, pp. 153–155.
14. Hummel, I, 30.
15. From the penetential decree of February 13, 1901, *CSL:KH*, 477:13–16b, tr. in Bland and Backhouse, p. 378.

program of reconstruction that became known as the Manchu Reform Movement. Professing penitence, she vowed to make amends for previous shortcomings by personally directing her officials in substantial reforms. A penitential decree issued in the name of the emperor on August 20,1900, a few days after the court's flight from Peking, admitted a "sense of our errors and deep remorse" and called upon all officials to rally speedily to the court's support in devising a reform program.[16] A more comprehensive decree, issued from Sian on January 29, 1901, has been termed "virtually the charter of the reform movement under imperial auspices which filled the remaining years of Tz'u-hsi's dominance."[17] That remarkable proclamation depicted the empress dowager as "now thoroughly bent on reform." She and the emperor were said to be convinced "of the necessity of blending into one harmonious form of administration the best customs and traditions of Chinese and European Governments." High officials were ordered to report within two months with their recommendations on "a constant supply of men of talent, a sound basis of national finance, and an efficient army."[18] Similar expressions of the intent to reform were voiced in another penitential decree of February 13, 1901.[19]

Despite these protestations of the empress dowager, there were both foreign and Chinese skeptics who questioned the sincerity of her intentions or the purity of her motives. Some felt that the wily old ruler, incapable of any genuine change of heart, sought only to hoodwink or impress the foreign powers and thereby ameliorate the pending Boxer settlement.[20] Chang Chih-tung may have been among the original doubters. If he did not mistrust the empress dowager's decrees, he at least had cause to mistrust some of her close advisers at the court. Chang was given to understand that although provincial officials had been ordered to memorialize upon reform, they should not stress "Western methods" (*hsi-fa*) in their replies. On February 12, 1901, the governor of Anhwei informed Chang that a secret report had been received in Anking from a secretary of the Grand Council, advising, "When sending the memorials on reform, do not unduly esteem Western methods." Chang replied to the governor: "What kind of reform would it be if we did not pay atten-

---

16. *CSL:KH*, 467:11–13; Bland and Backhouse, pp. 393–394.
17. Meribeth E. Cameron, *The Reform Movement in China, 1898–1912* (Stanford, Calif., 1931, p. 57.
18. *CSL:KH*, 476:8–10b, tr. in Cameron, *The Reform Movement in China*, pp. 57–58; Bland and Backhouse, pp. 419–424.
19. *CSL:KH*, 477:13–16b, tr. in Bland and Backhouse, pp. 376–381.
20. Cameron, *The Reform Movement in China*, pp. 60–62.

tion to Western methods?"[21] On February 27, 1901, Chang registered a protest with Lu Ch'uan-lin, president of the Board of Revenue. Chang reported having heard that a junior official of the Grand Council had telegraphed certain governors general and governors stating: "By all means do not talk much about Western methods." Chang pointed out that selection from the West had been clearly specified in the imperial edicts and decrees recently issued. He argued in favor of such a selection, declaring that without Western methods, "reform" (*pien-fa*) would become as devoid of meaning as had the "readjustment" (*cheng-tun*) attempted in the past. "What, after all, is the intention of the empress dowager?" he asked. He requested clarification on whether the provinces could memorialize thoroughly and truthfully.[22] Chang later received a telegram from Lu Ch'uan-lin, which stated: "Do not plagiarize the externals of Western methods and avoid giving cause for scandal."[23] On March 24, 1901, Chang sent a still stronger and longer telegraphic protest to Lu, outlining numerous advantages that could accrue from the application of Western methods, including the advantage of overcoming the Western view of the Chinese as "stupid, crude, lazy, weak, cunning, deceitful, and useless." With powerful nations in the world, Chang argued, China would perish if it remained isolated; if it were in harmony with others, it would survive.[24]

Chang Chih-tung's protests may have influenced the empress dowager toward fulfilling her decreed promises. At any rate, she soon took definite steps toward fulfillment, and Chang's fears of bad faith subsided. One of the empress dowager's first encouraging actions was to create the Office for the Management of State Affairs (Tu-pan cheng-wu ch'u) on April 21, 1901. She appointed as members of the office Prince Ch'ing; the Grand Secretaries Li Hung-chang, Jung-lu, K'un-kang, and Wang Wen-shao; and the Board president Lu Ch'uan-lin. Chang Chih-tung and Liu K'un-i were ordered to serve as "participants from a distance." The office was to function as a clearing house for reform proposals. Members of the office were to receive and consider memorials, select worthy suggestions, and make recommendations to the throne. Any decisions would be promulgated when the "Imperial carriage" returned to Peking.[25] Chang Chih-tung seemed to doubt the need of awaiting the return of the "Imperial carriage."[26] Otherwise he was pleased with the development,

21. *CC*, 170:34b.
22. *CC*, 171:3–3b.
23. *CC*, 171:23.
24. *CC*, 171:22b–24b.
25. *CSL:KH*, 481:4b-5.
26. *CC*, 172:19b.

When the Office for the Management of State Affairs was established, Chang was already planning reform proposals that he himself wished to submit to Sian. On March 31, 1901, he had telegraphed fourteen other leading officials of the southeast and southwest suggesting united action in the form of joint memorials. The more men who participated, he explained, the better would be the results. Liu K'un-i was the principal addressee of Chang's telegram, and Chang asked that Liu serve as the chief drafter of one petition emphasizing Western methods and another on reform of Chinese methods and institutions. Chang suggested nine topics that might be discussed under the heading of Western methods: foreign travel, study abroad, revision of the examination system, establishment of schools, Western-type troop training, employment of specialists, establishment of police, expansion of postal services, and use of silver dollars. Chinese reforms could be discussed under such headings as reduction of official salaries, reduction of clerical staffs, revision of the methods for selecting officials, and elimination of tax corruption. "If the memorial on Western methods is not approved," Chang stated, "we can at least hope for some slight change in the old [Chinese] methods."[27] Chang also approached Yüan Shih-k'ai on cooperation, but Yüan, feeling that the governors general should submit their individual views, decided to memorialize alone. Liu K'un-i, however, agreed to join Chang, but he insisted that Chang be the chief drafter of the petitions they would submit.[28]

Before submitting their major reform memorials of 1901, Chang and Liu made a preliminary but unsuccessful attempt to win approval for changes in the examination system. Because of the Boxer troubles, a number of provinces envisaged difficulties in presenting examinations according to schedule. Liu K'un-i suggested to Chang that the provincial examinations be temporarily suspended in fairness to all the candidates. But instead, Chang saw this as an opportunity to revive the argument for revision of the examination system. He proposed resurrecting his plan that had been approved during the 1898 reform movement and then dropped, the plan which specified different tests for the three sessions of an examination: tests on Chinese government and history; on foreign government, military affairs, agriculture, industry, and mathematics; and on the meaning of the Four Books and Five Classics. However, Chang wished to amend his previous ideas on including scientific topics such as

27. *CC*, 171:30b–32. The telegrams were sent to the governors general of Liangkiang, Szechwan, Liangkwang, Fukien, and Yunnan; the governors of Shantung, Anhwei, Hupeh, Kiangsu, Chekiang, Hunan, and Kweichow; the Ch'ing-chiang taotai in charge of grain transport; and Sheng Hsüan-huai in Shanghai.
28. *HNP*, p. 147.

physics, chemistry, and electricity, having come to the conclusion that knowledge in these subjects could not be tested adequately by written essays alone. Liu K'un-i agreed with Chang's ideas.[29] On June 2, 1901, they incorporated these ideas in a telegraphic memorial that defined their over-all purpose as encouraging practical learning without abandoning study of the classics. If the revisions were adopted, they wrote, scholars in the provinces where examinations might temporarily be suspended could use the time to study and prepare themselves for tests under the new regulations.[30] The proposals of Chang and Liu were not adopted, however.

In the meantime, Chang and Liu had been working on their major reform drafts. They consulted together frequently by telegraph and solicited opinions from subordinates and fellow officials elsewhere.[31] On July 12, 1901, they presented a long memorial attesting that "in political reform men of talent are the foremost need."[32] On July 20, 1901, they presented two additional memorials. One proposed twelve items for reorganizing the Chinese political system: promoting frugality, breaking down customary formalities [red tape], stopping contributions or payments to obtain office, examining officials and increasing their emoluments, removing useless clerical staffs, weeding out government servants and messengers, lightening punishments and imprisonment, reforming the method of civil service examinations, planning for the livelihood of the Manchu Bannermen, abolishing military colonies and garrisons, abolishing the Army of the Green Standard, and simplifying documents and laws.[33] The second memorial included eleven items on the adoption of Western methods: encouragement of foreign travel, adoption of foreign military drill, enlargement of military supply, improvement of agricultural administration, promotion of industry, adoption of new legal and penal codes, use of the silver dollar, use of the stamp tax, promotion of the postal administration, collection of opium duties, and more translation of Japanese and Western books.[34] A supplementary memorial of July 20 discussed the urgency of making plans for financing various

29. *CC*, 183:4.
30. *CC*, 83:6b–7b.
31. Preliminary discussion of the 1901 memorials may be found in *CC*, 171:32–32b, 37–38b, 172:19b, 20–20b. See also *HNP*, pp. 146–147.
32. *CC*, 52:9b–29. See excerpts of this document in Teng and Fairbank, *China's Response to the West*, pp. 197–198; Peake, pp. 37–39.
33. *CC*, 53:1–33. See also Teng and Fairbank, *China's Response to the West*, pp. 199–200.
34. *CC*, 54:1–32b. See also Teng and Fairbank, *China's Response to the West*, pp. 200–205.

reforms.[35] The first of these four documents outlined a national system of schools.

The 1901 Memorial on Educational Reform

Chang Chih-tung and Liu K'un-i used quotations from the classics to begin their 1901 memorial proposing a Westernized school system.[36] They pointed out that it was recorded in the *Book of Changes*, "The Way of Heaven changes or transforms itself, hence the movement of heavenly bodies is continuous. This is a great demonstration of self-strengthening." Mencius had noted that "men for the most part err and are afterwards able to reform. They are distressed in mind and perplexed in thoughts and then they arise to vigorous reform."

Referring to the Boxer crisis, the memorialists stated that recent times had been most perplexing and distressing to the rulers, scholar-officials, and people of China. Error should be followed by change and reform. If the empire remolded its own institutions and borrowed the best from other nations, it could achieve the mean glorified by the sages of the past.

After these opening words, Chang and Liu introduced the main theme of their 8,000-character memorial: that training men of ability should be the first consideration in carrying out political reform. They wrote: "China is not poor in resources but poor in men of ability, not weak in troops but weak in will. The scarcity of men of ability results because knowledge is not broad and learning is not solid. The weakness of will results because those who live in improper ease have no long-range plans for coping with danger and saving (the empire) from destruction, and those who are self-satisfied have no power of persistence in zealous studies. Protecting the state and achieving good government will be impossible without the men."[37] Chang and Liu stated that, after carefully considering both ancient and modern educational methods, they had decided upon four general proposals. They suggested the establishment of civil and military schools, revision of the civil service examination system, abolition of the military examination system, and the encouragement of study abroad.

In order to justify their proposal for establishing a network of new civil and military schools under state control, Chang and Liu argued that educational methods used in the West were not without merit. To sup-

---

35. *CC*, 54:32b–36.
36. Unless otherwise specified, the data on the 1901 memorial are drawn from *CC*, 52:9b–29.
37. *CC*, 52:10b.

port their generalization, they briefly surveyed the history of Chinese education. From the Han dynasty through the Sui dynasty, scholars had been selected for the civil service primarily by means of recommendation. From the T'ang and Sung dynasties through the Ming, the main method used had been examination. Both methods had a common characteristic: they selected men of ability already trained but did not provide the training. While family schools had offered a definite curriculum, official schools had only emphasized testing on subjects already learned. The old methods had worked fairly well when times were peaceful. Nevertheless, they were not in harmony with the system of schools that had existed during the Three Dynasties. Various classics also agreed that in the Chou dynasty, teaching and learning had encompassed virtue (*te*), conduct (*hsing*), the Way of Heaven (*tao*), and significantly, the practical arts (*i*). Students were trained in archery and charioteering as well as in rites, music, writing, and mathematics. Chang and Liu inferred that the curriculum of ancient times represented a combination of the substance (*t'i*) and utility (*yung*). Furthermore, the civil (*wen*) and the military (*wu*) had both been represented in education and accorded equal attention. "The old system of our ancestors is really adequate for 10,000 generations," the memorialists wrote. "Today in the methods of schools of all Western countries, there seem to be ideas handed down from the Three Dynasties. To say that we can recover our forgotten ceremonies from abroad is not wrong."

Having thus established a general case for Western educational methods by asserting the prior claim of the early Chinese dynasties, Chang Chih-tung and Liu K'un-i proceeded to describe contemporary Western schools as they understood them. They placed special emphasis on the schools of Germany and Japan, which they were convinced provided the best models for China to follow. "The power of Germany is the strongest, and the system of schools is the most highly developed in Germany," they wrote. "The rise of Japan has been the fastest, and the number of schools (there) is the greatest of any country in the East."

They recommended that China adopt a system similar to that which they described as prevalent abroad. They envisaged a Chinese system with schools at six levels, including both general and technological schools and both civil and military schools. The courses offered by all of these institutions would represent a combination of Chinese and Western learning. The learning would be presented to boys and young men. Although Chang Chih-tung later took action on behalf of education for women, in 1901 he and Liu indicated interest in training the sons of the gentry only. Their plan called for schools of the following types.

Kindergartens (meng-hsüeh). Kindergartens should be established by the departments and districts for boys eight through eleven *sui.* These schools would teach such subjects as recognition of characters, proper speech, reading aloud, and simple songs. While the children would read the Four Books, they would be required to study only one or two of the Five Classics. Family schools and free schools could be established privately by the gentry, but they would be expected to accept official guidance and inspection. They also would be required to submit annual reports to the authorities.

Lower primary schools (hsiao-hsüeh). Primary schools, also to be founded by the departments and districts, would provide a three-year course for boys of twelve through fourteen *sui.* Students would complete the Five Classics, with the main emphasis on simple explanation of classical meanings rather than memory work. General studies would include elementary Chinese and foreign geography, mathematics (not advancing beyond cubic measurement), surveying (not advancing beyond the measurement of level land surfaces), and beginning work in Chinese history. Calisthenics or "pliable exercises" (*ju-juan t'i-ts'ao*) would be required. Final examinations would be administered by an officer from the gentry.

Higher primary schools (kao-teng hsiao-hsüeh). These schools would accommodate students from the ages of fifteen through seventeen *sui.* The curriculum would include more advanced classical interpretation, geography, mathematics (through algebra), and surveying. Composition and essay-writing would be offered, as well as the study of foreign governments and more advanced Chinese history. The study of one foreign language would begin. The higher primary schools would require "calisthenics with equipment" (*ch'i-chü t'i-ts'ao*), and all schools would have a military drill ground (*ping-tui ts'ao-ch'ang*). After completing the course, students would sit for a prefectural examination, administered by a prefect, with a member of the gentry assisting him. Those with passing grades would receive diplomas and become "supplementary students" (*fu-sheng*). They could then enter prefectural schools. Those who failed the examination would remain in the higher primary schools.

Middle schools (chung-hsüeh). These schools, to be opened to students ranging from ages eighteen through twenty *sui,* would be established by the prefectural governments. In addition to higher primary school graduates, these schools would admit holders of the lowest purchaseable degree (*chien-sheng*), providing they paid tuition and took the same course as the supplementary students. Noncommissioned military officers and soldiers might be admitted if they could prove literacy and experience in mathematics and cartography. Students of the middle schools would review the classics, history, and geography and would study essay-writing, literary styles, and the styles of public documents and correspondence. Military men would be exempt from the study of literary styles. Courses would be offered in more advanced mathematics (including geometry and trigonometry), surveying (including military cartography), Chinese history and military affairs, and foreign history, language, science, and law (including the study of treaties). The elements of agriculture, industry, and commerce would be explained. Middle schools would require "military-style calisthenics" (*ping-shih t'i-ts'ao*) and would have military drill grounds. Graduates would be examined by the provincial director of education. Those passing the test would receive diplomas, become "salaried students" (*lin-sheng*), and be entitled to enter provincial high schools.

High schools (kao-teng hsüeh-t'ang). Three types of high schools would be established: general schools, technological schools, and military schools. Each would offer a three-year program of classroom work, to be followed by one year of practical training on the job or in the ranks. The general high schools would be opened in the provincial capitals. Those of the large provinces should accommodate two to three hundred students, and those of medium-sized and small provinces would take more than one hundred students. Where it was not feasible to build dormitories, branches of a provincial high school could be opened at two or three places. Only graduates of a middle school general studies program would be admitted. The high schools would be divided into seven departments: classical studies, including Chinese literature; history, including both Chinese and foreign history and geography; science, including astronomy (Chinese and foreign), physics, chemistry, electricity (*tien-hsüeh*), dynamics (*li-hsüeh*), and optics (*kuang-hsüeh*); political science, including Chinese and foreign political science, foreign law and finance, and international relations; military science, including foreign tactics, ordnance, administration, and medicine; agriculture; and engineering, including surveying and mathematics, cartography, road building, irrigation, fortifications, the manufacture of weapons and gunpowder, and similar subjects. Each student would enroll in one of the seven departments;

concurrently, he would study one foreign language. All of the schools would have military drill grounds. Students who completed three years of classwork in the high schools would be expected to spend an additional year as interns or trainees (*lien-hsi hsüeh-sheng*). Law students would be assigned to government offices that conducted foreign affairs, and military students would enter the army. Students of the remaining five departments could elect service with bureaus of agriculture, industry, commerce, or mining, so as to supplement their formal studies with practical experience. With regard to the study of medicine, the memorialists noted that, as Western medicine was not yet widely accepted in China, and Chinese medicine had its advantages, general study of the subject could be postponed. But there should be no delay in the promotion of military medicine, to be included in the department of military science.

As for the second category of high school, four special or technical schools (*chuan-men hsüeh-hsiao*) would be established in each province to teach agriculture, industry, commerce, and mining. They would have the necessary mechanical and laboratory equipment. Their curriculum would include review of the Chinese classics and literature. All of these schools would have military drill grounds. Graduates of middle schools would be admitted. After three years of study in the technical schools, students of agriculture would be sent to districts of their native provinces, mountain villages, or riverside villages for a year of practical training in agriculture. Students of industry would be assigned to Chinese or foreign factories, those of commerce to various ports, and those of mining to foundries or regions where natural resources were being exploited.

Each province would also have a special military preparatory school, the third type of high school proposed. Western methods would be taught in all military courses. Foreign languages would also be taught. Courses would be offered in the Four Books, Chinese history, and essay writing. Instead of operating a military preparatory school, some provinces might prefer to follow the Japanese example of setting up a school of armaments (*p'ao-kung hsüeh-hsiao*) to teach the manufacture of weapons. Students for the military schools would be selected from among the *lin-sheng* who had completed middle school. After three years of classwork, they would be assigned to the ranks for a year, serving six months as soldiers and six months as noncommissioned officers.

Universities (*ta-hsüeh*). Students completing the high school study programs would be examined by the governors general, governors, and education directors of their provinces. Those who passed the examination would become civil or military "tribute students by virtue of special merit" (*yu-kung-sheng*). Upon completing their year of practical training, they would be expected to pass an examination administered by an official sent from Peking. Those succeeding in this test would become "elevated men" (*chü-jen*). *Chü-jen* who had achieved grades ranking them among the upper half of the successful candidates could be sent to Peking to enter a university for civilian scholars (*wen-shih ta-hsüeh*) or a naval and military university (*shui-chün lu-chün ta-hsüeh*).[38] *Chü-jen* who had ranked in the lower half of the examination group would be eligible for civil service appointments as minor capital officials or assistant district magistrates or would be eligible for military appointments in the rank of lieutenant or second captain. If the higher ranking *chü-jen* did not wish to study at a university, they too would be eligible for minor appointments. If the lower ranking men did not wish to accept appointments, they could remain in their high schools until the next examination, in the hope that they could then qualify for university entrance. Chang and Liu explained that it would be impractical to try to accommodate all of the *chü-jen* of the empire in two universities. Such a procedure would be excessively expensive. As an economy measure, they proposed selecting only half of the group. The universities in the capital would be more advanced but would be organized into the same departments as the provincial high schools. The university program would last for three years. Upon completing it, students would be tested by an imperially appointed director general of the metropolitan examination (*hui-shih tsung-ts'ai*). Students who passed the metropolitan examination would become civil or military "presented scholars" (*chin-shih*). According to their standing in the examination, they would receive appointments as court assistants, board officers, district magistrates, captains, or second captains. After receipt of the *chin-shih* degree, students would be subjected to no further examinations; that is, the palace and court examinations of the old system would not be required for school graduates. A student could become a *chin-shih* between the ages of twenty-eight and thirty *sui,* which the memorialists claimed was not slow in comparison with the old system.

Ideally, Chang Chih-tung and Liu K'un-i claimed, Chinese schools should be established in this sequence, beginning with primary schools and gradually working up to the university level. Thousands of primary schools should be opened first, so as to graduate their students before the middle schools were established, and middle schools should be

38. The Peking Imperial University, established during the Reform Movement of 1898, had been destroyed during the Boxer Uprising. Hummel. II, 674.

opened before the high schools. However, Chang and Liu admitted, to follow this sequence would require too many years. A deviation from the logical order was demanded by China's urgent need for talent, scarcity of funds, and lack of qualified teachers. A need also existed for smoothly integrating into the new system those scholars trained by the traditional, classical educational methods. Chang and Liu therefore suggested that the initial emphasis be placed on the establishment of middle and high schools. These would be opened to young, intelligent, and healthy *sheng-yüan* from the old examination system. The *sheng-yüan* admitted to the middle and high schools at the outset would be offered a short-term or accelerated course (*su-ch'eng k'o*) modeled after such courses in Japan. Chang and Liu recognized that an abbreviated program, with lessons pared down to the absolute essentials, would mean some sacrifice of quality. But for the first stage of educational reform, they regarded speed and concessions to the existing *sheng-yüan* as the more important factors. While *sheng-yüan* were taking short-term courses in the middle and high schools, the building of the lower schools could proceed. When primary schools had become as numerous as the trees in a forest, then the proper educational sequence could be adhered to, step by step, with a full-time curriculum.

In their 1901 memorial Chang Chih-tung and Liu K'un-i stressed no radically new concept of the basic purposes of education. They proposed a school system that would lead students to a government career, just as Chinese education had done in the past. They still described schools as a training ground for the civil service and depicted school graduates as a reservoir from which to draw officials. Their proposed method for selecting officials would be by civil service examination, as in the past. Chang and Liu in effect suggested a new examination system that would operate parallel to the old system for a decade and then supplant the old system. The new system would have steps and degrees similar to the old, but it would be broader in scope, based on a variety of Western subjects as well as on the Chinese classics and history, and would not include the eight-legged essay.

In fact, a portion of the 1901 memorial submitted by Chang and Liu suggested elimination of the eight-legged essay from both the old system and the new. The memorialists presented three main arguments. First, some persons claimed that abolishing the eight-legged essay would mean that no longer would anyone read the classics, respect the ancient sages, or appreciate philosophy. Yet that essay did not become entrenched until the Ming dynasty, the memorialists observed. From the Han through the

Sung dynasties it did not exist; nevertheless, the classics were trans-mitted, the *tao* was preserved, and many famous scholars emerged. Others said that abolishing the eight-legged essay would mean the loss of the ability to write good literature. But China's best literature, Chang and Liu noted, was produced from the Chou through the Sung dynasties, which antedated this type of essay. Finally, opponents claimed that abol-ishing the eight-legged essay would mean that those who had already specialized in mastering the style would have no way to advance in their careers. Such critics failed to realize that former masters of this medium had been generally brilliant and generally vigorous in scholarship, the memorialists countered. Anyone capable of mastering this essay certainly should not find the recommended new studies difficult. Youth could easily adapt to the new system. Scholars from twenty-five to fifty *sui* should have no trouble with the new subjects, except possibly with foreign languages and advanced mathematics. If a man could not change his practices and pass examinations after the new system had been in effect for ten years, he would be naturally untalented and unambitious and would be of no use as an official anyway. However, in the transi-tional period, Chang and Liu suggested, experts in the eight-legged essay who could not make the adjustment easily might be given employment as teachers of the classics and literature in primary and middle schools. Those who took the new examinations and failed them might be shown special consideration and compassion by the throne. Those over sixty *sui* might be given honorary titles, while those under fifty might be given minor jobs after special examinations following recommendation by provincial officials.

As the new examination system would differ from the old in content and style, so its methods of administration would vary. Chang and Liu briefly mentioned several points. In the prefectural examinations (and presumably in the higher examinations as well) percentile marks would be awarded by the examiners, and the sealing (*mi-feng*) of examination papers would not be required. Here Chang and Liu referred obliquely to one of the safeguards against favoritism by an examiner or his collusion with a student—the old method whereby the corner of an examination theme was pasted down to hide the student's name.[39] Chang and Liu apparently looked upon announced percentile grades as a sufficient check on an examiner's integrity. Prefects and directors of education who would conduct examinations at the higher primary and middle school levels

39. On *mi-feng*, see Zi, *Pratique des examens litteraires en Chine*, p. 109.

would be required to assign and keep a careful record of grades. When the results of an examination were announced, those who passed would not simply be revealed by name. Beside each name, the percentile grade would have to be promulgated. In the provincial examinations for high school graduates, Chang and Liu noted, the number of candidates would be small. Students therefore could be tested in the presence of an examiner (*mien-shih*). Again there would be no need to paste over names. The new system would also eliminate the step whereby themes were copied (*t'eng-lu*) by a team of transcribers in order to prevent examiners from identifying the students' handwriting.[40]

The memorialists outlined the method by which the new examination system would gradually take the place of the old. Under the old system, the maximum number of civil service degrees that could be awarded following the different examinations was determined by fixed quotas. Chang and Liu proposed that school graduates who passed examinations under the new system be allotted a share of the quotas. Higher primary school graduates who passed prefectural examinations would receive their degrees from the quotas established for *sheng-yüan* taking *sui* and *k'o* examinations. High school students who passed the provincial examinations given by the imperially appointed chief examiners would receive their degrees from the quota for *chü-jen*, and university graduates who passed the metropolitan examinations would receive their degrees from the quota for *chin-shih*. A new quota for *yu-kung-sheng* would be established to provide for the degrees awarded high school graduates after their examination by provincial officials and before the examination for the *chü-jen* degree conducted by an imperial appointee. At the beginning one-third of the quotas for *chin-shih* and *chü-jen* degrees would be reserved for school graduates. One-fourth of the quota for *sheng-yüan* would be reserved for school graduates. The quota percentages for school graduates would be increased gradually in successive examinations over the course of a decade. "After ten years and three (triennial) examinations," Chang and Liu wrote, "the old quotas will be reduced to nothing, and all *sheng-yüan, chü-jen,* and *chin-shih* will come from the schools." When this stage was reached, the quota system would be abandoned altogether, and from then on percentile grades would determine whether a larger or smaller number of degrees would be awarded.

While the new school and examination systems would operate parallel to the old civil service examination system for ten years, Chang Chih-

---

40. This practice was abolished by a decree on November 12, 1901. *CSL:KH*, 488:2.

tung and Liu K'un-i were not in favor of permitting the old system to continue without some change in subject matter. Once again they revived the plan originally drafted by Chang in 1898 and resubmitted earlier in 1901, calling for different tests during the three sessions of an examination: one test on Chinese government and history, another on Western government and arts, and the third on the Four Books and Five Classics. Chang and Liu again explained that their motive in making the proposal was to provide for practical studies without neglecting the classics, or to provide for stress on both the *t'i* and the *yung*. The recommended amendments in the old civil service examination would help develop more useful talents for government service during the period when schools were being established.

At the same time, the memorialists saw no excuse for prolonging the old military examination system while effecting a gradual transition to the new methods of military training. They urged immediate cessation of the military examinations. "Clumsy bows, swords, and stones are absolutely useless in battle," they wrote. "The advantage of bows and arrows has been long lost to firearms. As for writing from memory from the military classics, most (candidates) employ substitutes to write for them. They do not even know what is being discussed." Declaring that graduates of the military examinations did more harm than good for the empire, Chang and Liu refuted supporters of the system with essentially the same arguments that Chang had advanced in 1898.

The final section of the 1901 memorial submitted by Chang Chih-tung and Liu K'un-i concerned the encouragement of study abroad. Chang had presented the basic ideas in previous memorials and in the *Ch'üan-hsüeh p'ien*. However, in the 1901 petition, study abroad was more closely linked to staffing the proposed new Chinese school system with faculty members. "If we wish to establish many (schools), there will be two difficulties," the memorialists wrote. "First, the funds required will be great. Second, we will have few teachers. The difficulty of finding teachers will be greater than that of raising funds." Encouraging study abroad, in schools already established, would hasten the training of faculty members for Chinese schools. Both privately financed study and study subsidized by the provinces should be encouraged, with some students sent for general civil and military training and some for special training in normal schools. Chang and Liu again especially recommended study in Japan: language problems would be fewer, Japan had more short-term courses than the West, and expenses, including travel, would be about two-thirds less than the cost of study in the West. All students returning from abroad, private students as well as government-subsidized scholars, could present their diplomas to the authorities, be reexamined, and if successful, earn *chü-jen* or *chin-shih* degrees. They then would be assigned to serve as teachers in the new Chinese schools.

Chang and Liu had relatively little to say about the difficulty of financing their proposals. Their principal memorial on "men of talent" mentioned but did not seriously discuss the problem. The supplementary memorial of July 20, 1901, on financing all of their proposed reforms, was primarily an exhortation. It urged that funds somehow be budgeted for reform projects, but included few concrete ideas on where or how to procure the money.

The memorial of Chang Chih-tung and Liu K'un-i quickly evoked endorsement by the empress dowager and resulted in imperial action. On August 29, 1901, an edict ordered that in civil service examinations thereafter, the Confucian classics must share a place with other branches of knowledge. Beginning in 1902, the first session of the provincial and metropolitan examinations would consist of five discussions (*lun*) on Chinese government and history. The second session would consist of five dissertations (*ts'e*) on foreign government and arts. The third session would consist of two explanations based on the Four Books and one on the Five Classics. The same edict provided for abolition of the eight-legged essay, beginning in 1902.[41]

Another edict of August 29, 1901, abolished the system of military examinations in its entirety. Holders of the second and third military degrees were ordered to apply for new training. Holders of the first degree and candidates for that degree were charged to join provincial forces until modern military schools could be established.[42] On September 11, 1901, a decree directed that all governors general and governors should establish military academies. Since Chang Chih-tung, Liu K'un-i, and Yüan Shih-k'ai already had military schools in operation, they were instructed to prepare regulations governing future military education. After being approved by the throne, the regulations would be promulgated as a model for other provinces to follow.[43]

An edict of September 14, 1901, called specifically for a national school system. It ordered that all academies (*shu-yüan*) in provincial capitals be converted to colleges (*ta hsüeh-t'ang*); that all prefectures and independent departments establish middle schools; and that all departments

41. *CSL:KH*, 485:13b–14b.
42. *CSL:KH*, 485:14b.
43. *CSL:KH*, 485:19b.

and districts establish primary schools and kindergartens. The schools were to have a Sino-Western curriculum.[44]

On September 16, 1901, another edict approved sending students abroad from all provinces and provided a strong incentive for men who received foreign diplomas. When graduates returned from overseas, they would be entitled to sit for a civil service examination. Those who passed the test would be awarded *chü-jen* or *chin-shih* degrees.[45]

Other educational reforms were decreed later in 1901 and after the court had returned from Sian to Peking on January 2, 1902. Chang Po-hsi was appointed superintendent of educational affairs, and on his recommendation, Wu Ju-lun was assigned the task of restoring the Imperial University, which had been destroyed during the Boxer Uprising.[46] Following the death of Wu Ju-lun on February 9, 1903, Jung-ch'ing, a Mongol Bannerman, was assigned to assist Chang Po-hsi in educational matters. In 1904 Sun Chia-nai, the first president of the Peking Imperial University, having been recalled from retirement, was ordered to join Chang Po-hsi and Jung-ch'ing in forming a three-man commission to direct educational affairs in the capital.[47]

Initial Achievements in Hukwang

Imperial approval opened the way for carrying out the school plan of Chang Chih-tung and Liu K'un-i, but it did not provide easy answers for specific problems faced by the provinces. The imperial orders of 1901 offered no immediate solutions for what Chang Chih-tung had defined as the two most crucial problems: financing schools and securing teachers. The initial decrees also failed to define the relationship that should exist between the new schools and the old examination system, and failed to provide degrees for the graduates of Chinese schools. Chang and Liu were later forced to press for clarification of these points. Nor were directives from the throne altogether sufficient to overcome a lingering prejudice against change harbored by many of the literati. Despite these deterrents, some immediate progress toward the establishment of schools was made in the provinces, especially in the areas governed by Chang Chih-tung and Yüan Shih-k'ai. Chang's efforts were enacted partly in Hukwang. However, he also devoted considerable attention to education when assigned to Liangkiang in 1902 and 1903 and to Peking in 1903 and 1904.

44. *CSL:KH*, 486:2–2b.
45. *CSL:KH*, 486:6–b.
46. Hummel, II, 871.
47. Hummel, II, 674.

Chang Chih-tung was transferred to Liangkiang to become governor general there on October 31, 1902.[48] Just before his transfer, he was able to report to the throne that he had "established" eleven different kinds of schools in Hupeh. Actually, many of his "new" schools represented reorganization of the various self-strengthening institutions he had previously founded, including the Self-Strengthening School, the Military Preparatory School, the Noncommissioned Officers' School, and schools of agriculture and industry. He had also added "practical studies" at the Liang-Hu, Ching-hsin, and Chiang-Han Academies.[49] Because of his previous efforts, Chang Chih-tung was in a better position than some governors general for immediate compliance with the imperial decrees ordering that schools be opened. He had a head start, and his old institutions formed the basis for the new.

The additional educational reforms carried out by Chang were executed despite a strain imposed on his treasury by the huge Boxer indemnity demanded of China. Hupeh was expected to pay Tls. 1,200,000 annually as its share of the indemnity. This made it necessary for Chang to devise new sources of revenue. He raised land and grain taxes, imposed new levies on rental properties and shops, and attempted to establish provincial control over opium sales through licensing decoction of the drug.[50] On October 31, 1902, he informed the throne that the educational reforms completed up to that time were being financed with funds already allocated for education; a contribution of Tls. 100,000 from Liu Wei-chen, a retired provincial commander; the sale of lottery tickets in Hankow; and school tuition payments.[51]

On January 11, 1902, Chang memorialized on experimenting with lotteries.[52] He claimed that an existing prohibition of lotteries in Hupeh could not be effectively enforced and had merely resulted in an underground traffic in tickets, many of them entering his domain from other provinces. Noting that lotteries were a common method of raising emergency funds in foreign countries, he proposed that they be legalized in

48. *CC*, 57:40–40b. For memorial of thanks on this appointment, see *CC*, 71:23b–24b.
49. On the addition of new studies at the Hupeh academies, see *CC*, 47:21b–22b, 152:-30b, 218:13b–14b.
50. For memorials on these financial measures, see *CC*, 55:21–25b, 56:8–9b.
51. *CC*, 57:10b–11b.
52. *CC*, 55:21–22. This was Chang's second experience with lotteries as a source of state revenue. When serving as governor general of Liangkwang in 1885, he had legalized and taxed examination lotteries. Lottery tickets were issued in Kwangtung to gamble on the *wei-hsing*, surnames of successful candidates in the next civil service examination. Persons who bought tickets could bet on a list of surnames. Those who guessed the most correctly won. Yang Lien-sheng, "Buddhist Monasteries and Four Money-raising Institutions in Chinese History," *Harvard Journal of Asiatic Studies*, 13, 1–2 (June 1950), 188.

Hupeh and sponsored by the provincial administration in collaboration with reliable merchants. Originally he intended to apply any lottery surpluses to the indemnity fund, but after receiving imperial permission to proceed with the scheme, he decided to apply the profits to education.

With regard to fees paid by Hupeh students, Chang reported that in foreign countries tuition was never charged for lower primary schools, this being a unique feature of "national people's education" (*kuo-min chiao-yü*). Nor were foreign normal school students charged tuition, since they would later be obliged to teach in primary and middle schools and refrain from entering other professions. All other foreign students were required to pay tuition, Chang stated. Hupeh could not follow this plan exactly, he continued, but primary school students of the province would never be charged tuition, and those of higher schools would not be expected to pay any fees for at least two years. However, tuition would be expected of students from other provinces. All would be charged 160 yuan a year, except those from Hunan, who would pay only 100 yuan. Forty students from Hunan would be accepted by the Hupeh normal school and thirty students each by the high school, civil and military middle schools, and the language school.[53]

In carrying out these educational reforms, one of Chang Chih-tung's first acts after submitting the 1901 memorial was to create a provincial office to administer the new school program. On July 24, 1901, at the same time that he assumed concurrent duties as the acting governor of Hupeh, he established the Hupeh Provincial Office of School Affairs (Hu-pei ch'üan-sheng hsüeh-wu-ch'u).[54] This office was given control over all provincial government and private schools. School inspection, curriculum, schedules, and faculty supervision were all within its jurisdiction. Two of Chang's most trusted subordinates were placed in charge of the office. Liang Ting-fen was appointed director general of civil schools (*wen-hsüeh-t'ang tsung-t'i-tiao*). Liang was the acting Wuchang prefect, and earlier most Hupeh academy and school affairs had been under his immediate supervision.[55] Huang I-lin, an expectant prefect who had studied military science in Japan, was made the director general of military schools (*wu-hsüeh-t'ang tsung-t'i-tiao*). The two men were also placed in charge of a translation bureau attached to the Office of School Affairs for the purpose of preparing textbooks.[56] Before the death of

53. *CC*, 57:10b–11b.
54. *CC*, 57:12–12b.
55. *CC*, 57:12b. See also Chang's recommendation of an award for Liang in 1907, *CC*, 70:18.
56. *CC*, 57:12b.

Liu K'un-i, he and Chang Chih-tung had planned the translation and issue of textbooks as a joint enterprise. Early in 1902 they established the Kiangsu-Hupeh Translation Bureau (Chiang-Ch'u pien-i-chü) in Nanking.[57] Huang Shao-chi was appointed chief editor of the bureau and was assisted by Miao Ch'üan-sun and Lo Chen-yü, a well-known scholar who lived until 1940.[58]

Another step preparatory to the reorganization of education in Hupeh was the dispatch of missions to inspect schools in Japan. In the fall of 1901 an eleven-man delegation headed by Chu Tzu-tse was sent to study Japanese military methods, schools, and factories.[59] Another delegation, sent to study schools and purchase textbooks in the winter of 1901, included Liu Hung-lieh, Lo Chen-yü, Ch'en I, Hu Chün, Tso Ch'üan-hsiao, and T'ien Wu-chao.[60]

On October 31, 1902, just before departing for Liangkiang to assume the post of governor general left vacant by the death of Liu K'un-i, Chang Chih-tung was able to report to Peking on the following progress in the establishment of Hupeh schools.[61]

Normal School. Realizing that teacher training was an essential for success in the Hupeh educational program, Chang Chih-tung gave priority to the establishment of a normal school in Wuchang. He selected a site in the eastern part of the city and constructed a building that was adjacent to a primary school, where students might gain experience in practice teaching. In addition to general studies, the school offered courses in education and teaching methods, school administration, and hygiene. An enrollment quota was set of 120 students ranging from twenty through thirty *sui.* Initially, however, capable civil students between the ages of twenty-five and thirty-five were selected for a short course of one year. The second class was to be offered a two-year course, and the third class a full course of three years. Liang Ting-fen was appointed concurrent supervisor (*chien-tu*) of the normal school. Appointed as principals (*t'ang-chang*) of the school were Hu Chün, a *chü-jen,* and Ch'en I, a *lin-sheng,* both honor graduates of the Liang-Hu Academy and members of the school mission that had visited Japan. One Japanese was employed to serve as general instructor (*tsung-chiao-hsi*) at the normal school.

---

57. *HNP,* p. 155. For documents on the translation of textbooks, see *CC,* 174:25b, 178:27–27b.
58. Hummel, I, 343–344.
59. *HNP,* p. 151; *CC,* 57:2b.
60. *HNP,* p. 153.
61. Unless otherwise specified, data in remainder of section are drawn from *CC,* 57:1–22b, 104:35–36b.

Primary Schools. In the West, Chang Chih-tung pointed out, lower primary schools were usually staffed by women who were capable of simultaneously teaching and caring for children. China, however, was already having trouble finding qualified male teachers, so that it would be even more difficult to obtain females. For the time being, therefore, Chang advised, lower primary schools in Hupeh would have to be left to private initiative. Family schools and free schools would be the responsibilities of the gentry, while the provincial educational system would start with the higher primary schools. To set an example for the departments and districts of Hupeh to follow, Chang opened five higher primary schools in different sections of Wuchang: the Northern, Southern, Western, Central, and Eastern Higher Primary Schools (the latter attached to the normal school). Quarters were found in government buildings already erected. Each school was to have one hundred students. Until a lower primary system was put into operation, the higher primary schools would admit boys from eleven through fourteen *sui* who had studied the Four Books and could read and write. Students would attend the higher primary schools for four years. The curriculum consisted of ethics (*hsiu-shen*), classical study, Chinese literature, mathematics, history, geography, science, map drawing, and physical education. Liu Hung-lieh, a secretary of the Grand Secretariat, was appointed director (*t'i-tiao*) of the higher primary schools.

Civil Middle School. The civil middle school that Chang Chih-tung reported he had opened in Wuchang represented an enlargement and reorganization of the former Self-Strengthening School. With an enrollment set at 240 men from fifteen through twenty-four *sui*, the middle school initially recruited most of its students from the old Liang-Hu, Ching-hsin, and Chiang-Han Academies (which were supplanted by the new institutions founded by Chang). In the future, it was planned, higher primary school graduates would be promoted to the middle school. The courses to be offered over four years were philosophy (*lun-li*), classical review, Chinese literature, foreign language, history, geography, mathematics, natural history (*po-wu*), physics and chemistry, law, map drawing, and physical education. The probationary taotai, Huang Shao-ti, was named supervisor of the middle school, and the probationary prefect, Kao Ling-wei, was appointed to serve as director.

Military Middle School. Chang Chih-tung selected a site south of Tang-tzu-shan upon which to build a military middle school, but he opened the school provisionally at the old Chiang-Han Academy. The enrollment of the school was set at 240. Initially "literate and healthy" students were sought for the school; later higher primary school graduates would be admitted. The age limits were fifteen through twenty-four *sui*. Chang described the curriculum as being much the same as that of the civil middle school, with the addition of work in such fields as military drill, target practice, riding, and swimming. Students in the military middle school were to study German or Japanese, while those in the civil middle school were to study English or Japanese. After four years in the military middle school, students would spend six months in the ranks. Huang I-lin was made concurrent supervisor of the school. He was to be assisted by graduates of Japanese military academies.

Civil High School. Chang Chih-tung reorganized the Liang-Hu Academy to form the Liang-Hu High School (Liang-Hu kao-teng hsüeh-t'ang). Mindful of the edict of September 14, 1901, which ordered the founding of provincial colleges, he pointed out that the school was the virtual equivalent of a college (*ta hsüeh-t'ang*). The high school was divided into eight departments: classical study, including ethics and literature; Chinese and foreign history; Chinese and foreign geography, including surveying; mathematics, including astronomy; physics and chemistry; law; finance; and military science. The first four departments, called "Sino-foreign studies," would be staffed by Chinese instructors. Japanese and Western teachers would present courses in the last four departments. The enrollment quota called for 120 students. Initially, superior students from the Liang-Hu, Ching-hsin, and Chiang-Han Academies were to be accepted. They would spend one year in general preparatory studies and three years in specialized studies. After graduation, they would be sent abroad to study for one year. Later, when middle school graduates could be accepted, the time required for graduation from the high school would be reduced to three years. A Hanlin compiler, Wang T'ung-yü, was appointed supervisor of the high school; Chi Chü-wei, the educational director of an independent department, was made assistant supervisor; and Wang Ping-en, an expectant taotai transferred from Kwangtung, was named director of the school.

Military high schools. Chang Chih-tung reported that two military high schools had been "established" in Wuchang, although both had been in operation before 1902. One was the former Military Preparatory School, with an enrollment of sixty students selected from among the first and second degree holders of Hupeh. The school had three German instructors under a Chinese director, Li Chung-chüeh, a former Kwangtung district magistrate, and a Chinese general inspector (*tsung-chi-ch'a*), Chiang Chieh, a departmental magistrate transferred from Shantung.

When the school was reorganized, students were accepted from the old Military Preparatory School. They were to be given one year of class-room work, followed by one year in the army, where six months would be devoted to practice as soldiers and six months to service as officer candidates (*hsüeh-hsi wu-kuan*). The first new class to be recruited would remain in school for three years, receiving both general and military training, and then would spend six months in the army as officer trainees. Once middle school graduates could be admitted, the term of training would be reduced to two years, with six months of assignment to the army. The curriculum of the Military Preparatory School included military tactics, geography, surveying, mathematics, physical education, ordnance, fortifications, infantry studies, cavalry exercises, and artillery studies.

The second military high school established by Chang Chih-tung was the former Noncommissioned Officers' School. It had five Japanese instructors, under the supervision of the Chinese officials, Chang Piao, leader of the Hupeh Defense Forces, and Huang Pang-chün, an expectant prefect. This school differed from the Military Preparatory School in that it offered training for literate military men who had already acquired experience in the armed forces. Because its students were experienced, Chang Chih-tung explained, its curriculum was broader and especially emphasized the application of principles. Courses included military systems (*chün-chih*), battle tactics (*chan-shu*), weapons (*ping-ch'i*), mathematics, hygiene, drill methods (*ts'ao-fa*), wall-building (*chu-ch'eng*), field exercises (*yeh-ts'ao*), "military chess" (*ping ch'i*), surveying and cartography, tactical practice (*chan-shu shih-shih*), boxing (*chi-chi*), and military medicine.

Language school. Chang Chih-tung established a language school for the primary purpose of training specialists in international relations. Resembling the former Self-Strengthening School, the new institution offered courses in English, French, German, Russian, and Japanese as well as geography, history, mathematics, international law, and international relations. The enrollment quota called for 150 students from fifteen through twenty *sui*, or thirty students for each of the five foreign language departments. Superior students from the Self-Strengthening School were selected to make up the first class. In the future, middle school graduates were to be admitted. Students would be graduated from the language school after five years of work. For the first two years of the school's operation, Chinese teachers would be used. Thereafter foreigners would be employed. The probationary prefect, Ch'eng Sung-wan, was appointed director of the school.

School of Agriculture. Chang Chih-tung reported that the former School of Agricultural Affairs had been moved to the outskirts of Wuchang so that it could be near an experimental farm, composed of two thousand mou of reclaimed public land. At the new site 120 students were to take courses in agriculture, sericulture, animal husbandry, and forestry. The first class of the reorganized school was composed of students who had not yet been graduated from the old school of agriculture. They were to undergo a two-year supplementary preparatory course and then devote another two years to the main program of the school. Sang Pao, a taotai of Honan province, was appointed general superintendent (*tsung-pan*) of the school. Wang Feng-ying, an expectant prefect, was named director, and Lo Chen-yü was appointed general manager (*tsung-ching-li*).

Industrial school. Chang Chih-tung reported that he had reorganized the former School of Industrial Arts on the site of the old Chiang-Han Academy. The school offered courses in physics and chemistry, machine manufacturing, weaving and dyeing, and architecture. The enrollment quota called for sixty engineering students and thirty craft apprentices. Students of the old school who had not yet been graduated would be offered a two-year supplementary preparatory course and then spend another two years in specialized fields. The expectant taotai Liang Tun-yen was appointed director of the school, and Chang Chih-tung requested that Ch'a Shuang-sui, a departmental magistrate, be assigned as the assistant director.

The School of Diligent Accomplishment (Ch'in-ch'eng hsüeh-t'ang). Chang Chih-tung established this school for older *sheng-yüan* who could not compete with young students in regular classwork or undergo the program of physical education prescribed for other schools of Hupeh. The school utilized the facilities of the former Chiang-Han Academy. It had no definite courses but arranged lectures and organized discussions based on the classics, histories, and useful books on Chinese and Western government and practical arts. No fixed term of study was specified, and there was no fixed enrollment quota. However, examinations were to be presented periodically, and those who passed would be recommended for commendations and awards. Yang Shou-ching, a secretary of the Grand Secretariat, was appointed chief professor (*tsung-chiao-chang*) of the school, while Yao Chin-ch'i, an unassigned secretary of the Board of Revenue, and Jao Shu-kuang, a Hanlin bachelor, were appointed assistant professors.

The Institute for Officials (Shih-hsüeh yüan). Chang Chih-tung established this institute to provide in-service training for Hupeh officials.

Provincial officers attended the institute to participate in discussions led by "lecturing fellows" (*chiang-yu*). Chang engaged Chinese scholars to conduct seminars in dynastic historical records, Hupeh geography, water conservation, and mathematics. Foreign lecturers were employed to discuss physics and chemistry, law, finance, and military matters. Ch'eng Chih-ho, an unassigned senior secretary of the Board of Works, was appointed supervisor of the institute.[62]

Statement of Guiding Principles

In the same memorial of October 31, 1902, in which Chang Chih-tung reported on Hupeh's initial progress in establishing schools, he discussed eight principles that had been adopted to govern the new educational system of the province.[63] Two of Chang's points were familiar themes—the need of a special period for classical study in the new schools, and the need for military drills and disciplines that would help unite the civil and military. Other points represented relatively fresh ideas. Among these were Chang Chih-tung's statements on the basic aims of education. In their memorial of 1901, Chang and Liu K'un-i had dwelt upon education as a means of obtaining better officials. Chang now spoke of education as a means of enlightening the people as a whole. In this and other reports by Chang, education for citizenship began to share a place with education for the bureaucracy. Chang wrote:

> The educators of all (foreign) nations say that training human talent as preparation for employment by the state is a secondary consideration. In regard to the first consideration, they say that pursuit of knowledge is a duty of the people, and enabling the people to attend schools is a duty of the state. Consequently, in all the (foreign) schools the full cost of lower primary education is borne by the governments. Their major purposes are (1) ethical, to provide everyone with a knowledge of the principles of righteousness; (2) patriotic, to enable everyone to know (the importance of) protecting the state; and (3) related to livelihood, to enable everyone to have the means of making a living. This is called "public education" (*i-wu chiao-yü*). It is also called "national people's education" (*kuo-min chiao-yü*) . . . Primary schools teach them to be good men, and middle schools and universities teach them to be useful men.

---

62. Chang also directed considerable effort toward having an Institute for Officials established in Peking under the direction of Chang Po-hsi. For his telegrams on the subject, see *CC*, 178:20b–21b, 26–27, 33–34, 179:3b–4.

63. Quotations and data in the following section come from *CC*, 57:12b–21b.

Westerners looked upon primary schools, Chang Chih-tung continued, as indices of enlightenment when judging a country. They attempted to determine the amount of public money spent for primary education, the length of the school program, and the percentage of the population enrolled in the primary schools. They were not so concerned about college graduates, although obviously if primary school enrollments were large, many students would go on to middle schools and universities. In their 1901 memorial Chang Chih-tung and Liu K'un-i had urged that China give priority to the establishment of middle schools. Chang now defined the establishment of primary schools as the most urgent task, while expressing a belief that primary schools were the institutions where knowledge and appreciation of the Chinese *t'i* could best be implanted. In Japan, he observed, school attendance had reached 80 percent (presumably of the eligible population), but the Japanese were still dissatisfied and made regular plans to increase the percentage. In view of the large number of Chinese children and the scarcity of educational funds, China could not hope to equal Japan immediately. But the immediate goal should be accommodation of 10 to 20 percent (of the eligible population) in primary schools. Since reaching the goal would depend largely on the availability of teachers, normal school training was presented by Chang as an integral part of the primary school plan. "As soon as we have trained teachers, we can have primary schools," he wrote. Normal school training should also be undertaken at once.

Chang summarized a guiding principle for Hupeh schools of all grades with the statement: "Do not compromise in regard to teachers." The faculty and administrative staffs of all the schools should be selected from men who were thoroughly conversant with educational affairs or those who had studied the educational methods of Japan and the West, who had inspected foreign school systems, traveled abroad, or established private schools.

Speaking again of all schools, those at both the primary and higher levels, Chang revealed a concern for uniform standards in school construction. He listed three "important matters" that should be taken into account in building schools. First, consider health and sanitation, because great harm could result unless attention were given to the purity of water and the cleanliness of grounds, the circulation of air and the adequacy of light. Second, to facilitate teaching, attention should be paid to the size of classrooms. A standard should be adopted that would prevent strain upon eyes and ears. For laboratories, arrangements should be made for "long tables" and other special equipment needed. Finally, with regard to the control of students, inspection would be difficult unless classrooms, dining halls, and dormitories were all in the same area. When classes were over, discipline would be difficult unless there were grounds for recreation. Chang reported that all the new schools in Hupeh had an auditorium (*li-t'ang*) and four to eight classrooms (*chiang-t'ang*), with laboratories adjoining the science classrooms. In addition, there were study rooms, bedrooms, dining rooms, washrooms, recreation rooms, infirmaries, guest reception rooms, libraries, and recreation grounds. He added that students had a definite place to assemble for meals, a definite time for rest and rising, and a fixed style of clothing, all in accordance with Western customs.

As another guiding principle, Chang Chih-tung stressed that careful attention should be paid to the selection and compilation of textbooks. "Learning emanates from the *tao*," he wrote, "and the *tao* changes with the times. Thus, there is an important relation between learning and the times." China had a wealth of old books, many of which could be used in the classrooms, but there was a dearth of up-to-date books on modern subjects. He continued:

> We definitely must translate and use foreign books. Japanese education fully imitates Western method, except that courses in religion (*tsung-chiao*) are changed to ethics (*hsiu-shen*) and philosophy (*lun-li*), for which the Japanese compile their own textbooks. For all other subjects, such as geography, cartography, mathematics, physics, and chemistry, most of the books are based on Western works. Recently it has seemed that they (the Japanese) are continually selecting, inspecting, and using them (the foreign books), and a wealth of human talent is steadily produced. This is using the books of other countries and obtaining great profits. Russian schools use textbooks of the French Rebublic, and their students repeatedly stir up trouble. This is using the books of another country and reaping great disadvantages. . . .
> Although we translate and use foreign books, we must also carefully consider revisions: (1) of interpretation and classification—for example, in geography we should consider China in detail and foreign countries in brief, and in zoology and botany we should first treat that which is familiar and then that which is strange; (2) of names—for example, in zoology and botany we should use native names and not transliterations, and in physics and chemistry we should use old translations and not completely new names; and (3) of literary style—the style should be enriched to make understanding clear; it should conform to China's ancient and modern literary methods and wording; we should not use the crooked and confusing expressions characteristic of most books translated literally.

Moving on to another principle, Chang Chih-tung stated that an additional aim of the new educational system should be the achievement of "real results" (*shih-hsiao*), a phrase he often contrasted with "empty talk" (*k'ung-t'an*). He defined three important requirements for effectiveness. First of all, officials should not begrudge expenditures on education. The *Analects of Confucius* warned that if one sought a petty advantage, he would fail in great affairs, and the philosopher Kuan Chung maintained that stinginess was waste. If economy were made the major consideration in building, equipping, and administering schools, then any expenditure would prove in the long run to be a useless extravagance. Second, Chang wrote, impatience should be avoided if real results were to be achieved. Lessons should not be too many, nor graduation too quick. In an eagerness to see results, students should not be allowed to enter middle school without completing primary school, nor enter college without completing middle school. Teachings should be presented in an orderly sequence, lest the toil of the teachers prove ineffective. If schools offered only new courses and neglected the classics, the obligations of filial piety, and the merits of good behavior, there would be no foundation to hold up the educational wall, and the wall would surely tumble. The *Analects of Confucius* advised that haste does not lead to benefit; Mencius warned against pulling up the sprouts to hasten growth of the plant. Third, Chang cautioned, the government should not be loathe to reward school graduates. Giving recognition and employment to the graduates would encourage and strengthen men of talent, while an opposite effect would result if the graduates were not used at all or were used in jobs for which they had not been trained.

Finally, Chang Chih-tung discussed three undesirable practices that should be avoided in the schools. All of these practices were related to preservation of the Chinese *t'i*. First, he stated, the classics should not be abandoned in the lower schools. "Foreign schools all have departments of religion," he declared. "The classics are China's religion." Some educators with a shallow understanding of Western method considered study of the classics a useless waste of time, but knowledge of the classics would strengthen the character of the Chinese people. However, Chang conceded again that elementary education could include a smaller number of the classics than in the past and that study should be concentrated on the general meaning of the classical works and not on memorizing. He estimated that if students read one hundred characters of the classics a day from the ages of ten to eighteen *sui*, they could complete the Four Books, one other small or medium-sized classic, and one of the long classics. Courses on "Western method" were organized in Hupeh primary schools to last four hours a day, and in middle schools to last six hours a day. Chang stated that Hupeh primary and middle school regulations required that two extra hours a day be devoted to the study of Chinese classical works. If one hundred characters were read during these two hours daily, the minds of the students would not be overtaxed. They might not fully comprehend the principles of righteousness, but deeper understanding would come with adulthood. "If the principles of China perish," Chang asked, "how can China itself survive?"

Another practice to be avoided was the study of foreign languages at too early an age. A dictum good for all times, Chang wrote, is, "That which enters first is master" (*hsien-ju wei-chu*). If nations did not observe this dictum, they would soon forget their language and literature and lose their ability to be independent and strong. Stretching his point, Chang charged that if the Chinese did not understand their own language and studied only foreign languages, they soon would be unable to read Chinese books, understand teachings handed down from the golden age of the past, write public documents, or pen personal letters. Foreign language study should therefore not begin until graduation from higher primary school. Students at fifteen or sixteen *sui* would still be "clever in speech" and could still learn foreign languages rapidly.

Concluding his statement of principles, Chang Chih-tung declared that Western philosophy should not be taught in Chinese schools. The numerous Western schools of philosophy, he wrote, were somewhat like the School of Names (*Ming-chia*) of the Warring States Period, but more closely resembled Buddhism, with arguments on the interaction of Heaven and man and the struggle between human feelings and logic, and love and hatred. Clever Western philosophers, vying with one another, had traveled different paths and gone to great lengths to seek out mysteries and probe into the obscure. What they contributed to an understanding of "the real customs of the world" or mundane problems was for the most part already included in the Chinese classics. Chinese philosophy, furthermore, was not to blame for China's decline. Rather, the decline could be attributed to the fact that fickle or excitable Confucian scholars had been concerned with obtaining selfish advantages or had engaged in reckless "empty talk" instead of extending their studies and pursuing the truth. "China's holy classics and esteemed commentaries embrace all (truthful) principles," Chang wrote. "How can the schools set aside the truthful principles of 4,000 years and indulge in empty talk (echoed) from several 10,000 li away?"

Further Educational Reforms

From the end of 1902 until 1907 Chang Chih-tung was active in administering a variety of additional educational reforms in Nanking, Peking, and Wuchang. He assumed office as the acting governor general of Liangkiang on November 8, 1902.[64] During the following month he established the Liangkiang Office of School Affairs, and in January 1903 he presided over examinations at the Natural Sciences Academy (Ko-chih shu-yüan)—a new name of the School for Gathering Talent that Chang himself had established in 1895 during his first tour of duty in Liangkiang.[65] But Chang's most important contribution to education during his second tour of duty in Liangkiang was the founding of the San-Chiang Normal School.[66] Planned as a large establishment that would cost about Tls. 100,000 a year to operate, the school was opened to serve Kiangsu, Anhwei, and Kiangsi. Chang hoped that the enrollment would reach nine hundred within three years, with five hundred students from Kiangsu, two hundred from Anhwei, and two hundred from Kiangsi. Perhaps the most unusual feature of Chang's plan was a faculty training program instituted while the San-Chiang Normal School was under construction. Twelve professors were recruited from Japan to teach education and science courses, and fifty Chinese teachers were employed for courses in ethics, history, geography, literature, mathematics, and physical education. The Japanese professors were assigned the task of studying the Chinese language and Chinese classics for one year before the opening of the normal school. During the same period, the Chinese faculty was to study science and the Japanese language. This program, Chang Chih-tung reported, would increase mutual respect among the faculty members as well as encourage mutual exchange of knowledge. After the school had opened, the Japanese professors' understanding of Chinese would obviate any obstacles to "questions and answers," interpreters could be dispensed with, and a saving of time and money would be effected.[67]

Before completion of the faculty training program for the San-Chiang Normal School, the empress dowager called Chang Chih-tung to Peking for an audience. Chang delivered the Liangkiang seal to his successor, Wei Kuang-tao, and began his journey to the north on March 20, 1903.[68]

---

64. *HNP*, p. 165.
65. *HNP*, pp. 167, 169.
66. See memorial on founding of the school, *CC*, 58:15b–18.
67. Other documents on the San-Chiang Normal School are in *CC*, 185:35–35b, 37, 186:1b–2b.
68. *CC*, 60:31b–32.

His stay in the capital extended until February 7, 1904.[69] Soon after his arrival in Peking, a memorial was submitted by Chang Po-hsi, praising Chang Chih-tung as the Chinese statesman with the deepest understanding of educational matters and asking that Chang Chih-tung be assigned to consult with him and Jung-ch'ing on drawing up regulations for the national school system.[70] The empress dowager granted the request and gave Chang Chih-tung the additional job of personally drafting regulations to govern study abroad by Chinese students.[71] Chang was assigned an office and given a competent staff.[72] For approximately nine months, he and his colleagues worked on the various regulations, revising some articles as many as ten times. For the last two months Chang labored day and night until he was physically exhausted and ill.[73] He submitted his regulations concerning study abroad on August 8, 1903, and on January 13, 1904, he and Chang Po-hsi presented a series of five memorials on education. One requested rewards for officials who traveled or studied abroad.[74] Another proposed a method whereby all new *chin-shih*, thirty-five *sui* or younger, created under the traditional civil service examination system, would be required to enter a School for Presented Scholars (Chin-shih kuan) in Peking and receive training in "general studies" before being assigned to office.[75] The third memorial requested that the throne appoint a controller of educational affairs (*tsung-li hsüeh-wu ta-ch'en*) and permit the incumbent superintendent of education (*kuan-hsüeh ta-ch'en*), Chang Po-hsi, to concentrate solely on his original duties as head of the Peking university.[76] A fourth memorial proposed revision of the civil service examination system, and the fifth presented the detailed school regulations that had been completed by the two Chang's and Jung-ch'ing. The school regulations, in twenty chapters (ts'e), covered all general schools through the university level, special and vocational schools, an Academy of Sciences (T'ung-ju yüan), and the School for Presented Scholars. They included rules on school administration and procedures and a summary of educational principles to be followed.[77] Chang Chih-tung personally wrote

69. *HNP*, p. 177.
70. *HNP*, p. 173.
71. *HNP*, p. 175.
72. *HNP*, p. 173.
73. See letter to Ch'ü Hung-chi, *CC*, 220:17b–18b.
74. *CC*, 61:19–21b.
75. *CC*, 61:22b–24.
76. *CC*, 61:22–22b.
77. For memorial on the school regulations, see *CC*, 61:15b–19. One available edition of the regulations is *Tsou-ting hsüeh-t'ang chang-ch'eng*, published in five ts'e, one han, in 1903 by the Chiang-Ch'u pien-i-kuan shu-chü.

the summary of educational principles and those regulations pertaining to the study of the Chinese classics and literature.[78] The basic educational philosophy set forth was given in brief in the memorial transmitting the regulations: "In establishing schools the general principle is that schools of all classes will take loyalty and filial piety as the root and study of the Chinese classics and histories as the foundation. When the minds of the students have become pure and upright, Western studies may be offered to increase their knowledge and refine their skills."[79]

His duties in Peking completed by February 7, 1904, Chang Chih-tung left the capital for a short visit to Nan-p'i, his ancestral home in Chihli. While there, he contributed money from his own savings as an endowment for a higher primary school in his native village.[80] Chang returned to his post as Hukwang governor general on March 29, 1904, and for the next three and one-half years he continued to work in Wuchang for the improvement of education in Hupeh and, to a lesser extent, in Hunan.[81] To facilitate the work and better divide responsibilities among his subordinates, he reorganized the Hupeh Office of School Affairs during 1904, placing the department under the direction of Liang Ting-fen and ordering Huang I-lin and Wang Feng-ying to serve as deputy directors. The Office of School Affairs was subdivided into six sections, each with a chief and one or more assistants. The six sections were concerned with textbook editing, general studies, special studies (the Institute for Officials, military schools, and medical studies), vocational studies (schools of agriculture, industry, and commerce), overseas studies, and accounting. The translation bureau, which originally had been attached to the Office of School Affairs, was transferred to a newly created Bureau of Foreign Affairs (Yang-wu chü).[82]

Chang Chih-tung also established an educational supply house in 1904. Until then equipment needed for the schools was bought in Shanghai or ordered from abroad—such items as "maps, books, instruments, charts, rulers, paper, pens, slates, specimens, models, tables, and benches." The materials were slow in reaching Wuchang, and the costs were high. Chang set aside a building for use as a storehouse and ordered the Office of School Affairs to start buying the needed equipment in large quantities. School supplies would then be resold to students at 20 percent below the

78. *HNP*, pp. 173, 180.
79. *CC*, 61:16b.
80. *CC*, 72:4b–6, 106:20–21b, 192:22–23; *HNP*, p. 179. Chang also made contributions to a school at his birthplace in Hsing-i, Kweichow. *HNP*, p. 203: *CC*, 221:19–20b.
81. *CC*, 62:1–2.
82. *CC*, 105:30–31, 32b–34.

original cost and to teachers at a 10 percent discount. School officials from other provinces would also be entitled to buy supplies from Hupeh at a 10 percent discount. All persons making use of this facility would be required to offer proof of their student or official status in order "to prevent commercial middlemen from deluding us."[83]

Chang Chih-tung opened several new institutions of learning after his return to Wuchang and adopted measures to attract more students from other provinces. Tuition fees for students from Hunan were reduced from 100 to 70 yuan a year, while the fees for students from all other provinces were cut from 160 to 100 yuan.[84] Among the new institutions, two represented experiments in women's education. However, neither revealed a very high evaluation of women or of women's rights. The two women's schools established were for the purpose of training governesses and nurses. During 1904 Chang Chih-tung ordered the Office of School Affairs to open the School of Reverence and Purity (Ching-chieh hsüeh-t'ang) and the School of Infant Rearing (Yü-ying hsüeh-t'ang). One hundred literate and moral women were to be selected for the first school, where they would attend lectures by a Japanese woman teacher on women's and home education. They would be prepared for employment as tutors in the homes of wealthy families. The second school was to admit one hundred literate nurses to receive instruction from a Japanese woman on child rearing and guidance. Students of this school would also be prepared for employment by rich families. Unmarried girls would not be admitted to either of these two schools, Chang decreed, for it was necessary to "exhibit restrictions and reflect discriminations." If young, unmarried girls were determined to enter a school, their fathers or elder brothers might consult with other relatives and clansmen on establishing a private girls' school at the home of the clan chief. If such private schools were founded, they would be required to report to the authorities on their enrollments and regulations.[85]

Another interesting experiment initiated by Chang was the Hupeh Railroad School (T'ieh-lu hsüeh-t'ang), established in Tokyo. Chang originally founded this institution as a school of railroads and mining in 1905, but the following year he reorganized it to eliminate mining from

83. *CC*, 105.29–30.
84. *CC*, 105:38–39. Chang made a special effort to accommodate 200 students from his native Chihli province. He first offered to pay one-half their expenses from his own savings if they would study in Hupeh. He later ordered that scholarships be paid from public funds. *CC*, 105:24b–25b, 107:2–2b.
85. *CC*, 105:16b–18.

the curriculum.[86] He provided funds for the railroad school, appointed Chinese supervisors, and hired Japanese teachers. Liao Cheng-hua was made director of the school, and Ch'eng Ming-ch'ao and Huang Kung-ch'ien were appointed to assist him. Full government scholarships were to be provided for sixty Hupeh students in Japan, and Hupeh would pay half of the expenses for twenty students from other provinces. After three years of training in railroad construction and management, the students would return to take jobs in Hupeh. Those who had received full scholarships would be expected to work for the Hupeh government for at least six years, while the students from other provinces would have to serve for at least three years.[87]

While Chang Chih-tung founded several other special schools between 1904 and 1907, he was chiefly concerned with rectifying an earlier error of judgment. In the first enthusiasm for educational reform, Chang and his subordinates had opened a number of general middle schools and high schools, only to discover that the problems of recruiting teachers and qualified students were even more serious than originally anticipated. To overcome the problems, Chang devoted his final years in Hupeh principally to promoting normal school and primary school education. Soon after returning from Peking, he reorganized the Liang-Hu Normal School. Delays had been experienced in constructing buildings in eastern Wuchang for this institution, founded by Chang in 1902, so that the school had begun operation in rented quarters. In the meantime, the Liang-Hu High School had begun operation on the spacious site of the old Liang-Hu Academy. In 1904 Chang turned the larger establishment over to the normal school. He estimated that this step would enable the normal school to attain an enrollment of one thousand students. The high school apparently was suspended until the site in eastern Wuchang could be readied.[88]

Near the beginning of 1905 Chang also merged the two military high schools that he had established in 1902 and created a single military normal school.[89] As another measure to provide more teachers for the province, Chang ordered the Office of School Affairs to open normal training centers (*shih-fan ch'uan-hsi-so*) in the provincial capital in 1904. Men sent to the centers by the gentry of the prefectures and departments

86. *HNP*, pp. 191, 199; *CC*, 196:6b.
87. *CC*, 109:8b–11b.
88. *CC*, 105:15b–16b.
89. *CC*, 106:21b–24.

would gain a "rough understanding" of the new educational methods before becoming primary school teachers. Chang designated the officials
who were to be in charge of the centers, and the project was launched.[90]
However, the plan did not work out well. A number of students were
enrolled, but by 1905 Chang had decided that the training offered at the
centers was too shallow and hurried. He therefore decided to organize six
branch normal schools (*chih-chün shih-fan hsüeh-t'ang*) in different
prefectures to present longer and more thorough training.[91]

New measures to promote elementary education included a 1904 order
that supplementary primary school courses be required for all middle
and technical school students who were not already primary school
graduates.[92] In 1906 Chang founded primary schools of agriculture, industry, and commerce; and in 1907 he drew up regulations for military
primary schools.[93]

In general, more progress in education reform was evident in Wuchang
than in the Hupeh hinterland. To encourage the opening of primary
schools in the departments and districts, Chang on September 8, 1904,
informed the officials of Hupeh's subdivisions that they would be ex-
cused from the annual levy of Tls. 1,200,000 for the province's share
of the Boxer indemnity. Chang would make the indemnity payments
from lottery profits and taxes on opium decoction and minting. The
amounts previously paid by the departments and districts should thereafter be applied to primary schools.[94]

On January 16, 1905, Chang's disappointment over the lack of progress
beyond Wuchang erupted in a furious circular to his prefects. He sternly
rebuked the prefects for lagging in the promotion of normal training and
the encouragement of primary schooling. Whereas the Wuchang prefecture had established a normal school, and the Shih-nan prefecture and
Ching-men department had opened normal training centers, all other
prefectures had done nothing but open middle schools. One prefecture
had a middle school with an enrollment of 240 students, and two prefectures had middle schools with more than 160 students. It was true
that the national school regulations had given three to four hundred
students as the optimum enrollment for middle schools, but the regulations had stated clearly that such a large enrollment should not be an
immediate aim. To establish middle schools without trained teachers

90. *CC*, 105:35b–36b.
91. *CC*, 107:3b–4.
92. *CC*, 106:13–14.
93. *CC*, 70:4–9b, 118:34–35.
94. *CC*, 105:25b–28.

to conduct them or students advanced enough to benefit from them reflected nothing but ignorance and stupidity, Chang declared. The prefectures were evading responsibility and "caring only for the front gate" (or the appearance of things). Middle schools might mean more prestige for a prefecture, but they were leading to an unhealthy and uneven development of education in Hupeh. The middle schools were like uprooted stalks. Furthermore, the concentration on middle schools was interfering with the extension of primary training in the departments and districts. The former indemnity funds that were earmarked for primary schools in the departments and districts were being used by the prefectures for middle schools. Chang ordered that the prefects call an immediate halt to the founding of middle schools. Those already in operation were to be converted to beginning normal schools, with an enrollment not to exceed sixty students from each of the large districts subordinate to the prefecture or forty students from the smaller districts. All students in excess of the allowable number enrolled in middle schools at the time of the conversion were to be sent back to receive lower or higher primary training. Middle schools would not be reopened until the primary schools had graduated enough students to justify the step.[95]

Among problems other than normal or primary education that occupied Chang Chih-tung from 1904 to 1907 were ceremonial practices for the new school system. The greater the number of schools established in China, Chang reflected, the greater the occurrence of disorder among the students. Rules of propriety, or rites (*li*), were needed to help create order.[96] As one means of fostering adherence to rites, Chang decided upon uniformity of dress for the students of Hupeh schools. He was shocked to observe that some students were wearing such odd garb as Western-style "short garments" and leather shoes. He personally had seen American graduation caps and gowns, which he took as evidence that even in the West students did not invariably wear "short garments." One of the school regulations adopted in 1903 had provided that all students of a given school should dress alike. Chang was intent upon seeing that the regulation be upheld in Hupeh. Uniforms for different occasions would create a proper awareness of "grades" and "distinctions" within the schools, Chang believed, and would help instill within the students a proper sense of "reverence and respect." They would also help create a "martial spirit" (*shang-wu chih ching-shen*). Furthermore, uniforms would increase the prestige of the student class, setting them apart from

95. *CC*, 106:16b–18b.
96. See memorial on school uniforms, *CC*, 68:21b–24b.

peddlers, servants, and coolies; people on the street would take one look at the students and know their status.[97]

During 1905 Chang promulgated detailed rules on student dress, which were to be adopted on an experimental basis.[98] The rules defined the proper ceremonial and classroom dress for civil and military schools of all grades. Styles for use on the exercise grounds and during formal drills and marches were also specified. As an example, the ceremonial dress for middle and high school students would consist of a big hat with woolen brim and red tassel for winter wear; a big hat of thin silk, with red tassel, for summer wear; a long outer robe of plum-colored camlet; a long gown of light blue glazed cotton (*chu-pu*) for spring, autumn, and winter; a long gown of light blue linen (*hsia-pu*) for summer; a stiff blue waist sash of woven cotton; and black satinette shoes. The classroom uniform differed in requiring no outer robe, substituting black cotton shoes for black satinette, and specifying a straw hat with a button of red knotted cord. After experimenting with the uniforms until May 27, 1907, Chang Chih-tung asked the throne for a decree ordering their general use on a permanent basis.[99]

To improve morale and discipline, indoctrinate Hupeh students in the aims of education, encourage feelings of "loyalty and love," and increase "self-strengthening" determination, Chang Chih-tung wrote a school song in 1905. Almost a doggerel version of the *Ch'üan-hsüeh p'ien,* the song consisted of thirteen stanzas with a total of 164 rhymed couplets.[100] The potpourri of couplets covered such topics as the aims and benefits of education, Chinese and world geography, Chinese history, courses offered in the schools, desirable habits, the benevolence of the Ch'ing empire, educational progress in Hupeh, the relationship between education and national strength, the causes of China's weakness, and the dangers of imitative radicalism. On January 11, 1905, Chang ordered that the song be distributed throughout Hupeh and that a copy be given to each student. The students were to chant the song as they marched in or out of classrooms or paraded on the drill grounds. They were to sing the first six words of each couplet slowly, taking one step for each word, pause briefly, then chant the last seven words quickly, as they took four brisk

97. *CC,* 68:22–22b, 23b.
98. *CC,* 107:16b–30.
99. *CC,* 68:22–22b.
100. See text of the school song, *CC,* 106:1–10b. Following it is an army song that Chang also wrote.

steps.[101] The first stanza of Chang Chih-tung's school song read as follows:

T'ien ti t'ai, jih yüeh kuang;
T'ing wo ch'ang-ko tsan hsüeh-t'ang.

Heaven and earth are vast,
 the sun and moon are bright;
Hear me sing a song in praise
 of schools.

Sheng T'ien-tzu, t'u tzu-ch'iang;
Ch'u-ch'ü hsing-hsüeh wu-pieh-fang.

The Holy Son of Heaven plans
 for self strengthening;
To make learning flourish is
 the only way.

Chiao t'i'yü, ti-i chuang;
Wei-sheng shih min ch'iang-chuang.

Teach physical culture as a
 first step;
Hygiene makes the people strong
 and healthy.

Chiao te-yü, hsien meng-yang;
Jen-jen ai-kuo min shan-liang.

Teach moral culture,
 starting at an early age;
If all love their country,
 the people will be good.

Hsiao fu-mu, tsun chün-shang;
Keng hsü kung-te lien szu-fang.

Honor father and mother, and
 respect the rulers;
Public virtue is especially
 needed to unify the empire.

Chiao chih-yü, k'ai yü-mang;
P'u-t'ung chih-shih p'o t'ien-huang.

Teach mental culture, and
 enlighten ignorance;
Popularize knowledge as never
 before.

Wu-li t'ou, chi-i ch'ang;
Fang chih mou-sheng ping pao-pang.

Understand science and master
 mechanical arts,
So as to know how to make a living and
 protect the state.

Abolition of the Examination System

While Chang Chih-tung was working on behalf of a new Chinese school system, he did not slacken the campaign that he and Liu K'un-i had begun in 1901 to modify the civil service examination system. His efforts led finally to a demand that the old examinations be abolished entirely and

101. *CC*, 106:10b.

immediately. The imperial decrees following the 1901 memorial by Chang and Liu had encouraged the establishment of schools but did not give clear or unequivocal approval to the memorialists' proposals on granting civil service degrees to school graduates.[102] Nor did the decrees approve the proposed gradual reduction in the award of degrees to successful candidates in the old-style classical examinations according to a quota system.[103] Chang and Liu had recommended that the titles of *fu-sheng, lin-sheng, yu-kung-sheng, chü-jen,* and *chin-shih* be conferred on the graduates of the new schools. They had proposed, furthermore, that upon adoption of the reform, the school graduates receive one-third of the *chin-shih* and *chü-jen* degrees for which quotas were established and one-fourth of the *hsiu-ts'ai* degrees. The school graduates' share in the degrees would be increased to 100 per cent over a ten-year period or by the end of three triennial examinations.

Chang Chih-tung and Liu K'un-i had submitted their original joint memorial on July 12, 1901, and by November 10, 1901, Chang was again agitating for the grant of degrees to school graduates. He and Liu K'un-i memorialized on the subject once more, and sent telegrams urging support of the plan to other provincial authorities, board officers, and the Grand Council.[104] In one message to the Grand Council, Chang pointed out that degrees obtained by civil service examination were the traditional patents for entrance to public office. Conferring degrees under the new system, with the promise of offices to come, would be a powerful incentive for students to acquire general education in the schools. Scholars would become more enthusiastic about entering those institutions that could best train "human talent" to meet the practical needs of the empire. Moreover, the degrees (which would entitle sons to a place in the bureaucracy) would serve as an incentive for private financial support of the new educational system. Carrying out the plan of founding schools in every prefecture and department of the empire would cost huge sums of money, Chang argued. Because of the shortage of public funds, the provinces at best could hope to open only a few schools in their capital cities to serve as "models" and "stimuli." Sizable local subscriptions or contributions would be required if the schools were to increase and flourish. If the throne issued a decree definitely providing that school graduates could become *chin-shih, chü-jen,* and *sheng-yüan,* the people

102. *CC*, 83:19b–21b; *HNP*, p. 152.
103. *CC*, 175:11.
104. *HNP*, p. 152; *CC*, 83:19b–21b, 174:8–8b, 11.

would voluntarily come forward with the money needed to create a prosperous school system.[105]

Chang's ideas were laid before the Office for the Management of State Affairs, which succeeded in gaining imperial approval of the basic plan. An edict of December 5, 1901, stipulated that provincial authorities could examine students who had been graduated successively from primary schools, middle schools, and provincial colleges. The best students would be selected and sent to the Imperial University, where they would be reexamined. Candidates chosen would receive either *chü-jen* or *kung-sheng* degrees, depending on their standing. After a number of *chü-jen* had been created, the university would again make a selection and send the best men to the Board of Rites. The Board would examine them and award *chin-shih* degrees to the successful candidates.[106]

A longer time passed before Chang Chih-tung witnessed a victory in his fight for reduction of traditional degree quotas and gradual abolition of the outmoded examination system. Having achieved no results by 1903, he enlisted the aid of Yüan Shih-k'ai, whom he asked to seek support from other governors general and governors. With Yüan as the chief memorialist, the plan of gradual abolition was again presented to the throne in a joint petition. The empress dowager directed on March 12, 1903, that the memorial by Yüan and Chang be submitted to the Board of Rites and the Office for the Management of State Affairs for consideration and recommendations.[107]

Chang interpreted this outcome as tantamount to tabling the proposal. In a telegram to Yüan Shih-k'ai, he blamed the blocking of the plan upon stubborn and insincere Hanlin academicians who feared that their livelihood would suffer if they lost their customary commissions as examiners.[108] Chang proposed a new strategy built around the idea: "If the examination system cannot embrace schools, schools still can embrace the examination system." It should be stressed that even though school graduation in the first instance would be predicated on the "total marks method" of grading, civil service examinations would be given to students after graduation. The examinations would still be administered by gov-

105. *CC*, 83:19b–21b.
106. *CSL:KH*, 488:15b–16. More detailed and different methods of examining and awarding degrees to school graduates were accepted in school regulations that Chang helped draft in 1903. See Franke, pp. 65–67.
107. *CSL:KH*, 512:8–8b; *HNP*, pp. 170–171. For translated excerpts from the 1903 memorial by Chang and Yüan, see Teng and Fairbank, *China's Response to the West*, pp. 206–207.
108. *CC*, 186:29–29b.

ernment representatives and special appointees, and those candidates who did not possess sufficient literary knowledge or orthodox learning (specialties of the Hanlin scholars) could still be eliminated. In other words, the vested interests of the Hanlin academicians would not be adversely affected.

Chang disclosed another tactic (and perhaps some insincerity himself) in a letter of September 29, 1903, to Ch'ü Hung-chi, an advocate of reform who in 1906 was sent with I-k'uang and Sun Chia-nai on a mission to study foreign governments preparatory to adopting a constitutional system. Asking that Ch'ü use his influence at court, Chang claimed that the opponents of any reduction in recruitment of officials by the old examination system were merely arguing: "The schools are no good, they have not been established on a broad scale, and they cannot quickly produce talent." However, the school regulations then being drawn up would provide for the protection of Chinese studies and include safeguards against heterodox influences. The opponents should realize that the proposed method of granting a portion of civil service degrees to school graduates was merely an experiment. If the experiment had not succeeded by the end of six years—if the schools had within that time become permeated with evil practices or had not produced real talent— then China could close the schools, revert to old practices of the examination system, and restore the old degree quotas.[109]

Chang Chih-tung did not win his case until January 13, 1904, when he and Chang Po-hsi submitted a joint memorial on gradually abolishing the old system.[110] In addressing the throne, the two Changs expressed their belief that the examination system was deterring progress in the establishment and operation of schools. They repeated the arguments that recruitments of officials from among school graduates would encourage private financial support of the schools and lead to greater school enrollments. With both a school system and an examination system in being, the minds of the people were confused, and the confusion would not be dissipated until the throne gave further evidence that it favored the first system over the second. Chang Chih-tung and Chang Po-hsi itemized their reasons for believing that the school system was superior to the examination system as a source of recruits for the bureaucracy. Examination essays for the most part were sheer plagiarism, while schools required real devotion to self-improvement. Passing the examinations represented "one day's luck," whereas graduation from schools

109. *CC*, 220:12–12b.
110. For text of the memorial by Chang Chih-tung and Chang Po-hsi, see *CC*, 61:24–28b.

represented years of proven cumulative achievement. The examinations were purely literary and provided no good way to judge a man's character, whereas conduct was under constant surveillance in the schools and was taken into account in the award of grades. It had been decided that the curriculum of all schools would include Chinese studies as well as Western studies; all that was taught under the examination system would be taught even better in the schools, and more would be added to it. Finally, there was no need for the literati to worry that the "total marks method" of grading used by the schools would lead to corruption. Everything done by the teachers would be obvious to the students. Student discussion and the pressure of public opinion would make it hard for a teacher to "gloss over" dishonesty or subjectivism and award grades on the basis of personal like or dislike or in consideration of personal profit or loss. A further safeguard against corrupt practices would be the examinations given by government officials after the students had graduated from the schools. The two Changs declared, "There will be no abolition of the examination system, but in reality an amalgamation of the examination and school systems."

They thereupon set forth practically the same plan that Chang Chih-tung and Liu K'un-i had originally proposed in 1901. Beginning in 1906, the quota for the provincial and metropolitan examinations would be reduced by one-third for the old-style literary candidates. Reductions of one-third would be made in each of the two succeeding triennial examinations, after which the traditional provincial and metropolitan examinations would be discontinued. Quotas would also be reduced by one-fourth for each of the four *sui* and *k'o* examinations held within the six-year period spanning two provincial examinations. When the quota had been reduced to zero, the *sui* and *k'o* examinations would cease. Thereafter the provincial directors of education would preside over examinations to select all *sheng-yüan* from among the new school graduates.

After the traditional examination system had come to an end, the director general of the metropolitan examinations would become an examiner of university graduates. Specially appointed provincial examiners would administer tests to high school graduates. Furthermore, the office of the provincial director of education would not be abolished after cessation of the examination system. But new duties would be assigned to the director. He would work with provincial authorities in carrying out educational reforms and would administer examinations to middle school graduates.

After final cessation of the examination system, old-style *chü-jen, kung-sheng,* and *sheng-yüan* under thirty *sui* would be required to enter the new schools, graduate, and pass the new-style examinations if they wished to receive higher degrees. Those from thirty to fifty *sui* could enroll in short courses in the normal schools. Two special recruitments of the type known as the "great selection" (*ta-t'iao*) and the "selection for advancement" (*chien-fa*) would be made from men thirty to fifty *sui* who did not wish to enter schools and from older men of fifty to sixty.[111] Those chosen by these means would be assigned to various offices to serve as copyists. Meritorious men, including the various "tribute students" (*kung-sheng*), still not placed by the above methods, might be recommended directly to the court and examined for minor bureaucratic positions. Others would be considered for jobs of teaching the classics or literature in the new schools, and aged degree-holders would be considered for brevet rank.

The 1903 memorial of Chang Chih-tung and Chang Po-hsi evoked an edict from the empress dowager which commanded that the reduction of the traditional examination degrees begin in 1906 as recommended. The edict declared that the examination system would be terminated once and for all as soon as schools were operating uniformly through the provinces and as soon as they had shown substantial results.[112]

Having taken the lead in the 1903 campaign for elimination of the examination system within ten years, Chang Chih-tung by 1905 was demanding that the system be abolished at once. As an experienced politician, he possibly had looked upon approval of the 1903 plan as gaining the first inch in the ultimate mile, a concession required before pressing his advantage further. Or possibly during the interval from 1903 to 1905 it had become obvious to Chang that the scheme for gradual elimination of the system had not provided the stimulus to schools originally envisioned. Whatever his reasoning, Chang was prepared by the summer of 1905 to join with Yüan Shih-k'ai in exerting pressure for more rapid action. In the summer of 1905 Yüan telegraphed Chang and suggested that they act together to call for immediate cessation of the examination system. Chang replied that he already had submitted an exceedingly large number of petitions during the year. He would assist Yüan but preferred that Yüan act as the chief memorialist.[113] Support was also solicited from Chao Erh-hsün, the military governor of Mukden;

---

111. *Ta-t'iao* and *chien-fa* were terms for two slightly different ways of selecting for office *chü-jen* who had several times been unsuccessful in the metropolitan examinations. See Franke, citing the *Kuang-hsü hui-tien shih-li*, 73, *shih-lang, ch'u-shou*.

112. *CSL:KH*, 523:19b–20b; *CC*, 61:28b–29.

113. *HNP*, p. 192.

Chou Fu, the acting governor-general of Liangkiang; Ts'en Ch'un-Hsüan, the acting governor-general of Liangkwang; and Tuan-fang, the governor of Hunan. On August 31, 1905, the six men presented their memorial to the throne.[114]

The memorialists declared that corruption of the old examination system was well known to Chinese and foreigners alike. They reiterated that the system was hindering schools and misleading men of talent. Even if the old examinations were stopped at once, a decade would pass before the schools could train an abundance of talent. Waiting one decade to eliminate the examination system and adding another decade for the schools to show substantial results would mean a lapse of twenty years before the urgent needs of the bureaucracy could be met. Immediate abolition of the examination system was needed as a contribution to greater state stability. The step would increase foreign respect for China. It would also reassure graduates of the new schools and men who had studied abroad. When these men could feel fairly certain that they would receive government jobs, heterodox ideas and reckless speech would diminish.

The memorialists devoted much of their petition to principles that should be observed once the examination system had ended. Study of the classics should not be neglected by the schools, special attention should be paid to conduct when awarding school grades, and normal school training should be accelerated. In general, no one should be admitted to the bureaucracy in the future unless he had graduated from a school. During the transitional period, however, concessions should be made to accommodate scholars who had prepared for the old examinations; otherwise their poverty and grievances would result in trouble for the empire. It was proposed that during the next ten years three examinations be given for the degree of *yu-kung-sheng* and one examination for *pa-kung-sheng*. The old classical requirements and the old quotas for these degrees would remain in effect for the ten-year period. A certain number of men who already held *chü-jen* or *kung-sheng* degrees could be sent to the capital once every three years for a metropolitan examination on the classics and histories and one "foreign" specialty. Candidates

114. The 1905 memorial does not appear in the works of Chang Chih-tung, although a digest is given in *HNP*, pp. 192–194. Among other places, the full text may be founded in *Chin-tai Chung-kuo chiao-yü shih-liao*, ed. Shu-Hsin-ch'eng (Shanghai, 1923), 4:124–128. For an English translation, see John C. Ferguson, "The Abolition of the Competitive Examinations in China," *Journal of the American Oriental Society*, 27 (January–July 1906), 79–84.

who obtained degrees by these special processes would be entitled to employment as district magistrates or given other jobs. The transition to a single school system and a new method of bureaucratic recruitment thus would be effected without causing great hardship for the old literati.

When the regular examinations were eliminated, the supply of scholars trained only in the classics would soon be exhausted, and talent would then be drawn only from the schools. The memorialists presented an idealized description of the future school system, to the effect that establishing schools was not solely a matter of gathering talent for the bureaucracy, but also of increasing the knowledge of the people. If everyone was able to obtain a general education, all would share common knowledge and abilities. Those who were above would give devoted, loyal service to the empire. Those who were below would be able to improve their livelihood. There would be enough men of great talent to aid the rulers; and those lower down would not be lost as good subjects. Soldiers, farmers, artisans, and merchants all would know their rightful duties and devote themselves to their professions. Women and children. would not be forced to live in retirement but would receive education at home. In no place would there be no learning, and no man would go uneducated (*wu-ti wu-hsüeh, wu-jen pu-hsüeh*). If this plan were carried out, the country would be prosperous and strong. To achieve these results, extending schools must be the first step; and to extend schools, abolishing the examination system must be the first step.[115]

The empress dowager was prepared to take these first steps. On September 2, 1905, an imperial edict ordered that the provincial and metropolitan examinations be halted, effective with the tests scheduled for 1906.[116] Lower examinations were also to end, and men who already held degrees were to be eligible for integration into the bureaucracy according to the methods recommended. An institution that had stood since the T'ang dynasty was overthrown in one of the most significant reforms of modern Chinese history. Chang Chih-tung had helped inspire and secure the overthrow, but he soon appeared somewhat frightened by what he had done.

115. *HNP*, pp. 192–194.
116. *CSL:KH*, 548:4–5. See translation of the edict by Ferguson, pp. 84–86.

8 The Elder Statesman
(1905–1909)

Chang Chih-tung's final years were marked by anxiety and disappointment over the general trend of Chinese polity. In the government, constitutionalism was surgent, and Chang continued to look upon this movement with skepticism, even if not with the open hostility he had demonstrated in 1898. In the field of education, he reported, memorials were requesting that the Four Books and Five Classics be set aside in the new schools. Some primary and middle schools had arbitrarily dropped classical studies from the curriculum, and certain normal schools had altered their regulations to eliminate courses on the classics. To Chang, abandoning the classics meant abandoning loyalty, filial piety, and other great moral obligations. If this trend continued, the eventual result would be "rebellious ministers and wicked sons," he predicted. By 1907 Chang was writing: "There are all kinds of queer and evil practices which one cannot bear to observe."[1] He also expressed a few regretful second thoughts over the passing of the examination system.

From 1905 to 1909 Chang Chih-tung was engaged in a protest over alleged misunderstandings of his intentions. All along, he stated, he had advocated a balance of the *t'i* and the *yung*, a Sino-Western equilibrium. But the imbalance was becoming ever more pronounced, with the difference that the scales, formerly weighted heavily in favor of the *t'i*, were now tipping far too much to the *yung*. Many officials, scholars, and students had heeded only the half of Chang's proposition that demanded the acceptance of innovations based on Western institutions and methods. In their eagerness to imitate the West, they were despising their own Chinese cultural heritage. Too many were "taking delight in the new and forgetting the root" (*hsi-hsin wang-pen*). They were discarding the first and the proper and neglecting the right and the true. The study of Western learning in schools should not be permitted to eclipse totally the study of China's classics, histories, and literature. "Saving the situation [by practical, Western means] and preserving the old at the same time are not necessarily contradictory," Chang declared. The past and the present were interrelated. He quoted Confucius: "Review the old and know the new" (*wen-ku erh chih-hsin*).[2] In coping with the problems of education during the last years of his life, Chang Chih-tung struggled to halt the

1. *CC*, 68:31b–32.
2. *CC*, 190:3, 68:29.

decline of respect for Chinese tradition. His acts were viewed by many as an old man's retreat to conservatism and a final repudiation of his earlier reforming zeal, but they were actually consistent with his lifelong emphasis on Confucianism as the heart of Chinese civilization.[3]

Chinese students abroad continued to worry Chang with their rebellious activities. He became highly disturbed in 1905 when it was reported that eight thousand students had gone on strike against a set of regulations issued by the Japanese Department of Education. The regulations, governing the school registration and residence of all foreign students in Japan, were taken by the young Chinese as a repressive curtailment of their freedom and an insult to their national pride. In protest, more than four hundred of the students returned to China at once.[4]

Chang viewed the regulations as being in the best interest of maintaining peace and order among foreign students in Japanese schools. He accepted the interpretation of the Chinese minister to Japan that the strike was incited by three to four hundred agitators who had sworn to die for the rebel party of Sun Yat-sen. Using the Japanese regulations as a pretext, the rebels were seeking to beguile more students into their movement for overthrowing the Manchu dynasty. This was just one of the rebellious schemes recently exposed in Japan, Chang charged—schemes that would make a loyal official's hair stand on end.[5]

Before receiving details of the strike, Chang cabled an appeal to Hupeh students in Japan to behave in a peaceful manner befitting Confucian scholars with an understanding of propriety (*li*) and righteousness (*i*).[6] He became furious when he learned the reaction of Li Pao-sun, successor to Ch'ien Hsün as the superintendent of Hupeh students in Japan. Li had advanced two to three months' tuition and allowances to the Hupeh students who wished to return home. Having acted without first requesting authority, he was guilty, according to Chang, of "stupid and absurd anticipation." To make matters worse, he had the temerity to ask for a telegraphic remittance of about 50,000 yuan more to pay the homeward fares for other students. Chang decreed that those students presently on their way home would never again be permitted to study abroad. Officers would be sent to meet them in Shanghai and escort them to their homes, so that they could not loiter in the foreign concessions of Shanghai to invent new rebellious schemes. Those students still in Japan were not

3. Hummel, I, 31.
4. *CC*, 195:17b. For the strike, see also Hackett, pp. 153–154; Ernest P. Young, "The Chinese Student Strikes in Japan, 1905," unpub. seminar paper, Harvard University, 1959.
5. *CC*, 195:17–19b.
6. *CC*, 195:11–11b.

to sail for home but were to wait quietly for a settlement of the strike. The "intimidated students" in Tokyo were to "go into hiding" until order had been restored, whereupon they would re-enter their schools.[7]

Chang sent a special commissioner, Shuang Shou, to Japan to help restore order, and he urged the governors general and governors of Liangkwang, Hunan, Szechwan, Honan, Shantung, and Kweichow to follow suit by sending their own representatives. Chang also tried to organize a telegraphic campaign, directing Hupeh gentry to wire officials in Peking to press for the appointment of an imperial mediator.[8] The Chinese student strike lasted for a month, after which Chang's representatives in Tokyo informed him that a compromise settlement had been reached.[9] "One disgrace is hard to overcome," Chang replied on receiving the news. But after all, he added, "Study is the most important thing."[10]

Near the end of 1905 Chang also went on record against abolition of the Hanlin Academy. Earlier in the year the academy had asked for an increased appropriation in order to revive its researches. The request brought forth several counterproposals, including memorials advocating that the academy be dissolved. Chang, who a short time before had criticized academy members for opposing new schools, now contended that the academy represented China's chief storehouse of talent capable of interpreting ancient learning. The academy therefore had a great responsibility to fulfill. Though large provinces had been requested to supply Tls. 1,000 a year to subsidize studies at the academy, Chang declared that this was not enough. He voluntarily committed Hukwang to provide Tls. 10,000 a year.[11]

In December 1905, Peking created a Ministry of Education (Hsüeh-pu), as Chang Chih-tung and Chang Po-hsi had earlier recommended. Chang Chih-tung telegraphed his congratulations to Jung-ch'ing, the Mongol bannerman selected to head the new agency. Jung-ch'ing's appointment, Chang wrote, somewhat allayed his fears that China would soon be embroiled in a great rebellion and that the teachings of the sages would perish.[12]

A short time later Chang recommended to the Ministry of Education the perpetual selection of "tribute students by virtue of special merit"

7. *CC*, 195:16–17, 18b.
8. *CC*, 195:19–19b.
9. Terms of the settlement are not given in Chang's collected works. Waning enthusiasm of the students may have brought about the end of the strike. Hackett, p. 154.
10. *CC*, 195:19b.
11. *HNP*, p. 196.
12. *CC*, 195:10b–11.

(*yu-kung-sheng*) and "tribute students by virtue of special selection" (*pa-kung-sheng*), in a modified extension of the old examination system.[13] In their 1905 memorial on abolishing the examination system, Chang and Yüan Shih-k'ai had proposed that the award of these special degrees be temporarily continued to accommodate scholars who had already acquired training under the old educational system. Chang now stated that he and Yüan had not considered the matter with enough care. The special selection of *yu-kung-sheng* and *pa-kung-sheng* should be continued forever to provide a way, external to the schools, for preserving the Chinese heritage, as the licentiates would be conversant with the Chinese classics and histories. Again Chang asked what hope there would be of retaining the Chinese *t'i* if the Chinese *wen* ceased to exist. As late as the Hsüan-t'ung reign, Chang was still supporting this small-scale examination system. In 1909 he learned that the governor of Kwangtung had launched a campaign to halt the *yu-kung* and *pa-kung* selection. Discontinuing these tests, Chang protested, would be tantamount to ending the study of "national literature" (*kuo-wen*). It would mean an end of classical study and produce a dearth of teachers for Chinese studies in the schools; "in less than ten years there would not be a single literate man in the Empire."[14]

During 1906 Chang Chih-tung became active in the movement that resulted in the imperial edict placing sacrifices to Confucius on the same plane with those to Heaven and Earth.[15] In that year Chang also received an imperial mandate to make the plans for building a classical school at Ch'ü-fou, the Shantung birthplace of Confucius. The project had been suggested to the throne by Liang Ting-fen, Chang's chief subordinate in educational matters. The Shantung treasury was ordered to advance Tls. 100,000 for building the school, and the Hupeh director of education, Huang Shao-chi, was instructed to work with Chang in making other arrangements. The school was established in 1907, after Chang had consulted with the Ministry of Education on faculty, curriculum, and regulations, but a biography of Chang states that in the end only a "rough model" was achieved because of troubles experienced in obtaining professors.[16]

School for Preservation of Antiquity

Within Hupeh, Chang's most ambitious undertaking for strengthening the *t'i* was to found the School for the Preservation of Antiquity (Ts'un-

13. *HNP*, p. 197.
14. *CC*, 195:10b–11.
15. Hummel, I, 31.
16. *HNP*, pp. 201, 208.

ku hsüeh-t'ang). Chang had conceived the idea of this school as early as 1904, but it was not until July 9, 1907, that he formally revealed his plans in a memorial to the throne and not until August 28, 1907, that the school actually opened its doors.[17] In explaining the purposes of the school, Chang wrote:

> Today the schools of all countries in the world place special emphasis on departments of national literature. National literature includes the written and spoken language of a given country and the books handed down through history. Among the books there are some not fully suitable for use in times that have changed; but they also must be preserved and transmitted. Their destruction absolutely cannot be permitted. The finest of a country's teachings, skills, rites, doctrines, and customs which are especially treasured and protected are called the "national essence" (*kuo-ts'ui*). (Other countries) attach special importance to preservation (of the national essence). They do so in order to nourish feelings of patriotism and an awareness of one's own kind. Actually the source (of strength) of the powerful nations in the East and West may be found herein. This cannot be disregarded.[18]

The essence of Chinese culture, including both the useful and ornamental, was to be found in China's classics, histories, and creative literature, Chang continued.[19] The educational regulations adopted in 1903 provided that courses in *kuo-wen* be offered in the new schools. However, there was a shortage of qualified teachers for such courses, and the shortage would become more acute with time. As schools increased, the need for teachers of classical courses would increase. Yet future graduates of the schools, having been merely introduced to Chinese studies without going into them deeply, would be unqualified to become instructors. China could not hope to produce famous teachers like those of the Chou and Ch'in dynasties who transmitted the classics, but only doctors (*po-shih*) like those of the Han dynasty who established schools. Hupeh had two to three hundred schools stressing Western learning, Chang stated; at least one institute was therefore needed to specialize in Chinese studies and perfect teaching talent that could contribute substantially to the preservation of China's "national essence." For these reasons Chang Chih-tung had decided to establish the School for the Preservation of Antiquity.

17. *CC*, 190:3–4, 68:26–32b, 200:16b.
18. *CC*, 68:26–26b.
19. The following comments are based on Chang's memorial on establishing the school, *CC*, 68:26–32b.

The school was housed in the former Ching-hsin Academy in Wuchang. Chang made repairs and additions and drew up plans for a library that would keep old books, manuscripts, bronzes, tablets, and artifacts of earlier generations. The school was opened to graduates of the old examination system and higher primary schools. Chang planned to enroll 240 students under 35 *sui*. They would be subject to the same discipline as other students in Hupeh, and the administration would differ from that of the old-style academies. "In the classrooms all of the lecturers will ask questions and receive answers and write on the blackboard," Chang explained. "Each day there will be military drill. There will be times for entering and leaving, times for rising and rest, fixed class hours, and regulations on assembling for meals and receiving guests." Professors would administer monthly tests. Grades, calculated by percentages, would be checked by school officials, sent to the provincial director of education, and then forwarded to the governor general, who would examine the standings and announce the results of the tests. The final annual examination would be administered personally by the governor general. Students would graduate after seven years of study. They might then go on for university training, but at the end of their education they would be expected to serve as teachers of the classics, history, or literature.

The schools that Chang Chih-tung had opened before 1907 theoretically stressed Western studies without neglecting the Chinese classics. The reverse was to be the case with the School for the Preservation of Antiquity: it would stress Chinese subjects without neglecting Western studies. Chang divided the school into three main departments: classics, including the study of divination, lexicography, and phonology; history, including the Twenty-four Histories, the *T'ung-chien*, *T'ung-k'ao*, and records of the Ch'ing dynasty; and literature, including the study of various styles of prose, poetry, and calligraphy. In addition, students were to devote some time to reading ancient and modern philosophers and to the study of mathematics, geography, foreign history, natural science, physics, chemistry, foreign government, law, finance, foreign police and prison systems, agricultural sciences, industry, commerce, and physical education. Students needed a knowledge of these subjects, Chang explained, although it was not necessary to become experts in them at the School for the Preservation of Antiquity. Students who elected to study a foreign language would be permitted to enroll as part-time students in the nearby Wuchang language school. During the summer of 1907 Chang Chih-tung sent to the Ministry of Education a detailed report on the proposed curriculum.[20]

20. *CC*, 109:20b–31b.

Chang Chih-tung planned to staff the school with four professors (*tsung-chiao*), four assistant professors (*hsieh-chiao*), and six instructors (*fen-chiao*). He experienced problems in engaging teachers, however, just as he had in the case of the Ch'ü-fou school. He issued a number of invitations that were declined and apparently succeeded in recruiting only one professor before official opening of the school.[21] The "lecture mat" was almost empty on opening day.[22] Six months later the school was having problems in obtaining students. On March 1, 1908, in a wire from Peking to his successor in Wuchang, Chang Chih-tung reiterated the importance that he attributed to the school. "It must not be allowed to fall into ruins, and you must take charge of obtaining men for it," Chang directed.[23]

Minister of Education

Founding the School for the Preservation of Antiquity was one of Chang Chih-tung's final contributions to education in Hukwang. On July 23, 1907, the throne appointed him a grand secretary, and on September 4, 1907, he was made a grand councillor.[24] On August 10 he received orders to proceed to Peking for an audience.[25] Before beginning his journey north, Chang requested a round of awards for Liang Ting-fen and numerous other subordinates who had assisted him ably in educational reform.[26] He also directed that the schools of Hupeh stop displaying images of himself.[27] On September 9, 1907, Chang handed over his seal as the Hukwang governor general for the last time and, at the age of seventy, departed from the Wuchang yamen where he had been stationed as a viceroy for approximately fifteen years. He arrived in Peking on September 12.[28] On September 31, the empress dowager commanded him to take charge of the Ministry of Education. In thanking the throne for the new appointment, Chang spoke once again of the Chinese educator's responsibility for both reviewing the old and introducing the new.[29]

During Chang Chih-tung's short tenure as officer-in-charge of the Ministry of Education, some progress was made toward compiling textbooks and revising earlier school regulations. Approval was granted to

21. *CC*, 190:3–4, 200:16b, 210:18b–19; *HNP*, p. 208.
22. *HNP*, p. 208.
23. *CC*, 201:1b.
24. *CC*, 72:15–17b; *HNP*, pp. 203, 205.
25. *HNP*, p. 204.
26. *CC*, 70:18, 18b–19.
27. *HNP*, p. 206.
28. *CC*, 70:19b–20; *HNP*, p. 209.
29. *CC*, 71:18b–19.

organize the Peking Imperial University into eight departments; a women's normal school was established in Peking; and plans were made to increase Chinese literacy through simplified training courses. But illness overtook Chang and forced him to take much leave. He was saddened by the death of the empress dowager on November 15, 1908. Less than a year later he submitted a valedictory memorial and requested release from duty. On the same day, October 4, 1909, he died.[30]

An imperial edict was promptly issued in praise of Chang for his loyal service, honest character, and great help rendered to the state in troubled times.[31] Memorials reached the throne lauding him and requesting honors on his behalf.[32] He was canonized as Wen-hsiang kung, the second highest posthumous title. The foreign press also noted his passing. In Shanghai the *North China Herald* commented: "He sought for what he thought would be the greatest advantage to his own country, being in this, as in all his conduct, an unswerving patriot on whom there was cast no suspicion."[33] More critically, the London *Times* said that it would not be easy to find another Chinese official of the nineteenth century "in whom were united so many of the qualities which account for the solidarity of the Chinese system of government and so many of the defects which contributed to its inherent weakness."[34]

The configuration of Chinese education changed radically during Chang's lifetime, and his own efforts were crucial in this metamorphosis. During the first thirty years of his life, he underwent the rigors of the examination system, to emerge with a conviction that the system badly needed overhauling. As a provincial director of education, he served for a decade as a repairman, attempting to cleanse the system and inject into it new vitality. He achieved limited success, but bitter political experiences between 1877 and 1882 convinced him that more drastic remedies were necessary to strengthen China. He turned to the construction of specialized schools to train young Chinese in Western military methods, foreign languages, science, and technology. Through the *Ch'uan-hsüeh p'ien*, he challenged the Chinese intelligentsia to awaken to new opportunities, without forgetting their heritage. As he did so, however, it became obvious that the old system was a serious obstacle to acceptance and advance of the new. He therefore lent his support to abolition of the

30. For Chang's final memorial, see *CC*, 70:24b–26b.
31. For text of the edict, see *CC, chüan-shou shang*, pp. 1–2, tr. in the *North China Herald*, n.s., 93 (Oct. 9, 1909), 77.
32. For memorials lauding Chang, see *CC, chüan-shou shang*, pp. 9–18.
33. *North China Herald*, Shanghai, n.s., 93 (Oct. 9, 1909), 67.
34. *The Times*, London, Oct. 6, 1909.

civil service examinations, with the proviso that the best of Chinese culture be transmitted through a reformed educational system.

Structurally and organizationally, Chinese education of the twentieth century is indebted to Chang Chih-tung. In the areas of educational administration and teaching methods he made a contribution through his promotion of new courses of study and his emphasis on such matters as regular school terms, explanation versus rote learning, objective grading, and tuition payments. By his latter-day stress upon general, public, and "national people's" education, he shared in broadening the scope and spreading the benefits of schooling in China. He was furthermore a warrior in the struggle against a number of ingrained social concepts that Chinese leaders and educators are still combatting. Although Chinese Communists today patly categorize Chang as a bureaucratic tool of feudal dictatorship and foreign imperialism,[35] he anticipated them in urging higher status for the Chinese soldier and artisan and in criticizing the reluctance of Chinese students—the educated class—to engage in manual labor.

In his broadest aim, Chang Chih-tung failed. He was unable to dam the flood of change that he himself had helped unleash or to channel it through his *t'i-yung* formula for the preservation of the Confucian state. The fallacy of the formula was described by Joseph Levenson: "Chinese learning, which was to be the *t'i* in the new syncretic culture, was the learning of a society which had always used it for *yung*, as the necessary passport to the best of all careers. Western learning, when sought as *yung*, did not supplement Chinese learning—as the neat formula would have it do—but began to supplant it. For in reality, Chinese learning had come to be prized as substance because of its function, and when its function was usurped, the learning withered."[36] Western *yung* challenged the literati's way of life, offered him the commercial-industrial alternative and republican-democratic ideas, and ultimately sapped his conviction in the indispensability of Confucian learning and the sanctions it provided for Manchu rule.

Several of Chang Chih-tung's contemporaries recognized the fallacy in their own way. Yen Fu, the prominent translator of Western thought, wrote: "The *use* of the *body* of an ox is to carry heavy burdens; the *use* of the *body* of a horse is to run fast. I have never known of an ox's body being used to perform the function of a horse . . . Chinese doctrines have

---

35. See, for example, Chang Hui, "Chang Chih-tung pan yang-wu" (Chang Chih-tung manages foreign affairs), *Ta-kung pao*, Hong Kong, Sept. 30, 1965; March 3, 1966.
36. Levenson, *Confucian China*, p. 61.

their body and use, just as Western knowledge has. As long as we keep the two strictly apart, they will both function and live; once we arbitrarily mix them together and let the body of one do the work of the other, both will become useless and inert."[37]

Less than a month after Chang's death a relatively new journal, the *Chiao-yü tsa-chih* (Education magazine), assessed the statesman's relationship to Chinese education. It protested that Chang had not understood "educational theory." With his "neither old nor new" policies, he had retarded the progress of Chinese education and stifled its expansive spirit.[38] This judgment, while unfair, was indicative of a new generation's mood.

Two years after Chang's death, republican revolution broke out in Wuchang. Ironically, the battleground was the former viceroy's capital. Pressed into service as chief of the rebel military forces, and later President of the Chinese Republic, was Li Yüan-hung, assistant commander of the new-style Hupeh army that Chang had created.[39] A leader of the revolutionary political forces, second only to Sun Yat-sen, was Huang Hsing, a former student at Chang's Liang-Hu Academy and one who had been sent to study in Japan at government expense.[40] The revolution emanated in part from the very reforms that Chang Chih-tung had labored so long to effect and tried so hard to control.

37. Jerome Ch'en, *Yüan Shih-k'ai (1859–1916)* (Stanford, Calif., 1961), p. 246, citing Chou Chen-fu, *Yen Fu ssu-hsiang shu-p'ing,* 1940, p. 2.
38. "Chang Wen-hsiang-kung yü chiao-yü chih kuan-hsi," *Chiao-yü tsa-chih,* 1:10 (ninth lunar month, 1909), 19–23.
39. Li Chien-nung, pp. 247–248.
40. Li Chien-nung, p. 202.

Bibliography

Glossary

Index

Bibliography

Chinese and Japanese Works

Chang Chih-tung 張之洞. *Shu-mu ta-wen* 書目答問 (Answering questions on bibliography), with *Yu-hsüan yü* 輶軒語 (Light carriage talk). 5 chüan, 3 ts'e. Hunan Hao-shang shu-chai, 1877. The *Shu-mu ta-wen* also appears in *Chang Wen-hsiang-kung ch'üan-chi*, ch. 206–209, and is available in other editions, with supplements. For the *Yu-hsüan yü*, see also *Chang Wen-hsiang-kung ch'üan-chi*, ch. 204–205.

———. *Ch'üan-hsüeh p'ien* 勸學篇 (Exhortation to learning). 2 chüan in 1 ts'e. Liang-Hu Shu-yüan, 1898. Also appears in *Chang Wen-hsiang-kung ch'üan-chi*, ch. 202–203, and is available in other editions.

———. *Chang Wen-hsiang-kung i-chi* 張文襄公遺集 (Works of the late Chang Wen-hsiang-kung [Chang Chih-tung]), ed. and pub. Hsü T'ung-hsin 許同莘. 150 chüan, 65 ts'e, 10 han. Peking, 1920.

———. *Chang Wen-hsiang-kung ch'üan-chi* 張文襄公全集 (The complete works of Chang Wen-hsiang-kung, ed. and pub. Wang Shu-t'ung 王樹枏. 229 chüan, 120 ts'e, 20 han. Peiping, 1928.

———. *Ch'uang-chien Tsun-ching shu-yüan chi* 創建尊經書院記 (Memoirs on establishment of the Tsun-ching Academy), in *Chang Wen-hsiang-kung ch'üan-chi*, 213:18b–29b.

Chang Chung-ju 章中如. *Ch'ing-tai k'ao-shih chih-tu* 清代考試制度 (The examination system of the Ch'ing dynasty). Shanghai, 1932.

"Chang Wen-hsiang-kung yü chiao-yü kuan-hsi" 張文襄公與教育關係 (Chang Wen-hsiang-kung's relation to education), *Chiao-yü tsa-chih* 教育雜誌 (Education magazine), 1. 10 (ninth lunar month, 1909), 19–23.

Chang Wen-hsiang-kung yung-ai lu 張文襄公榮哀錄 (A collection of tributes in memory of Chang Wen-hsiang-kung). 4 ts'e. Peking, undated.

Ch'en Ch'ing-chih 陳青之. *Chung-kuo chiao-yü shih* 中國教育史 (History of Chinese education). 2 vols. Shanghai, 1936.

Ch'en Kung-lu 陳恭祿. *Chung-kuo chin-tai shih* 中國近代史 (History of modern China). Shanghai, 1935.

Ch'ien Shih-fu 錢實甫, comp. *Ch'ing-chi chung-yao chih-kuan nien-piao* 清季重要職官年表 (Chronological tables of important officials of the late Ch'ing dynasty). Peking, 1959.

Chin-tai Chung-kuo chiao-yü shih-liao 近代中國教育史料 (Historical materials on modern Chinese education), ed. Shu Hsin-ch'eng 舒新城. 4 vols. Shanghai, 1933.

Ch'ing-chi wai-chiao shih-liao 清季外交史料 (Historical materials on foreign relations in the late Ch'ing period), comp. Wang Yen-wei 王彥威 and Wang Liang 王亮. 218 chüan for the Kuang-hsü reign. Peiping, 1932–1935.

Ch'ing-shih 清史 (History of the Ch'ing dynasty), comp. by Chang Ch'i-yün 張其昀 et al. 8 vols. Taipei: Academia Sinica, 1960.

Ch'ing-shih kao 清史稿 (Draft history of the Ch'ing dynasty), comp. Chao Erh-hsün 趙爾巽 et al. 536 chüan. Peiping, 1927–1928.

Ch'ing-shih lieh-chuan 清史列傳 (Biographies from Ch'ing history), comp. Chung-hua Book Co. Shanghai, 1928.

Ch'ing-tai k'ao-shih chih-tu tzu-liao 清代考試制度資料 (Source materials on the examination system of the Ch'ing dynasty), ed. Chang Chung-ju. Shanghai, 1934.

Chou Ssu-chen 周思真. *Chung-kuo chiao-yü chi chiao-yü ssu-hsiang shih chiang-hua* 中國教育及教育思想史講話 (Lectures on the history of Chinese education and educational thought). Shanghai, 1943.

Chūgoku bunka-kai jimbutsu sōkan 中國文化界人物總鑑 (Who's who in the Chinese cultural world), ed. Hashikawa Tokio 橋川時雄. Peiping, 1940.

Chung-Fa chan-cheng 中法戰爭 (The Sino-French War), ed. Shao Hsün-cheng 邵循正 et al. Shanghai, 1957.

Fang Chao-ying 房兆楹 and Tu Lien-che 杜聯喆. *Tseng-chiao Ch'ing-ch'ao chin-shih t'i-ming pei-lu* 增校清朝進士題名碑錄 (Enlarged revision of the Ch'ing dynasty record of the names of *chin-shih*). Supplement No. 19 of the Harvard-Yenching Institute Sinological Index series. Peiping, 1941.

Han Pin-tu 漢濱讀, ed. *Chang Wen-hsiang mu-fu chi-wen* 張文襄幕府紀聞 (Memoirs of Chang Wen-hsiang's [Chang Chih-tung's] private secretaries). 2 ts'e. 1910.

Hsiao Kung-ch'üan 蕭公權. *Chung-kuo cheng-chih ssu-hsiang shih* 中國政治思想史 (History of Chinese political thought). 2 vols. Shanghai, 1945-1946.

Hsieh En-hui 謝恩禪. "Chang Hsiang-t'ao chih ching-chi chien-she" 張香濤之經濟建設 (Chang Hsiang-t'ao's [Chang Chih-tung's] economic construction), *Ching-chi hsüeh-pao* 經濟學報 (Economics studies journal), no. 2 (June 1941), pp. 105–148.

Hsü T'ung-hsin. *Chang Wen-hsiang-kung nien-p'u* 張文襄公年譜 (Chronological biography of Chang Wen-hsiang-kung). Chungking, 1944.

Hsüeh-t'ang chang-ch'eng 學堂章程 (School regulations), comp. Chang Chih-tung 張之洞, Chang Po-hsi 張百熙 and Jung-ch'ing 榮慶. 5 ts'e. Hu-pei hsüeh-wu ch'u, 1904.

Hu Chün 胡鈞. *Chang Wen-hsiang-kung nien-p'u*. 2 ts'e. Peiping, 1939.

Hu-pei t'ung-chih 湖兆通志 (Gazetteer of Hupeh province), comp. Chang Chung-hsin 張仲炘 et al. 3 ts'e. Shanghai, 1934.

Ku Hung-ming 辜鴻銘. *Chang Wen-hsiang-kung mu-fu chi-wen* 張文襄公幕府紀聞 (Reminiscences of a secretary of Chang Wen-hsiang-kung). 2 ts'e. 1910.

Li Han-chang 李瀚章. *Ho-fei Li Ch'in-k'o-kung cheng-shu* 合肥李勤恪公政書 (Official writings of Li Ch'in-k'o-kung [Li Han-chang] of Hofei). 10 ts'e. Pub. his family, 1900.

Liu K'un-i i-chi 劉坤一遺集 (Works of the late Liu K'un-i), ed. No. 3 Historical Office, Chinese Academy of Sciences. 6 vols. Peking, 1959.

Liu Po-chi 劉伯驥. *Kuang-tung shu-yüan chih-tu* 廣東書院制度 (System of academies in Kwangtung). Shanghai, 1939; reprint, Hong Kong, 1958.

Nan-p'i-hsien chih 南皮縣志 (Gazetteer of the Nan-p'i district), comp. Wang Pao-shu 汪寶樹. 8 ts'e. 1888.

Nan-p'i-hsien chih, comp. Liu Shu-hsin 劉樹鑫. 8 ts'e. 1932.

Pao-ping-t'ang ti-tzu chi 抱氷堂弟子記 (Memoirs of the Pao-ping-t'ang disciples), in *Chang Wen-hsiang-kung ch'üan-chi*, ch. 228.

Pao Tsun-p'eng 包遵彭. *Chung-kuo hai-chün shih* 中國海軍史 (History of the Chinese navy). Taipei, 1953.

Pei-chuan chi pu 碑傳集補 (Supplement to the Collection of epitaphs), comp. Min Erh-ch'ang 閔爾昌. 24 vols. Peiping: Harvard-Yenching Institute, 1931.

Shang Yen-liu 商衍鎏. *Ch'ing-tai k'o-chü k'ao-shih shu-lu* 清代科學考試述錄 (Description of the Ch'ing dynasty examination system). Peking, 1958.

Sheng Lang-hsi 盛朗西. *Chung-kuo shu-yüan chih-tu* 中國書院制度 (The system of Chinese academies). Shanghai, 1934.

Ta-Ch'ing chi-fu hsien-che chuan 大清畿輔先哲傳 (Biographies of eminent scholars of the great Ch'ing metropolitan area), comp. Hsü Shih-ch'ang 徐世昌 et al. 46 chüan, 22 ts'e. Tientsin, 1917.

Ta-Ch'ing hui-tien 大清會典 (Collected statutes of the Ch'ing dynasty), comp. K'un-kang 崑岡 et al. 100 chüan for the Kuang-hsü reign. 1899.

Ta-Ch'ing li-ch'ao shih-lu 大清歷朝實錄 (The veritable records of the successive reigns of the Ch'ing dynasty). 597 chüan for the Kuang-hsü reign (*Ta-Ch'ing Te-tsung Ching-huang-ti shih-lu* 大清德宗景皇帝實錄). Photolithographic edition by the Manchukuo State Council, 1937–1938.

T'ang Chih-chün 湯志鈞. *Wu-hsü pien-fa jen-wu-chuan kao* 戊戌變法人物傳稿 (Draft biographies of personalities of the 1898 reform movement). 2 vols. Peking, 1961.

Teng Ssu-yü 鄧嗣禹. *Chung-kuo k'ao-shih chih-tu shih* 中國考試制度史 (History of the Chinese examination system). Nanking, 1938.

Ting Chih-p'in 丁致聘. *Chung-kuo chin ch'i-shih-nien lai chiao-yü chi-shih* 中國近七十年來教育記事 (Chronology of Chinese education during the last seventy years). Shanghai, 1935.

T'ing-yü-lou chu-jen 聽雨樓主人 (Master of the listen-to-the-rain study). *Hsin-ch'u Chang Wen-hsiang-kung shih-lüeh* 新出張文襄公事略 (The career of Chang Wen-hsiang-kung, a new publication), ed. T'ao Tso-t'ing 陶佐庭. Shanghai, 1909.

Tou Chen 竇鎮, ed. *Kuo-ch'ao shu-hua-chia pi-lu* 國朝書畫家筆錄 (Sketches of writers and artists of the Ch'ing dynasty). Soochow, 1911.

Tso Shun-sheng 左舜生, comp. *Chung-kuo chin-pai-nien shih tzu-liao ch'u-pien* 中國近百年史資料初編 (Chinese historical materials for the last hundred years, first collection). Taipei, 1958.

————, comp. *Chung-kuo chin-tai-shih tzu-liao chi-yao* 中國近代史資料輯要 (A source book of important documents relating to the modern history of China). Shanghai, 1945.

Tsou-ting hsüeh-t'ang chang-ch'eng 奏定學堂章程 (School regulations, as memorialized and decided upon), comp. Chang Chih-tung et al. 5 ts'e. Chiang-Ch'u pien-i-kuan shu-chü, 1903.

Wu-hsü pien-fa 戊戌變法 (The reform movement of 1898), ed. Chien Po-tsan 翦伯贊 et al. 4 vols. Shanghai, 1953.

Yang Chia-lo 楊家駱. *Min-kuo ming-jen t'u-chien* 民國名人圖鑑 (Sketches of famous men of the republic). 2 vols. Nanking, 1937.

Yang-wu yün-tung 洋務運動 (The foreign affairs movement), ed. Chinese Historical Society. 8 vols. Shanghai, 1959.

Western Works

Allan, C. Wilfrid. *Makers of Cathay.* Shanghai: Kelly & Walsh, 1936. Ch. 23: "Chang Chih-tung, Scholar and Educationalist."

Ardsheal, tr. "Reminiscences of a Chinese Viceroy's Secretary, Being the Opinions and Recollections of a Secretary on the Staff of the Late Viceroy Chang Chih-tung for over Twenty Years," *Journal of the North China Branch of the Royal Asiatic Society*, 45 (1914), 91–109; 46 (1915), 61–76.

Beresford, Lord Charles. *The Break-up of China.* New York, 1899.

Biggerstaff, Knight. *The Earliest Modern Government Schools in China.* Ithaca, N.Y.: Cornell University Press, 1961.

———. "The T'ung Wen Kuan," *Chinese Social and Political Science Review*, 18.3 (October 1934), 307–340.

Bland, J.O.P. *Li Hung-chang.* New York: Holt, 1917.

———, and E. Backhouse. *China under the Empress Dowager.* Philadelphia: J. B. Lippincott, 1910.

Bodde, Derk. "Harmony and Conflict in Chinese Philosophy," in *Studies in Chinese Thought*, ed. Arthur F. Wright, pp. 19–80. Chicago: University of Chicago Press, 1953.

Bone, Rev. C. "The Kwangnga University, Canton," *The East of Asia Magazine*, 1.4 (1902), 326–327.

Boulger, D. C. *The Life of Sir Halliday Macartney.* London: J. Lane, 1908.

Britton, Roswell S. *The Chinese Periodical Press, 1800–1912.* Shanghai: Kelly & Walsh, 1933.

Brunnert, H. S., and V. V. Hagelstrom. *Present Day Political Organization of China*, rev. M. T. Kolessoff, tr. from Russian by A. Beltchenko and E. E. Moran. Shanghai: Kelly & Walsh, 1912.

Cameron, Merebith E. "The Public Career of Chang Chih-tung, 1837–1909," *Pacific Historical Review*, 7.3 (September 1938), 187–210.

———. *The Reform Movement in China, 1898–1912.* Stanford, Calif.: Stanford University Press, 1931.

Chang Chih-tung. *China's Only Hope: An Appeal by Her Greatest Viceroy, Chang Chih-tung, with the Sanction of the Present Emperor, Kwang Sü*, tr. Samuel I. Woodbridge. New York: Fleming H. Revell, 1900.

———. *K'iuen-hio p'ien: exhortations à l'étude*, tr. Jérome Tobar, *Variétés sinologiques* no. 26. Chang-hai, 1909.

Chang Chun-shu. "The Development of the Early 19th Century Ching-shih Thought and Tseng Kuo-fan's Learning," unpub. seminar paper, Harvard University, 1959.

Chang Chung-li. *The Chinese Gentry: Studies on Their Role in Nineteenth Century Chinese Society.* Seattle, Wash.: University of Washington Press, 1955.

Chang Yu-chuan. "The Kuo Tzu Chien," *Chinese Social and Political Science Review*, 24.1 (April–June 1940), 69–106.

Chen Shih-hsiang. "An Innovation in Chinese Biographical Writing," *The Far Eastern Quarterly*, 13.1 (November 1953), 49–62.

Ch'en Hsien-ting. "Chinese Students in Japan (1905) and the Japanese Government's Policy toward Them," unpub. seminar paper, Harvard University, 1954.

Ch'en, Jerome. *Yüan Shih-k'ai (1859–1916)*. Stanford, Calif.: Stanford University Press, 1961.

China, Imperial Maritime Customs. *Decennial Reports* (Statistical Series, No. 6). Shanghai; 1882–1891, 1892–1901, 1902–1911.

Chronicle and Directory for China, Corea, Japan, etc. Hong Kong; 1891, 1892, 1893, 1898, 1900, 1906, 1907, 1909.

Chu Djang. "War and Diplomacy over Ili," *Chinese Social and Political Science Review*, 20.3 (October 1936), 369–392.

Chyne, W. Y. *Handbook of Cultural Institutions in China*. Shanghai: Chinese National Committee on Intellectual Co-operation, 1936.

Cordier, Henri. *Histoire des relations de la Chine avec les puissances occidentales*. 3 vols. Paris: F. Alcan, 1901–1902.

Cornaby, W. Arthur. "Morning Walks around Hanyang," *The East of Asia Magazine*, 2.3 (1903), 279–283.

Doolittle, Justus. *Social Life of the Chinese*. New York, 1865.

Douglas, R. K. *Society in China*. London, 1894.

Eastman, Lloyd E. "Ch'ing-i and Chinese Policy Formation during the Nineteenth Century," *Journal of Asian Studies*, 24.4 (August 1965), 595–611.

———. *Throne and Mandarins: China's Search for a Policy during the Sino-French Controversy, 1880–1885*. Cambridge, Mass.: Harvard University Press, 1967.

Evans, E. W. Price. *Timothy Richard*. London: The Carey Press, 1945.

Fairbank, John K., ed. *Chinese Thought and Institutions*. Chicago: University of Chicago Press, 1957.

Ferguson, John C. "The Abolition of the Competitive Examinations in China," *Journal of the American Oriental Society*, 27 (January–July 1906), 79–87.

Franke, Wolfgang. *The Reform and Abolition of the Traditional Chinese Examination System*. Cambridge, Mass.: Harvard University Press, 1960.

Frechtling, L. E. "Anglo-Russian Rivalry in East Turkestan," *Journal of the Royal Central Asian Society*, 26 (1939), 471–488.

Fung Yu-lan. *A History of Chinese Philosophy*, tr. Derk Bodde. 2 vols. Princeton, N.J.: Princeton University Press, 1952–1953.

Galt, Howard S. *A History of Chinese Educational Institutions*. London: A. Probsthain, 1951.

Giles, H. A. *A Chinese Biographical Dictionary*. Shanghai, 1898.

Grieder, Jerome B. "The Abolition of the Classical Examination System in China: The Edict of September 2, 1905—Introductory Remarks," unpub. seminar paper, Harvard University, 1957.

———. "The Educational Reform Movement after 1901 and the Abolition of the Examination System," unpub. seminar paper, Harvard University, 1957.

Gundry, R. S. *A Retrospect of Political and Commercial Affairs in China and Japan during the Five Years 1873 to 1877*. Shanghai, 1878.

Hackett, Roger. "Chinese Students in Japan, 1900–1910," *Papers on China*, 3 (1948), 134–169. East Asian Research Center, Harvard University.

Hao Chang. "Liang Ch'i-ch'ao and Intellectual Changes in the Late Nineteenth Century," *Journal of Asian Studies*, 29.1 (November 1969), 23–33.

Hao Yen-p'ing. "Cheng Kuan-ying: The Comprador as Reformer," *Journal of Asian Studies*, 29.1 (November 1969), 15–22.

———. "A Study of the Ch'ing-Liu Tang: The 'Disinterested' Scholar-Official Group (1875–1884)," *Papers on China*, 16 (1962), 40–65. East Asian Research Center, Harvard University.

Ho Ping-ti. *The Ladder of Success in Imperial China: Aspects of Social Mobility, 1368–1911.* New York and London: Columbia University Press, 1962.

Houn, Franklin H. "The Civil Service Recruitment System of the Han Dynasty," *Ch'ing-hua hsüeh-pao* (Tsing Hua journal of Chinese studies), n.s., 1.1 (June 1956), 138–164.

Howard, Richard C. "The Chinese Reform Movement of the 1890's: A Symposium —Introduction," *Journal of Asian Studies*, 29.1 (November 1969), 7–14.

Hsiao Kung-chuan. "Weng T'ung-ho and the Reform Movement of 1898," *Ch'ing-hua hsüeh-pao*, n.s., 1.2 (April 1957), 111–243.

Hsiao, Theodore E. *The History of Modern Education in China.* Shanghai: Commercial Press, 1935.

Hsieh Pao-chao. *The Government of China (1644–1911).* Baltimore: The Johns Hopkins Press, 1925.

Hsü, Immanuel C. Y. *China's Entrance into the Family of Nations: The Diplomatic Phase, 1858–1880.* Cambridge, Mass.: Harvard University Press, 1960.

———. *The Ili Crisis: A Study of Sino-Russian Diplomacy, 1871–1881.* Oxford: Oxford University Press, 1965.

Hsüeh Chün-tu. *Huang Hsing and the Chinese Revolution.* Stanford, Calif.: Stanford University Press, 1961.

Hucker, Charles O. "The Tung-lin Movement in the Late Ming Period," in *Chinese Thought and Institutions*, ed. John K. Fairbank, pp. 132–162. Chicago: University of Chicago Press, 1957.

Hummel, Arthur W., ed. *Eminent Chinese of the Ch'ing Period (1644–1912).* 2 vols. Washington, D.C.: U.S. Government Printing Office, 1943–1944.

Jansen, Marius B. *The Japanese and Sun Yat-sen.* Cambridge, Mass.: Harvard University Press, 1954.

Kennedy, Thomas L. "The Kiangnan Arsenal, 1895–1911: The Decentralized Bureaucracy Responds to Imperialism," *Ch'ing-shih wen-t'i*, 2.1 (October 1969), 17–37.

Kiernan, E. V. G. *British Diplomacy in China, 1880 to 1885.* Cambridge: Cambridge University Press, 1939.

Kracke, E. A. *Civil Service in Early Sung China, 906–1067, with Particular Emphasis on the Development of Controlled Sponsorship to Foster Administrative Responsibility.* Cambridge, Mass.: Harvard University Press, 1953.

———. "Family versus Merit in the Chinese Civil Service Examinations under the Empire," *Harvard Journal of Asiatic Studies*, 10.2 (September 1947), 103–123.

———. "Region, Family, and Individual in the Chinese Examination System," in *Chinese Thought and Institutions*, ed. John K. Fairbank, pp. 251–268. Chicago: University of Chicago Press, 1957.

Ku Hung-ming. *The Story of a Chinese Oxford Movement*, 2nd ed. Shanghai: Shanghai Mercury, 1919.

Kuo Ping-wen. *The Chinese System of Public Education.* New York: Teachers College, Columbia University, 1915.

La Fargue, Thomas E. *China's First Hundred.* Pullman, Wash.: State College of Washington, 1942.

Legge, James, tr. *The Four Books: Confucian Analects, The Great Learning, The Doctrine of the Mean, and The Works of Mencius, with Original Chinese Text, English Translation and Notes.* Reprint of 1923 Shanghai edition. New York: Paragon Book Reprint Corp., 1966.

Lewis, Charlton M. "The Hunanese Elite and the Reform Movement, 1895–1898," *Journal of Asian Studies,* 29.1 (November 1969), 35–42.

———. "The Reform Movement in Hunan, 1896–1897," unpub. seminar paper, Harvard University, 1961.

Lewis, Robert E. *The Educational Conquest of the Far East.* New York: Fleming H. Revell, 1903.

Levenson, Joseph R. *Confucian China and Its Modern Fate.* 3 vols. Berkeley and Los Angeles, Calif.: University of California Press, 1965–1966.

———. " 'History' and 'Value': The Tensions of Intellectual Choice in Modern China," in *Studies in Chinese Thought,* ed. Arthur F. Wright, pp. 146–194. Chicago: University of Chicago Press, 1953.

———. *Liang Ch'i-ch'ao and the Mind of Modern China.* Cambridge, Mass.: Harvard University Press, 1953.

Li Chien-nung. *The Political History of China, 1840–1928,* tr. and ed. Ssu-yu Teng and Jeremy Ingalls. Princeton, N.J.: D. Van Nostrand, 1956.

Liebenthal, Walter. *The Book of Chao.* Peiping: Peking Catholic University, 1948.

Lin Yutang. *A History of the Press and Public Opinion in China.* Chicago: University of Chicago Press, 1936.

Lo Jung-pang. *K'ang Yu-wei: A Biography and a Symposium.* Tucson, Ariz.: University of Arizona Press for Association for Asian Studies, 1967.

Lobanov-Rostovsky, A. *Russia and Asia.* New York: Macmillan, 1933.

Martin, W. A. P. *A Cycle of Cathay, or China, South and North, with Personal Reminiscences.* Edinburgh, 1897.

———. *Hanlin Papers; or, Essays on the Intellectual Life of the Chinese.* Edinburgh, 1880.

———. "Report on the System of Public Instruction in China," U.S. Bureau of Education, Circulars of Information, 1877, no. 1.

Mayers, W. F. *The Government of China, a Manual of Chinese Titles, Categorically Arranged and Explained,* 3rd ed., rev. G. M. H. Playfair. Shanghai, 1897.

Michael, Franz. "Military Organization and Power Structure of China during the Taiping Rebellion," *Pacific Historical Review,* 18 (November 1949), 469–483.

Michie, Alexander. *The Englishman in China.* 2 vols. Edinburgh: W. Blackwood & Sons, 1900.

Morgan, Evan. *A Guide to Wenli Styles and Chinese Ideals.* Shanghai: Christian Literature Society for China, 1912.

Morrison, Esther. "The Modernization of the Confucian Bureaucracy: An Historical Study of Public Administration," unpub. diss., Harvard University, 1959.

Morse, H. B. *The International Relations of the Chinese Empire*. 3 vols. London and New York: Longmans, Green & Co., 1910–1918.

Nivison, David S. "Protest against Conventions and Conventions of Protest," in *The Confucian Persuasion*, ed. Arthur F. Wright, pp. 177–201. Stanford, Calif.: Stanford University Press, 1960.

——. "Protest against Conventions and Conventions of Protest: Some Effects on Chinese Thought of the Mode of Education and the System of State Examinations from T'ang through Sung," paper (mimeo.) presented to the Third Conference on Chinese Thought, Stockbridge, Mass., September 5–12, 1957.

—— and Arthur F. Wright, eds. *Confucianism in Action*. Stanford, Calif.: Stanford University Press, 1959.

Odontines, L. "Chang Chih-tung and the Reform Movement in China," tr. from German by E. Zillig, *The East of Asia Magazine*, 1.1 (1902), 19–42.

Papers Relating to the Foreign Relations of the United States. Washington, D.C.: U.S. Government Printing Office, 1880.

Peake, Cyrus H. *Nationalism and Education in Modern China*. New York, Columbia University Press, 1932.

Powell, Ralph L. *The Rise of Chinese Military Power, 1895–1912*. Princeton, N.J.: Princeton University Press, 1955.

Purcell, Victor. *Problems of Chinese Education*. London: K. Paul, Trench, Trubner, 1936.

Rankin, Mary Backus. "The Manchurian Crisis and Radical Student Nationalism, 1903," *Ch'ing-shih wen-t'i*, 2.1 (October 1969), 87–106.

Rawlinson, John L. *China's Struggle for Naval Development*. Cambridge, Mass.: Harvard University Press, 1967.

Richard, Timothy. *Forty-five Years in China*. New York: Frederick A. Stokes, 1916.

Ross, E. A. *The Changing Chinese*. New York: Century Co., 1912.

Sakai, Robert K. "Politics and Education in Modern China," unpub. diss., Harvard University, 1953.

Schwartz, Benjamin. *In Search of Wealth and Power: Yen Fu and the West*. Cambridge, Mass.: Harvard University Press, 1964.

Sivin, Nathan. "The Translation Bureau of the Kiangnan Arsenal," unpub. seminar paper, Harvard University, 1959.

Smith, Arthur H. *Village Life in China*. London, 1899.

Smythe, E. Joan. "The Tzu-li Hui: Some Chinese and Their Rebellion," *Papers on China*, 12 (December 1958), 51–68. Center for East Asian Studies, Harvard University.

Sun, E-tu Zen. *Chinese Railways and British Interests, 1898–1911*. New York: King's Crown Press, Columbia University, 1954.

——. *Ch'ing Administrative Terms*. Cambridge, Mass.: Harvard University Press, 1961.

Swann, Nancy Lee. *Food and Money in Ancient China*. Princeton, N.J.: Princeton University Press, 1950.

Taam, Cheuk-woon. *The Development of Chinese Libraries under the Ch'ing Dynasty, 1644–1911*. Shanghai: Commercial Press, 1935.

Tan, Chester C. *The Boxer Catastrophe*. New York: Columbia University Press, 1955.

T'ang Leang-li. *China in Revolt*. London: N. Douglas, 1927.

Teng Ssu-yü and Knight Biggerstaff. *An Annotated Bibliography of Selected Chinese Reference Works*. Cambridge, Mass.: Harvard University Press, 1950.

——— and John K. Fairbank. *China's Response to the West: A Documentary Survey, 1839–1923*. Cambridge, Mass.: Harvard University Press, 1954.

Translation of the Peking Gazette, reprinted from the *North China Herald*, annually. Shanghai, 1880–1885.

Wen Ching. *The Chinese Crisis from Within*. London: G. Richards, 1901.

Wen Yuan-ning. "Ku Hung-ming," *T'ien-hsia Monthly*, 4 (April 1937), 386–390.

Who's Who in Japan, with Manchukuo and China, 1941–1942, ed. Tsunesaburo Kameska. Tokyo: The Who's Who in Japan Publishing Office, 1941.

Wilhelm, Hellmut. "The *Po-hsüeh Hung-ju* Examination of 1679," *Journal of the American Oriental Society*, 71 (January–March 1951), 60–66.

———. "The Problem of Within and Without: A Confucian Attempt in Syncretism," *Journal of the History of Ideas*, 12 (January 1951), 48–60.

Williams, S. Wells. *A History of China*. New York: C. Scribner's Sons, 1897.

———. *The Middle Kingdom: A Survey of the Geography, Government, Literature, Social Life, Arts, and History of the Chinese Empire*. 2 vols. New York: C. Scribner's Sons, 1901.

Wittfogel, K. A. "Public Office in the Liao Dynasty and the Chinese Examination System," *Harvard Journal of Asiatic Studies*, 10.1 (June 1947), 13–40.

Wright, Arthur F., ed. *The Confucian Persuasion*. Stanford, Calif.: Stanford University Press, 1960.

———. "The Formation of Sui Ideology, 581–604," in *Chinese Thought and Institutions*, ed. John K. Fairbank, pp. 71–104. Chicago: University of Chicago Press, 1957.

———, ed. *Studies in Chinese Thought*. Chicago: University of Chicago Press, 1953.

Wright, Mary C. *The Last Stand of Chinese Conservatism*. Stanford, Calif.: Stanford University Press, 1957.

Wright, Stanley F. *Hart and the Chinese Customs*. Belfast: W. Mullan for Queens University, 1950.

Yang Lien-sheng. "Buddhist Monasteries and Four Money-raising Institutions in Chinese History," *Harvard Journal of Asiatic Studies*, 13.1–2 (June 1950), 174–191.

Young, Ernest P. "The Chinese Student Strikes in Japan, 1905," unpub. seminar paper, Harvard University, 1959.

Yung Shang Him. "The Chinese Educational Mission and Its Influence," *T'ien-hsia Monthly*, 9 (October 1939), 225–256.

Yung Wing. *My Life in China and America*. New York: H. Holt, 1909.

Zi Etienne. *Pratique des examens litteraires en Chine*, in *Variétés sinologiques* no. 5. Chang-hai, 1894.

———. *Pratique des examens militaires en Chine*, in *Variétés sinologiques* no. 9. Chang-hai, 1896.

Glossary

a-k'o-te'-mi 阿喀特米
Aisin Gioro 愛新覺羅

Ch'a Shuang-sui 查雙綏
chai-chang 齋長
Chan-shih-fu 詹事府
chan-shu 戰術
chan-shu shih-shih 戰術實施
chan-t'u 戰圖
Chang Chih-tung 張之洞
Chang Chih-wan 張之萬
Chang Ch'üan 張權
Chang Jen-chi 張仁霽
Chang Jen-ch'üan 張仁權
Chang Jen-chun 張仁準
Chang Jen-hui 張仁會
Chang Jen-k'an 張仁侃
Chang Jen-li 張仁蠡
Chang Jen-shih 張仁實
Chang Jen-t'ing 張仁遐
Chang Jen-yüeh 張仁樂
Chang Kuang-ya 張廣雅
Chang P'ei-lun 張佩綸
Chang Piao 張彪
Chang Po-hsi 張百熙
Chang Shu-sheng 張樹聲
Chang T'an 張檀
Chang Ts'ung 張璁
Chang Wen-hsiang-kung ch'üan-chi 張文
襄公全集
Chang Ying (father of Chang Chih-
tung) 張鍈
Chang Ying 張英
Chang Yüan-chi 張元濟
Chang Yün-ch'ing 張澐卿
Ch'ang-yen pao 昌言報
Chao Erh-hsün 趙爾巽
Chao I 趙翼

Chao Shu-ch'iao 趙舒翹
ch'ao-k'ao 朝考
Ch'en I 陳毅
Ch'en Li 陳澧
Ch'en Liang 陳亮
Ch'en Pao-chen 陳寶箴
Ch'en Pao-ch'en 陳寶琛
Ch'en Pi-kuang 陳璧光
Ch'en San-li 陳三立
cheng (right) 正
cheng (government) 政
cheng-ch'üan 正權
Cheng Hsiao-hsü 鄭孝胥
Cheng hsüeh-pao 正學報
cheng jen-hsin 正人心
cheng-ming 正名
cheng-shih 徵實
cheng-t'i 正體
cheng-tun 整頓
Cheng Tun-chin 鄭敦謹
Ch'eng Chih-ho 程志和
Ch'eng I 程頤
Ch'eng Ming-ch'ao 程明超
Ch'eng Sung-wan 程頌萬
Ch'eng T'ing-kuei 程廷桂
ch'eng-ts'ai 成材
chi-chi 技擊
Chi Chü-wei 紀鉅維
chi-shih pen-mo 紀事本末
chi-ssu 繼嗣
chi-t'ung 繼統
ch'i-chieh 氣節
Ch'i-chü-chu kuan 起居注館
ch'i-chü t'i-ts'ao 器具體操
chia-shu 家塾
Chiang Chieh 蔣楷
Chiang-Ch'u pien-i-chü 江楚編譯局
Chiang-Han ping-ling chi 江漢炳靈集

Chiang-Han shu-yüan 江漢書院
chiang-i 講義
Chiang-nan kao-teng hsüeh-t'ang 江南
　高等學堂
Chiang Piao 江標
Chiang-pien hsüeh-t'ang 將弁學堂
chiang-t'ang 講堂
chiang-yu 講友
ch'iang 強
Ch'iang-hsüeh hui 強學會
Ch'iang-hsüeh pao 強學報
chiao-an 教案
chiao-hsi 教習
chiao-kuan 教官
Chiao-pin-lu k'ang-i 校邠廬抗議
chiao-shou 教授
chiao-wang 教王
chiao-yü 教諭
Chiao-yü tsa-chih 教育雜誌
chieh-yüan 解元
chien-fa 楝發
chien-sheng 監生
chien-tu 監督
chien-yüan 監院
chien-yüeh 儉約
ch'ien 錢
Ch'ien Hsün 錢恂
Ch'ien-lung 乾隆
Ch'ien Te-p'ei 錢德培
chih (wisdom) 智
chih (treatise) 志
chih-ch'ih 知恥
chih-chü 知懼
chih-chün shih-fan hsüeh-t'ang 支郡師
　範學堂
chih-li 知禮
chih-li chou 直隸州
chih-li ming-chieh 砥礪名節
chih-pen 知本
chih-pi chih-chi 知彼知己
chih-pien 知變
chih shen-hsin 治身心
chih t'ien-hsia 治天下
chih-yao 知要
chih-yen chi-chien 直言極諫
ch'ih-chiao 斥教
chin ch'i-yung 盡其用

Chin-chiang shu-yüan 錦江書院
chin-shih 進士
Chin-shih kuan 進士館
Chin-ssu lu 近思錄
Ch'in-ch'eng hsüeh-t'ang 勤成學堂
ching-chi 經濟
ching-chi-k'o chin-shih 經濟科進士
ching-chi-k'o chü-jen 經濟科學人
ching-chi sui-chü 經濟歲舉
ching-chi t'e-k'o 經濟特科
ching-chieh 經解
Ching-chieh hsüeh-t'ang 敬節學堂
Ching-hsin shu-yüan 經心書院
ching-i 經義
Ching-i shu-wen 經義述聞
Ching-ku shu-yüan 經古書院
ching-li 經理
ching-lun 經論
ching-shih 經世
Ching-shih ta-hsüeh-t'ang 京師大學堂
ching-shuo 經說
ching-ts'e 經策
ching-wen 經文
Ch'ing-chi wai-chiao shih-liao 清季外交
　史料
ch'ing-i 清議
ch'ing-liu 清流
Ch'ing-liu tang 清流黨
Ch'ing-p'ing t'uan-lien 清平團練
Ch'ing-shih 清史
chiu 舊
chiu-hsüeh 舊學
chiu-hsüeh wei t'i, hsin-hsüeh wei yung
　舊學為體，新學為用
chou 州
Chou Fu 周馥
chu-ch'eng 築城
Chu Feng-piao 朱鳳標
Chu Hsi 朱熹
chu-k'ao kuan 主考官
chu-pu 竹布
Chu Shao-en 朱紹恩
Chu Tzu-tse 朱滋澤
ch'u-teng 初等
Ch'u-ts'ai hsüeh-t'ang 儲才學堂
chü-jen 學人
Ch'ü Hung-chi 瞿鴻禨

ch'ü-kou 去苟
ch'ü-ti 取締
ch'ü-wang 去妄
chuan 傳
chuan-men hsüeh-hsiao 專門學校
chüan 卷
Ch'üan-hsüeh p'ien 勸學篇
Ch'üan Tsu-wang 全祖望
chuang-yüan 狀元
Ch'uang-chien Tsun-ching shu-yüan chi 創建尊經書院記
Chüeh-lo kuan-hsüeh 覺羅官學
chün-chih 軍制
chün-hsiu 俊秀
Ch'un-ch'iu 春秋
chung 中
Chung-hsüeh ching-chi 中學經濟
Chung-hsüeh hsi-hsüeh chih hsüeh-hsiao 中學西學之學校
chung hsüeh-t'ang 中學堂
Chung-hsüeh wei t'i, hsi-hsüeh wei yung 中學為體, 西學為用
Chung-hua chih so-i wei chung 中華之所以為中
Chung-yung 中庸
Ch'ung-hou 崇厚
en-k'o hui-shih 恩科會試
en-kung-sheng 恩貢生

Fan Ming-ho 范鳴龢
Fang-hai hsin-lun 防海新論
fang-ying pien-yung 防營弁勇
fei-kung pu-wei kung 非工不為功
fen 分
fen-chiao 分教
Feng Kuei-fen 馮桂芬
Feng Tzu-ts'ai 馮子材
fu (prose-poetry) 賦
fu (prefecture) 府
fu-chiang 副將
fu-k'ao 府考
fu-kung-sheng 副貢生
fu-kuo 富國
fu-sheng 附生
fu-shih 覆試
Fu Yün-lung 傅雲龍
Han-Chan ta-k'ao 翰詹大考

Han Ch'ao 韓超
Han-lin ssu-chien 翰林四諫
Han-lin yüan 翰林院
Han-shu 漢書
Ho Shou-tz'u 賀壽慈
Ho Yang-yüan 何養源
hsi 西
hsi-fa 西法
hsi-hsin wang-pen 喜新忘本
hsi-hsüeh ching-chi 西學經濟
hsi-hsüeh tsung-chiao-hsi 西學總教習
Hsi-i hsüeh-t'ang 西藝學堂
hsia-pu 夏布
Hsiang hsüeh-pao 湘學報
hsiang-shih 鄉試
Hsiao-che 孝哲
Hsiao-ching 孝經
hsiao hsüeh-t'ang 小學堂
hsiao-k'ai 小楷
hsiao-lien 孝廉
hsieh-chiao 協教
hsien 縣
Hsien-feng 咸豐
hsien-hsieh 閑邪
hsien-ju wei chu 先入為主
hsien-liang fang-cheng 賢良方正
hsin 新
hsin-cheng 新政
hsin-hsüeh 新學
hsing 行
hsiu-chuan 修撰
hsiu-hsing 修省
hsiu-shen 修身
hsiu-ts'ai 秀才
Hsiung Hsi-ling 熊希齡
Hsü Chih-ching 徐致靖
Hsü Chih-hsiang 徐致祥
Hsü Ching-ch'eng 許景澄
hsü-hsin 虛心
Hsü Jen-chu 徐仁鑄
Hsü T'ung 徐桐
Hsü Ying-k'uei 許應騤
hsüan-chü 選舉
Hsüan-t'ung 宣統
hsüeh-an 學案
hsüeh-cheng (departmental director of education) 學正

hsüeh-cheng (provincial director of education) 學政
hsüeh-chih 學制
Hsüeh-hai t'ang 學海堂
hsüeh-hsi wu-kuan 學習武官
hsüeh-hsiao 學校
Hsüeh-pu 學部
hsüeh-sheng 學生
hsüeh-t'ang 學堂
hsün-hsü 循序
hsün-tao 訓導
Hu Chün 胡鈞
Hu Lin-i 胡林翼
hu-ming 糊名
Hu-pei ch'üan-sheng hsüeh-wu-ch'u 湖北全省學務處
Hu-pei hsüeh-sheng lüeh 湖北學生略
Hu-pei hu-chün 湖北護軍
Hu Ssu-ching 胡思敬
Hua-hsüeh hsüeh-t'ang 化學學堂
hua-min erh ch'eng-su 化民而成俗
Huang Hsing 黃興
Huang I-lin 黃以霖
Huang Kung-ch'ien 黃恭謙
Huang Pang-chün 黃邦俊
Huang Shao-chi 黃紹箕
Huang Shao-ti 黃紹第
Huang T'i-fang 黃體芳
Huang Tsun-hsien 黃遵憲
Huang Tsung-hsi 黃宗羲
Hui 回
hui-shih 會試
hui-shih tsung-ts'ai 會試總裁
hui-t'ung 會通

i (righteousness; interpretation) 義
i (art) 藝
i-chih 益智
I-ching 易經
I-hsin. See Prince Kung 奕訢
i-hsüeh 義學
I-huan. See Prince Ch'un 奕譞
i-k'o 藝科
I-k'uang. See Prince Ch'ing 奕劻
I-li i-shu 儀禮義疏
I Nai 易鼐
i-shu 義塾

I-shu chü 譯書局
i-wu chiao-yü 義務教育

Jao Shu-kuang 饒叔光
jen 仁
jen-jen-che chih, jen-fa-che luan 任人者治, 任法者亂
jen-p'in 人品
jen-ts'ai 人才
jen wu pu-hsüeh, hsüeh wu pu-shih 人無不學, 學無不實
jih-chi 日記
jou-juan t'i-ts'ao 柔輭體操
ju-hsüeh 入學
ju-shu 儒術
Juan Yüan 阮元
Jung-ch'ing 榮慶
Jung-ch'üan 榮全
Jung-lu 榮祿

k'ai feng-ch'i 開風氣
k'ai-wu ch'eng-wu 開物成務
Kang-i 剛毅
K'ang-hsi 康熙
K'ang-Liang tang 康梁黨
K'ang Yu-wei 康有為
Kao Ling-wei 高凌霨
kao-teng 高等
kao-teng hsiao-hsüeh 高等小學
kao-teng hsüeh-t'ang 高等學堂
k'ao-ch'ai 考差
Ko-chih shu-yüan 格致書院
Ko-lao hui 哥老會
k'o 科
k'o-chü 科學
k'o-chü chih-tu 科學制度
k'o-k'ao 科考
Ku-ching ching-she 詁經精舍
Ku Hung-ming 辜鴻銘
ku-wen 古文
Ku Yen-wu 顧炎武
Kuan Chung 管仲
kuan hsüeh-sheng 官學生
kuan-hsüeh ta-ch'en 管學大臣
Kuan Ts'un-yüan 管存元
kuan-tu shang-pan 官督商辦
k'uan-ta 寬大

Kuang-an shui-chün 廣安水軍
Kuang-chia 廣甲
Kuang fang-yen kuan 廣方言館
Kuang-hsü 光緒
kuang-hsüeh 光學
Kuang-sheng chün 廣勝軍
Kuang-ya shu-chü 廣雅書局
Kuang-ya shu-yüan 廣雅書院
K'uang-wu hsüeh-t'ang 礦務學堂
kuei-chü 規矩
Kuei O 桂萼
K'un-kang 崑岡
kung-hsüeh jen-yüan 工學人員
kung-hsüeh-sheng 工學生
kung-i 公議
Kung-i hsüeh-t'ang 工藝學堂
kung-kung chih hsüeh 公共之學
kung-li 功利
kung-sheng 貢生
kung-shih 貢士
Kung-yang chuan 公羊傳
k'ung-t'an 空談
K'ung-tzu kai-chih-k'ao 孔子改制考
kuo-chiao 國教
kuo-min chiao-yü 國民教育
Kuo-shih kuan 國史館
Kuo Sung-tao 郭嵩燾
kuo-ts'ui 國粹
Kuo-tzu-chien 國子監
kuo-wen 國文

la-k'o 拉搞
lan-shan 藍衫
li (profit) 利
li (rites) 禮
li (one-third mile) 里
li (reason) 理
Li Chan-chuang 李占椿
Li-chi 禮記
Li-chih hui 勵志會
Li Chung-chüeh 李鍾珏
Li Han-chang 李瀚章
li-hsüeh (Neo-Confucianism) 理學
li-hsüeh (dynamics) 力學
Li Hua-lung 李化龍
Li Hung-chang 李鴻章
Li Hung-tsao 李鴻藻

Li Pao-sun 李寶巽
li-p'in 立品
Li Ping-heng 李秉衡
li-t'ang 禮堂
Li Tuan-fen 李端棻
Li Tz'u-ming 李慈銘
Li Wei 李衞
Li Wen-t'ien 李文田
Li Yüan-hung 黎元洪
Liang Ch'i-ch'ao 梁啟超
Liang-Hu kao-teng hsüeh-t'ang 兩湖高
    等學堂
Liang-Hu shu-yüan 兩湖書院
liang-neng shou-chih 量能授職
Liang Ting-fen 梁鼎芬
Liang Tun-yen 梁敦彥
Liao Cheng-hua 廖正華
Liao P'ing 廖平
lien-hsi hsüeh-sheng 練習學生
Lin-k'uei 麟魁
lin-sheng 廩生
Lin Tse-hsü 林則徐
Ling-te t'ang 令德堂
Liu En-jung 劉恩榮
Liu Fen 劉賁
Liu Hung-lieh 劉洪烈
Liu Jui-fen 劉瑞芬
Liu K'un-i 劉坤一
Liu Kung-mien 劉恭冕
Liu Shu-nien 劉書年
Liu Wei-chen 劉維楨
Liu Wen-yao 劉問堯
Liu Yung-fu 劉永福
Lo Chen-yü 羅振玉
Lu Chiu-yüan 陸九淵
Lu Ch'uan-lin 鹿傳霖
Lu-chün hsüeh-t'ang 陸軍學堂
Lü Hsien-chi 呂賢基
lüeh 略
lun 論
lun-li 論理
lun-li k'o 倫理科
Lun-yü 論語

Ma Tuan-lin 馬端臨
Mao Ch'ang-hsi 毛昶熙
Mao Tse-tung 毛澤東

meng-hsüeh 蒙學
Meng-tzu 孟子
mi-feng 彌封
Miao 苗
Miao Ch'üan-sun 繆荃孫
mien-shih 面試
min-ch'üan 民權
ming ch'i-li 明其理
Ming-chia 名家
ming-ching 明經
Ming-ju hsüeh-an 明儒學案
ming-kang 明綱
ming-t'i erh ta-yung 明體而達用
mou 畝
Mu-tsung 穆宗

Nan-hsüeh-hui 南學會
Nan-shu-fang 南書房
Nan-yang ta-ch'en 南洋大臣
nei 內
nei-p'ien 內篇
Nien-erh-shih cha-chi 廿二史劄記
Nien-fei 捻匪
nien-p'u 年譜
Nung-wu hsüeh-t'ang 農務學堂

Ou-yang Hsiu 歐陽修

pa-ku 八股
pa-ku wen 八股文
pa-kung-sheng 拔貢生
P'an Tsu-yin 潘祖蔭
pang-yen 榜眼
pao-kuo 報國
Pao-ping-t'ang ti-tzu chi 抱冰堂弟子記
Pao-t'ing 寶廷
Pao-yün 寶鋆
p'ao-kung hsüeh-hsiao 礮工學校
p'ei pen-ken, hou feng-su 培本根, 厚風俗
pen 本
p'eng-t'u 朋徒
P'eng Yü-lin 彭玉麟
pien fa 變法
pien-hsiu 編修
pien k'o-chü 變科學
p'ien 篇

p'in-hsing 品行
ping-ch'i (military chess) 兵棋
ping-ch'i (military weapons) 兵器
ping-pei tao-t'ai 兵備道台
ping-shih t'i-ts'ao 兵式體操
ping-tui ts'ao-ch'ang 兵隊操場
p'ing-teng 平等
po-hsüeh hung-tz'u k'o 博學宏詞科
Po-hsüeh kuan 博學館
po-shih 博士
po-wu 博物
Prince Ch'ing (I-k'uang) 慶親王 (奕劻)
Prince Ch'un (I-huan) 醇親王 (奕譞)
Prince Kung (I-hsin) 恭親王 (奕訢)
Prince Li (Shih-to) 禮親王 (世鐸)
Prince Tuan (Tsai-i) 端親王 (載漪)
p'u-chi chiao-yü 普及教育
p'u-t'ung hsüeh 普通學

San-chiang shih-fan hsüeh-t'ang 三江師範學堂
san-kang 三綱
san-kuan k'ao-shih 散館考試
Sang Pao 桑寶
shan-chang 山長
shang-wu chih ching-shen 商武之精神
Shang-wu chü 商務局
Shang-wu hsüeh-t'ang 商務學堂
Shao Yu-lien 邵友濂
she-hsüeh 社學
Shen Pao-chen 沈葆楨
sheng 省
Sheng Hsüan-huai 盛宣懷
Sheng-pao 勝保
Sheng-yü 盛昱
sheng-yüan 生員
shih 詩
Shih-chi 史記
shih-chiang 侍講
shih-chiang hsüeh-shih 侍講學士
Shih-ching 詩經
shih-fa 史法
shih-fan ch'uan-hsi-so 師範傳習所
shih-hsiao 實效
Shin Hsü 石煦
shih-hsüeh 實學
Shih-hsüeh kuan 實學館

Shih-hsüeh yüan 仕學院
shih-kuan hsüeh-hsiao 士官學校
shih-lun 史論
shih-shih 事實
Shih-to. See Prince Li 世鐸
shih-tu hsüeh-shih 侍讀學士
shih-wen 時文
shih-wu 時務
Shih-wu hsüeh-t'ang 時務學堂
Shih-wu pao 時務報
shih-wu ts'e 時務策
shou-yüeh 守約
shu 疏
Shu-ch'ang kuan 庶常館
shu-chi-shih 庶吉士
Shu-ching 書經
Shu-hsüeh hui 蜀學會
Shu-mu ta-wen 書目答問
shu-yüan 書院
Shuang Shou 雙壽
Shui-ching chu 水經注
Shui-chün lu-chün ta-hsüeh 水軍陸軍大學
Shui-lu-shih hsüeh-t'ang 水陸師學堂
Shun-t'ien-fu chih 順天府志
ssu-chien-ch'en 四諫臣
Ssu-ching-chü hsi-ma 司經局洗馬
Ssu-k'u ch'üan-shu tsung-mu 四庫全書總目
Ssu-ma Ch'ien 司馬遷
Ssu-ma Kuang 司馬光
Ssu-shu i 四書義
Su Ch'e 蘇轍
su-ch'eng k'o 速成科
Su Shih 蘇軾
sui 歲
sui-k'ao 歲考
sui-kung-sheng 歲貢生
Sun Chia-nai 孫家鼐
Sun Ching 孫敬
Sun Yat-sen 孫逸仙
Sung Po-lu 宋伯魯
Sung-Yüan hsüeh-an 宋元學案

Ta-hsüeh 大學
ta hsüeh-t'ang 大學堂
ta-i 大義

ta-t'iao 大挑
T'ai-hsüeh 太學
T'ai-p'ing 太平
T'an Chi-hsün 譚繼洵
T'an Chung-lin 譚鍾麟
t'an-hua 探花
T'an Ssu-t'ung 譚嗣同
t'ang-chang 堂長
T'ang Shu-i 唐樹義
T'ang Ts'ai-ch'ang 唐才常
tao 道
tao-k'o 道科
Tao-kuang 道光
tao-t'ai 道台
te 德
Teng Ch'eng-hsiu 鄧承修
t'eng-lu 謄錄
t'i 體
t'i-fu 提覆
t'i-tiao 提調
T'ieh-cheng chü 鐵政局
t'ieh-ching 帖經
T'ieh-lu hsüeh-t'ang 鐵路學堂
tien-chih 典制
tien-hsüeh 電學
Tien-pao hsüeh-t'ang 電報學堂
tien-shih 殿試
T'ien-hsiang-ko shih-erh-ling ts'ao 天香閣十二齡草
T'ien Wen-ching 田文鏡
T'ien Wu-chao 田吳炤
ting-pen 定本
ting-t'i 定題
t'ing 廳
t'ou-teng shih-ch'en 頭等使臣
tsa-wen 雜文
Tsai-i. See Prince Tuan 載漪
Tsai-t'ien 載湉
Ts'ai Hsi-yung 蔡錫勇
ts'ai-neng 才能
ts'ao-fa 操法
ts'e 策
ts'e-wen 策問
Ts'en Ch'un-hsüan 岑春煊
Tseng Chi-tse 曾紀澤
Tseng Kuang-fu 曾廣敷
Tseng Kuo-ch'üan 曾國荃

Tseng Kuo-fan 曾國藩
tseng-sheng 增生
Tso-chuan 左傳
Tso Ch'üan-hsiao 左全孝
Tso Tsung-t'ang 左宗棠
Ts'ui Kuo-yin 崔國因
Tsun-ching shu-yüan 尊經書院
Ts'un-ku hsüeh-t'ang 存古學堂
tsung-chi-ch'a 總稽察
tsung-chiao 宗教
tsung-chiao-chang 總教長
tsung-chiao-hsi 總教習
tsung-ching 宗經
tsung-ching-li 總經理
tsung-li hsüeh-wu ta-ch'en 總理學務大臣
tsung-pan 總辦
tsung-ts'ai 總裁
Tsungli Yamen 總理衙門
Tu-ch'a yüan 都察院
Tu-pan cheng-wu ch'u 督辦政務處
Tu T'ung-chien lun 讀通鑑論
Tuan-fang 端方
Tung Chung-shu 董仲舒
Tung Hsün 董恂
Tung-shu tu-shu chi 東塾讀書記
t'ung 通
T'ung-cheng ssu 通政司
T'ung chien 通鑑
T'ung chih 通志
T'ung-chih 同治
T'ung-ju yüan 通儒院
T'ung-k'ao 通考
t'ung-k'ao-kuan 同考官
t'ung-shih 童試
T'ung-tien 通典
T'ung-wen kuan 同文館
tzu-ch'i 自欺
tzu-ch'iang 自強
Tzu-ch'iang chün 自強軍
Tzu-ch'iang hsüeh-t'ang 自強學堂
Tzu-chih t'ung-chien 資治通鑑
tzu-chu chih ch'üan 自主之權
tzu-jao 自擾
tzu-sai 自塞
Tz'u-an 慈安
tz'u-ch'en 詞臣

Tz'u-hsi 慈禧

wai 外
wai-p'ien 外篇
Wai-wu pu 外務部
Wan Ch'ing-li 萬青藜
Wang Chung-jen 王仲任
Wang Feng-ying 汪鳳瀛
Wang Fu-chih 王夫之
Wang I-jung 王懿榮
Wang Jen-k'an 王仁堪
Wang K'ang-nien 汪康年
Wang P'eng-yün 王鵬運
Wang Ping-en 王秉恩
Wang P'u 王朴
wang-tao 王道
Wang Tsu-yüan 王祖源
Wang T'ung-yü 王同愈
Wang Wen-shao 王文韶
Wang Yin-chih 王引之
Wei Kuang-tao 魏光燾
wen 文
wen-chang 文章
Wen-hsiang 文祥
Wen-hsiang kung 文襄公
Wen-hsien t'ung-k'ao 文獻通考
wen-hsüeh-t'ang tsung-t'i-tiao 文學堂總提調
wen-k'o 文科
wen-ku erh chih-hsin 溫故而知新
wen-li 文理
wen-shih ta-hsüeh 文士大學
Wen-yü 文煜
Weng T'ung-ho 翁同龢
wu 武
Wu Ch'ang-ch'ing 吳長慶
Wu-ching i 五經義
Wu-ching po-shih 五經博士
Wu Chung-hsiang 吳仲翔
Wu-hsü pien-fa 戊戌變法
wu-hsüeh-t'ang tsung-t'i-tiao 武學堂總提調
Wu Ju-lun 吳汝綸
Wu K'o-tu 吳可讀
Wu-pei hsüeh-t'ang 武備學堂
Wu Ta-ch'eng 吳大澂
Wu T'ang 吳棠

wu-ti wu-hsüeh, wu-jen pu-shüeh 無地
  無學, 無人不學
Wu Wen-jung 吳文鎔

Yakub Beg 阿古柏
yang 陽
Yang Feng 楊鳳
Yang Jui 楊銳
Yang Shen-hsiu 楊深秀
Yang Shou-ching 楊守敬
Yang Tu 楊篤
yang-wu 洋務
Yang-wu ch'u 洋務處
Yang-wu chü 洋務局
Yao Chin-ch'i 姚晉圻
Yao Hsi-kuang 姚錫光
yeh-ts'ao 野操
Yen Fu 嚴復
Yen Hsiu 嚴修
yen-lu 言路

yin 陰
yu-chi 游擊
Yu-hsüan yü 輶軒語
yu-kung-sheng 優貢生
Yü-ch'ing kung 毓慶宮
Yü-lei hsüeh-t'ang 魚雷學堂
Yü-p'i t'ung-chien chi-lan 御批通鑑輯覽
yü-te 育德
Yü-ying hsüeh-t'ang 育嬰學堂
yüan 元
Yüan Ch'ang 袁昶
yüan-k'ao 院考
Yüan Shih-k'ai 袁世凱
Yüan T'ai-tsu 元太祖
yüeh-chüan ta-ch'en 閱卷大臣
yung (utility) 用
yung (courage) 勇
Yung-cheng 雍正
Yung-lo 永樂
Yung Wing (Jung Hung) 容閎

Index

Academies: converted to colleges, 215; founded by Chang Chih-tung, 54–62; in Ch'ing educational system, x, 16. *See also* Academy

Academy (*shu-yüan*): Chiang-Han, 55, 60*n*, 217, 220, 221, 223; Chin-chiang, 56; Ching-hsin, 55, 57, 60*n*, 189, 217, 220, 221; Ching-ku, 55; Hsüeh-hai, 56, 58; Ko-chih, 131, 229; Ku-ching, 56; Kuang-ya, 58–59, 60*n;* Liang-Hu, 60–62, 125, 127, 129*n*, 140*n*, 144, 148, 189, 217, 219, 220, 221, 233, 254; Ling-te, 57–58, 143; Nan-ching, 50*n;* Tsun-ching, 51, 56–57, 147*n;* Wen-ch'ang, 55*n*

Academy of Sciences (T'ung-ju yüan), 230

Aisin Gioro clan, 25

Alexander II, 81, 83, 91

Alexander III, 91

Analects of Confucius, 11*n*, 13, 55, 151, 227

Annam: crisis over, 70, 92–97; French encroachments in, 80, 156. *See also* France: war with China (1884–1885)

Army of Green Standard, 180, 204

Baclé incident, 93

Balluseck, Minister, 79

Banner Forces, 180, 204

Barclay, J. R., 131*n*

Beresford, Lord, 115, 119, 120

Bernstorff, W., 128*n*

Berthemy, Minister, 79

Black Flag bandits, 92, 94

Bland, J. O. P., 7

Blyhofer, 115*n*

Board: of Admiralty, 155; of Civil Appointments, 10, 78; of Punishments, 87, 143*n;* of Revenue, 77, 78, 202; of Rites, 10, 11, 25, 30*n*, 63, 65, 143, 174, 175, 188, 239; of War, 78, 96, 176, 182; of Works, 23, 78. *See also* Six Boards

Bodde, Derk, 3, 4

Bolschacoff, S. T., 128*n*

Book of Rites, 11*n*, 157

Boxer Uprising: indemnity for, 217, 234, 235; influence on educational reform,

196, 205; influence on Noncommissioned Officers' School, 120; influence on studies abroad, 134; origins and development, 197–200; role of Chang Chih-tung in, 196–200

Britt, G. D., 132*n*

Bruce, Minister, 79

Buddhism: and heterodox ideas, 172, 185, 228; and proposed property expropriation, 161–162; and *t'i-yung* philosophy, 3

Burlingame, Minister, 79

Burma, 156

Butzow, Eugene, 82, 83

Calligraphy (*hsiao-k'ai*), 12, 184, 187–188

Censorate, 77

Ceylon, 167

Chan-shih-fu. *See* Supervisorate of Imperial Instruction

Ch'an Shuang-sui, 223

Chang Chih-ch'eng, 20*n*

Chang Chih-ch'ing, 19*n*, 20*n*

Chang Chih-tung: academies founded by, 54–62; and Annam crisis, 94–95, 97; and Boxer Uprising, 196–200; and Kuanghsü succession, 70–74; and problems of student discipline, 44–50, 189–195, 246–247; and Pure Group, 65–70, 72–74, 75–79, 85–88, 94–97; and relations with Tz'u-hsi, 6, 28, 72–74, 144, 193, 199, 200, 229, 251; and "self-strengthening" movement, 97–99, 100–104; and *t'i-yung* formula, 3–5, 151–152, 253–254; and *Ch'üan-hsüeh p'ien,* 151–173, 182–188; appointed assistant examiner, 31, 40, 41; director of education, 40, 41; grand secretary and councillor, 251; Hukwang governor general, 105, 112; Liangkiang governor general, 97, 105, 113, 131, 217, 229; Liangkwang governor general, 97; minister of education, 251; Shansi governor, 74, 97; appointed to Hanlin Academy, 30, 64–65; to Office for Management of State Affairs, 202; assessments of, 1–8, 252–254; becomes *chin-shih,* 29; *chü-jen,* 22–23; *kung-shih,* 28; *sheng-yüan,* 22;

Harvard East Asian Series